The Islamic Middle East

A contemporary Bedouin and his son in traditional clothing, Jordan.

The Islamic Middle East

Tradition and Change

REVISED EDITION

Charles Lindholm

Blackwell
Publishing

350 Main Street, Malden, MA 02148-5018, USA
108 Cowley Road, Oxford OX4, 1JF, UK
550 Swanston Street, Carlton South, Melbourne, Victoria 3053, Australia
Kurfürstendamm 57, 10707 Berlin, Germany

First edition published 1996
Revised edition published 2002 by Blackwell Publishers Ltd, a Blackwell Publishing company

Library of Congress Cataloging-in-Publication Data is available for this book.

ISBN 1-405-10146-6 (paperback)

A catalogue record for this title is available from the British Library.

Set in 10 on 12 pt Sabon
by Kolam Information Services Pvt. Ltd, Pondicherry, India.
Printed and bound in the United Kingdom
by MPG Books Ltd, Bodmin, Cornwall

For further information on
Blackwell Publishers, visit our website:
http://www.blackwellpublishing.com

Contents

Illustrations

Maps

Figures

Plates

To the memory of Ernest Gellner

Preface to the Second Edition

After the collapse of the Soviet Union, it was said that a stable new world order was in place, with the United States claiming to hold uncontested sway as both leader and exemplar for the rest of humanity. But after September 11 it appears that much of the West, and certainly the United States government, has found in militant Islam a threat to this so-called new world order and an opponent to fill the role left vacant by the disappearance of the "communist menace." Several years ago this shift was predicted by the conservative theorist Samuel Huntington, who made an immense impact with his portrait of a "clash of civilizations" in which the West – characterized by Huntington as rational, capitalistic, individualistic, and egalitarian – was seen as destined to struggle with other cultures motivated by competing value systems – especially those inspired by the religious edicts, patriarchal attitudes and tribal ethics of Islam. Similarly, other political scientists have foreseen a battle of "MacWorld" versus "Jihad" – the Western forces of technology, efficiency, and change warring against Islamic forces represented as zealotry, irrationality, and tradition. These dismal predictions would seem to be borne out by President Bush's declaration of a crusade against terrorism and by the American-led campaign against the Taliban in Afghanistan.

This book is my attempt to resist this widely held and one-sided perspective. For me, such simplistic divisions of us against them ignore the fundamental values that the West in general, and, as I argue, the United States in particular, share with Middle Eastern culture; values that have often fueled dispute, but could and should also provide a basis for dialogue and reconciliation. This is not to deny deep-rooted cultural and historical differences between the two cultures (particularly in social organization and in the structure of the family), but it is to affirm that fundamental Western principles of equality, freedom, and individualism have their parallels and even their historical origins in the Middle East, dating back to the very first stirrings of civilization in ancient Sumeria. These precepts animate the great religions of the West, from Judaism to Christianity, as well as informing the ethical prophecy of Muhammad, and serve as reminders of a common heritage.

In practice, what this heritage means within the Middle Eastern context is that even the mightiest king has never been accepted as a deity; no matter how powerful, the ruler has always been recognized as merely mortal. Muhammad and his disciples too lived and died like ordinary men and women; they were emissaries and spokesmen of God, not emanations to be worshipped. Such modesty is extremely rare in world history. The Kings and Prophets of ancient China, India, Southeast Asia, and South America were usually reckoned by themselves and their followers to be gods who provided order to the cosmos; they were surrounded by pious ritual and worshipped by those beneath them.

Most complex premodern civilizations also were marked by caste divisions that organized humankind into preordained orders ranked by their supposedly innate spiritual purity. In sharp contrast, everyone in the Islamic Middle Eastern world, regardless of status, position, wealth, or family history, has long been thought to possess a divine soul and to have an equal capacity to attain salvation through ethical action and God's grace. In the dominant culture of the Middle East, independence, not subservience, has been highly valued for millennia; the capacity for freedom of choice and of action have been requisites for self-respect; honor has meant never admitting the right of power to impose itself, never accepting the inherent superiority of another individual. This prevailing egalitarian ethic is quite at odds with the misinformation so widely disseminated in the West about Middle Eastern values, and equally at odds with the conditions found in other more hierarchical world civilizations. As I will show; it has deep historical roots, and is correlated with the ecological, economic, political, and structural conditions characteristic of the region.

The value system of individualism, equality, and freedom, which resists secular authority and favors competition between co-equals, ought to sound familiar to Americans, since it is precisely the ethic that is widely celebrated within American society. In other words, "Live Free or Die" is not just the motto of the state of New Hampshire. But if the United States and the Middle East share fundamental beliefs, they do not share a history of political freedom. Rather, despite its pervasive ethic of egalitarianism and individualism, the Middle East has long been burdened by oppressive tyrannies, and remains home to various despots.

The how and why of this paradox is one of the major topics I explored in the pages to follow. In this inquiry, I was inspired by Alexis de Tocqueville, whose understanding of the ambiguities and implications of the passion for equality remains unsurpassed. Using the United States as his example, Tocqueville worried that the pursuit of purely personal success would lead egalitarian individualists to withdraw from participation in the larger public sphere. This in turn would ease the development of a tyranny. For him, the solution was the development of local level civil society that would give people practice in voluntary self-government. This answer, while arguably adequate for the United States, is not sufficient in the Middle East, where state tyranny flourishes despite the ubiquitous existence of unofficial local level voluntary organizations and civic associations. In part, this is because egalitarianism requires trust in the representative character of the state if it is to lead to democratic government. For various reasons explored in the text, this trust does not exist in the Middle East; thus, when the state asserts authority, it is felt to act immorally, and the citizenry obey only under duress. Lacking popular support, states must resort to oppression to maintain authority, which further erodes their legitimacy. Of late, the spiral of popular mistrust and state despotism has been intensified by foreign intervention, but it is indigenous in origin. Egypt, Syria, Iraq, Morocco, and Jordan are only some of the modern Middle Eastern states where variations on ancient forms of secular tyranny continue to prevail. Although thinly justified by various means (sacred and aristocratic lineages in Morocco and Jordan, the need for military protection in Syria and Iraq, bureaucratic expertise in Egypt) all of these regimes rely primarily on coercion and fear to maintain them. Insofar as they have popular support, it is in lieu of any viable alternative, and on the principle that injustice is better than chaos.

In this context, the upsurge of Islamic religious fanaticism that so frightens the West is best seen as a modern version of an ancient popular reaction against conditions of repression and tyranny. Stifled in their efforts to gain a voice in a secular polity that is seen to be corrupt and coercive, and disenchanted with the promises of nationalism, communism and capitalism, populist reformers in the Middle East have looked back to the era of the Prophet, who conquered the cruel rulers of Mecca and instituted a golden age of justice and equity. The use of violence to recapture this millennial moment has a long history in the Middle East, dating back to the very first days of Islam, when the third Caliph, Uthman, was murdered for favoring his relatives and acting unjustly to the community or when a radical assassinated Ali, the fourth Caliph, (the first Caliph of the Shi'ites) who was also the Prophet's son-in-law and cousin, on the grounds that he had betrayed the faith. The same justifications for murder are given by modern assassins, often using almost the same words as their predecessors.

The pattern of religiously motivated insurgence is associated with the problem of maintaining authority among equals. The logic is as follows:

where no one has an intrinsic right to rule, governments are likely to be fragile and dominate through sheer force. But such coercive violence stands at right angles to the religious ethic of brotherhood as originally enunciated by Muhammad and his disciples, who ruled by religious authority and thereby transcended the competitive ethos of egalitarian individualism. The messages of charismatic leaders who claim to offer a return to this remembered era of peace and unity have always been tempting to a citizenry fatigued by official oppression and injustice.

Unhappily, pretenders to piety have rarely been able to offer a more equitable government than the rulers they have replaced, and have themselves been repudiated by the same people who believed in them in the first place. This is what happened in Afghanistan, where the Taliban lost support when their much-touted moral rigor was contradicted by corruption and power seeking. Similarly, in Iran, Ayatollah Khomeini's Islamic revolution has been adulterated by popular resistance to the arbitrary authority of religious zealots. And, in Saudi Arabia, the purity of Wahhabism has been tainted by the fabulous oil wealth and luxurious lifestyles of the Saudi elite. As their moral claim to religious authority has evaporated, the Saudis have been obliged to impose more tyrannical rule, and so have exposed themselves to accusations not only of repression, but also of hypocrisy. It is in this crucible that Osama bin Laden was formed.

In the following pages I trace the vicissitudes of power – both secular and sacred – within the Middle Eastern cultural universe, where equality and individualism have long been the predominant value-orientations, and where authority has generally been justified either by pure force or by claims to charisma. Although I have updated this edition to take account of recent events, I have not focused on contemporary problems; I have undertaken instead a cultural analysis of historical case studies to reveal a variety of ways in which the so-called superiority of some and the inferiority of others has been justified, tolerated, or hidden in a social universe where all people can, in principle, claim to be independent agents and spiritual equals. I show what types of government and religion have occurred within this ethical environment, and consider how invidious distinctions of race, sex, and ethnicity have been perceived, transformed, and negotiated. Finally, I ask how people have attempted to escape from the tensions and contradictions of their condition through friendship, love, and worship.

This work makes extensive use of historical and political material, which I hope will be of some use and interest to those students unfamiliar with the Middle Eastern world. But I am no historian or political scientist. My field is anthropology, and I have done my research in a very remote corner of the region. This gives me a frontier perspective that I hope usefully balances out the more common urban and textual perspectives of my colleagues. Furthermore, my main interest is in developing, rethinking, and applying theory, not in recapturing the past or making policy. The more I have read, however, the more my respect has grown for those who have collected, presented, and analyzed the material that I have only been able to skim in my own writing. I hope I have been able to do some meager justice to the labors of these scholars, and would be very pleased indeed if my book might stimulate some of my readers to a more detailed study of Middle Eastern history and politics than I have been able to undertake here. At the same time, I hope that the kind of approach I have followed may have value for other disciplines, if only to inspire them to take anthropological research and theory into account in their work.

Although I do not focus on contemporary issues, I do strongly believe my historical-cultural interpretation of the dialectical interplay between values and circumstances has practical political implications. For example, the argument I have developed indicates to me that the solution to the Arab-Israeli conflict hinges on Israeli (and American) recognition that the personal honor of Palestinians has been sullied and must be made whole again. This does not necessarily require wholesale repatriation or the return of land. For egalitarian individualists, restoring dignity is far more important than simply regaining property. Therefore, to achieve a lasting peace, the Israelis and their allies must swallow their pride, tone down their rhetoric of justification, and eliminate their practices of expansion and violent suppression of all forms of resistance, which only lead to further escalation of conflict as the Arabs seek to reassert their honor by acts of revenge. After stepping back from aggression, symbolic reparations can be offered as a recognition and vindication of the lost honor of the Palestinians. This kind of reconciliatory gesture could greatly contribute to establishing a *modus vivendi* between peoples who have, in truth, much more in common than either likes to admit – which is a big part of the problem, since Israelis are Middle Easterners too, and just as unwilling as Palestinians are to accept what looks like a loss of honor.

My argument also implies that the United States should not be quick to favor and fund despots whose main claim to American loyalty is their anti-Islamic rhetoric. As I noted above, in the Middle East political activism tends to become religious fanaticism when confronted with repressive regimes – all the more so when the regime is seen as un-Islamic. But when Islamists do take power, their legitimacy is very likely to be eroded by the necessities of rule and they must either collapse or accommodate. Thus, American support of oppressive regimes in Egypt and Saudi Arabia has led directly to the massive popularity of radical Islamist movements in these two societies, and to equally massive anti-American sentiment. Similarly, Turkish military force used

against triumphant Islamic parties has ended only in increased radical-
ization, while in Algeria the suppression of a moderate and democratic
Islamic movement resulted in an upsurge of religious fervor, increased
polarization, and years of bloody civil war that is only now abating.
Meanwhile, in Iran, which has actually experienced a religious revolution and has also had the disenchanting experience of clerical rule, pro-
American feeling and democratic political activism are both on the
increase. In fact, Iran may yet offer the world an example of a new
form of democratic state in which popularly elected governments can
co-exist and function alongside an Islamist judiciary and military.

To conclude, simplistic notions of the clash between the rational
West and a monolithic and irrational Islamdom do nothing except contribute to hostility and aggression between "us and them." Such one-
sided notions fail to do justice to the actual issues at stake, and ignore
the shared values that provide a language for argument and agreement.
The real question is: can stable and legitimate governments take the
place of the secular tyrannies or millenaristic movements that have so
long struggled for rule in the Middle East? This is a question that
cannot be properly articulated, let alone answered, without developing
an adequate historical-cultural understanding of the various ways in
which power has been sought, contested, retained, and lost within the
moral universe of this ancient cultural complex. My updated second
edition is offered as a modest contribution to that increasingly imperative project.

Acknowledgments

The author and publisher acknowledge the following with regard to the reproduction of figures and photographs.

Frontispiece (Jordanian Bedouin), 2.1 (camel train): photos by Tom Barfield.

1.1 (suq in Aleppo), 9.1 (Umayyad mosque), 9.3 (old man with beads), 11.1 (Shi'ite mosque): photos by Vanessa Maia Rangel.

2.2 (Yemeni town), 14.2 (headdress variations) are from: Carsten Niebuhrs, 1774. *Reisebeschreibung nach Arabien und andern umliegenden Ländern*, vol I. Copenhagen: Nicolas Moller.

4.1 (Shaikh and his men), 6.1 (cavalry man) are from: Paul Gaffarel 1883. *L'Algérie: Histoire, Conquête et Colonisation*. Paris: Librarie de Firmin-Didot.

5.1 (Allah amali) is from: Yasin Hamid Safadi, 1978. *Islamic Calligraphy*. London: Thames and Hudson.

5.2 (the mosques of Mecca and Medina) is from: Suraiya Faroqhi, 1990. *Herrscher über Mekka*. Munich: Artemis Verlag. Reprinted from Johann Bergk, 1799. *Arabien und syren....*Berlin.

7.1 (qizilbash), 8.1 (prisoner), 14.1 (slave) are from: Rayhaneh Shahrestani, 1987. *Iran in Days of Old: a pictorial Record*. Tehran.

9.2 (invocation of Muhammad), 9.4 (profession of faith), 12.1 (huwa Allah), (endpiece, p. 271) are from: A. Schimmel, 1984. *Calligraphy and Islamic Culture*. New York: New York University Press.

10.1 (expert reciting Quran), 13.1 (religious mendicant), 15.1 (bridal procession), 15.2 (women at a funeral), 17.1 (boys): photos by Cherry Lindholm.

Every effort has been made to name all the copyright holders but if any have been inadvertently overlooked the publishers will be pleased to make the necessary arrangement at the first opportunity.

One of the most appealing things about traditional scholarship in the Middle East was the close attention paid to intellectual genealogy. Every writer was careful to give credit to his teachers and influences. Unfortunately, it would take too many pages for me to fully follow this convention; I can only mention a few people who have been most helpful to me.

Intellectually, I owe much to my colleague Fredrik Barth, who preceded me as a fieldworker in Swat. One could not wish for a better exemplar as an ethnographer or as an anthropologist. The clarity and rigor of his logic and the range of his knowledge has been a great inspiration to me. I also am pleased to acknowledge my debt to Ernest Gellner, whom I knew only slightly, and whom I disagreed with occasionally, but whose formidable intellectual power was combined with a willingness to engage in a way that was truly admirable. I have dedicated this book to his memory.

I am glad to give due credit to my advisors at Columbia, Abraham Rosman, Paula Rubel, and Robert Murphy in the Department of Anthropology, Ainslie Embree and Howard Wriggins in the South Asian Institute, Richard Christie in the Department of Psychology. They encouraged me and nurtured me in ways that only now am I beginning to appreciate.

My fellow scholars at Boston University, Merlin Swartz, Tom Barfield, and Herbert Mason, kindly read the manuscript over in draft, suggested valuable new sources, and saved me from serious errors and solecisms. My former colleague at Harvard, Carl Lamberg-Karlovsky, was generous in offering me expert advice that helped me immeasurably in my research on the ancient history of the region. I also was much aided by the historians who read the text for Blackwell, especially David Morgan, whose criticisms made me rethink and rework some crucial chapters. Deborah Tooker first proposed that I consider the social consequences of egalitarian ideals, while Pnina Werbner, Juan Cole, Jeff Wientraub, Nadav Kennan, and John A. Hall (among others) offered criticism of earlier work on this topic. Dick Norton helped me in writing the chronology. In a review, Richard Tapper pointed out a number of errors in the first edition, which I have tried to correct in this one. I am very appreciative indeed for the assistance of all of these scholars, and hasten to add that the mistakes remaining are wholly my own responsibility.

I am grateful as well to John Davey, my former editor and present friend, who asked me to undertake this project, and who encouraged me throughout, despite many distractions. I owe a debt to Anthony Grahame for his patient, tolerant, and careful copy-editing of the first edition. I would also like to thank Amy Yodanis, who championed this new edition, and Jane Huber, whose enthusiasm, intelligence, and editorial skill were instrumental in bringing it to fruition. Tom Barfield, Vanessa Maia Rangel, and Cherry Lindholm provided the wonderful photos that enliven the pages of the book, and I am thankful to them. It is a pleasure to acknowledge the role of the University Professors Program at Boston University, which supported my research by funding my assistant, Rebecca Norris, who was a careful and tireless researcher, fact-checker, critic, and colleague. Finally, and as always, my deepest gratitude goes to my wife Cherry for her unfailingly good editorial judgment and equally unfailing moral support.

Glossary

abid: Slave. Also used for a person who is black, and for all humanity as "slaves of God".

adab: The manners, bearing, proper behavior, and courtesy of a courtier. Also applied to the spiritual discipline of a Sufi.

aga: Turkish term for elder brother. Also indicates chief, leader, master.

ahl al-hadith: People who know and repeat the traditions of the Prophet.

akhbari: Shi'ite school favoring the primacy of the study of tradition over interpretation. Opposed to and defeated by the *usuli* school.

al-dawa al-hadiyya: The "rightly-guided mission" of the Ismaili Imam.

Alids: Descendants of Ali, the Prophet's cousin, whom Shi'ites believe have the spiritual mandate to rule all Muslims.

al-rida: Consultation and communal choice.

amin: Trustworthy. A title applied to Muhammad.

Ana l-haqq: "My 'I' is God!" Ecstatic cry of the mystic al-Hallaj.

ansar: "Helpers". The people of Medina who joined Muhammad.

asabiyya: Group feeling; the sense of unity and obligation of a group of patrilateral kin.

askeri: The military elite of the Ottoman world. Those who practice the "Ottoman way".

ayatollah: The "miraculous sign of God" – the Shi'ite religious scholar recognized as the most spiritually elevated and learned by his peers.

baqa: Remaining in the world while transfigured by God.

baraka: Divine grace; thought to emanate from a holy man or from his tomb and relics.

barara: The "true" – refers to clans who joined the early Muslim *jihad* en-masse.

barzakh: In esoteric doctrine the archetypical forms seen in dreams and reverie.

batin: The inner significance of holy text, available only to initiates.

begherata: Pukhtu term meaning without honor, a cuckold, passive homosexual, or man who is unfree.

bila kayf: Without being able to specify meaning. A doctrine of textual analysis among traditionalist scholars, who argued the sacred word must be accepted as it stands.

bint amm: Father's brother's daughter. In Middle Eastern marriage systems, a young man usually has a marriage claim over his *bint amm*.

burqah: Afghan style of veil. It completely covers the face and body.

Caliph: "Deputy". Ruler of the community of Islam.

dai: A "summoner"; missionary of a Shi'ite movement.

daif: Weak, requiring protection, without noble pedigree.

dar al-harb: The "house" of the infidel. The land of war.

dar al-hums: Trade alliance inaugurated by Hashim, Muhammad's ancestor.

dar al-Islam: The "house" of Islam. Opposed in holy war to *dar al-harb*.

dawla: "Turn"; a dynasty or regime.

devshirme: Levy of Christian children trained to serve the Ottoman administration as *janissaries* or bureaucrats.

dhikr: "Remembrance". Sufi discipline involving recitation of the names and attributes of God.

dhimmi: Protected non-Muslim minorities.

dost: In Persian, friend.

dullah: The characteristic Pukhtu pattern of dualistic political alliances. Equivalent to Berber *liff*.

Eid al-Adha: The "greater festival" commemorating Abraham's sacrifice by the slaughter of a sheep. The last day of the *hajj*.

Eid al-fatr: The "lesser festival" celebrating the end of *Ramadan*. A time of feasting, gift-giving and unity.

emir: Military leader, Islamist commander.

fana: The state of self-annihilation. One of the highest stages of mystical awareness.

faqih: A scholar of Muslim law; jurist.

fatwa: A legal opinion given by a *mufti*.

fiqh: Religious law.

fitna: Chaos, also means sexual promiscuity. Used to refer to the early wars that rent the Muslim community.

futuwwa: Qualities of young men; refers to the ideologies of clubs associated with urban residential quarters in the traditional Middle East.

ghazi: Warrior for the faith

ghulam: Young man, servant, slave, warrior.

hadith: A "report" of the sayings and deeds of the Prophet.

hajj: Annual pilgrimage to Mecca, enjoined for all Muslims who are able to undertake it.

hajji: An honorific applied to one who has undertaken the *hajj*.

hakam: A traditional judge-arbiter.

hal: Ecstatic moment granted by God to the mystic.

haram: A sacred place. Forbidden, set aside. Traditionally, a spot where trade is protected and disputes are mediated. The area around the *kaaba* is *haram*.

harem: Protected female part of the household.

hbel shitan: The "rope of satan". Moroccan term for women.

hijra: The "flight" of Muhammad and his followers to Medina in 622 to avoid persecution. The Muslim calendar begins with this event.

hilm: The quality of restraint and rationality that makes a man a good mediator-leader.

hiyal: "Permissions" or legal manipulations allowing an evasion of the letter of the law.

hubb udhri: Chaste (udhiritic) love – as supposedly practiced by the Bedouin Banu Udhra tribe in the seventh century.

hojjat: Persian term for a proof beyond contradiction.

hojjat al-Islam: The "proof of Islam" – a high-ranking Shi'ite religious scholar.

huddam: Servant.

hurriyya. Freedom. Also implies noble and generous.

hurma: Honor.

ijma: Consensus. The basis of the Muslim community's acceptance of an interpretation of law.

ijtihad: "Exertion to the greatest degree". The use of reason and analogy to reinterpret the law. The opposite of *taqlid*.

ikhwan: Wahhabi warriors.

ilm: Knowledge.

ilm al-rijal: The "science of men". Moral judgments reached through the use of biography.

imam: For Sunnis, the *imam* is the leader in prayer. For Shi'ites, the *Imam* is the supreme leader of the community, given miraculous powers by Allah.

iqta: An assignment of land for revenue predominant under the Seljuks and (under different names) in later dynasties as well. *Iqta* was temporarily awarded by the Sultan to generals and administrators in return for their services.

Islam: Submission to God. The religion of Muslims (those who submit).

Ismailis: Shi'ite sect who follow the spiritual leadership of Ismail, a son of Jafar, the sixth *Imam*. Branches include the Qarmati, the Nizari, and the Fatimids.

isnad: The "chain" of transmitters of *hadith*.

istina: System of fictional kinship initiated by the Buyids.

jahiliyya: Pre-Islamic era of religious ignorance.

janissary: Member of the elite Ottoman slave infantry. (From the Turkish *yeniceri*.

javanmardi: Member of a men's club. The Persian equivalent of *futuwwa*.

jihad: "Striving". Holy war against non-believers. Sometimes interpreted as the struggle against one's own weakness.

jinn: Malevolent or capricious spirits. Plural *jnun*.

jirga: A counsel of elders among the Pukhtun.

kaaba: The sacred black stone and sanctuary in Mecca that is the focus of Muslim pilgrimage and prayer.

kafaa: Legal doctrine requiring equal status between husband and wife. Can be taken to prohibit inter-racial marriages.

kafir: Infidel.

kalam: Formal theological proofs of religious beliefs.

karamat: Miracles which validate the *baraka* of a Sufi saint.

khan: A Turkish title for ruler.

khaniqa: A Sufi lodge, often centered around the tomb of a saintly founder.

kharijites: "Those who go out". Muslim anarchistic and egalitarian rebels who opposed all ascribed statuses in favor of rule by the most able and pious.

khiyara: The "select" – refers to clan sections who joined the early Muslim *jihad* prior to other sections of the same group.

khuwa: Protection fees demanded by tribesmen of caravans and peasants.

kul: Slaves of the Ottoman ruler. Except for the religious judiciary, all administrators and military men officially belonged to this category.

la dustur illa l-Quran. "No constitution except the Quran!" The demand of the Muslim Brotherhood.

la hukm illa li llah: "No judgment but God's!" The cry of the early *kharijites*.

laylat al-miraj: The night of Muhammad's living ascent to heaven and his meeting with God.

liff: The characteristic Berber pattern of dualistic political alliances. Equivalent to Pukhtun *dullah*.

madhhab: A "chosen way". One of the four Sunni schools of Islamic law: Malikite, Shafite, Hanifite, Hanbalite. The Shi'i have equivalent legal schools.

madrasa: A college of Islamic law.

Maghreb: The Western regions of the Islamicate. Especially refers to North Africa.

mahar: Gift donated by groom's family to the bride.

mahdi: The "rightly guided" redeemer who will appear at the end of time.

mamluk: One who is owned. Refers to slave warriors and bureaucrats. *Mamluks* could and did gain great political power, and established their own dynasties in Egypt.

maqam: A stage on the path to mystic enlightenment.

marifa: State of intuitive awareness of God sought by Sufis.

marja al-taqlid: A "guide to imitate" – a Shi'ite spiritual leader and legal scholar.

masjid: Arabic term for mosque – the "place of prostration".

mawla: Client or servant. Plural is *mawli*.

mufti: One whose learning permits him to issue a legal opinion (*fatwa*).

muhajirin: Those who accompanied Muhammad on the *hijra* to Medina. Also applied to religious students.

Muharram: The Shi'ite ceremony mourning the martyrdom of Husain at Karbela.

mujtahid: Man of knowledge and sactitity, capable of interpreting the law. The Shi'ite equivalent of *faqih*.

mulid: Birthday celebration at the tomb of a saint. A major ritual of Sufi brotherhoods.

murid: A Sufi disciple.

murjia: "Those who defer". A quietist movement of early Islam.

murshid: A Sufi spiritual guide.

muta: Temporary marriage permitted in twelver Shi'ism.

nafs: The passions.

nai: A barber (Pukhtu).

nasab: Pedigree, lineage.

nass: Secret spiritual knowledge. In Shi'ism this knowledge is passed on to the *Imam* and validates his authority.

nisba: Tribal name.

pir: A Sufi spiritual guide.

purdah: The practice of veiling and female seclusion.

qabaday: Modern equivalent of *futuwwa*. Also means thug, local bully.

qadi: A government appointed judge.

qanat: Water tunnel in Iran.

qawm: Clan, patrilineal kinship unit.

qibla: The direction of the *kaaba* in Mecca, toward which all Muslims face in prayer.

qizilbash: "Red-heads". Military devotees of the Safavids.

Quran: Muslim scripture, dictated by God to Muhammad.

qutb: In Sufi lore, the "pivot" of the universe; the "perfect man" at the top of the spiritual hierarchy of initiates.

qutb-al-aqtab: The "pole of poles". Center of the mystical universe.

rahm: The womb. Symbol of shared community.

Ramadan: The ninth month of the Islamic calendar. Fasting is obligatory for all Muslims during this month.

reaya: Subjects of Ottoman rule. Literally, "sheep at pasture."

ridda: Secession. The *ridda* wars were rebellions by tribesmen who refused to acknowledge the legitimacy of Muhammad's successors.

salafism: The return to "true Islam" preached by modern intellectual reformers. Strongly anti-Sufi.

sahw: Sobriety. Opposed to *sukhr* (intoxication) by mystics favoring *baqa*, remaining in the world, over *fana*, self-annihilation.

salat: The five daily prayers enjoined for Muslims.

salik: A "wayfarer" – a Sufi student.

sama: Music intended to induce ecstatic states.

sayyid: Descendant of Ali's second son Husain. More broadly, a prince or chief.

shahada: The Muslim profession of faith – "There is but one God, and Muhammad is his Prophet".

shaikh: An elder, a tribal leader, a Sufi spiritual guide.

shah: Iranian term for King.

shah khel: In Pukhtu, a leather-worker.

Sharia: The "path." The total corpus of Muslim law.

sharif: Noble, capable of protecting the weak; more narrowly, the descendants of Ali's first son Hasan. The plural is *ashraf* or *shurfa*.

Shi'ites: The "partisans" of Ali and his family as the rightful holy leaders of the Islamic community.

silsila: The spiritual genealogy of a Sufi saint.

siyasah: The art of politics; literally, the grooming of animals.

Sufi: Muslim mystic.

sukhr: Intoxication. Opposed to *sahw* (sobriety) by mystics favoring *fana*, self-annihilation, over *baqa*, remaining in the world.

Sultan: "Power" – the standard title for Muslim secular rulers.

sunna: "The trodden path" – the custom and practices of Muhammad and the original community of Muslims – to be emulated by all believers.

Sunnis: The majority of the Islamic community who accept the rule of the first four caliphs; as opposed to the partisans of Ali.

sura: Quranic verses

taqiyya: Dissimulation – practiced by Shi'ites for self-protection and to hide esoteric knowledge from the vulgar.

talib: Student in a college of law.

taqlid: "Imitation" of established doctrines. The opposite of *ijtihad*.

tarbur: The Pukhtu term of reference for father's brother's son. Also implies enemy.

tariqa: A Sufi "pathway" or school.

tawakkul: Absolute trusting obedience, enjoined for Sufi disciples in their relations with their *pirs*.

ulema: The religiously learned. Those who have *ilm*.

umma: The sacred community of Muslim believers. More broadly, any demarcated group.

usuli: Shi'ite school favoring the primacy of interpretation over imitation. Opposed to, and eventually triumphant over, the more traditionally oriented *akhbari* school.

wajd: "Findings". The sudden experience of ecstasy experienced by Sufis in communion with God.

walayat-e-faqih: The "rule of the jurist". The official doctrine of modern Iran.

wali: A "friend" of God.

wali-e-faqih: The supreme jurist – a title applied to *ayatollah* Khomeini.

waqf: Property set aside in a perpetual inalienable endowment. Often used to pay for maintaining religious institutions, such as *madrasas*.

wazir: Prime minister.

yashmaq: The light veil worn by Ottoman women.

zahir: Outward appearance. The literal meaning of holy text, as opposed to *batin*, its inner significance.

zakat: Obligation to pay alms to maintain the Muslim community.

Zanj: Ethiopian, but commonly applied to mean all blacks.

zawiya: A Sufi lodge among Berbers, centered around the tomb of a saintly founder.

zina: Fornication.

Part I

Introduction

1

The Middle East:
Assumptions and Problems

The Middle East in Western Eyes

Writing a general book about the Middle East is a daunting task, not only because of the enormous complexity of the subject, but also because of the pervasive prejudice in the West against the region and its peoples. In recent years, the Iranian revolution, the war with Iraq, and the rise of Osama bin Laden have all served to fuel western anxiety, and the situation has been exacerbated by the long-term influx of Muslim immigrants into those European countries that want their labor, but do not want to accommodate their culture or give them full rights as citizens. Events such as the uproar in France over Muslim girls wearing headscarves in school and xenophobic violence directed against Muslim workers in Germany indicate the present extent of western dread of and hatred toward Islam.

Contemporary western enmity, however, is not simply a consequence of modern conflict. It is a reflection of the thousand-year rivalry between the Muslim Middle East and Christian Europe for economic, political and religious hegemony over the western hemisphere and beyond – a contest dominated until recently by Islam. Through the sixteenth century, Europe was terrified by the specter of a reverse crusade, a Muslim invasion into the heart of Christendom that would repeat the earlier Islamic conquest of Spain. These fears seemed all too well-founded as the Ottoman army, under the leadership of Sulieman the Magnificent, marched on Vienna in 1529 and arrived before the city walls in September. Only the reluctance of the Turkish troops to spend the winter away from home prevented their victory, and it appeared likely they would return again the next year to resume their siege, reduce Vienna to a satrapy, and threaten the whole heartland of Europe.

It was not until 1571 that the myth of the Sultan's invincibility was dispelled as Hapsburg galleys defeated the Ottoman fleet in the Battle of Lepanto. But this setback hardly ended the Ottoman challenge to

Christendom. Only in 1606 did the Sultan deign to treat a European power as an equal, signing a treaty with the Hapsburgs to end a costly stalemate on the Danube. As late as 1683 another vast Ottoman army again besieged Vienna, and was only vanquished due to its lack of heavy artillery. Soon thereafter, in 1699, the treaty of Karlowitz obliged the Sultan to give up Transylvania and Hungary – the first time Ottoman territory was returned to Christian control. Although not recognized at the time, the balance of power had decisively shifted. The Ottoman retreat marked the end of Muslim conquest in Europe and the beginning of the slow development of western domination over the Middle East; domination definitively signaled by Napoleon's conquest of Egypt in 1798. The great Ottoman Empire, which had aspired to convert the world to Islam, now was obliged to look to the West for inspiration; instead of being Europe's nemesis, it soon would be its "sick man."

really?

Although from the modern western vantage point the eventual victory over the Ottomans seems inevitable, at the time the reverse result appeared more likely. Unlike the fragmented, provincial, superstitious, and often incompetent European dynasties, the Ottoman Empire had a centralized Imperial court, capable leadership, a relatively efficient bureaucracy, and a magnificent, loyal and well-organized army. Given these circumstances, the "natural" triumph of the European powers was actually far more problematic than it now seems, and the panic of sixteenth and seventeenth-century Europe was well justified.

The historical memory of this great and costly struggle for domination remains potent in the Occidental cultural unconscious, and has most recently been summoned up in what used to be Yugoslavia by the self-styled protectors of Christendom who slaughtered their Muslim neighbors in order to defend Europe against a new Islamic *jihad* (holy war). The hysterical fear of Muslim "fundamentalism" that is so widespread today in Europe and America arises, at least in part, from the same historical source, and takes its place within a venerable tradition of the demonization of Islam itself. The Prophet Muhammad, regarded by Muslims as the Messenger of God, has regularly been portrayed in western literature as a lecherous and grasping villain, as an agent of the devil, and even the anti-Christ. No other leader of any great religion has ever been so systematically vilified and reviled or treated with greater contempt in the West than Muhammd, nor has any other religion, save perhaps Judaism, been held in such scorn.[1]

Simultaneous with the disparagement of the Muslim religious annunciation, the civic life of the Middle East has also been roundly condemned by western theorists. Since they first became a threat, the Muslim Empires of the Middle East have been depicted in Europe as vast tyrannies where political action was completely suppressed under the iron rule of a despot; the West, in contrast, was seen to favor citizenship and participatory government. This perspective was perhaps most famously stated by Hegel, who was contrasting the Ottoman Empire with his own country of Germany when he wrote in *Reason in History* that "the Orientals knew only that *one* is free, the Greeks and Romans that *some* are free, while we know that *all* men absolutely, that is, as men, are free."[2]

This mode of western discourse continued into the nineteenth century, even though western imperial power was well established in the Middle East and the Ottoman Empire enfeebled. In these changed circumstances, as fear gave way to patronage,[3] the great sociologist Max Weber described the typical Middle Eastern state as an arbitrary, personalized kingship, marked by overlapping, incoherent and whimsical administrative and judicial institutions staffed not on the basis of ability but on the basis of loyalty to the ruler. The Sultan himself reigned without any purpose beyond simple retention and enjoyment of the pleasures of domination; his minions existed merely to curry his favor and to extract plunder from the realm, and the people were an inert source of revenue. For Weber, the legitimacy of this inefficient and cruel form of authority was "irrational", based only on the populace's passive acceptance of tradition and the leader's coercive power.[4] From this point of view, Iraq's Sadam Hussain is an unexceptional representative of a long lineage of arbitrary Oriental tyrants who serve as reverse images of the western democratic tradition.

These dark assessments are typical of much of the standard scholarly European understandings of premodern (and modern) forms of Muslim government in the Middle East. Their accuracy will be evaluated in later chapters; here I only note that the prevailing denigration of Muslim polity and religion has often been utilized to validate a glorification of the virtues of western culture and rule as more humane and more efficient than anything found in Muslim society. Having subdued and colonized the Middle East, Occidental observers no longer saw power, but only gross inefficiency and corruption. The Ottoman Empire, the prototypical Middle Eastern despotism, became a pathetic sight, incapable of responding to the challenges of the contemporary world, governed by irresponsible incompetents prone to lust and greed. As Marshall Hodgson writes, from a colonial perspective, in the late Ottoman era "everyone in a public position seemed to be for sale except as he might be checked by brute fear of an unscrupulous tyrant."[5] European rulers could therefore easily justify their rule as necessary for stemming the abuses endemic to the Middle Eastern state.

Within this ideological context, Europeans believed that Muslims could not achieve reforms for themselves since they were fundamentally incapable of rational thought and reasonable action. As Lord Cromer, British consul-general of Egypt from 1882 to 1907 complacently stated,

"the want of mental symmetry and precision...is the chief distinguishing feature between the illogical and picturesque East and the logical
West";[6] and elsewhere he wrote flatly that "somehow or other the Oriental generally acts, speaks, and thinks in a manner exactly opposite to the
European."[7]

We can say then that the western imagination of the Middle East and
of Islam that is prevalent today has been shaped by a long and antagonistic history. Precisely because of its record as a military and ideological
rival to European domination the Middle East has served as a negative
standard against which the Occidental imagination could define itself;
hostility (as well as attraction) toward the Muslim world is part of the
process of western self-construction. As Edward Said has famously
written, the western understanding of the Islamicate "has less to do
with the Orient than it does with 'our' world."[8]

However, Said has also argued that any western representation of the
Middle East as a culturally specific entity must be seen as an expression
of hegemonic authority, applied to dominate the disenfranchised, dehumanized and voiceless Muslim "Others" by turning them into objects
and "types" who can be manipulated and exploited.[9] This radical perspective may be heroic, but recognition of the power and cultural hegemony of the West does not require as a correlate the rejection of the
possibility of constructing general comparative arguments about Middle
Eastern culture, nor does it require negating the real historical and
cultural patterns of Middle Eastern society simply because that society
has been viewed through western eyes.

The real question ought to be: what does Middle Eastern culture con-
sist of? Are its constituents too vague to be useful, too far removed from
ordinary reality to be compelling? Perhaps so. But, as Rodney Needham
argues, we can limit the field of inquiry by focusing on those aspects that
"evoke...some sharper sense of the quandary of human existence";[10]
that is, on the manner in which persons within cultural worlds seek to
gain a respite from mortality through winning distinction for themselves
and respect from their peers. This quest springs precisely out of the
existential human tension between self and other, between autonomy
and participation, and begins with the simple question "what sort of life
ought a person live?" Or, put more abstractly "what are the notions of
individual and society that are pre-eminently valued in a given cultural
milieu?" Starting from this point, we can then consider sympathetically
the ways Middle Eastern people try to live out their ideals – how they
fail, how they succeed, and the sorts of strains and paradoxes that arise
in response to the demands of their ethical world.

Where is the Middle East?

But before proceeding on this pathway, some basic terms need to be clarified. To this point, I have used the words "Middle East" and "Muslim" as if their meanings were self-evident and as if the Middle East and Islam were coterminous. Of course, neither is the case. Obviously the Middle East cannot be defined simply as Muslim society, since more Muslims live in Indonesia, Bangladesh and India, as well as in sub-Saharan Africa, than live in the Middle East. Yet at the same time, it is clear that the territory of the Middle East and the religion of Islam are closely intertwined, since it was from Arabia that Islam originated and spread, as the Prophet Muhammad's charismatic annunciation of a new shared belief system created a new mode of being in the world that permanently reconfigured the region's previously existing cultural models for living.

It is also true that, although the Arabic of the Quran is recited everywhere in the Muslim world, regardless of the local language, the spirit of Islam is nonetheless strongly effected by the cultural milieu in which it finds itself. The same is the case for Islam over time; the way the Quran is understood and interpreted today is not the same as it was in the past; nor is the Islam promoted by authorities the same as that preached by populists.

If simply being Muslim is not enough to define the Middle East, then what is? Following Said, postmodern theorists have argued that any such designation is necessarily pernicious, since it obscures local and even personal differences for the purpose of making categorizations which serve to divide "us" from "them", with "us" as necessarily superior. Because such distinctions are destructive and dehumanizing it follows that to categorize the Middle East as a cultural region, or to understand Middle Easterners as having a distinct cultural heritage, is an act of aggression. Such an approach makes any sort of comparison impossible, and turns the Middle East into a conglomeration of local particularities and specific individuals, without any historical or social continuity. This is a falsification of the experience of Middle Easterners themselves, who understand their world as having exactly the sort of unity and identity that postmodern theorists deny them.

More appealing and useful is the pragmatic argument made by the influental historian Marshall Hodgson for "Islamdom" to be defined as the area of the Nile on the west to the Oxus on the east. This, he said, was the cultural core region of Muslim society because it was here that the most authoritative states and courts held sway during the heyday of Islamic rule and provided the cultural models which the rest of the Muslim world followed.

The traditional anthropological demarcation of the Middle East has generally followed Hodgson's notion of a cultural core, but moved the center to the west, excluding the Oxus region and placing it in Central Asia, while expanding the Middle East to include North Africa (the so-called *Maghreb*, or "west"). For anthropologists, this distinction made sense because of marked differences between the two regions in terms of material culture and social practice. These differences led anthropologists to argue that the people of the Oxus belong to a different "trait complex" than the people of the Maghreb, Arabia, and Persia. From this perspective it is not the pomp of the court, but local knowledge, material culture, and typical patterns of action that determine a culture area.

If we accept the "trait complex" perspective we can delimit, albeit provisionally, the spatial range of the Middle East, which can be pictured as centered on the axis of north latitude 38, and extending from the southwest to the northeast over an expanse of approximately seven million square miles. It is bounded on the west by the Atlantic beaches of Morocco and stretches east across North Africa, into Arabia, through Iran, and finally merges into Central Asia and south Asia in northern Pakistan and southern Afghanistan. In the southwest, the region does not reach beyond the Sahara and in the southeast is halted by the Arabian Sea. In the north, the frontier is naturally set by three inland seas: the Mediterranean, the Black, and the Caspian, and then finally by the peaks of the Hindu Kush mountains.[11]

It will be immediately recognized that this is the heartland of the early history of Western civilization. It is here that goats, sheep (and pigs!) were first domesticated; here that agriculture was discovered and the Neolithic revolution changed men and women from hunters and gatherers into farmers and pastoralists. It is from this region that many of the foods we take for granted were first cultivated: wheat, rye, barley, onions, garlic, olives, grapes, melons, apples, plums, figs, dates, apricots, pears, peaches, chick peas, broad beans, walnuts, almonds. It was also in the Middle East that the first literate urban civilizations arose, greatly extending the productivity and power of humanity, but also subordinating the many to the few. These imperial civilizations built huge monuments to honor the glory of their dynasties and rulers, and they used the new invention of writing to keep accounts, tell stories of men and Gods, and record the histories of the rise and fall of empires.

This is obviously an enormous, ancient, highly complex and varied region. Its past is marked by the vicissitudes of thousands of years of human history; it is the home of the first literate culture, and has within it not only three major language groups – Arabic, Persian, and Turkic – but also other smaller but distinct linquistic units, such as Kurdish, Pukhtu and Berber. It is the mother country of Judaism, Christianity and Zoroastrianism, along with the now dominant religion of Islam, which

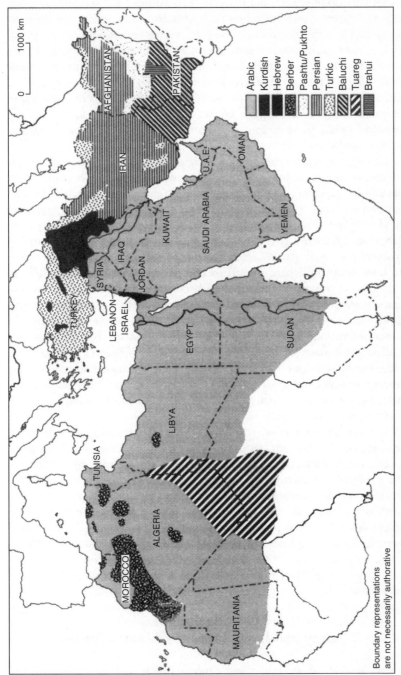

Map 1.1   Modern states and major languages in the Middle East.

Boundary representations
are not necessarily authorative

is itself divided between mainstream Sunnis and Shiʿi sectarians, along with a number of smaller subsects, offshoots and heresies. The territory has within it huge inland seas, great deserts and harsh mountain ranges, but contains too a portion of the world's most fertile farming areas. Its populace include some of the wealthiest people in the world, and some of the poorest; they work as camel nomads, shepherds, peasant farmers, fishermen, merchants, and at the numberless occupations to be found in the great urban centers; they live in distinct and occasionally warring states governed by divergent polities – socialist, nationalist, religious, and monarchical.

In short, the region shows such a range of different ecologies, histories, social organizations, beliefs and governments that uniting all of them under one label would seem highly tendentious, despite the fact that certain traits, such as tent style and kinship organization, are very widely shared throughout. But the trait complex method lumps together all attributes as if they had equal value: tent style and kinship structure are equivalent as characteristic indicators, and one searches to see how many traits are shared to compile a list of groups which are more or less typical. This sort of anthropology has gone out of fashion ever since it was wittily derided by Edmund Leach as a butterfly collector's approach to the study of society, that is, as a sterile compilation of ever-proliferating categories to be put against one another in the ethnographic equivalent of museum exhibit cases.[12] Leach's critique has force, but he did not mean it to preclude generalization and comparison entirely; his concern was to discover deeper structural patterns beneath surface appearances, which would then allow for more meaningful correlations and more significant comparisons.

The real question is whether these shared traits are expressions of some deeper and pivotal cultural and moral continuity. As I have mentioned, I believe we should look for this continuity in the manner in which Middle Eastern people face the existential problems involved in constructing their ethical choices and self-identities through what Muhammad Arkoun calls the "cultural imaginary"; that is, the deeply-held indigenous values that provide the most salient and strongly motivating bases for action, feeling and thought among Middle Easterners themselves, inspiring them in their ordinary lives, in their symbolic and religious experiences, and in their dialectical interaction with the rest of the world.[13]

Equality and Individualism as Central Values

In this book, I argue that these central values include egalitarianism, competitive individualism, and the quest for personal autonomy – values that are shared with the West, and especially with America, but that are not to be found in most cultures. Far more prevalent historically and cross-culturally is the deification of authority, so that the right to command is ascribed to a certain sacralized social stratum, which is set apart from and above the rest of the society. To hold superior rank in such a society one must be born or adopted into the elect, whom all the rest are morally obliged to obey. Acceptance of sacralized ranking finds its most radical expression in the caste system of India,[14] but can be found in all cultures where an elite group is marked off permanently from the hoi polloi. The pattern of ascriptive hierarchy is, in fact, taken by many scholars to be the defining characteristic of pre-industrial society.[15]

But among Middle Easterners, as among Americans, such rating is anathema; for both, moral equality is taken for granted as an essential human characteristic; rank is to be achieved by competition among equals, not awarded at birth to members of an aristocratic social stratum. Americans and Middle Easterners also share a faith that all human beings are equal in the eyes of God, and that all humans are born as free and autonomous human agents, who struggle to gain positions of honor and respect among their fellows and salvation in the afterlife.

Shared values of egalitarianism and competitive individualism are to be found in any number of ethnographic and historical accounts of the region. Typical is Henry Rosenfeld's description of the Bedouin nomads, among whom "each kin group, not accepting exclusive control of resources, fundamentally considers itself the equal of others in regards to prestige, honour, status, and in rights."[16] And elsewhere, among Jordanian villagers, Richard Antoun notes that the average fifteen-year-old "man" "regards himself now as no man's servant and only undertakes chores out of the generosity of his own heart for his friends, and out of a sense of obligation for his kinsmen."[17] Similarly, among the Pukhtun of northern Pakistan every man "thinks he is as good as anyone and his father rolled into one,"[18] and local proverbs continually stress the equality of the tribesmen, who, like rain-sown wheat, "all come up the same".

It might be argued that these rural people are egalitarian because they are, in fact, all equal – equally impoverished. But what is remarkable is that in the Middle East, even in the face of distinctions in status and wealth, the same ideology holds. For instance, among the sedentarized Lur of Western Iran, where a small elite own almost all the land and animals, Jacob Black reports that:

> All Lurs consider each other on a footing of intrinsic equality; that is to say, the status of any given individual at any given moment is seen as achieved. No-one is born politically superior to anyone else. All Lurs believe that individual industry is the key to personal achievement and

that only ineptitude, sloth or bad luck can prevent a man from attaining the highest goals, or, alternatively, can bring a man of importance and standing into straitened circumstances.[19]

And in urban Morocco, despite vast differences in wealth and power, Paul Rabinow tells us that poverty "indicates only a lack of material goods at the present time, nothing more. Although regrettable, it does not reflect unfavorably on one's character."[20]

The same egalitarian ethos is reflected in the absence of honorifics in the Muslim world. As Bernard Lewis notes: "From the beginning to the present day, there are no hereditary titles, other than royal, in the Islamic lands, except on a very limited and local scale, and even there by courtesy rather than by law."[21] This egalitarianism even extends to rulers, who are never referred to as fathers to their people; the most recognition given to the Sultan is the Ottoman title of "aga": elder brother (an appellation that, as we shall see, reflects a distinctive Turkic kinship structure). This again indicates the absence of any absolute ideological distinction between ruler and ruled. Meanwhile, the people are typically referred to as "brothers" or "sons" of the nation, which is then imagined as similar to a tribe, with its members equal co-participants under the aegis of the state.

In this environment all men, regardless of standing, can and do meet and interract without deference. This pervasive value is expressed in the Muslim salutation "Peace be upon you" which does not refer to the status of the other; nor is there any bowing and genuflecting when persons of different social rank meet. The handshake and the embrace, which are signs of equality and intimacy, are Middle Eastern institutions. Even the legitimacy of the king was marked by a simple handshake given to him by his advisors and the *ulema* (the learned); this handshake affirmed the equivalence of the contracting parties at the very moment that power was officially conferred on the ruler. If the ruler was in theory equivalent to his entourage, who only ceded him power, the entourage also were fundamentally equal to one another in their pursuit of the ruler's personal commendation. In the Middle East the acquisition of political power was never thought of as rising up through set degrees of hierarchy. That imagery is limited to spiritual ascent.

It is with this background in mind that Lewis writes: "This is a society which always in principle, and often, at least to some extent, in practice, rejects hierarchy and privilege, a society in which power and status depend primarily on nearness to the ruler and the enjoyment of his favor, rather than on birth or rank."[22] Similarly, Marshall Hodgson states flatly that in the Islamicate "equality was the basic principle, above all among free adult males"; in this context "every free Muslim should be accorded that personal liberty and dignity which was expected by the Arabian tribesman – being bound to obey no man without his own assent...(therefore) all free Muslims ought to be treated on an essentially equal basis."[23]

The ideal of equality was carried over into the ecclesiastical realm where, more than any other faith, Islam demands recognition of the elemental equivalence of all believers before God and the dignity and personal responsibility of the individual in fulfilling his religious duties. Even the Prophet was no more than a man, and worship of him, or anthropolatry of any sort, is forbidden as the worst of sins. Ideally speaking, in Islam there is no ecclesiastical hierarchy, no ordained clergy, no central church structure, nothing to stand between the individual Muslim and Allah. In its radical affirmation of the direct confrontation between man and God, Islam goes even further than Calvinism.

Equality and competitive individualism are not the sole values of Middle Easterners, but coexist and correspond with a high estimate of the importance of bravery, independence, and generosity; a personal honor code based upon self help, hospitality, blood revenge, sanctuary, and rigid sexual mores of female chastity and seclusion. It is also crucial to note that honor is not only personal, but is also inextricably located within the patrilineal and patriarchal families, clans, and tribes into which men and women are born, and to which they owe obligations of loyalty and support. As we shall see, these ideals also coincide with strong cultural assumptions about female weakness and inferiority, with negative racial and ethnic stereotyping, and with notions of noble and base lineages – all of which contradict the premise of human equality. This ambiguous blend of beliefs and values is intertwined with and causally implicated in a shared ethos of mercantilism, social mobility, cosmopolitanism, and calculating rationality.

The culture of the Middle East is therefore not an empty reflection of western domination, as some have claimed; nor is it only a conglomeration of random individuals, each unique, separate, irreducible and impenetrable, as a postmodernist approach might indicate. Rather, the Middle East has at its core many of the values that are presently believed to be essential characteristics of the modern western world: egalitarianism, individualism, pluralism, competitiveness, calculating rationality, personal initiative, social mobility, freedom; but these are set within a distinctive historical context based upon chivalric honor, female seclusion, and patrilineality and that also favored invidious distinctions between men and women, whites and blacks, tribesmen and peasants, nobles and commoners, free men and slaves.

From this perspective the Muslim "Other" is not unrecognizable to the westerner; quite the contrary. In fact, our antagonisms are all the more deeply felt for the very fact of our likenesses, which challenge any claims by either party to absolutely separate realities and identities. By

Plate 1.1   A recent photograph of the suq (bazaar) in Aleppo, Syria.

considering the ways in which the taken-for-granted faith in equality
and individual freedom effect social reality in the political, religious,
and personal realms in the Middle East, we can discover how subordination and hierarchy are legitimated, hidden, or denied within a cultural
milieu that like our own, assumes the intrinsic equality of all participants.[24]

But before this discussion can take place, we need to consider, in
brief outline, the social, historical, and ecological context in which this
special value system that we share with our Middle Eastern cousins
arose and prevailed. This is the task of the following chapters.

Part II

Preconditions for Egalitarian Individualism

2

Ways of Living

The Ecological Framework

The most critical things to notice about the Middle East are the thrusting young mountain ranges that jaggedly divide the region into localities: the Rif and the Atlas Mountains in Morocco, Algeria, and Tunisia; the Zagros and Elburz range in Iran; the Sulaimaniya and Hindu Kush in Afghanistan and Pakistan, with lesser peaks found in every country save Kuwait. Although not high enough to block caravan passage, they are rugged enough to provide refuge for outlaws and rebels; they supply as well lush sheltered valleys for cultivation and summer forage for lowland herds. Even more importantly, these mountain ranges create barriers to the flow of precipitation blown west in the winter months by the prevailing Monsoon winds. Because of the climatic effect of the mountain barricades, the Middle East is characterized by arid near-desert or desert conditions for most of its territory, with rain becoming ever more scant the further west one goes. Everywhere the amount of rainfall, even in the rainy winter season, is unreliable, and winter crops grown without irrigation can often fail.

As the Monsoon turns and winter rapidly becomes summer, the winds begin to blow across the desert, eliminating rain altogether and bringing the fiery heat that is normal in most of the Middle East during this season. Only in a very few areas can any significant summer rainfall be relied upon. Much of the water that does fall lands as snow in remote high mountain valleys, where harsh conditions make permanent residence difficult or impossible. Other areas of high rainfall are generally located where the land is sandy, or steep, or remote and extremely difficult to cultivate. In fact, because of the climatological constraints of the region, only about 14 percent of the vast land mass in the Middle East is suited for cultivation, almost all of it to be found within the oases, high mountain vales, and especially in the plains and deltas of the great rivers where water supply is sufficient and

Plate 2.1   Camel traffic during the annual spring nomad
migration in northeast Afghanistan.

relatively reliable: the Nile, the Tigris–Euphrates, the Karun, and the
Helmand.

But even in these relatively rich areas, cultivation in the Middle East
can be extremely demanding and precarious; farmers must carefully
husband and control whatever water is available. This frequently requires the building of complex irrigation systems or underground water
tunnels stretching for miles (called *qanats* in Iran). But the use of these
ancient technologies has its dangers: there is an ever-present risk that
breakdowns of the system due to silting, salinization or simple neglect,
coupled with climatic shifts due to deforestation, can lead to desertifi-
cation of fertile land. Due to these processes, Uruk, the first great city
of the world, now is an uninhabitable ruin sweltering in the midst of a
desolate wasteland. The huge and fertile wheat fields of the Tigris–
Euphrates Delta that made Iraq the breadbasket of the ancient world
have also been largely returned to the desert as a result of the silting up
of the ancient irrigation system.

Despite the severity of conditions in the inhospitable deserts and
mountains, and the fragility of cultivation even in the valleys, for thousands of years Middle Eastern people have managed to find ways to eke
out their livings; fearing the power yet relying upon the resources of the
ancient urban city-states.[1] Understanding the ecological constraints on
their lives, the modes of production they have developed to cope with
these contraints, and their complex long-term interrelationships with the

valley civilizations, will go a long way toward helping us to understand the roots of the egalitarian and individualistic values of Middle Eastern culture.

The Bedouin Option

One remarkable adaption to the conditions found in the hinterlands is camel nomadism, which has been culturally influential far beyond the number of its practitioners. Perhaps as long as 2,500 years ago[2] the introduction of the camel, with its incredible ability to withstand thirst and heat, permitted an expansion of patoralists into the deep desert. Nomadic camel herders could gather at fertile oases in the deep desert during the dry summer, scatter to search for water in the winter, and find enough grazing to raise large herds of camels for use as reliable transport in trade. Their adaption to the desert obliged the nomads to evolve a fluid social organization permitting considerable individual autonomy within an overarching clan structure, since family units sharing a tent had to count on themselves and their close allies during the search for winter grazing, although they would later unite with their larger kin group in summer.

Between 500 and 100 BC the invention of the camel saddle allowed these nomads to ride their camels; this was a significant innovation, since it enabled them to transform themselves into the mobile warriors of the desert who became famous as the Bedouin. Similar adaptions were made in the Sahara by the people now known as the Tuareg and in the deep deserts of Iran and Pakistan by the present-day Baluch and Brahui. Now, with new mobility, the armed camel riders could not only raid one another, they could also improve their lives by offering "protection" to trading convoys and extorting similar tribute (*khuwa*) from sedentary villagers. These relations of protection and tribute could extend to the state itself, which might pay the Bedouin for their silence and cooperation, rather than attempt to pursue and subdue them in their desert domain. Even today, the al-Murrah of the Saudi Arabian Empty Quarter need not sell their camels, since they are given a regular stipend as members of the national guard maintaining the peace of the borders. The state, then, could be seen by the Bedouin not only as a danger, but also as an exploitable resource, while the state might regard the nomads as both threats and as potential allies.

The moral values of these nomads can be, in some measure, correlated with the ecological conditions they face. The vaunted courage and love of personal independence found among camel herders are a consequence of their need to range widely during the winter to take advantage of scattered rainfall and pasturage. For instance, the contemporary al-

Murrah Bedouin travel as much as 1,900 kilometers in their search for winter pasture.[3] Individuals in this arid country have always had to be willing and able to act on their own, prepared to deal with unforeseen contingencies on their long migrations, and ready to stand up bravely to predators and occasional armed opposition. Honesty, honor, self-control, and a capacity to mediate are necessities in a world of uncertainty, where a man's reputation is his only guarantee of esteem, and where there are no police to enforce rules. Courage in love and war, and a willingness to use violence, are highly valued as well, since mediation and personal integrity cannot substitute for masculine strength and assertion in a competitive world. Generosity and hospitality are also adaptive responses to a harsh and unpredictable environment, where the wealthy of one day may be impoverished the next. Similarly, careful observation of the character of one's friends and foes, and of strangers, is required to assess their possible future actions and the sorts of relations one can expect from them.[4] The nomads therefore have long had a passion for biography and narratives of deeds and incidents that illustrate the complexities and contradictions of human personality – both heroic and base.

Most importantly for my argument, the conditions of the desert correlate with the deep-seated resistance of camel nomads to hierarchy and stratification. For example, The Bedouin shaikh traditionally organized attacks and oversaw defense, but his authority was purely a matter of voluntary agreement among his co-equals. He had no power of coercion whatsoever. As Ibn Khaldun, the great fourteenth-century Muslim philosopher of history, writes about the Bedouin: "The leader is obeyed, but he has no power to force others to accept his rulings...There is scarcely one among them who would cede his power to another, even to his father, his brother, or the eldest member of his family."[5] Even today, the King of Saudi Arabia, with his vast riches and power, is addressed by the Bedouin without honorifics, as an equal.

William Irons, among others, has argued that the opposition to ranking is a direct result of the nomadic life-style, where the absence of large-scale economic production or distribution activities, coupled with a relatively low population density and high mobility "make the development of an institutionalized political hierarchy improbable...hierarchical political institutions are generated only by external political relations with state societies, and never develop purely as a result of the internal dynamics of such societies."[6] Hierarchy, then, is contingent; it is a product of the mobile and fluid nomadic community's confrontation with the state or with other competing social structures. In this situation, elevated rank is not given by God, but is to be achieved by men of character and good fortune.

Bedouin values are important in the Middle East because of the disproportionate part they have played in Middle Eastern and Muslim history. As we shall see in more detail in a later chapter, it was in great measure through the aid of the Bedouin that Muhammad came to power in his own society. The Bedouin camel cavalry were the unstoppable military arm of Islam; their triumph and prestige was so total that the camel completely replaced older forms of transport throughout the Middle East, to the extent that wheeled vehicles utterly disappeared.[7]

With the victories of the Muslim armies, the camel nomad and his brethren from the remote oases were transformed from backward barbarians into the conquerors of the world and the bearers of the great transformative message of the Prophet. They defeated and settled among the farmers and pastoralists of Iraq, Syria, Iran and Egypt, whom they ruled, and with whom they eventually intermingled. As Ernest Gellner writes, in this manner the tribal "wolves" were transformed into tame "sheepdogs" by the state which employed them.[8] But for some generations at least they self-consciously retained their wolfish natures; and even when thoroughly tamed, the ideals of equality, independence and warrior notions of honor still kept a hold on the consciousness of the tribesmen–soldiers, who soon also became local administrators and notables. The values held by these dominant soldiers provided a kind of cultural template for the ideal life throughout the regions they ruled; a template which included distaste for all forms of submission and high evaluation of personal strength, the pursuit of honor, and self-assertive displays of courage. In this way the nomadic value system was propagated throughout the Middle Eastern world.

But not all nomadic influence was from above; much of the tribal ethos was disseminated from below. The tribal regions have never been capable of supporting all the people born there, and those who lost their herds have always migrated into cultivated areas, where poor nutrition and unhealthy conditions created a high death rate and a never-ending need for manpower. The cities and towns have been populated from time immemorial by immigrants who traced their ancestry back to the people of the hinterlands. Despite their own impoverishment and low status in the city, even today these migrants still try to maintain their lineage connections and rights, and are proud to cherish the values of their tribal forefathers.[9]

Of course, the ideal of the tribe is not without its ambiguities; for the Middle Eastern urbanite, the hinterlands remain places of poverty, violence, and crudity – one would not like to leave the luxury and sociability of city for the harsh life of the tribesman. But the remote oases of Medina is where Islam was nurtured, and the desert tribes were Islam's warriors; the wilderness is also often the place where one's own ancestors were born. Because of this history, the wilderness has long been viewed as the locus of purity and honor, despite its dangers and discomforts. There integrity, pride and virtue can best be realized, while the city, with all its luxury and variety, is the locus of corruption, venality and compromise.

Evidence of the moral authority of nomad may be found in the fact that the term "Arab", now taken as a linguistic and ethnic designation for the whole of the Arab-speaking world, was originally used by the Bedouin to refer only to themselves, and is still used by them in this way; it was appropriated by Arab nationalists in the last century in an effort to associate the whole society with Bedouin self-esteem and pride. Another indication is that, to this day, city boys in many Middle Eastern countries are sent to the desert for training in manhood and rectitude. Traditionally, elite urban infants were also raised by a tribal wet nurse, who established a near blood tie with her charges. Muhammad himself had fictive kinship with a clan of the Hawazin Bedouin, who had nursed him as an infant.[10] Although the Bedouin has often been portrayed as cruel and primitive, the generally positive literary image of the tribal periphery is unique among world cultures. Consider, in contrast, the contempt and horror felt by the urban Chinese or Romans or even modern Europeans for the vulgarities of rural barbarians.

Shepherds and Confederacies

Camel nomadism, though much lauded in legend and important in Muslim expansion, is only one form of tribal adaptation to the harsh conditions of the wastelands. Much more ancient (dating from at least 6,500 BC) and far more numerous are the shepherds living on the desert permimeters and at the edges of the mountains, pursuing more reliable pasture than their deep desert cousins (many of whom, in fact, also may keep sheep and goats in oases and on the desert fringes). Present-day groups which follow this pattern of life include many of the Berber tribes of the Atlas, the Lurs, Basseri, Bakhtiari, Qashqai and some Kurdish and Arab pastoralists, all herding in the Zagros and Elburz ranges, as well as the multitude of other shepherding peoples from Afghanistan to Morocco.

These shepherds, who may use camels, donkeys or horses for transport, drive their flocks of sheep and goats into the rainy highlands every summer, following fairly regular migration routes and sometimes doing some farming as well in their summer campsites, which may also be set up as second homes, depending on the fertility of the soil and the severity of the climate. Scarcity and unreliability of grazing also correlate with differences in family structure, as those shepherds in more productive areas of Iran, Turkey and Afghanistan favor joint families, where fathers and married sons work together to care for the herds. In the more sparse environments of southern Iran and in Baluchistan, in contrast, shepherds distribute the risk through a division of the herd among small nuclear families who, like camel nomads, are extremely independent of one another.[11]

But in general sheep and goat nomadizing has always been more restricted and orderly than camel nomadism, since it may require the movement of extremely large herds (Fredrik Barth estimates that the annual sheep migration in Fars, southern Iran, involves more than one million animals) to the proper places at the proper times, in the proper sequence, sometimes through the territory of potentially unfriendly farmers who may try to stop or impede the migration. They must also cope with efforts by states to dominate them as they traverse their territory. The size of their migration, the regularity of their lives, and intrusiveness of the state makes the lives of these nomads quite different from their Bedouin cousins.

As Barth writes, "a prerequisite for the development of a land use pattern such as this is a political form that ensures the disciplined and coordinated migration of large populations by regular routes and schedules. This requires the development of strong and effective coordinating authorities."[12] As a result, pastoral tribes and patrilineal clans have tended to gather together in loose confederations under powerful central leadership, often recruited from outside the tribal structure.[13] These leaders could organize the complex migratory procedure, and could serve as well to mediate with interfering state systems and local peasant communities. Such centralized confederations had considerable capacity to command significant manpower and to develop complex internal hierarchies. With this strong base, these shepherds, like their deep desert brothers, managed to resist state power to a large degree, and to assert their own independence as confederacies, while holding dependent peasant farmers in contempt.

The development of independent confederacies is not the only form of adaption the tribes have made to organize their migration and aid them in their eternal struggles with the state. In some circumstances, the confederacies have accommodated themselves to state power, and, like nomadic "sheepdogs" cited by Gellner, have kept a modicum of freedom by serving as guardians of the center. Sometimes, as well, they too have risen up against the state, and have managed to conquer it. Historically, most of the states of the eastern half of the Middle East originated in conquest by herdsman and horse nomads migrating down from the steppes of Central Asia; the pre-Islamic Achaemenid, Parthian, and Sasanid regimes were all products of such nomadic invasions, as were the Muslim Seljuk, Qajar, and Ottoman Empires, among others.

Other adaptations occurred when the state was too strong to be conquered or held at bay. Then the shepherds, following the motto "divide that ye may not be ruled," could scatter into the more remote and forbidding periphery, breaking apart into small unruly clans impossible for the center to control. In each instance, the tribe and state changed shape in a continuous dialectical relationship as the herdsmen sought to adjust to circumstances while still maintaining as much of their autonomy as possible.[14]

Even when a paramount chief did manage to gain ascendancy among the shepherds his inferiors nonetheless obstinately refused to accept their subordination. Like their camel-herding cousins, they still claimed to be all equals, in spite of the existence of objective hierarchies. This has caused considerable consternation among Marxist anthropologists, who consider the ideology of equality to be "a political chimera which serves to attenuate an unpalatable *status quo*."[15] Yet this "chimera" nonetheless retains its hold throughout the Middle East. Simply to dismiss these beliefs as false consciousness risks reducing deep-seated cultural values to ideological manipulations by a self-serving elite. This is not to deny that such beliefs may indeed further elite interests by masking invidious distinctions; that is evident. But if the actual distinctions being masked are so obvious to us, isn't it very likely that they are also obvious to *them* as well? Why then continue with the charade?

In part, resistance to recognizing class and status distinctions is due to the conditions of the nomadic existence, where the rich of today may be the poor of tomorrow, since wealth located in animals is notoriously unreliable. Furthermore, the client herding his patron's animals may actually feel no sense of oppression whatsoever, since the patron's stable capital primarily comes from the way he uses the profits from sale of animals in urban trade opportunities and in the purchase of farmland. All the poor herdsmen does is care for his patron's herd, an honorable and manly job. In return, the shepherd can take his pay in animals, which, with luck, will multiply and give him the possibility of independence in the future. Hence, from the point of view of the ordinary shepherd, the wealthy man is just someone who has succeeded in the pathway he himself hopes to follow.

One must also take into account the way in which local authority has actually operated, especially within the large tribal confederacies of Iran, where complex governing administrations were ruled by powerful *khans*. There too, despite the khans' objective authority, the nomads retained strongly egalitarian ideologies, and did not accept their leaders as intrinsically superior to them. Even among the greatest and most hierarchical pastoral confederacy, the Qashqai of Iran, "tribespeople often viewed tribal leaders as necessary (although sometimes unwelcome) mediators against what they perceived as the illegitimate, exploitative rule of the state."[16] The local leader's power came from his capacity to mobilize men for military action, a capacity that was limited by the fact that "tribespeople who were discontented could effectively deny support to leaders, ultimately by severing ties and joining other units or forming their own."[17]

In other words, the contractualism found among pastoralists was not limited to worker–employer relationships, but extended to the relationship between chief and subject, and, more crucially, between military commander and soldier. All were understood as contingent agreements between equals, which could be voided by either party at any time. The arbitrary power of leaders in these shepherd communities was therefore sharply limited by their well-founded fear of their fellow tribesmen, who might decide to eliminate, or at least abandon, an overly-ambitious or oppressive "authority".

As a result, leaders generally intervened little at the level of local politics, and contented themselves with ratifying the clans' own choices for headmen; also, relatively little was exploited from the ordinary tribesmen, as the khans and their minions gained their primary wealth not from taxation of their followers, but from urban investments, trade, and the purchase of farmland. Under these circumstances, the yoke of authority did not weight very heavily on the tribesman, and the great and wealthy khan was respected but not deified, and was regarded as a man like any other. Nor did the fall of an elite lineage mean much to the supposed subjects, who continued to live their daily lives as before.[18]

Independent Farmers of the Mountains

A final adaption to the geography of the hinterlands is not nomadic; it is found among the people who farm the isolated mountain valleys that are at the very boundaries of state control. The Kabyle Berbers of Algeria, the Kurds of Iran and Turkey, the Berbers of the highlands of the Morocco and the Pukhtun of Pakistan and Afghanistan are people who live in environments of this sort. If water is plentiful and soil good, these remote valleys can be remarkably productive and densely populated. Swat, in Northern Pakistan, where I did my fieldwork with the Pukhtun, had approximately 1,600 persons per arable square mile – more than Bangladesh!

Like the rest of the people of the wilderness, these mountaineers expound values of hospitality, honor, integrity, generosity, bravery, and so on. They also are deeply egalitarian, and have a strong antipathy to submitting to any form of state authority; the Pukhtun, for instance, defined independence to me as "not paying taxes"; they make an invidious distinction between "yaghestan", the vaunted land of freedom where they live, and "hukomat", the despicable land of governance, where peasant farmers live. Similarly, the Berber mountaineers distinguish between "siba" where men are free, from "makhzen", the "treasure house", where men are enslaved by taxation.

This is not to say leaders never appear in the highlands. They do. Swat had a king while I was first working there. In Morocco, the Glawi ruled what amounted to a state within a state during the Protectorate. But, as among pastoralists, when secular authority does arise it is usually due to external causes – often occurring when a leader is required to rally the tribes against invasion. A capacity for unity in defense is the source of the remarkable ability of these mountain groups to keep their independence, and to this day mountain tribes, more than any others, have proven extremely resistant to state takeover. The early Arab conquests came to a grinding halt in the mountains of Afghanistan, as did invasions by India, Britain and, most recently, the Soviet Union. The Kurds continue even now to resist the authority of Turkey and Iran. But the warriors who directed resistance generally have not left dynasties behind them. Unless preserved by external alliances, their authority vanished soon after the threat was over. More long lasting were the ruling lineages that arose when mountain people managed to invade the lowlands to set up their own kingships. The Buyid dynasty in Iraq was founded by mountaineer tribesmen, and the mountain Berbers too have contributed many regimes, and were the main arm of the Muslim conquest of Spain.

The mountain tribes pose a puzzle for ecological determinism. If we can partially explain the Middle Eastern nomads' egalitarian values as a consequence of the low population density, mobility, and variable productivity characteristic of nomadism everywhere, combined in the Middle Eastern cases with a complex interrelationship with the ancient power of the state, how can we understand the perpetuation of these same values among the hill tribes who are farmers, not nomads, who may produce considerable surplus, who have a high density of population, and who generally do not have a similar symbiotic relationship with the power of the state?

One answer may be that mountain tribes are simply settled nomads who are carrying on, in altered form, their traditional mode of life in an environment that is more suited to peace and the acceptance of an ordering authority.[19] However, not all mountaineers claim a nomadic past, including some of the most independent and egalitarian; there is absolutely no evidence for instance, that the bellicose Afridi of the Afghan-Pakistan border were ever nomads.

A better answer is that the mountain tribes, like their nomadic cousins, live in situations of what John Davis has called "shifting indeterminacy" and "endemic competitiveness" in which there is no overarching power structure or prescribed set of statuses, nor any possibility of achieving uncontested and permanent domain over others. An assertion of equality can be seen as a consequence of this restriction. As Davis puts it, "thwarted in their attempts to gain dominance, men settle for the next best – 'we are all equal': at least they can resist other's assertion of dominance."[20] In a blocked social world, the struggle for honor through demonstrations of bravery and generosity is a way of asserting distinction when other avenues are unavailable. Davis associates this type of egalitarian competitive social ethic with an intense struggle for scarce resources in an undiversified economy among undifferentiated people who are incapable of real social mobility or of challenging the status quo.[21]

But while Davis's portrait of the mountaineer's mode of production is accurate, his moral perspective is most appropriate for European peripheral peoples, who have long been subjects of a dominant state that oppresses them and restricts their potential. Their assertion of equality is the assertion made by peasants seeking to hide their weakness and resist government power by presenting a solid front of corporate unity. As Davis says, "Vis-a-vis outsiders, of course, they are all equals, all equally powerless."[22] This has never been the case in the Middle Eastern tribal context. Although these mountain people, and their nomadic comrades, clearly demarcated themselves in opposition to the center, they certainly did not feel themselves powerless in relation to the state – at least until fairly recently. On the contrary, their own history tells them that they can sometimes conquer the state and that their way of life is purer and better than urban life. For these mountain tribesmen, as for the pastoralists, the faith in human equality and the pursuit of personal honor are more than defenses against impotence; they are the essence of the proper way of being, and cannot be derived purely from ecological constraints, though these contraints are crucial factors. As I shall argue in later chapters, we must take into account structural, scriptural, and historical influences as well.

But for the moment, let me reiterate that Middle Eastern peripheral peoples – camel nomads, shepherds, and mountain farmers – unanimously maintain ideologies of egalitarianism and personal independence. Note that it is not nomadism *per se* that is valued, but the freedom, integrity and personal independence that is associated with the nomad's life – the same freedom found in remote mountain villages and tribal oases, where men also claim a right to the respect and honor due to a warrior. The characteristic tribal values continue to be held in spite of attempts by the state to dominate, and in spite of the hierarchies that arise within the tribes – hierarchies which themselves are largely a way to mobilize against the state and maintain autonomy in the face of its demands.

The Dialectic of Desert and Sown

But the locally asserted dichotomy between tribe and state, desert and sown, center and periphery, does not tell the whole story. If it did, only the people of the margins would hold the values that I have argued are central to the Middle Eastern cultural milieu. Yet the same values are held just as deeply by the majority who live in the great lowland river valleys that have permitted intensive agriculture, a dense population growth, and the rise of ancient centralized state systems. Tribal peoples have been involved for thousand of years with these ancient city-states; they have always known of the city's treasure houses, harlots, scholars and artisans, and of its rulers and their ambitions. For millennia, tribesmen could go to the city for merchandise, learning and pleasure; if they lost their herds or land, they could find work there; if they became powerful, they could hope to plunder it or perhaps settle down in a mansion and intermarry with the urban elite; if the state had strength, they had to fear its expansion. The city center in the Middle East has always provided a model of sophistication, wealth, power and knowledge, as well as corruption and tyranny, against which the people of the hinterlands could measure themselves, against which they could struggle, and toward which they could turn both for inspiration and as an example of depravity.

Yet despite the radical ideological distinction made between city and country, the typical Middle Eastern city was in actual fact not so very much different from the tribal world surrounding it. The Muslim town was defined by the mosque, market and bathhouse (all independent of civil rule[23]) and by the variety of persons who lived within it: merchants, craftsmen, scholars, administrators, warriors. Yet the city itself hardly had a civic identity; there was no mayor, no town council. As Ira Lapidus puts it, Middle Eastern cities "were simply the geographical locus of groups whose membership and activities were either larger or smaller than themselves."[24] The fragmentation of the city was indicated by its structure. It was divided into walled quarters, which, as in rural areas, were generally inhabited by members of the same patrilineal kin group, often composed of immigrants from the surrounding hinterlands, who maintained their relationships of alliance and factionalism in the urban environment. Although there were exceptions, in general the whole city was overseen and exploited by formerly tribal military rulers who lived in a garrison-palace complex nearby, and who also kept up their own tribal values.

Ordinary governance rested within the separate quarters and was multiplex according to the matter at hand. Local elders, wise men, officials of occupational groups, leaders of youth clubs, and the heads of religious orders all acted in mediating disputes and laying claim to

Plate 2.2 A Yemeni town in the mid-eighteenth century.

whatever authority was possible within the civil space left by the absolute, but little exercised, control of the ruler and his bureaucratic administration. In these circumstances, tribal loyalties and values did not vanish with urbanization; they were maintained in the quarters, sometimes cross-cut and at other times intensified by bonds of guild affiliation, association with Sufi brotherhoods, membership in chivalric young men's clubs (the *futuwwa*),[25] and participation in local factions. But on the level of ordinary individuals, the notions of honor, personal agency, and the independence of equal actors bound together by kinship, contiguity and religion remained as potent in the city as in the hinterlands.

This characteristic attitude was furthered by the predominance of trade in the economy of the city, as caravans negotiated the desert, restricted only by access to water and by the mountain ranges. This has been so since ancient times, partly due to the geology of the area, which is mostly limestone and sandstone, with few deposits of metallic ore and other useful materials. Ancient demands for obsidian led to trade with Armenia, while jade for cutting tools was brought from Turkestan, and lapiz lazuli imported from Afghanistan. One can trace such expeditions back to ancient Sumeria. Records show merchant caravans and trading posts set up by the Sumerians in the surrounding mountains and deserts of Persia and Arabia, where they traded grain for raw materials, such as timber and stones, as well as for metals and gems.

The expansion of this early trade was the source of the vast Middle Eastern wealth in the premodern era. Again, the map shows why. The Middle East is the crossroads of the old world; met on the northwest by southern Europe and on the north-east by Russia and Central Asia, on the southeast by the Indian subcontinent, and in the southwest by sub-saharan Africa. Land trade and sea trade to and from any of these regions passed through Middle Eastern territory, providing the slaves, tin, timber, precious metals, and luxury goods that were necessary for the great urban centers to thrive. The craftsmen of the bazaar, the merchants, the ruling warriors and the state bureaucrats all were dependent on this extensive trade for their livelihood. In the heyday of the Middle Eastern merchant, Muslim entrepreneurs from Baghdad and Cairo pursued profit as far afield as China, India, Central Asia and Indonesia.

Reliance on trade had several important consequences. Production was generally in the hands of skilled individual artisans doing piece work in small shops under the tutelage of a master who was also the shop-owner. In these shops differences of rank were blurred as artisans and masters labored side by side in the same modest establishment, were usually members of the same guild and religious sect, lived in the same neighborhoods, and often had fictive (or real) kinship relationships. Like the shepherd and the khan, the worker was bound to his master by a mutual contract which either could repudiate, and the relationship was conceptualized as one of partnership, with, as Chardin puts it, "the Master having always the Liberty to turn away his 'Prentice,' and the 'Prentice' to leave his Master."[26]

This mode of craft production favored the growth of self-governing and ideologically egalitarian craft guilds everywhere in the Middle Eastern city. The growth of independent guilds was furthered by the fact that surplus was drawn primarily from trade, not from labor; the government left working people to govern themselves, much as shepherds of tribal confederacies were left alone by their khans. In the multiplicity of small-scale local egalitarian or quasi-egalitarian organizations for fellowship, worship and production that flourished in this laissez-faire environment individuals could interact with one another within a community of comity and ideological equality, following their own popularly elected leaders and governing themselves by shared consensus while minimizing distinctions of wealth and power.

The mercantile economy was also characterized by a peculiar moral stance that is typical of people who live by trade – an attitude that is individualistic, calculating, risk-taking, and adaptive to circumstances. As among tribesmen, personal relationships and a careful weighing of character have always been crucial in this world, where a man's word is his bond, and where informal ties of trust cement together an international trade network.[27] Nor have merchants and artisans ever had much tolerance for aristocratic professions of moral superiority, favoring instead an egalitarian ethic of the open market, where steady hard work, the loyalty of one's fellows, and entrepreneurial skill make all the difference.[28] And, like the pastoralists, the Middle Eastern merchant or craftsman unhappy with his environment could simply pack up and leave for greener pastures – an act of self-assertion wholly impossible in most other civilizations – including feudal Europe,[29] the former Soviet Union and modern China.

Finally, dependence on long-distance trade meant the great empires of the Middle East were built both literally and figuratively on shifting sand. The central state, though often very rich and very populous, was intrinsically fragile, since the development of new international trade routes could undermine the monetary base and erode state power, as occurred when European seafarers made an end run around Ottoman merchants after the voyage of da Gama. The ecology of the region also permitted armed predators to prowl the surrounding barrens, which were almost impossible for a state to control. Peripheral peoples therefore held a trump card in their dealings with the center, making governmental authority insecure and anxious.

Under these circumstances, whether in the wilderness or in the bazaar, a pervasive sense of the precariousness of life and the tenuousness of power, coupled with a disrespect of aristocratic privilege, a competitive urge, a faith in the essential equality of persons, and a belief in the potential for individual empowerment and honor in the face of arduous odds, have been the pervasive undercurrents of Middle Eastern culture. As we shall see in the next few chapters, these currents have a very long history indeed.

3

Traditions of Authority and Freedom

Continuities with *Jahiliyya*

For devout Muslims, the period prior to the advent of Muhammad was a time of jahiliyya, an era of religious ignorance and barbarism, completely transformed by Islam. However, despite the vast changes wrought by the Muslim explosion, obvious continuities do exist with the past. Persians today persist in reading the adventures of great pre-Islamic kings and heroes in their national epic the *Shahnamah*, while Arabs still recite the magnificent poetry of the warriors of jahiliyya.[1] The ancient Near Eastern gnostic tradition has been tremendously significant in the development of esoteric Islam, and Greek thought underpinned the work of the Muslim philosophers who translated Aristotle and Plato into Arabic. It is because of translations and commentaries on Greek authors by the scholars known to the West as Averroes (Ibn Rushd) and Avicenna (Ibn Sina) that Greek philosophy came first to Spain, and then to the rest of Europe. Greek intellectual methods have also been appropriated into Islamic *kalam*, or theological debate, tightening categories and increasing rationalization within the relatively narrow boundaries of expert formal discourse.[2]

But for many commentators the major influence from the past has not been literary, gnostic, or philosophic but rather the proud monarchical heritage of Sasanid Persia, which was conquered by the expanding Arab Muslim empire. H. A. R. Gibb argued that the gradual replacement of the egalitarian and millenarian ideals of the Arabian desert tribes by Persian notions of universal and absolute authority is the source of the "inner disharmony" he found in Middle Eastern political and social life.[3]

Persians believed the function of the king was to defend a God-given social order. In contrast to the Islamic message that "everybody regardless of his birth could attain whatever social postion was within the reach of his ability,"[4] the Persian social order was not based on freedom and mobility, but on an immutable ranked caste-like segmentation of society into priests, warriors, farmers, and artisans. Even the Persian term "azad", usually translated as "free", actually meant a man born into the proper social strata.

Ideally, the Persian ruler had the duty of preserving the proper distinctions and harmony amongst these ranks in order to maintain prosperity. His job was to dispense justice and sustain the necessary balance between the superior and inferior elements, all of whom had their necessary part to play in the social cosmos. Justice was understood as the continuation of the hierarchical status quo, which had a sanctified foundation. The ruler was portrayed as a mediator between groups, assuring them their appropriate dues and protecting their rights. The deity favored Persia with protection as long as the king and the people acted as they should, keeping the sacred order of the Sasanid realm.

On the one hand, the subject's role in this context was to accept the decrees of the authorities, since those decrees, emanating from the hereditary elite, were believed to have the ultimate purpose of keeping the whole sacredly sanctioned society peaceful and wealthy.[5] On the other hand, the ruler's edicts had to remain within the religious framework, and the king was viewed, in essence, as a servant of the whole – a kind of sacred functionary, surrounded by an elaborate ritual performance that served both to manufacture and to sustain his divinely appointed authority. In their caste-like hierarchy and in the absolute authority of their kings, the Sasanids are often pictured by scholars as the complete opposites of the egalitarian and competitive Arab Muslim tribesmen.

Such polarization obscures some essential similarities between the two polities. In both Persia and Arabia the notions of justice, of the contract between God and man, and of the active role of God and humanity in the world, remained paramount. Although Persian theory saw the king as a representative of the divine, nonetheless, the king was *not* divine himself; as in Arabia, he was conceptualized as a mediator balancing the relationships between the various social segments; also temple and palace were clearly distinguished – the priest was protected by the king, but was *not* the king, nor was the palace a microcosm of the universe, though it was definitely a center of power and justice.

The image of a monolithic Sasanid autocracy also misses elements of resistance that existed within Persian society. Despite self-inflating rhetoric, the royal ideal in Persia was not as powerful and pervasive as the scribes of the court presented it to be and often existed more in the imperial imagination than in reality. Even at their peak of power, the Sasanid kings did not have full control over their people, and their power when it did exist was often arbitrary, coercive and opportunistic, even though rulers attempted to legitimate their rule with sacred trappings of diadems and thrones, and with banquets and receptions where the royal foot was kissed and ornate gifts were distributed among elegant courtiers.

This was because in Persia, as elsewhere in the Middle East, intractable nomads and mountain tribes retained very considerable independence from the state; these dangerous people were sometimes accommodated by being recruited into the army – wolves becoming sheepdogs in an age-old pattern – while at other times they could threaten the empire itself. Within the heart of the Sasanid kingdom as well, outcries against the excesses of the hereditary aristocracy were heard, most loudly in the communistic reform movement led by Mazdak in the fifth century, which temporarily won over the king himself to a program of wealth redistribution, including (according to opponents) the sharing of wives, in the name of universal brotherhood.[6] This revolutionary regime was later overturned and Mazdak and his followers slaughtered, but the movement shows the limits of the Sasanid claims to sacred sanctions for their power and the existence of very strong populist impulses toward more egalitarian forms of moral order. The Persian rhetoric of the divine mission of kings should therefore not be taken at face value, but must be understood, at least in part, as propaganda serving to buttress unstable and often repressive regimes.

After the downfall of the Persian Empire, the Sasanid model was appropriated by many Muslim secular kings and princes seeking to legitimize their powers, who adopted the customs and luxuries of the Sasanid court and portrayed themselves as ideal rulers according to Persian political theory. Handbooks on rule based on reinterpretation of Sasanid kingship (the so-called "mirrors for princes") became a well-known genre as intellectuals tried to inspire their sultans (which literally means "powers") to emulate ideal Persian kings of the past by defending the nation through arms and ordering it through justice.[7] This appropriation of Persian courtly etiquette and political theory was not, as has often been claimed, a triumph of Persian absolutism and opportunism over Arab egalitarianism and millenarianism. As we shall see, Arabs, like Persians, have always tried to develop authoritarian states whenever they could – they were simply less successful. Taking over Persian forms was only one more step in a continued effort by Arab leaders to establish and ratify their rule.

But these attempts were doomed to failure. In both Arabia and Persia any assertion of absolute state power has always been countered by religious and popular affirmations of the dignity of all persons, regardless of social position. We have already seen how such claims fueled Mazdak's millenarian revolution; they remain potent today, and predate the conflict between Islamic revelation and Persian autocracy. Demands for equity and justice are embedded in an ancient Middle Eastern ethical tradition enunciated by Moses, Jesus and the Persian prophet Zoroaster, who all warned of the evils of Godless tyrannies and called for moral action by true believers against a corrupt world.

As Ira Lapidus notes, these charismatic prophets addressed themselves to the consciences of individuals, not nations, asserting "a personal relationship to the gods, and a personal responsibility for upholding the impersonal order of society and cosmos."[8] Within the embrace of these charismatic annunications, men and women were bound together in egalitarian and universalistic communities of worship; faith and deeds, not heredity and power, were the true measure of humanity, and all mankind was united by the imperative of ethical action.

Muhammad did not attempt to cut Islam off from this great ethical past, nor did he wish to be seen as an innovator; he understood his mission to be the correction and completion of the divine messages borne by those who had come before him, returning monotheism to the Abrahamic path from which it had strayed.[9] Like the prophets who preceded him, Muhammad too spoke for an omnipotent God who called upon the faithful to act morally in the world and to transform it, and themselves, through the abolition of injustice and inequity, which are affronts to the deity. By opposing despotic and oppressive rule Muhammad consciously took his place as the last in a series of ethical prophets who have demanded righteous government and justice and equity for all.

Emissaries and Exemplars: Types of Prophecy

Muhammad's prophecy, like earlier Middle Eastern annunciations, can usefully be understood as a particular type of religious message specific to the conditions of Middle Eastern civilization. In order to make this clear, let me first turn to Max Weber's famous distinction between emissary prophecy and exemplary prophecy.[10]

The exemplary prophet, Weber says, is found in the Orient. The type case is Buddha, who demonstrated the way to salvation through his person. To vastly simplify a complex tradition, we can say that in order to escape from the suffering caused by clinging to the hopes and cravings of mundane human experience, Buddhists imitate the Buddha's own examples of passive contemplation and detachment. Salvation in this tradition is understood as the withdrawal and extinction of all desire and the cultivation of indifference to sensation. The goal is to realize the illusory nature of the world, of time, and of the self, thereby achieving nirvana, which is pictured as a negation of all attributes, a merger into absolute nothingness. In this tradition, the deity has no character or moral message, but is pervasive, static, immanent, and abstract.

In aiming to become the empty vessel of the depersonalized universal truth, the practitioner disavows ethical action as a snare that keeps human beings entangled in the world. The seeker instead must focus on the techniques of enlightenment found in meditation and other methods for eliminating desire. Exemplary religions are typically religions of a virtuoso elite whose aspiration is attainment of self-loss in a mystical state of union which is encompassing, timeless, and indescribable. In popular understanding, the exemplary saint is a magical being; a God on earth granted special powers as a result of a spiritual identification with the supernatural.[11]

If exemplary mysticism is typically Asian, ethical emissary prophecy is characteristic of the Middle East. Judaism, Christianity, and finally Islam are the great emissary religions, each with its moral prophets bringing instructions for action and promises of redemption to the faithful. In this form of religious annunciation the prophet is not God's vessel, but His instrument; for him God is omnipotent, transcendent and personal, far beyond human ken, but nonetheless active and moral, ordering humanity onto the right path. To attempt to become one with God would be a blasphemous act of pride, and a misunderstanding of the role of believers as active agents following God's ethical pathway in the world.

The message of the emissary is not one of static merger; it is a dramatic revelation that portrays history as a struggle between good and evil – a struggle which shall end in the apocalypse of Judgement Day. All human beings have a role to play in this cosmic drama, making their own moral choices during the course of an entire lifetime in hopes of gaining eternal paradise after death. Withdrawal from the contest is impossible, since the wrathful, jealous, yet compassionate God commands human beings to live in this world, which He has made for them. They must fulfill their sacred duty here and now, in daily life, acting righteously within the community of believers for the glory of God.

The emissary prophet's calling is to lead humanity onto that arduous ethnical path of piety, and to help all people who heed him toward their ultimate salvation. Emissary religion is consequently egalitarian, preaching universal brotherhood within the congregation, and requiring the participation of all the faithful in the quest for redemption, which is God's just reward to the devout. The prophet as an emissary is not an ecstatic mystic nor a magician, but a sober messenger bringing God's warning and promise to the world, forming the moral community of the righteous who are personally responsible for acting on God's world.[12]

In its eschatology and in the character of its Prophet, Islam in its mainstream form is the emissary religion *par excellence*.[13] In orthodox Islam, Allah is understood as a transcendent and personal God delivering a universal and eternal moral code for humanity that is laid down for all to read in the Quran. This code enjoins people to act properly and make ethical decisions in the world – to "promote the good and prohibit evil"; every person is individually responsible for his or her own moral choices and deeds, and will be called to account for every action before God on Judgment Day, when justice will be meted out.

Just as Allah stands above all humanity, so ought all humanity to stand together, united as equal participants in a community of worshipful believers. Muhammad is the messenger of this supramundane and unifying God, but, as we have already noted, so radical is Islam's humanism and egalitarianism that in his annunciation of universal brotherhood the Prophet denied his own spiritual virtuosity; he is not a God himself, not even God's companion, but only an ordinary man whom God has appointed as His spokesman, His "warner."

Weber's explanation for the rise of exemplary and emissary prophecy relies on specific ecological and social conditions in the distant past. He begins by noting that, in contrast to the Middle East, in Asia farming was by far the dominant mode of production; independent tribes and urban merchants had little influence on the general social formation. Furthermore, in Asia, agriculture was primarily regulated by the periodicities of rainfall and river flow, which could not be effected by human intervention. Political authority and action were constructed within a relatively undifferentiated agrarian social environment where human action had minimal impact in the natural world. According to Weber, under these conditions innate anxiety over human impotence was alleviated by conceptualizing rulers as nature deities in charge of the regulation of rain, the rising of the rivers, and other naturally occurring processes.

Regulation of nature was achieved in this context only symbolically, through elaborate formalized rituals and public performances of possession trance demonstrating that the rulers and their entourages actually embodied the impersonal energies of nature in themselves. While in trance, the ruler–shamans could be placated and worshipped by the apprehensive populace. The basis of both virtuoso mysticism and the deification of ancient kings in the Orient is located by Weber in a deep sense of the futility of human activity and a corresponding veneration of the magical individuals who manifest in trance the spiritual powers necessary for the continuance of the fertility of the fields. But the God–king's range of action is paradoxically quite limited, since he is imprisoned within the framework of rigid ritual practices that allow him to be possessed by abstract, inhuman and (in fact) unmanageable forces.[14]

Weber's intuitive historical account of the shamanistic Asian sovereign has gained greater credence in recent years through the research of archaeologists and anthropologists who have discovered that the rulers of ancient China and India, as well as Mesoamerica, were indeed considered by their subjects and by themselves to be manifestations of the gods of nature, and that these leaders did actually spend much of their lives playing roles in the highly elaborated public ritual perform-ances in which they exemplified and embodied their sacred statuses as demiurges.[15]

The cities and states of these archaic kingdoms were literally con-structed as symbolic expressions of sacred cosmologies, with the king and his court enacting the necessary ceremonies at the center, purport-edly ordering an integrated universe by their actions.[16] This does not mean that struggles for power and domination were non-existent in the court, but it does mean that the emphasis in politics was on the sacred fusion of gods, kings, and the state; government functioned as a sym-bolic vehicle for expressing this cosmic union. With many variations, the theatrical and deified symbolic king who served as an expressive conduit to the sacred seems to have predominated throughout the ancient world.

The Near East was an exception. Weber's reasons for this irregularity again are premised upon the relationship between humanity and the natural environment. Unlike Asia, the arid lands of the Near East re-quired *creating* the habitable world through the laborious construction of irrigation canals that transformed the desert into farmland.[17] The hero-king, with the help of his people, built these vital canals. Because it was regulated by creative action, nature was not understood as an eternal and impersonal essence which individuals can only pretend to control through symbolic rituals of identification; on the contrary, it was seen as malleable and conditional, molded for human benefit by the incessant work of human beings under the inspiration of their own personal warrior-leader.

Within this world view, the bold hero-king validates his individual dominion by his achievements and the gains he accomplishes for his following, who give him obedience and labor in return. His right to command is legitimized by his personal strength and abilities, and is ratified in a written legal code that sets down the terms of the compact between ruler and ruled, as well as the duties of the people toward one another and toward the king, who is singular, not plural; personal, not abstract.

According to Weber, this type of earthly authority provides a different paradigm for imagining divinity. The deity, like the hero, is pictured in the ancient Middle East as a freely acting, ethical, and personally cre-ative being who can fashion a productive world out of nothingness. Salvation is accomplished through moral activity in the mundane world which, since it is created by an active God for his subjects, cannot be totally repudiated. God also has a contract or covenant with his people; they do His work for Him in the world and He will provide paradise for them in return. This God is differentiated from his people; He cannot be possessed, nor can anyone claim self-deification on pain of persecution for heresey (or treason). Yet, at the same time, God is manly, active, powerful, and concerned with equity and justice.

Although Weber did not do so, we can postulate that the appearance of a king who served as a model for such a God is correlated not only with a particular ecology which required concerted and organized action to tame it, but also with the development of different and competing status groups and with the rise of trade. As in Asia, the Middle East relied upon farming for its productive base, but as we have seen, Middle Eastern farmers also had to live in close relationship to independent and threatening nomads and other peripheral peoples; simultaneously, urban commerce was decisive and prevalent from a very early period. The hero was not simply concerned with maintaining agrarian production, he also built the walls that protected the merchants and artisans, he led the armies that fended off the barbarians at the gates, he conquered the hinterlands and brought its treasures back to his city.

Perhaps even more important than defense and conquest was the hero's role as mediator and judge – a role that may actually precede and imply political leadership. Nomads, farmers, and tradesmen have disparate interests and values. Nomads and farmers are especially liable to come into conflict over land use rights, and, rather than risking continual destructive conflict, require someone to arbitrate equitably between them. The mediator-judge is likely to be a priest whose isolation from the mundane struggles over land and power insures his impartiality. The holy arbitrator is in an especially good position to coordinate the activities of those who rely on him for conciliation; this allows him to supervise labor projects and to lead the united groups in wars against less-organized neighbors. Wealth is thereby increased, and the leader-mediator gains ascendance and prestige through his successes. The position of priestly mediator and judge can elide gradually into that of heroic ruler, military general, and law-giver. As we shall discover, this is indeed a pattern that recurs in Middle Eastern history.

To reiterate: the Middle Eastern heritage of emissary prophecy rests on the rise of powerful expansive states and coincides with a heroic view of personal human action that is born of the struggle for survival in the harshness of the arid environment. The ruler in this vision is a man among men, a warrior who organizes a community of egalitarian followers for defense against enemies and for the heroic construction of cities and irrigation networks. This active and creative ruler serves as a model for a similarly imagined deity who stands above mankind, interceding for the benefit of his community of followers while smiting down their opponents. Rulers are also mediators and judges within the community, bound by contractual obligation to dispense justice to the contesting groups they lead. God too fulfills a similar role, so that the dispensation of equal justice to all is a central preoccupation of emissary prophecy.[18]

The Legacy of Gilgamesh

The Middle Eastern world is remarkable for its truly impressive continuity over very long stretches of time. As the archeologist Philip Kohl writes, the "Bronze Age world systems coincide to a surprising extent with the area encompassed by the initial spread of Islam . . . The original Bronze Age world systems did not simply collapse, but left a complex, web-like legacy of political, economic, and, in the broadest sense, cultural interconnections which, in turn, were acted upon and influenced later historical developments."[19] Do the values outlined above have similar continuity?

The Bronze age webs Kohl refers to originally knit together the great literate empires of Egypt, Mesopotamia, and the Indus. Egypt, long portrayed as the radiant core from which all other civilizations emanated, arose within the uniquely protected and rich valley of the Nile, where from time immemorial regular flooding permitted tremendous and stable agricultural production. Outside the valley, conditions did not favor the growth of powerful nomadic groups, and threats from desert tribes were relatively easily handled, though there was always danger from the warrior people of the Upper Nile. The culture that grew up in the Nile valley was, generally speaking, static, homogenous and well-protected, with a strong sense of its own ethnic superiority, continuity, and longevity.

Authority when it evolved in the Egyptian context had an absolute and sacred character. As Henri Frankfort writes, the "Pharaoh was of divine essence, a god incarnate . . . His coronation was not an apotheosis but an epiphany."[20] In this sacred polity, the primary task of the God-ruler was to enact rituals maintaining the regularity of the seasons and the unity of the cosmos; death itself was alien to him. Embalmed in his sacred tomb, he would live forever in an unchanging paradise ruling over his subjects for eternity. Obviously, this is far cry from Weber's notion of emissary prophecy, and is more like exemplary Asian kingship – Egypt is therefore best understood not as the paradigm for the rest of the Middle East, but as an extraordinarily potent deviant case.

Rather than Egypt, it is in ancient Mesopotamia that we find the historical and moral core of the Middle Eastern world. Located in the delta of the Tigris and Euphrates rivers, Mesopotamia was the home of the pre-literate Ubaid culture who built the urban center of Eridu in approximately 5,000 BC. It was in Eridu that Enki, the creator God of water, gave men the universal laws that defined reality for all time – a notion of truth as a set of ethical proscriptions and regulations issuing from a divine source that is echoed again and again in all later revelations of the Middle East. The Sumerians recognized Eridu as the first city, and the Ubaids as their ancestors.

It is in the fertile delta, the home of the Ubaids and their Sumerian descendants, that we find ecological and productive conditions characteristic of the Middle East in general. As Henri Frankfort writes, in contrast to the bounded, secure and regular world of Egypt, this region "lacks clear boundaries and was periodically robbed and disrupted by the mountaineers on its east or the nomads on its west... Mesopotamia is, for much of its grazing, dependent on an uncertain rainfall and possesses in the Tigris an unaccountable, turbulent, and most dangerous river."[21]

In these difficult circumstances, a sort of ruler far removed from the omnipotent Pharaoh appeared. He is portrayed in the first written epic, the story of the warrior–hero Gilgamesh who built the walls of the great city of Uruk, killed the giant Humbaba, hewed the great cedars of the upland forests and slew the bull of heaven. "Supreme over other kings, lordly in appearance, he is the hero... Two-thirds of him is god, one-third of him is human"; Gilgamesh is "the shepherd of Uruk-Haven... bold, eminent, knowing." Yet, unlike the Egyptian Pharaohs, Gilgamesh, for all his qualities, cannot conquer death. He himself says, "Only the gods can dwell forever with Shamash. As for human beings, their days are numbered, and whatever they keep trying to achieve is but wind!"[22]

Gilgamesh was not a dehumanized ceremonial performer above the plane of ordinary human action. "It was he who opened the mountain passes, who dug wells on the flanks of the mountain... who restored the sanctuaries (or cities) that the Flood had destroyed!" His motivation was a desire for glory and honor: "I will face fighting such as I have never known, I will set out on a road I have never traveled... I will establish for myself a name for eternity!" Yet his power was not untrammeled. In his quest for renown, he sought the advice of the "noble counselors" of Uruk. And when Gilgamesh "struts his power over the people like a wild bull" he was reproved and reminded of his responsibilities as shepherd.[23] When Gilgamesh continued his tyranny, the gods heard the peoples' outcries and created the savage Enkidu, who emerged from the wilderness to challenge the king. Enkidu was narrowly defeated by Gilgamesh, who then took him as his friend and boon companion. Enkidu's death stirred Gilgamesh to bitter regret and a fruitless quest for eternal life.

In this epic we see many of the elements Weber predicted. The king, in the first place, is a mortal man, despite his greatness and heroism. He is motivated by a desire for glory and acts in the world to gain the respect of other men and a place in the memories of future generations.

He is not only a brave warrior fighting against the savages of the hinter-land, but also a builder who tames the wilderness and turns nature into culture. He is the shepherd of his people and builds the walls around their town, which is literally called "Uruk-the-Sheepfold". But the people are not simply his possessions; they protest his injustice, and he must heed the moral demands of the community, which are conveyed through a town assembly and a counsel of elders; trade too is important, and Gilgamesh confers with the town counselors in the marketplace.

The epic of Gilgamesh, as we now know it, is a transformation of very ancient stories and is reflective of later dynastic attempts to validate kingly rule in Mesopotamia; as such it shows a strong urban and literary perspective for which we must make corrections. However, archaeolo-gists who have studied this ancient polity find the tensions outlined in the epic to be seminal throughout the millennia-long span of literate Meso-potamian history. They find as well that modern elements of Middle Eastern social organization have a very long history indeed.

For instance, as Jacobsen notes, the earliest Sumerian myths and texts reveal a remarkably egalitarian ideology wherein all human beings are alike in their shared bondage to the gods. These gods make their decisions together in democratic assemblies similar to those of the town council of Uruk and to the public meetings held in the other Sumerian villages.[24] Jacobsen also argues that the very first temple complexes, like the local communities from which they arose, were primarily or-ganizations of mutual aid, taking shared responsibility for the well-being of the participants gathered together under the authority of the protective deity.[25]

The archeological record of housing shows as well a transformation from the small nuclear family houses of pre-literate Ubaid society to more extended family dwellings, which themselves were united into residential quarters. It is likely that these extended families were struc-tured by lineage; a pattern that continued in the urban centers of imper-ial Sumeria, where texts show that property holding in a quarter was restricted to members of a lineage group. An egalitarian kin-based or-ganization served as the basic building block of the burgeoning Sumer-ian city, just as it continued to do throughout the Middle East in urban and rural environments.[26]

The larger dwellings of extended lineages combined over time into village complexes, which employed more complex and efficient irriga-tion canals. As H. W. F. Saggs writes: "This called for a substantial well-organized labour force, and this need constituted a factor which was eventually to have a fundamental effect upon the way society developed, since the larger the group and the better organized it was, the more land could be irrigated and the more prosperous the whole community would be."[27] In this setting, as Henri Frankfort puts it, governance was by an "assembly of all free men" who, "in times of emergency...chose a 'king' to take charge for a limited period...The source of the king's authority was his election by the assembly."[28] The men elected in this process took charge of defense, or oversaw canal-digging, or the rituals of the New Year. They were the recognized best among their cohort, first among equals, whose temporary power to organize their fellows was a direct reflection of their personal abilities and capacity to win respect.

The organizational centers of this new and efficient mode of production were the cooperative temple complexes, which allocated labor and distributed goods, as well as supervising and supporting craft specialization and underwriting the risks of long-distance trade. As Carl Lamberg-Karlovsky argues, these self-sufficient temples can perhaps best be seen as public utilities, offering concrete as well as spiritual returns to those individuals who participated in them. People belonged to them as they did to a household, but these organizations brought a new capacity to amass surplus and organize the populace for public works, trade, and war. They were as well the first institutions of credit capital. Those who were not attached to a temple took up subsistence farming for themselves on the community land, or perhaps traded goods on consignment, paying the temple 20 percent of the proceeds and keeping the rest as personal profit.[29] As cities comprised of several distinct temple corporate enterprises evolved in the fertile southern Mesopotamian plain, the temples competed with one another for workers and profits, in a spirit of rivalry that continues to pervade throughout the region. We can see as well here the nascent combination of individualism with corporate membership that is so typical of Middle Eastern culture.

The Russian archeologist I. M. Diakonoff believes that at first the temples and local kin groups may have been one and the same, both governed by democratic consensus of the elders of the temple community.[30] Frankfort even speaks of a "theocratic communism".[31] But over time the temples became relatively autonomous, and priestly families became hereditary elites within the temple complex, acquiring land and privileges for their services. The temple also gained its own inalienable land (much like *waqf* in Islamic times, which is also inalienable land consigned to a mosque or another "non-profit" religious institution) which could constitute considerable estates. The benefits accruing to the temple could easily turn into benefits garnered by the dominant priestly family, a blurring of public and private that is again to be found throughout Middle Eastern history.

By 3500 BC, Uruk, the city of Gilgamesh, expanded explosively, drawing immigrants from all over the region. This was very possibly due to the invention of writing, which allowed a new efficiency in administration, better centralized control over irrigation networks and the accumulation of greater wealth. It is noteworthy that the purported inventor of writing, Gilgamesh's ancestor Enmerkar, was also the mythical originator of long-distance trade, and that Uruk was a society where the merchants were extremely influential.

As I argued in chapter 2, the mercantile ethnic of egalitarianism, social mobility, competitive individualism and puritanism has always opposed the aristocratic ethic of display and hereditary authority. On the other hand, the merchant relies on the state to provide an atmosphere of calm in which trade can go on, while the state counts on commerce to supply its luxury goods and much of its surplus. The uneasy balance between the interests of court and bazaar found in early Sumeria would also remain predominant right through the Islamic era.

The sudden urban expansion of Uruk and the new pattern of life involved in it led to a long chaotic period in which rival city-states and the temples within them struggled with one another for dominance while immigrants scattered throughout the region to establish colonies and seek trade. Already during this era, the region was marked by the competitiveness and relative fragility of any central hierarchy that would continue to be characteristic of the Middle East throughout history, since no temple complex could permanently dominate all the others. The importance of trade and the populist status ethic of merchants further undermined any local claims to absolute authority, as did the continuous threat of nomad invasion.

A limited exception, however, was the city of Nippur, universally recognized as the home of Enlil, the "father of the Gods". Nippur had no coercive power over other city-states, but by virtue of its spiritual superiority was exempt from both political rivalries and taxation. Due to their special holiness and genealogical priority, the priests of Nippur also served a function which we will see repeated by religious figures in later centuries; for a thousand years Nippur's clerics acted as arbitrators of disputes and offered refuge for exiles. It was also in Nippur that the gods sat in consultative councils that imitated the popular assemblies of the basic kinship community.

But the mediated balance between antagonistic temples in southern Mesopotamia was challenged from what is now known as al-Jezira, the "island" in the north on the wide plain between the two great rivers. Here, on the hilly plateau, adequate and regular rainfull made dry farming and nomadism the dominant modes of production. No communal temple complexes overseeing irrigation and crafts production arose here, nor was there an expansive trade complex; instead a single city, Kish, was predominant, ruled by warriors with no claims to sacred sanction.[32] Their power came from their own individual ability to command the loyalty of their comrades-in-arms. The tombs of Kish, dating from 2800 BC, contain weapons and treasure, showing the personal accumulation of wealth and power by warrior-heroes and their households. The social organization of Kish, based on the force of conquerors and their capacity to inspire a following, posed a threat to the internally divided world of the south. A fragmented and corrupt center menaced by the invasion of cohesive peripheral warrior peoples also will be a repeated motif in Middle Eastern history.

The Limits of Authority

It was in Kish that, as the Sumerians put it, "kingship descended from heaven" and made its permanent imprint on the history of the region. United around their secular warrior leaders, the northerners threatened Sumerian independence. The southerners could no longer afford their eternal internecine struggles in the face of the threat from Kish, and elected their own warrior–rulers to lead them into combat. These leaders developed into a new military class that was in competition with the already existing sacred temples for the loyalty and labor of the local communities.

The military elite gained popular approval by opposing the now oppressive temple order, enlarged their power by conquest and by taxation, and broke the sacred boundaries drawn between cities by the mediation of Enlil; they also sponsored expanded trade through which they and their allies profited. Temple land was confiscated and became crown estates, to be overseen and exploited by military dependents. An increase in individual landholding went along with greater differences in individual wealth. Monumental architecture and the development of wide-ranging trade by well-connected, profit-seeking individuals coincided with spiraling landlessness, debt slavery and oppression of the masses.

At the pinnacle of military domination, the warrior–king Naram Sin (2254–2218 BC), seeking legitimacy, had himself declared a supreme god, commanding all the gods of the cities, displacing the authority of the priests of Enlil and momentarily fulfilling the kingly ideal of a universal and centralized political authority legitimized by religion. The rapid and catastrophic fall of his dynasty to invasions by the "dog-headed" nomadic Guti was portrayed by Sumerian priests as divine retribution for Naram Sin's arrogance, foreshadowing the manner the invasion of Mongols was to be interpreted by clerics in Muslim times and the skepticism with which all later claims by warrior kings to sacredness would be viewed by the priesthood and the general Middle Eastern populace.

The processes of centralization and increased kingly authority nonetheless continued apace. After the Guti were ousted, imperial rule became more and more arbitrary and heavy-handed. During Ur III (2112–2006 BC), the royal house finally expropriated all temple land, and large-scale production of every sort became a state monopoly supported by state bureaucrats and a priestly class now encapsulated as clerkly dependents of the state. Nonetheless, despite even this increased centralization, and despite the first known (and first failed) attempt to build a great wall to keep the nomads out, another nomadic tribe, the Amorites, once again broke the power of the empire.[33] It is from within the ranks of the Amorites that Hammurabi arose to take command in Babylon.

Seeking popular support in their continuous power struggles with the temples, with each other, and with nomadic invaders, secular rulers in Sumeria continually tried to displace the old religion by turning themselves into gods – an effort doomed to miscarry as the dynasties rapidly fell and the ruler's grandiose claims proved patently false. The longest-lived dynasty (Ur III) lasted a mere century, and even the famous Hammurabi's empire collapsed in the lifetime of his son (1792–1750 BC).

Aside from abortive claims to godhood, another method for gaining the support of the community was the institution of reforms, canceling debts and liberating people from indentured servitude at annual New Year festivals.[34] For instance, the stele of Ur-Nammu, who founded the despotic Ur III dynasty in 2112 BC, guarantees that "the orphan was not given over to the rich man; the widow not given over to the powerful man; the man of one shekel was not given over to the man of one mina."[35] These proclamations were certainly intended to gain the confidence of the masses by promising them relief from fiscal oppression.

Yet, despite their propagandistic intent, the inscriptions on imperial markers nonetheless entail promises that were understood then, as now, as pledges to be redeemed; the principles of equity (nig.sisa) and justice (nig.gina) spoke to pre-existing local aspirations and became touchstones for critique of any later regime, setting the moral premises of Middle Eastern rule off from other cultural regions where the king has no such compact with his subjects, and where justice is simply maintenance of the status quo.

Kingly proclamations of equity and justice also show the expectations of the populace, who did not accept the rights of despots to absolute power. At the height of despotic hubris, when Naram Sin declared himself a god, Diakonoff tells us that "the ruler's authority beyond the territory which he controlled directly (i.e. beyond the temple estate and, later, crown land) was neither autocratic, despotic, nor unlimited. On the contrary...the state system of ancient Sumer can hardly even be called monarchic."[36] Even during these periods of absolutism members of self-governing local communities retained a fair degree of independence, and proudly proclaimed themselves to be "men" obeying customary law, as opposed to those who were "prostrated in submission" and reliant on the state to adjudicate for them[37] – an invidious contrast between the "free" and the "dependent" that will retain its resonance for Middle Easterners afterwards.

To recapitulate: The history of Mesopotamia is a history of warring city states ruled by warrior kings and temple cadres who struggled for power amongst themselves, while fending off raids from neighbors and from armed nomads, contending with a fertile, but fickle, environment through irrigation projects, and competing with one another both in battle and in pursuit of long-distance trade. Social mobility was great in this world, as daring warriors from the periphery took power from weak kings, only to lose power themselves to another invading upstart; immigrants, drawn by possibility of wealth, gave up nomadizing and moved into the city; slaves could be freed, or a free man enslaved for debt; risk-taking merchants won or lost fortunes; lucky administrators were granted estates, while the ill-starred were dismissed in disgrace. No one individual or group could plausibly claim any intrinsic superiority in this fluid environment, and even the lowest could dream of greatness. The pervasive values of competitive individualism were furthered by the egalitarian, puritanical, and cosmopolitan outlook of the merchant, who has been an essential feature of the Middle Eastern landscape from the very earliest days.

In this context, the state could not simply assert sacred legitimacy for itself, but had to appeal to the values of free communities for validation, offering in return legal codes defining the rights of the people and the obligations of the government to its citizens. As Lamberg-Karlovsky argues, such concepts as "freedom, equity, and justice" are the legacy of this social balance of forces – and the West, no less than the Middle East, is in debt to this ancient heritage for our central values.[38]

Finally, in spite of the despotic claims of rulers, ancient Mesopotamian communities of free men retained strong values of equality and autonomy; recognition of secular command also remained conditional, so even the mighty Babylonian "king of kings" was regarded as no way different in his essential nature from his fellow men. As Henri Frankfort writes, this great civilization was plagued like no other ancient society by "the ambiguity, the unsolved problem of how to regard a king who, though a mortal, yet stands apart from other men";[39] a quandary that is still at the core of Middle Eastern political life – and our own.

4

The Social Construction
of Egalitarianism

Ibn Khaldun's Theory of Authority

The thinker who made the greatest contribution to understanding the dynamics and contradictions implicit in the ancient riddle of authority in the Middle East was born in Tunis in 1332 and died in 1406 AD. Ibn Khaldun, a North African judge, bureaucrat, adventurer and scribe, had first-hand experience of the vicissitudes of power. During his career he served as tutor to the heir apparent of the shrinking Muslim state of Grenada and later as advisor to other petty courts of North Africa. At one point he recruited and led a force of desert Arabs in support of his employer. Defeated, he spent three years among mountain tribesmen as a refugee under their protection. He finished his life in the highly respected post of Grand Qadi of the Malikite school of law in Cairo.

Ibn Khaldun's stormy history was somewhat unusual but certainly not extraordinary. Such picaresque ups and downs were common among government functionaries throughout Middle Eastern history, where, as we have seen, dynasties have often rapidly ebbed and flowed, elevating or destroying those attached to them. What was unusual was Ibn Khaldun's response. Disillusioned by his failure to make a mark on the state, he tried instead to gain a theoretical grasp of the unstable world in which he was immersed. His time among tribesmen and his experience in the courts, along with his background in Greek philosophy, gave him a perspective that led his thoughts in a new direction.

Ibn Khaldun's radical methological contribution was to apply the techniques of philosophical science to the study of history. In his era, the actual events of the world were seen by philosophers as meaningless and contingent, hardly worth the attention of a logical mind, which should occupy itself instead with the higher realms of the eternal. As opponents of the philosophers, Muslim theologians were extremely interested in the past, but their concern was with moral biography, not the logic of history.

Neither of these approaches was acceptable to Ibn Khaldun. The wilful philosophic ignorance of history denied the importance of actual lived human reality, while the theologian's emphasis on personality ignored social patterning. A critical scientific historical method was needed that could allow both intelligent discrimination between truth and falsehood, and adequate understanding of historical processes. This was what he set out to achieve.

His great book, the *Muqaddimah*, was intended as an introduction to a larger study of history; in it he sought to build a basic framework for understanding the rise and fall of dynasties in North Africa and in the rest of the Middle East. As I have in this study, Ibn Khaldun starts his work with the common-sense premise that "the differences of condition among people are the result of the different ways in which they make their living."[1] Given his own experience with geography and ecology, he then postulates two essential and contrasting ways of "making a living" that give rise to complementary and intertwining forms of culture: the Bedouin civilization of the deserts, mountains and wastelands, and the sedentary civilization behind the walls of cities and towns. The main distinction he stresses here is *not* between nomad and farmer (the Bedouin, he rightly says, are often farmers); it is a distinction between a crude world in which individuals interact as equals and a complex world of distinctive ranks and statuses.

For Ibn Khaldun, the admirable equality of Bedouin life is primarily a consequence of its austerity, simplicity, and harshness. In this impoverished environment, wealth and power cannot be accumulated and distinctions between individuals are purely a result of personal characteristics, so that people are more or less equivalent. The primitivity of their circumstances means that the Bedouin necessarily live a life of individualism, independence, poverty and purity, as well as savagery; sedentary urban life, on the other hand, is built on the development of crafts and commerce, it favors both luxury and decadence. It also requires greater co-operation and complex divisions of labor, and therefore the evolution of distinctions and rank. In particular, sedentary life necessitates royal authority to curtail the violence of persons who naturally are aggressive and rivalrous. In the desert, innate human aggression is easily channeled away from the closely knit kin group and outward to warfare against the tribal enemies, but in the city human violence is not limited in this manner and must be forcibly restrained under the absolute command of the ruler.

Ibn Khaldun says the virtue and purity of the Bedouin is not intrinsic, but is a natural consequence of a rural culture that is based on scarcity. Like Rousseau, Ibn Khaldun traces the Bedouin fall from grace to exposure to the distinctions and *amour propre* of the city. But where Rousseau portrays this as a gradual and irreversible process, with the noble savage inevitably becoming depraved and civilized, in Ibn Khaldun's world the savage and the civilized exist simultaneously – the Bedouin isolated in the desert, the refined mixed promiscuously together in the city.

"Because all the necessities of civilization are not to be found among the people of the desert"[2] some Bedouin are inevitably drawn to the wealth and comfort of the urban world. By accepting the authority of the ruler and his minions they lose their courage, while their fortitude is "corroded by education or authority."[3] Even more importantly, the Bedouin's sense of belonging to a unified and egalitarian tribe is fragmented in the city by new multiple, overlapping associations and by new distinctions of rank and wealth.

Due to the softening and socially disintegrative effect inherent in sedentary life, Ibn Khaldun sees a consistent tendency for any urban dynasty to crumble over time and to be defeated by the more robust, aggressive and united tribes of the hinterlands. The new ruling tribal group will inevitably follow the same trajectory of decadence and be itself conquered in turn. The only way in which this eternal cycle can be broken is through the inspirational messages of prophets, who can unite city and country under the cause of God and regulate them by the ethically compelling internalized laws of religious revelation. Without prophetic intervention the cycle will continue; and even prophecy will be forgotten and diluted over time, leading to secularization, decadence, and a renewal of the eternal dialetic.

In his theory of the cycle of secular rule, Ibn Khaldun is especially concerned with the transformation of governance from a tribal to a bureaucratic base. At first, the conquering tribal leader relies upon his co-equal kinsmen and tribal allies for support, but after several generations the conqueror's descendant "seeks the help of clients and followers against the men of his own people."[4] The gradual disenfranchisement of his kinsmen occurs because the ruler fears that they, as his co-equals and tribal brothers, can and will make claims on his sovereignty. In response, he slowly replaces them with slaves, clients, and hired employees who are directly reliant on him for their positions. The ruler's aim is to increase his authority by exchanging his potential rivals for a covey of dependents.

The case for this strategy was plainly put by the Abbasid ruler al-Mansur: "When I sit in public audience, I may call a *mawla* (client) and raise him and seat him by my side, so that his knee will rub my knee. As soon, however, as the audience is over, I may order him to groom my riding animal and he will be content with this and will not take offence. But if I demand the same thing from somebody else, he will say: 'I am the son of your supporter and intimate associate' or 'I am a veteran of your cause' or 'I am the son of those who were the first to join your cause'."[5]

Plate 4.1   Nineteenth-century French lithograph of an Arab Shaikh and his men. Note the black tent in the background.

Despite its advantages for the ruler, Ibn Khaldun argues that the eventual effect of the systematic downgrading of one's kin and close tribal allies in favor of dependent clients is negative. The ruler does gain more leeway for exercising his own autocratic authority by dispensing with those who had helped his ancestors to victory. But, according to Ibn Khaldun, without these kinsmen and allies of his own people to support him, he is instead surrounded by flatterers and sycophants, and can be easily ousted by more aggressive and unified tribal opponents invading his realm from the periphery. This is because clients, slaves and hangers-on lack the essential ingredient that promotes social solidarity and self-sacrifice: this ingredient, the ephemeral secret of conquest, is what Ibn Khaldun calls *asabiyya*, which is usually translated as "group feeling."

Asabiyya is the magical element which is key to the process of history. "Group feeling produces the ability to defend oneself, to offer opposition, to protect oneself, and to press one's claims."[6] With it, one can conquer; without it, one is destined to collapse. It is eroded in the city, but is strong in the country, among the Bedouin. What is it?

Group Feeling: the "Band of Brothers"

Ibn Khaldun clearly understands asabiyya to be a product of the sort of kinship linkages and blood ties that prevail in Bedouin tribal areas. He argues that the Bedouin naturally obey their elected shaikhs and fight for self-defense because:

> They are a closely knit group of common descent. This strengthens their stamina and makes them feared, since everybody's affection for his family and his group is more important (than anything else). Compassion and affection for one's blood relations and relatives exist in human nature as something God put into the hearts of men. It makes for natural support and aid, and increases the fear felt by the enemy. Those who have no one of their own lineage rarely feel affection for their fellows... Group feeling results only from blood relationship or something corresponding to it... The purpose of group feeling, which is defense or aggression, can be fulfilled only with the help of a common descent.[7]

This does not mean that Ibn Khaldun believes there is an innate socio-biological bond between blood kin. Rather, "a pedigree is something imaginary and devoid of reality. Its usefulness consists only in the resulting connection and close contact... The real thing to bring about the feeling of close contact is social intercourse, friendly association, long familiarity, and the companionship that results from growing up together, having the same wet nurse, and sharing the other circumstances of death and life."[8]

Yet, although the ties of descent are imaginary ways of conceptualizing and realizing bonds of mutual help and affection, this does not mean that kinship is irrelevant. The *concept* of descent *is* important, since it is through the figuring lens of kinship ideology that one constructs one's relationships. A person who is simply attached as a subordinate to a lineage is not bound to the others by "affection, the rights and obligations concerning talion and blood money, and so on."[9] Conversely, a client or ally who is initiated as a full member of the group is eventually conceptualized as a blood kin, and a pedigree may be manufactured to facilitate incorporation. Rights and duties are legitimized in terms of blood relationships that, in time, will become accepted as "real," that is, as kin ties, by the tribe.[10]

The use of kinship as a defining paradigm for personal relationships is very ancient. In Mesopotamia, "kings conventionally addressed each other in family terms, as either 'father', 'son' or 'brother'. To call another ruler 'my father' implied acceptance of his seniority; to address one as 'my brother' was a claim of equality."[11] This is an important datum, since it means that for millennia brothers in the Middle East have been conceptualized as equivalent and were not ranked by seniority. Similarly, "brotherhood" in the tribe has always, in this region, meant sharing all tribal obligations and rights with one's co-equals.

As remains the case today, members of brotherhoods had co-responsibility for bloodshed. If one of their number killed someone of another lineage, any is liable to be killed in revenge; likewise, if one of the lineage is killed, all of them have the obligation to help slay a member of the murderer's group. The Bedouin sum it up by saying that lineages "pursue and they are pursued together."[12] The extent of accountability among agnatic kin varies in different social contexts, and can be manipulated for advantage, but the concept of shared blood-debt was and remains a powerful incentive for social solidarity and the control of violence within the lineage group.

Honor also is shared with one's line. The heroic stories of the Bedouin are not only of one's own daring and greatness, but also of the famous deeds of one's siblings and ancestors; their honor is one's own, and is often associated with deeds of blood revenge. Similarly, the shame or cowardice or promiscuity of one's lineage mate is a stain on all the group alike. More concretely, farm land, or grazing rights, or timber entitlements, are usually held by the lineage as a corporation, and even private property may have certain family ties attached to it; for instance, a "brother" may be obliged to give his lineage mates first chance to bid if he wishes to sell his land.

Since "brothers" share in inheritance and in other kinship rights and responsibilities, they are very likely to live contiguously or at least in close proximity. Camp sites of nomads are almost always made up of men of the same patrilineage, since only lineage mates have grazing rights and usage of oases, while in towns and cities it is assumed that one's neighbors somehow "must" be one's kin, since only kin, in principle, have the prerogative to hold land and property contiguously and links may be manufactured if necessary to prove this shared heritage to be the case.

Although Ibn Khaldun made a radical distinction between desert and sown, the tribal ethic is not so absent from urban life as he indicated. Instead, as we saw in chapter 2, throughout the Middle East a sense of "group feeling" prevailed among the localized urban guilds, neighborhoods and Sufi brotherhoods, who used ties of kinship (both real and fictive) in a way very much like the "tribal" organization Ibn Khaldun valorized, binding themselves together in "dislocated, self-contained and almost self-governing groups, subject only to the overriding authority of the temporal and spiritual powers."[13]

We can conclude that asabiyya is central in the "cultural imaginary" of the Middle Eastern world, both in the city and the country. We have discovered already that, from earliest times, extended lineages were the basic building blocks of the local communities, and lineages held sway in urban quarters. Now we find from Ibn Khaldun that the strength of a solidary kinship ideology, metaphorically expressed through asabiyya, is the factor that permits the expansion of tribal groups into positions of power in the city, while its decline propels those same groups into disintegration and defeat.

Middle Eastern Kinship and Descent

But Ibn Khaldun never discussed the structure of asabiyya. For him, there was only one form of kinship organization; the one he knew and took for granted. A major contribution of comparative anthropology is to demonstrate that the ways people relate to one another in families and the extensions of these relationships to the outside world are highly variable across cultures, and that these variations alter the deepest ways in which the world is understood, lived in and acted upon.

The Middle East has a characteristic descent system. Save for a single exception (the Tuareg), it is strongly patrilineal. This means that lineages are traced only through the father. Men and women drawing up their genealogies will typically only follow the male line back. It is through the male line that membership in the lineage comes, with all its rights and obligations, its honor and pride. This is not to say that ties through women are not known. They are. But it is to say that lineage ties are privileged over relationships of alliance,[14] as members of the patrilineage tend to be separated out terminologically from maternal relatives, and one's father's brother and one's mother's brother are often known by different terms.

Coincidental with patrilineality is a strong and parallel tendency toward patrilocality, that is, residence by men within the village or camp that "belongs" to one's father's lineage; wives move to be with their husbands, and not the other way around. To compensate, men often marry "close to the bone", to their own father's brother's daughters, in order to keep them in the patrilineage. Father's brother's daughter marriage is highly preferred in the Middle East, so much so that the father's brother's son must be asked permission if his *bint amm* is to marry elsewhere. This favored marriage pattern very strikingly sets the region off from all those surrounding it, where such parallel cousin marriages are frowned upon. It has the covert function of permitting fission between very near patrilineal relatives, who divide in disputes over marriage; it thereby enhances the flexibility of the lineage structure.[15]

As in the American kinship system, in the Middle East there is no distinction in the terminology to mark elder and younger or senior and

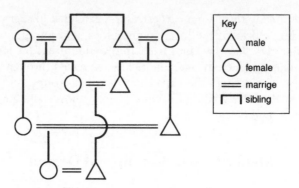

Figure 4.1   Parallel cousin marriage over two generations.

junior. This coincides with an egalitarian system of inheritance, where all the brothers inherit equally and have equal status. Texts indicate this is a very ancient pattern, but it is not "natural" by any means. For example, in Central Asian and Turkic kinship seniority among siblings is terminologically marked. This simple distinction will make a vast difference in Middle Eastern history, as we shall discover in a later discussion of the Ottoman Empire.

Middle Eastern kinship terminology coincides with and helps to construct a characteristic local-level political structure that is both egalitarian and capable of concerted political action. Anthropologists know it as the segmentary lineage system. These societies, which exist in profusion around the world, do not rely on stratification and rank to organize themselves; instead people act according to the principle that close patrilineal relatives should unite together if in dispute with more distant relatives. In the western cognatic kinship structure, where both male and female lines are of equal importance, this would be impossible, since the claims of the maternal and paternal lineages (and the multiple kindred they ramify into) are conflicting (see figure 4.2a).

This contrast can be easily visualized. Each American stands at the point of an inverted genealogical cone, expanding ever-outward in all directions into the past and mingling into multiple other kinship groups. But because relatives and ancestors in the Middle East are traced through one line only, the patterns of relationship are unambiguous. Rather than standing at the nadir of a gigantic upside down pyramid, the Middle Easterner is one node at the base of a triangle, which reaches its apex in the single mythical progenitor. All individuals in the system know or can discover their exact genealogical distance from every other individual in it by tracing back to the common ancestor and then down again to the person in question (see figure 4.2b).

As Elizabeth Bacon has argued, this means that segmentary lineages have no absolute boundaries (save, perhaps, at their outer limits), but

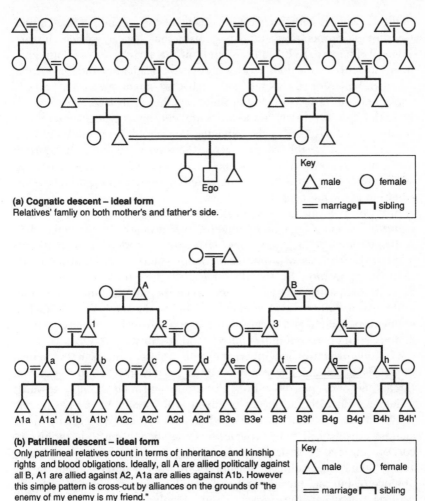

(a) Cognatic descent – ideal form
Relatives' famliy on both mother's and father's side.

Key
△ male   ○ female
══ marriage ⌐¬ sibling

(b) Patrilineal descent – ideal form
Only patrilineal relatives count in terms of inheritance and kinship
rights and blood obligations. Ideally, all A are allied politically against
all B, A1 are allied against A2, A1a are allies against A1b. However
this simple pattern is cross-cut by alliances on the grounds of "the
enemy of my enemy is my friend."

Key
△ male   ○ female
══ marriage ⌐¬ sibling

Figure 4.2 The Middle Eastern segmentary lineage system:
(a) cognatic descent – ideal form; (b) patrilineal descent – ideal form.

expand and contract, permitting the flexibility required in this highly
mobile and fluid social order.[16] This characteristic is evident in Middle
Eastern tribal personal names, which shift according to one's relationship with the inquirer. Where I worked, an individual might call himself
Yusufzai if speaking to someone from outside the region, Pindakhel if
talking to someone from a nearby district, Malikhel if his questioner is
from his own home area, Mushurkhel to a man from his village.

In this system, political action is ideologically constructed by using the
idiom of blood relations: brothers ought to aid brothers against patrilateral cousins, while brothers and first-degree cousins should act together

in disagreements with patrilateral cousins of the second degree – a relationship of cooperation and antagonism that has an ancient history. Julius Wellhausen, in his famous study of the early years of Islam, gives many instances of jealous rivalry among the leaders of the Qays tribal alliance, but informs us that "although they might play each other ill tricks, they nevertheless held faithfully together against foreign clans."[17] Note that kinship closeness and territorial contiguity coincide: in the city brothers lived together in the extended household, first cousins were in the same local neighborhood, second cousins were somewhat farther away, and so on. In fact, everywhere it is assumed that those closest in space are one's closest allies – or closest enemies – depending on the situation at the moment.

In its ideal form, this system is one of "complementary opposition" between lineage groups of equal genealogical depth. It is stimulated by confrontation but lacks any rigid structure or leadership. Hypothetically, all descendants of a mythical founding father of the group could unite in opposition to outside forces. At the same time, there is a boundless capacity for fission, "since even the nuclear family is a miniature of the larger social system."[18] This is the indigenous model of segmentary society and is the source of asabiyya, the capacity to unify and yet retain personal independence and equality.

Certain properties are inherent within this system as a theoretical model. First, alliances generally occur negatively in reaction to external threats. Second, quarrels within the group will tend strongly towards stalemate, since the segments involved will usually be approximately equal in size. Third, since the whole society can potentially unite against outsiders, it may become an expanding system, defeating, incorporating and/or enslaving neighboring groups which lack this capacity.[19] The final implicit feature of the segmentary system is the absence of internal means for ending feuding. Once fighting has begun between segments, the numerical and ideological equivalence of the opponents prohibits a severe defeat. Without the imposition of external authority to stop fighting, one would expect segmentary society to be weakened by continuous internal quasi-guerrilla warfare. In the Middle East, this difficulty is met by the use of sacred mediators, who are set off from the warring clans and can arbitrate disputes. As we have already seen, these individuals can sometimes rise above the general leveling propensity of the culture at large.

To reiterate, the characteristics of the segmentary society in its simplest formal operation include: equal opposing units, flexibly structured by expansive patrilineal genealogies, confronting close neighbors and kin in relations of reciprocal antagonism and occasional alliance against more distant aggressors. Complementary opposition allows considerable cohesion without any overarching authority save the moral authority of a sacred mediator, who has the potential to gain power within the egalitarian and competitive, yet balanced segmentary system.

Complications in the Model

The ideal pattern is just that – an ideal. In reality, it is complicated by differentiation in the vital matters of revenge and warfare. Among the nomadic Bedouin of Cyrenaica, for example, the nuclear family is not responsible for blood vengeance. That duty falls upon the co-resident lineage segment which is related to the victim up to the fourth or fifth ascending generation (sharing a great or great-great grandfather). Likewise, the members of this group share blood money and are held culpable for any homicide committed by a member.[20] More inclusive segments function only as landholding units and rarely, if ever, unite in blood disputes, while lineage groups within the co-resident segment appear to fission rather than fight. A similar distinction is seen among recently sedentarized Bedouin in Iraq.[21]

The level of violence against close patrilineal relatives also varies according to the competitive pressure felt within the culture. For instance, among the farming Berbers of the Rif, as David Hart remarks, "vengeance killings within agnatic lineage groups" occurred too often simply to be dismissed as exceptions to the rule.[22] Similarly, the agrarian Pukhtun have a high level of violence among close kinsmen who are rivals over the small plots of land left them by their common ancestors. In fact, among the Pukhtun, the term of reference for the father's brother's son is *tarbur*, which also means "enemy".

These differences are correlated with the mode of production. In general, we can say that nomads have larger units of blood revenge, and act corporately more often than do farmers, since their way of life requires greater cohesion in the seasonal herding of animals, as well a unified defense against raiders. At the same time, nomadic mobility permits an escape from the immediate proximity of irritating relatives, and the fecundity of their animals allows each herdsman to expand his resource base independently. Farmers, on the other hand, are usually permanently cheek to jowl with close patrilateral relatives who stand to inherit their plots of land from them should they die. Except at harvest time and perhaps during irrigation work, farmers rarely need each other's constant help in growing crops and maintaining their fields, which in any case cannot be carried off by outside attackers. Face-to-face confrontation with close relatives is therefore the norm in farming communities organized by patrilineal descent, while among nomads the confrontation is between rival clans.

These differences do not mean that the kinship system does not serve as the operant idiom structuring social relations, even in societies, such as the Pukhtun, where violence is most often between near relatives. There tribesmen modulate their antagonistic relations according to geneaological and spatial distance, and each more inclusive patrilineal segment has its own specific rules of violence for hostilities with segments of equal scale. Moreover, relations involving revenge take precedence over other forms of violence and opposition, so that a death in a village factional dispute dissolves the parties and leads to a personal vendetta between two nuclear families. In inter-village wars, as well, murders by close cousins are avenged, while those by more distant enemies are not.[23]

By way of comparison, Cyrenaican co-resident groups are relatively peaceful, becoming more violent with genealogical and spatial distance, moving from "indiscriminate murder and pillage" at the outer limits, to "unrestricted engagement in raids" and finally to relations of formal feud among closely related clans.[24] As Donald Cole writes, whatever the internal disagreements among kinsmen and whatever the categories of violence that are permissible, it remains the case that "in any showdown (a tribesman) is expected to fight with his blood relatives" against outsiders.[25] Not to do so means repudiating one's blood and forfeiting one's honor – the worst possible fate.

Alongside the complications introduced by the social organization of violence, the segmentary model is also often cross-cut by a dual system of political and marriage alliances, as each genealogical unit is split into two opposed factions, which are in turn allied with other factions in partisan blocs. These dualistic parties are found throughout Middle Eastern history, with the most famous probably being the ancient rivalry between Qays/Mudar and Yemen, which is still invoked to rally factional allies in Arabia. These parties are named after Bedouin tribes, but actually referred to interest groups that overlapped and cut through tribal boundaries. The dyadic *liff* of the Berbers and the dual *dullah* of the Pukhtun are similar in structure,[26] as are the dual factions, often bound to schools of law and to residential quarters, which have regularly divided Middle Eastern cities into warring camps.

These opportunistic bloc alliances have sometimes been taken as the foundation of the social structure, rendering lineage ties and segmentary ideology irrelevant, whereas in actuality these dual parties are an artifact of intra-lineage rivalries between close male relatives. We have seen already that among farmers a man's most salient opponent is a close patrilineal cousin, who is a co-inheritor of land. Among herdsmen and urbanites too, cousins and close rivals compete for leadership in the localized lineage, though generally without the fragmenting violence so common in farming communities. In all instances, competitors rally more distant allies according to the ancient Middle Eastern political axiom (recorded in Sumerian times) that "the enemy of my enemy is my friend."

Three crucial components are really involved here: the manipulating political individual, his temporary allies, and his temporary opponents. Each person is acting according to what he understands to be his own personal interests against his most salient opponents and will switch sides with alacrity when advantage is perceived. For instance, if one individual is very successful in his political maneuverings, he will find his erstwhile allies joining his enemies to humble him. This zero-sum game leads to a long-term balance of opposition, as Fredrik Barth has elegantly shown to exist among the Pukhtun.[27] The same pattern can be seen on a larger scale, and accounts for the perpetuation of shifting dualistic factional struggle that has so prevailed throughout Middle Eastern history.[28]

These political alliances are crucial for ordinary political life, but do not supersede blood ties, and a man must take revenge if a close cousin who is a factional opponent is killed by a genealogically more distant political ally;[29] the blood tie remains the most important bond between individuals, while blocs are arenas in which antagonism generated between local lineage rivals are extended into dual networks of very fluid and shifting factional coalitions.

Other variations also occur. As Ibn Khaldun had already noted, in real life kinship is manipulated, and relationships may be forgotten or remembered according to needs of the moment. A close relative who has moved to a distant territory may be forgotten, while a useful non-relative living nearby might be called a long-lost kinsman. A relative who is a troublemaker may be repudiated, while a nebulous kin affiliation may be claimed with the wealthy and powerful. Unevenness between kin groups can occur, as one becomes more powerful than its "brothers", breaking the symmetry ideally required of an egalitarian structure.

Citing these many deviations from the ideal, Emrys Peters has forcefully argued that the segmentary system is a product of "faulty reasoning" derived from a desire to "comprehend...complexity only by thinking in terms of a kind of average behavior."[30] His study, based on fieldwork with Cyrenaican Bedouins disorganized and depopulated by World War II, led many anthropologists since to discredit the segmentary structure altogether and to concentrate instead on the personal interests and strategies of self-seeking individuals.

But if the idea of tribal asabiyya is a product of faulty reasoning, as Peters alleges, it is the reasoning that has been locally in use for millennia, and continues as the organizing principle most referred to by the people themselves; as such, it tells us a great deal about the premises on which Middle Eastern people seek to construct a sensible and livable world. According to the indigenous logic of group feeling each person stands at the center of a traceable network of putative lineal kinsmen that loosely integrates everyone into a vague cultural unity. Inside this entwining net of kin, as Paul Dresch writes, "formally equal elements are defined by contradistinction, and formal inequality is admissible only in terms of the inclusion of subsets in larger sets."[31]

Personal struggles reflect the individualistic and egalitarian logic of the kinship structure, constrained only by obligations of blood and loyalty to one's own. Asabiyya, modeled on the contentions and alliances of near relatives, endures in the Middle East as the deepest paradigm for human action. The relationships and attitudes of asabiyya coincide with a moral environment where authority was achieved, not ascribed, and where rulers were treated with no great awe or obeisance. Such a debunking egalitarian ethic cannot legitimize the actual relations of hierarchy and command which must exist in any complex social formation. For Middle Easterners, the question remains: Who should be followed, and why?

Part III

State and Society:
Prophets, Caliphs, Sultans,
and Tyrants

5

The Prophetic Age

The Rise of Islam

The portrait we have drawn so far of the Middle East is one in which all forms of secular authority have always been questionable and unstable; obedience is won by the strong and clever, and asabiyya is the sole restraint on personal force. For Ibn Khaldun the only escape from this condition was the rise of a sacred leader who could unite all the warring tribes under a God-given mandate. In stating this hope, Ibn Khaldun was reiterating the promise of Muhammad, who sought to overcome the divisiveness of clans and the coerciveness of rulers by establishing the government of God on earth. The manner in which this attempt was made, and its fate, tell us much about the enduring cultural values of the Middle Eastern peoples.

The history of the foundation of Islam is now clothed with the veils of legend and obscured by multiple conflicting accounts that make its true outline all but impossible to discern with any clarity. But it is incontrovertible that Northern Arabia prior to Muhammad was a predominantly tribal environment, structured by exigencies of camel herding, trading, feuding, and raiding. In this personalized world, a tribesman's only permanent possession was his own hard-won self-respect and the honorable deeds of his ancestors, proclaimed in poems of valor and romance. As Julius Wellhausen puts it: "There was thus, in reality, not a state, but only a people; not an artificial organization, but simply a full-grown organism; no state officials, but only heads of clans, families and tribes. The same bond – that of blood, held together the people and the family; the only difference was their size."[1]

The "civilized" area of Arabia was not in the heartland where Islam was born, but rather had long been located in the coastal south and along the gulf.[2] There, in a pattern that has repeated itself throughout Middle Eastern history, tribal confederations established small kingdoms precariously uniting peripheral mountaineer warriors to lowland urban centers, while combining irrigation farming with control over the long-distance trade in incense and other goods passing through the Arabian peninsula.[3] Inland, the only possible location for development of any sort of state was in the impoverished and remote region dominated by Mecca and the Quraysh clan, where ancient pilgrimage centers protected markets in perfume, leather, and other trade goods. But no such development occurred until the advent of Muhammad, who was born around 570, received his first revelations at the age of forty, undertook his momentous journey to Medina (the *hijra*) in 622 (year one in the Muslim calendar)[4] and died in 632, having led his people in the conquest of the whole Arab peninsula, and having initiated their great and ultimately successful war against the surrounding Sasanid and Byzantine empires.

Who was this leader who could unite the Arabs as they never had been united before or ever were to be united again? Though his history is clouded by legend, we nonetheless do know with some degree of certainty a few facts about Muhammad's life. Muhammad was born a member of the elite Quraysh lineage who had dominated Mecca for generations; but as a posthumous child he was in a weak and exposed position and had to rely on the protection of more distant and potentially antagonistic relatives during his early years. Only the help of his first wife, the successful and much older tradeswoman Khadija, allowed him to escape poverty and obscurity and to become a well-to-do merchant, much respected for his integrity, good judgment and fairness by his fellows, who called him *al-Amin*, the trustworthy.

During a meditative retirement on Mount Hira, the life of the truthworthy entrepreneur was transformed as he was gripped by the first of the uncanny revelations that would eventually be collected into the Quran. In his vision, the angel Gabriel spoke to him, commanding him to "Proclaim! In the name of thy Lord and Cherisher, who created – created man out of a leech-like clot."[5]

Later revelations occurred at intervals, sometimes convulsing the Prophet into epilepsy-like fits, at other times blandly manifested in words or tinkling noises he could interpret upon arousing. Muhammad's waking recitations of his visions, which were often phrased in rhyming prose of surpassing beauty and novelty, were then written down and memorized by his close followers. The collection of his recited messages, the Quran, became the central holy text of Islam.

In Mecca, Muhammad's revelations at first had relatively little influence. His original converts were his wife and some of his closest relatives, but most of the early believers were those who were poor, disenfranchised and humble. They were drawn to the Quran's condemnation of excessive riches, to its advocacy of generous donations to care for the disadvantaged, and to its repudiation of the arrogance and selfishness of

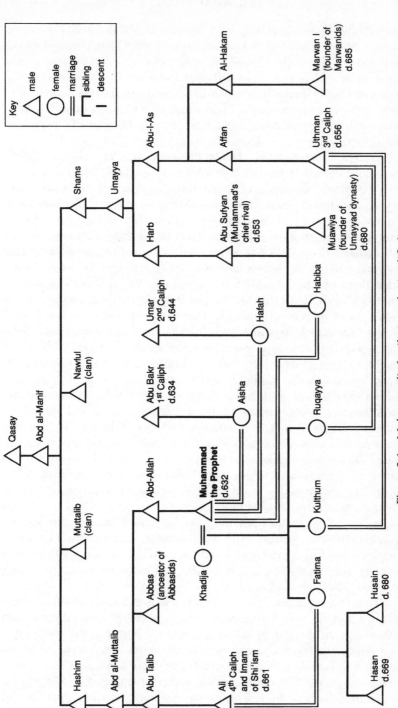

Figure 5.1 Muhammad's family (greatly simplified).

the wealthy. They accepted Islam's message of obedience to the rule of sacred law as enunciated by the Prophet (the word Islam literally means "submission").[6] Yet the Quran also had a place for the interests of the upper strata. According to Muhammad's revelation, wealth and power were not bad in themselves – only greed, arrogance and an absence of community responsibility. As M. A. Shaban puts it: "Cooperation between rich and poor is the basic tenet of all Muhammad's preaching just as Love is for that of Jesus Christ."[7]

However, in general the Meccan populace were unwilling to follow the Islamic demand that they pay *zakat* (a tax to be redistributed to the community of believers), cease to hoard, participate in community charity, and refuse interest on loans. Many were especially angered at Islam's absolute denial of the might of their clan gods in favor of the complete domination of Allah – a threat to the basic structure of their patriarchal society. Also galling for them was the Quranic demand that the great humble themselves in prayer to the Almighty God who would judge them on the Last Day. As Abu Talib, the Prophet's uncle and protector, said: "I do not like to prostrate so that my hindquarter is higher than (the rest) of me." The importance of this issue is indicated by the fact that Musaylima and Tulayha, two "false prophets" who later competed with Muhammad for the loyalties of the Arabs, both sought to gain converts by having their congregation "perform the prayer upright, in the manner of noblemen."[8]

After the death of his defender and uncle, Abu Talib, Muhammad and his followers suffered increasing persecution in Mecca and looked for refuge elsewhere. At first they attempted to spread the message of Islam to the neighboring oasis of al-Taif, but were ridiculed and expelled. Only in 622 did the Aws and Khazraj tribes of the agricultural oasis of Yathrib (later called Medina), anxious for a leader who could help them to resolve their interminable feuds, call on Muhammad to migrate there. Muhammad, fearing for his life in Mecca and hopeful of increasing his following, accepted this invitation, and undertook the hijra to Medina with his followers. It was in this desert sanctuary that he built the foundations of his holy empire, eventually returning to conquer his Meccan relatives and opponents, obliging them to pledge allegiance to Islam's one God, Allah, and to himself as that God's final Prophet.

Muhammad's success, while not reducible to external causes, occurred within a specific historical setting. Prior to his birth, Sasanid Persia and Byzantium, the great imperial competitors for power in the region, had long sought to wrest control over Arabia from the Arabs. Byzantine influence was indirect, exercised through their Ethiopian allies, who invaded Arabia in the fourth century, and returned again in 525, almost conquering Mecca. In response, the Sasanids subdued Yemen and established military colonies in all major ports on the peninsula by

Muhammad's birth in 570, taking control over external trade almost completely, though they were not able to extend their rule into the desert, where the tribes retained their freedom and their social mores.

This freedom was a precondition for the foundation of Islam. The isolation of the Arabs meant that the religious belief systems of the Sasanid and Byzantine world had not gained ascendance among them, although the concepts of God and of prophecy were well-known from Judaic, Christian and Zoroastrian sources. In fact, the Arab tribes traced their own genealogical charter back to Abraham and Hagar, and therefore had a mythical history of monotheism. But in actual practice they were polytheistic, worshipping a plethora of local gods who were almost indistinguishable from nature spirits.[9] These gods, who were territorial and associated with particular kin groups, were honored insofar as they offered their believers protection from their unpredictable environment. In truth, religious life sat lightly on these ancient tribespeople; they invoked their deities in emergencies, but had little in the way of ceremony, shrine, or mythology. The major role of their gods apparently was to act as divine guardians during certain holy months when clan feuds were set aside, as traders wearing special garb undertook pilgrimages to temporary markets set up on sanctified ground. It is in this guise that the tribal gods had their shrines in Mecca, where they guarded the sacred area around the *kaaba*, the holy black stone that is the goal of Muslim pilgrimage today.[10]

It is clear that Arabia at the time of Muhammad was a polytheistic backwater in a monotheistic universe; a very small, insular, and minor part of a far larger social world. Although influenced by the rivalries and ideologies of the vast Byzantine empire in the northwest and the Sasanid regime to the northeast, it retained its provincial and tribal character. Its people were poor, illiterate, without exploitable resources, and dangerous; from the perspective of the great cosmopolitan centers, all Arabia had to offer was its poetic tradition and the revenue from the trade that passed through it. Certainly a Sasanid of the sixth century would have laughed at the idea that this inchoate, uncouth and impoverished pagan wilderness could offer a threat to his proud empire. Yet a century later, the great Persian kingdom was reeling from the assault of Islam, and would soon yield, while Byzantium would be driven north, eventually to fall to the Ottomans.

How could this happen? There are two distinct theories about the basic preconditions that favored the rise of Islam out of the tribes of Arabia. The first, associated with Montgomery Watt, focuses on economic change, and begins with the decline of coastal trade in Arabia due to piracy and raids. As a result, Watt argues, following the accounts of al-Kalbi, luxury trade in incense and related products was rerouted inland to Mecca. Profiting from the situation, Muhammad's great-

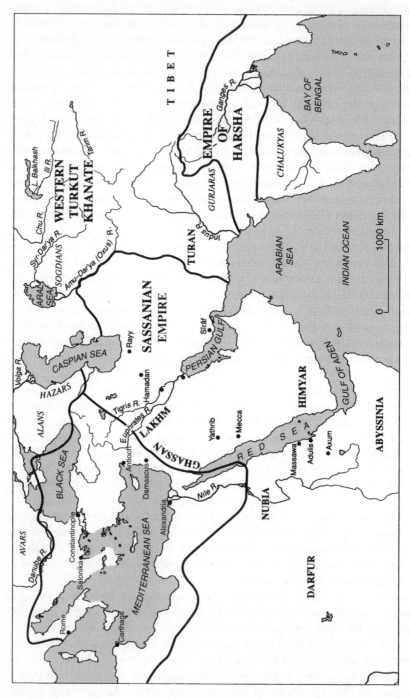

Map 5.1   The pre-Islamic world c. AD 600.

grandfather, Hashim, negotiated with the Byzantine emperor for a safe conduct to allow Meccan merchants to enter Syria. He then initiated a new trade alliance that transformed the old tribal system of segmentary opposition. This alliance brought together neighboring unrelated tribes who agreed to protect caravans going to Syria in the summer, Yemen in the winter. The pact was guaranteed by the holiness of the Meccan sanctuary overseen by Hashim's clan, the Quraysh, and by Allah, their patron deity, who was now recognized by the participants in the alliance (the *dar al-hums*) as the supreme God who guaranteed rights and agreements across tribal lines. In this way, a commonwealth of unrelated allies was united under a single moral authority, while the local cults of clan gods were still preserved intact.[11] Hashim's plan permitted Mecca to expand rapidly from a local market to an international commercial center and begin the process that had already occurred in the great states to the north. His plan also served as a template for the later Islamic revolution, gathering groups with no shared tribal origins into a sacred community united under Allah's shield.

At first the alliance was a highly equitable venture, as profits were redistributed to the impoverished among the participating tribes. But Watt argues that new distinctions between rich and poor, patron and client, soon evolved as participants in the trading network gained wealth and power beyond that of other tribesmen, leading to deep contradictions within the egalitarian Meccan community. As he writes:

> The traditional values of nomadic society (which was that of the most recent ancestors of the Meccans) were proving inadequate in the prosperous mercantile economic of Mecca, and were fading away. The wealthy merchants, who were also the leading men of the clans, were neglecting the traditional duty of caring for the needy and unfortunate among their kinsmen. Their great wealth made them proud, arrogant and presumptuous, ready to oppress and take advantage of any who were in any sense weak.[12]

According to Watt, the growth of market towns and the expansion of limited partnerships for control of trade also led to heightened tensions as those tribes excluded from this lucrative business wanted to take a share, while those already taking part wished to keep their monopoly. Confederation members undermined lineage solidarity as they allied themselves with their Meccan partners against their nomadic cousins; meanwhile struggles between clients led to hostilities between their patrons. In these altered circumstances, tribal asabiyya was challenged and a moral malaise prevailed throughout Arabia, laying the groundwork for Muhammad's unifying revelation.

The second theory is more political in nature, and has been forcefully made by Patricia Crone. She argues that Meccans did not trade in luxuries over long distances, but rather "exchanged pastoral products for those of the settled agriculturalists within their reach."[13] These meager resources, she believes, could not have developed the great and iniquitous class differences that Watt has claimed. Nor, Crone says, is there convincing evidence for the trade pacts that Watt offers as the center-piece of his analysis. Instead, earlier traditions about Meccan trade are deeply contradictory, and if anything, show that Mecca may have been less a trade center than a transfer point for goods carried to outlying tribes by Qurayshian itinerant merchants, who were not particularly associated with the sacred, except insofar as they kept the kaaba in repair and supplied food and drink for pilgrims meeting there. Crone also denies that Allah was the Qurayshian high God – why should they have fought against Muhammad if this was so?

From Crone's perspective, Islam did not triumph because it challenged class distinctions among the Quraysh merchants of Mecca, who in any case were Muhammad's major opponents. She notes that Muhammad only gained a significant following after his celebrated exile to Medina, an oasis inhabited by Bedouin tribesmen and their clients. According to Crone, "Islam originated in tribal society, and any attempt to explain its appearance must take this fact as its starting point." What Islam offered these tribespeople, she writes, was "the idea of a divinely validated state structures; and it was Muhammad's state, not his supposed blueprint for social reform, which had such powerful effect on the rest of Arabia."[14] Muhammad, repudiating his own ancestral gods in favor of the worship of Allah, the God of Abraham and thus of all Arabs, offered his followers a universal deity that conformed to the existing patrilineal ethos of the society. The appeal of his message was especially compelling during this period because of the recent unprecedented advances of the Sasanids, who, as noted above, had occupied Yemen and the Arab ports. Fearful of domination, the divided Arabs were ready for a prophecy – in Arabic – proclaiming that they were divinely predestined to gain victory over their powerful enemies.

Crone therefore postulates that Islam is best understood not as a response to an economic crises, but as a nativist movement: a reaction to external invasion that brought together previously unorganized tribal groups into one community under the authority of a charismatic leader who both reaffirmed and yet transformed local values, and who inspired his followers to war against outside influences and established a new indigenous state in the process.[15] The call to war was particularly effective in Arabia, where the feuding tribesmen were well accustomed to combat and pillage. As Crone writes, "Muhammad's God thus elevated tribal militance and rapaciousness into supreme religious virtues... It is precisely because the material interests of Allah and the tribesmen coincided that the latter obeyed Him with such enthusiasm."[16]

At this late date, and given the obscurity of the data, it is not possible to say which of these accounts has the most right on its side; what is evident is that both assume that the Arabs were won over because the Muslim message fit into and transubstantiated their already existing view of the world. It is no diminution of Muhammad's tidings to say that this was the case: the Prophet must speak in a language that will be recognized by those who hear him, so it follows that the creed must be one that reconfigures a universe that is already known. In the mainly illiterate world of the past, this universe, in its most essential existential reality, is not to be discovered in the writings of the lettered urban scribes, philosophers and courtiers, but rather in the way life was lived and understood by ordinary people in their daily experiences.

The Reconfiguration of Ordinary Life under Islam

To understand the appeal of Islam, then, we need to consider the context in which that appeal was made. In large part, the pre-Islamic perspective that Muhammad referred to was derived from the ecological and political situation outlined in the preceding chapters: mobile, armed nomads and oasis dwellers standing in a relation of interdependence with a mercantile city-state; guarding their own autonomy, yet reliant on the town as a market place, a center for needed crafts, and as a sanctuary. It was a world of considerable violence and uncertainty, as different groups and individuals manipulated for power and prestige without any overarching system of restraint, save for the limits imposed by lineage ties, tribal codes of honor and the sacredness of the market, where feuds were suspended under the protection of the local gods.

Part of the genius of the Islamic message was in reconceptualizing this daily reality. Instead of ratifying distinctions that were repugnant to the independent and egalitarian tribesmen of the desert and the roving merchants of Mecca, the Quran emphasized the spiritual equivalence of all persons, who are held to be responsible for their own destinies and who will be judged as individuals by Allah on the Last Day. As we have seen, in Islam there are no priests, no church, no monks, no difference between clergy and laymen. Everyone is alike in the eyes of the transcendent and absolute God to whom all must submit. The radical egalitarianism of Islam applied even to the Prophet, who was at pains to deny any sacred or superhuman status to himself. When doubters asked Muhammad to verify his revelation by miracles, he replied that the miracle of the Quran was sufficient, and that he was "but a man: It is revealed to me by inspiration, that your God is one God."[17] Nor did he claim to have any special knowledge. "I tell you not that with me are the

Treasures of Allah, nor do I know what is hidden. Nor do I tell you I am an angel. I but follow what is revealed to me."[18] In Islam, the Prophet does not even have the right to demand obedience from other human beings, as his prophesy clearly states: "Therefore do thou remind for thou are one to remind. Thou art not one to manage (their) affairs."[19] Some will listen to the warning, others will not, since God "leaves straying whom He pleases, and He guides whom He pleases."[20]

In the Quranic annunciation, individuals are required to take full responsibility for all their activity in the world; agency and accountability are not limited to obeying or disobeying commandments. For instance, in response to Muslim complaints about persecution by unbelievers, the Quran makes an angry rebuke: "Was not the earth of Allah spacious enough for you to move yourselves away (from evil)?"[21] This remark assumes social mobility, individual initiative and a pragmatic attitude toward life that is characteristic of the Middle East, but not of a medieval Europe locked in bonds of status rights and feudal obligations. A similar outlook is found in the often quoted remark of the Prophet to a Bedouin who asked him whether he should tie up his camel or count on God to keep it from wandering. "Count on God," said the Prophet, "and tie up your camel."

Alongside their individual freedom and responsibility, Muslims were also required to subordinate themselves within the community of believers. Old ties of kinship were replaced with affiliation to a single sacred community; the notion of personal honor was transformed into sacred duty; and the protection of the marketplace was extended to all believers. The communitarianism of Islam was symbolized in the requirements of zakat (the tax on believers) and the obligation of all men to perform military service. The noble generosity of the Bedouin was transmuted from a personal display to a community act, while the virtue of courage was channeled into a holy war for the faith. As Crone puts it, the Muslim creed "endorsed and ennobled such fundamental tribal characteristics as militance and ethnic pride."[22] In return, individual Muslims, though alone before God, were not left isolated; they were made a part of an encompassing sacred and superior congregation offering support, guidance, and protection.

In its most radical departure from tradition, the new assembly of Islam required a severing of the lineage ties that had previously provided men and women a minimum of refuge in the harsh and competitive world. Yet, as Hamid Dabashi tells us: "Muhammad's charismatic authority established a new order of social solidarity. It substituted brotherhood-in-faith for brotherhood-in-blood, which went against traditional Arab practices."[23] Severance of one tie and establishment of a new one was symbolized in the crucial event of the hijra to Medina, which meant "leaving the 'protection' of one group and entering that of another" in a

Plate 5.1   *Allāh amalī*, "God is my hope" – in Tumar style.

manner that both built upon and transformed Bedouin traditions of refuge and clientship.[24]

The new sacred community in which Muslims found protection was called the *umma*, the assembly of believers. Joining the Muslim umma was a voluntary matter; as the Quran says, "there is no compulsion in religion."[25] But once the faith was accepted then a Muslim was forever committed, and could not repudiate membership on pain of death as an apostate – Islam is easy to join, impossible to leave. This reflects Muhammad's struggle to build a following and to replace kinship bonds with something equally compelling. Lacking the potent ideology of asabiyya to bind it together, the umma relied on the sanction of the oath to maintain its unity; its members were linked not by common ancestry nor by pseudo-kin ties to patrons, but by common and absolute submission to the one God – the only tie that could supersede descent. Like kinship, it was a tie that was unbreakable – to deny it was to deny one's own identity; the most heinous of offenses.

Many of the functions of the clan and lineage were replicated and expanded in the new community. Among the tribesmen, the asabiyya of shared kinship linked members together in a group within which the shedding of blood was forbidden and co-responsibility was enjoined – it was, as Ibn Khaldun said, the unit of aggression and defense for the Bedouin. Similarly, co-responsibility for the other members of the umma was required of all members, who were also strictly prohibited from exploiting, injuring or enslaving one another; they were obliged as well to share their resources through charitable contributions which would be redistributed to the community at large.

We have also noted that tribal unity in the Middle Eastern context is activated primarily in matters of contestation as patrilineages solidify to struggle with competing patrilineages. So too in Islam the opposition between the realm of faith and the realm of unbelief implied a continuous battle, jihad, between *dar al Islam* (the unified house of Islam) and *dar al harb* (the house of the infidel). In this battle, Muslims must aid Muslims, just as patrikin help patrikin in the segmentary system – an extension of kinship that helped solidify the Bedouin warriors into a world-conquering army.

As Islam transmuted and universalized tribal structures of cooperation and duty, it simultaneously revolutionized relations of authority. In place of perpetual feud between lineages and disputes among co-equal men over who should hold command, the umma was indisputably governed by Muhammad, whose judgments were validated by their heavenly source. As Allah tells the faithful, "if ye differ in anything among yourselves, refer it to Allah and His Messenger."[26] Muhammad tied the umma to him as recipients and beneficiaries of his sacred communications; without his message and moral example, they would return to interminable and unwinnable wars amongst themselves. With him, they became invincible. It is with this aspect of Islam in mind that Crone writes: "Muhammad was neither a social reformer nor a resolver of spiritual doubts; he was the creator of a people."[27]

The first indication of Muhammad's relationship to his community is to be found in the business-like "Constitution of Medina", the earliest known written document in Islam, composed soon after Muhammad and his party were ensconced in their new home. The "Constitution" was negotiated and signed by all concerned, and consisted of a contract linking the tribes and their clients together in a cooperative and protective confederation, with Mohammed accepted by all as adjudicator and arbiter. The constitution also protected the rights of the Jewish tribes who lived in the oasis. Their religion was to be tolerated, and any harm done them was considered equivalent to harm done to their patrons (only later were the Jews expelled and warred against). The new confederation was centered around a sacred spot (*haram*) where violence was prohibited and justice was dispensed – a duplication of the harams surrounding pilgrimage marketplaces elsewhere in Arabia. The agreement was accepted after discussion and cemented by oath.

In form, the "Constitution" much resembles agreements made between tribes and saintly lineages in contemporary southern Arabia to provide protected locations for trade and mediation between segmentary rivals; arrangements which are also found in other Muslim tribal regions where pilgrimage sites are privileged loci for trade.[28] R. B. Serjeant, basing his argument both on this ethnographic data and textual evidence, contends that "Muhammad acted in accordance with Arabian political patterns in existence from the remote past. In one sense he is simply a judge-arbiter, a *hakam*, like his series of ancestors, and he was responsible for but few modifications to Arabian law and society."[29]

But Muhammad's community, though resembling those of other saintly hakam in its external form, was actually something completely different internally. In their own imagination of themselves, the early Muslims were not another tribal grouping gathered around a sacred marketplace; they belonged to the "party of God" – others were infidels. Nor was Muhammad one judge among many; he presented himself as the ultimate and final judge in a millenaristic movement that aimed at nothing less than transformation of the world. The shift from particular to universal, which is the necessary ingredient for a great religion, had now taken place. Islam had reconfigured Bedouin tribal social organization by turning the local clan into the unrestricted and encompassing umma, transforming the hakam into the Prophet, bringing a new ethical norm to transmute tribal virtues of bravery, generosity, and honor. Muhammad's reforms favored individual agency and responsibility within a framework of communal responsibility, and recast the deep egalitarian values so characteristic of Bedouin life into a religious message of universal brotherhood.

Also ratified and transformed by Islam were the urban mercantile values Muhammad had grown up with in Mecca. The Quran does not repudiate commerce, nor did the growth of Islam destroy trade and markets. On the contrary, Muhammad's message favored entrepreneurship, and integrated the ethics of the merchant into Islamic virtue through an expansion of the co-operation of the pragmatic trade confederation inaugurated by Hashim into all walks of life. Profit, if fairly made and appropriately spent in the service of God and to help the deprived, is praised in the Quran, while the absolute right of individuals to own and dispose of personal property is assumed, as is the right to make contracts.

In fact, the Quran is permeated with the imagery of the marketplace, which must have appealed directly to the individualistic mercantile values of the people of the time, both urban and rural, who were all accustomed to trade for their livelihoods. The pervasive Quranic ratification of rational calculation and free enterprise has been described by Torry as follows:

> Allah is the ideal merchant. He includes all the universe in His reckoning. All is counted, everything measured. The book and the balances are His institution, and He has made himself the pattern of honest dealing. Life is a business, for gain or loss ... The Muslim makes a loan to Allah; pays in advance for paradise; sells his own soul to Him, a bargain that prospers. The unbeliever has sold the divine truth for a paltry price, and is bankrupt. Every soul is held as security for the debt it has contracted. At the resurrection, Allah holds a final reckoning with all men. Their actions are read from the account-book, weighed in the balances; each is paid his exact due, no one is defrauded.[30]

Plate 5.2   The holy sites of Medina and Mecca in the late eighteenth century.

From its very beginnings, Islam therefore combined the urban-mercantile ethic of Meccan tradesmen with the traditions of the nomads, mediators and warriors of the periphery, as represented by Medina and the Bedouin. As we have seen, Watt focuses on the first aspect of Islam; Crone on the second. But these perspectives are not necessarily mutually exclusive. As I have argued, merchant and tribesmen alike value personal independence and see themselves as individual agents within the overarching context of their kin, acting to maximize desired ends (profit for the merchant, honor for the tribesman). Tribesmen and merchant are similarly pragmatic, mobile, and flexible. Both have a distaste for the pretensions of aristocracy and a faith in an egalitarian morality. Both are equally susceptible to the message of the Quran, which spoke to all of their concerns by bringing humanity under the aegis of a universal ethical prophecy as enunciated by the charismatic Prophet Muhammad.

The State in Early Islam

To understand Islam we also have to realize that it spread a wider political net than any previous religious annunciation. From the very beginning, Muhammad was not, like Jesus, willing to "render unto Caesar"; instead he rebelled against the authority of his kinsmen and sought to conquer the Meccan confederation that had repudiated him. Following his inspiration, he rallied his following to struggle against the odds, defeating a much larger Meccan army at the battle of Badr in 624, successfully raiding Meccan caravans, and threatening Meccan commercial dominance. Finally in 630 the Muslim army occupied Mecca itself, as Muhammad's Quraysh opponents were obliged to convert to his cause.

Muhammad's successful battle convinced many warlike Bedouin to come to his side, so they too could share in the glory and the spoils of Islam. These men, some sincere believers, some adventurers, most of them a combination of both, served as the main tool for the expansion of Islam out of Arabia. Fortuitously for the Muslim armies, by this time the Sasanid and Byzantine Empires had worn one another down; weakened by centuries of interminable war and the blockage of trade, they were vulnerable to Muslim raiders. After the death of Muhammad in 632 expansion was rapid; in 638 Jerusalem fell, and in the next thirty years all of ancient Mesopotamia, Egypt and most of Iran were conquered, while other Muslim armies pressed north-west into Byzantine territory. The continued success of Muslim troops solidified Islam's hold on recently converted warriors, who saw that the Muslim brotherhood, united in religion, was far superior to Bedouin tribes fragmented into warring clans. They now carried the Quran in place of their clan banner in battle, and their faith was substantiated by their continued victories.

The Muslim explosion which burst from the hinterlands of Arabia to overwhelm the Sasanid empire and to press the Byzantines back to their strongholds in Anatolia was historically unparalleled, and miraculously solved the old regional problem of economic and political impasse by forcibly dissolving the two competing deadlocked opponents into Islamdom, abruptly uniting the Middle East into one open trade area and paving the way for the rapid creation of new prosperity. At the same time, the Muslim message of the equality of all believers struck a cord with the common people of the empires, who, theoretically at least, were liberated from their inferior status by the simple act of conversion.[31] The rise of Islam was both an economic and social revolution, offering new wealth and freedom to the dominions it assimilated under the banner of a universal brotherhood guided by the message of the Prophet of Allah.

Remembering their glorious world-conquering past, Muslims have not pictured the "City of God" in the Christian manner as beyond ordinary ken, achieved in the radiant future by faith and renunciation. For them, God's mandate was actually realized in historical reality, under the authority of the Prophet himself and the four pious rulers after him: Abu Bakr (d. 634), Umar (d. 644), Uthman (d. 656), and Ali (d. 661) – who united the community of the faithful in their successful holy jihad against the unbelievers.[32] To compare the Muslim experience with Christianity, it is as if Jesus had commanded an army that subdued Jerusalem, and Peter had become Emperor of Rome.

Because the Muslim state originated in a charismatic movement of unparalleled political success, government has been given a remarkable ethical significance by Muslims. As A. R. Cornelius writes: "the purpose of the Islamic state, at its very inception, was the general good with the superior aim of achieving the 'highest good'...under divine sanctions."[33] The *Caliph*, (the "deputy of God") was the human instrument who guarded the community and executed the law, which, being divine, could not be altered. As Crone and Hinds put it, "Prophets and Caliphs alike are seen as God's agents, and both dutifully carry out the tasks assigned to them, the former by delivering messages and the latter by putting them into effect."[34] The ruler's responsibilities were clear; he had the obligation to see the law was properly promulgated and enforced and to assure the defense of the community. He was, as the poets put it, the "tent peg" of the umma, holding it together; he was also "God's rope" the faithful could cling to in order to insure their salvation.

Although the Caliph was reputed to have extraordinary spiritual powers as the deputy of God and exemplar of righteousness, as a ruler his capacity for initiative was minimal. The office itself was contracted by a handshake with fellow Muslims who were co-equal brothers in the faith; in theory, his power could be canceled if he were unfit. This was explicitly stated by the first Caliph, Abu-Bakr, who said: "I have been given authority over you but I am not the best of you. If I do well, help me, and if I do ill, then put me right...Obey me as long as I obey God and His apostle, and if I disobey them you owe me no obedience."[35]

In the memory of Muslims ever since, this period appears as a divinely ordered social formation flowering under the benign regime of the community's duly elected representative – the Caliph. A letter from the last generally accepted authentic Caliph, the Prophet's son-in-law, Ali, to his newly-appointed governor of Egypt gives some of the flavor of the ethics of the ruler in these early years. Ali writes:

> Let the dearest treasure to you be the treasure of virtuous acts. Control, therefore, your desires and appetites...Let your heart be imbued with mercy for your subjects as well as love and kindness for them...and never say, "I am your overlord (because) I order and am obeyed", for such ideas corrupt the heart and weaken the faith...And when the power you enjoy produces vanity and arrogance in your mind, look at the greatness of the kingdom of God above you...for God humiliates every tyrant or oppressor and disgraces every braggart.[36]

Muslim thought is saturated with longing for a return of this idealized era when ordinary men and women are imagined (in the soft glow of collective memory) to have acted together selflessly under the leadership of just and divinely guided Caliphs to realize the will of Allah in the world of human beings – a realization validated concretely through the vast power and wealth acquired by the victorious army of the faithful. Recalling their millennial past, the Muslim devout, unlike their Christian cousins, have never inwardly consented to the disjuncture between the religious experience of the community of believers (equal before God, led by the Prophet and his deputies) and the reality of power-seeking secular rulers prone to political intrigue and the use of physical coercion. The remembered unity of politics and religion during the first years of Islam has always remained available as an inspiration to Muslim reformers and as a rebuke to secular politicians.

Tensions and Divisions

But even in the original umma tensions existed. Although Muslims repudiated all divisions amongst themselves when they joined the party of God, internal distinctions based on pre-existent tribal ranks remained as models for dividing the faithful, though they were overlain with the new rhetoric of Islam. For instance, the Caliph Umar argued that since Muhammad is the most noble man, his people, the Quraysh, must be the most noble clan, and "for the rest, it follows proximity. The Arabs were ennobled by the Apostle of God."[37] Comparable traditions include: "If the Arabs become weak, Islam will become weak" and "Love the Arabs for three reasons: because I am Arab, because the Quran is Arabic and because the people of paradise speak Arabic."[38]

As we have seen, such proud reference to one's pedigree is an ancient part of Middle Eastern culture, where noble tribes made their major art form the recitation of poetry praising their ancestors, and where marriage was as "close to the bone" as possible in order to maintain the purity of the paternal blood line. According to their belief, true men were only to be found among armed chivalric tribesmen such as themselves; merchants, artisans, peasants and dependents were despised as the *daif* who must be protected, while the noble *sharif* did the protecting. Muhammad himself was a member of one of these aristocratic sharifian lineages, the Quraysh, who were elevated even more by their role as rulers of Mecca, caretakers of the kaaba and, later, by their kinship with the Prophet.

Within the Arab patrilineal and ethnic status hierarchy, noble lineages, such as the Quraysh, prided themselves on their blood purity, and bragged that kinship connections were sought with them, while they, as the most noble Arabs, did not initiate ties with others. This was so even in Medina where, despite the Muslim ideal of religious communalism, marriages with the *ansar*, the people of Medina, were rare indeed among the early Meccan migrants, who preferred to avoid contaminating their noble *qawm* (clan) with inferior blood.[39] Meanwhile, lesser groups manipulated genealogies to forge alliances with powerful lineages. As Wellhausen notes, "the poets in particular had a weakness for claiming kinship with those in high places."[40] The old entrenched faith in aristocratic blood lines, intrinsically contradictory to the egalitarian ideology of the umma, continued as tribes became Muslims en masse, following their leading men, and persisted in making claims for their clan's nobility. With conquest, the ideology of pure blood was translated to structure other hierarchical ties, so that Arabs did not marry non-Arab converts, while believers at large disdained marriage with infidels.[41]

Yet claims to superiority through noble blood have never been accepted with equanimity in the Middle East where, in Wellhausen's words, "every witness is inclined to regard the station of his own tribe as the center-point, and to ascribe the chief glory to the heroes of his tribe."[42] Even the claims of the Quraysh to pre-eminence were opposed by jealous rivals who argued that the nobility of the clan was blemished when the majority of them initially denied Muhammad's prophecy and fought hard against him. Base-born Muslims said that, as early converts, they actually had spiritual primacy over the late-arriving Quraysh, who in turn bitterly resented the pride of those whom they saw as upstarts.

It is with these conflicts in mind that Umar concludes his previously quoted discussion of spirituality by stating: "If the non-Arabs should come with works and we should come with none, then they will be closer to Muhammad than us on the Day of Judgment."[43] Similarly, reformist clerics often cited leveling traditions such as: "God is one, the religion is one and the ancestor is one. Lo, Arabic is not our father, or mother; it is merely a language; he who speaks Arabic is an Arab" and "at the Day of Judgment God will abolish the *nasab* (pedigree of noble tribes) and establish His nasab. The most honoured will be a God-fearing man."[44] The Quran itself says: "The most honoured of you in the sight of Allah is (he who is) the most righteous of you."[45] The glaring contrast between statements that ratify the innate elite status of the Arabs and the Quraysh, and other statements (appearing even within the same discourse)[46] that explicitly deny any type of superiority save personal moral superiority shows once again the deep and pervasive tensions that exist around acceptance of authority among egalitarian individualists.

But during the reign of the Prophet in the original umma no claims to superiority through ancestry or any other source were accepted. Among his companions the certainty of the Prophet's speech permeated the community and made debates over authority and hierarchy impossible. God spoke through His messenger and the believers obeyed wholeheartedly, convinced by Muhammad's immediate presence and by the pragmatic success of his newly formed political organization. One's status as noble or slave, black or white, wealthy or impoverished, Arab or Persian, was irrelevant for one's salvation in the charismatic community united by shared devotion to Allah and His Prophet. Holding fast to their egalitarian faith, these early Muslims saw they could vanquish the world. But governing what they had conquered while keeping their ideals intact was another matter.

6

Early Struggles for Authority

The Rule of the Righteous

Many of the first Muslims believed that with the death of Muhammad, the world would come to an end. In a sense, they were right. After Muhammad died in 632 the millenarian age was over – the Prophet's charismatic authority had been self-evident, but this was not true of his close companions, and the question of succession which inevitably plagues charismatic annunciations at once came to the fore. His immediate followers could make no claims to hearing divine voices in their minds. All they could say was that they would emulate Muhammad and act as devout Muslims.

The tension generated in the Muslim community over the question of naming of a new leader reveals the problematic nature of religious leadership in the Middle Eastern social environment. Immediately after the death of the Prophet, the Khazraj tribe convened to name one of their own as the new *emir*, meaning, apparently, a military commander. In doing so they hoped to forestall any power play by the rival Aws tribe and to take control over military expansion themselves. Uthman and other companions of Muhammad, fearing that the community would be torn apart, prevailed on the Khazraj to negotiate with the Aws, the Meccans, and the other Muslims of Medina on the question of the Prophet's successor.

After consultation, the parties decided on a compromise candidate, the good-natured and pious merchant Abu Bakr, the Prophet's father-in-law. He was not a clansman of either of the rival tribes, nor was he one of the Meccan elite. His qualifications were "closeness" to the Prophet, long commitment to Islam, and membership in the Quraysh (but in a cadet branch). Abu Bakr had also led the public prayers when Muhammad could not do so. And finally, he was known for his vast knowledge of tribal genealogies. The latter qualification is particularly interesting, since it indicates how important genealogy remained, even within the community of the faithful. Abu Bakr, as a genealogist, could work to reconcile disputes by showing old ties between groups, a talent which proved especially useful during the wars of secession (*ridda*) that soon followed, as some Arab tribes declined to obey the new Caliphate, arguing that their fealty was only granted to Muhammad personally, not to his successors.

As A. J. Wensinck writes, the opponents to the regime of Abu Bakr were divided between "those who followed religious or political adventurers and therefore turned their backs on Medina and Islam and those who cut the links with Medina without associating themselves with any new religious leader. This latter group did not, in all probability, reject Islam... What they rejected was zakat (taxation)."[1] New prophets from the hinterlands who reject the religion of the state and tax revolts by rural Muslims occur again and again in later Islamic kingdoms. The wars of seccession also illustrate another enduring component of Middle Eastern culture: the personalism of authority, which is conceived as a freely contracted mutual relation between individuals, to be rescinded or renegotiated when one of the parties dies. It is precisely such individualism that Islam attempted (with limited success) to supersede through the invocation of a sacred community that would live on after the death of Muhammad.

In these early years, Abu Bakr and the first Caliphs were severely limited in their power to control their closest associates, much less command the rebellious Arab tribes. For six months, until the community decided to contribute to his sustenance, Abu Bakr was a part-time leader in Medina, continuing his usual work as merchant, and milking his neighbors' sheep for additional income. Later Caliphs were not much more powerful. Abu Bakr's successor, Umar, was obliged to count the camels sent as tribute by himself, with only voluntary help.

Weakness at the center meant the wars of secession were won and the Muslim community sustained not by powerful rulers, but by warriors in the field who decided that the new order was preferable to the old and spontaneously acted to put down rebels and expand the dar al-Islam. During this period, commanders of Bedouin troops used their own judgment, and acted with little concern for higher authority in Medina. Their sense of independence was heightened when the military chief was a member of the old Meccan elite who did not wish to defer to the upstarts anointed in Medina as Muhammad's successors. When the Medina government sought to assert its authority, the field officers resisted, and struggles for power and control over booty began to divide the community of believers.

Other types of differentiation and opposition also arose due to the organization of the Muslims into a new society in which, as Wellhausen writes, "the citizen list was the army register, the tribes and families

Plate 6.1   Romantic nineteenth-century French portrayal of an Arab cavalryman.

forming the regiments and companies."[2] In the Muslim military machine, Clan structures were transformed as some members of kin
groups decided to go to battle, while others stayed home. If a whole
clan joined the jihad against the unbelievers, they were called "*barara*",
the "true"; if a section joined they were entitled "*khiyara*", the "select"
– leading to further hierarchies of rank among the Arabs.

Meanwhile some smaller clans were necessarily gathered together in
new military units based on reputed genealogical connections tenuously
traced to remote ancestors. These mixed groups of warriors were then
settled at the frontiers of the conquered zones in the newly-built garrison
towns of Basra, Kufa, and Fustat, where they were placed into residential
quarters made up of large tribal divisions of roughly equal size, with an
appointed leader for each. This enforced artificial consolidation was not
the end of tribal organizations; rather, it led to tribal alliances at a level
that had previously never existed in Arabia and facilitated the development of the large-scale factions, based on ancient Arabian tribal divisions
between north and south (usually expressed as Qays/Mudar versus
Yemen, Kalb, or Qahtan). Following a pattern we have already noted in
segmentary tribal society, these dualistic factional alliances henceforth
divided the empire by their continuous and fruitless struggles for power.[3]

Other internal divisions also arose. Tribes which had attempted to
secede from Islam in the ridda wars were prohibited from participation

in profitable and glorious invasions, while loyal groups were rewarded by being the first to partake of the plunder. Pensions were also allocated by the center on the grounds of priority in conversion. These new distinctions fueled resentments, especially since many of those penalized were from tribes with "noble" genealogies and strong lineage pride. Resentment simmered too over the center's appropriation of wealth from the conquests, which was doled out in stipends. Those who fought wondered if this redistribution was fair, and took exception to giving up their shares.

Levels of violence increased as Muslim Arabs settled pre-Islamic scores between themselves and their traditional rivals, regardless of the commands of the Prophet sanctioning peace among the believers. Well-hausen captures the tenor of the times when he quotes a warrior–leader who exhorted his kinsmen to attack a settlement of their ancient enemies, now supposed to be their Muslim brothers, by crying: "You have the choice between hell, if you follow me, and disgrace if you don't."[4] Needless to say, none chose disgrace, and the settlement was wiped out. Despite the rosy glow cast by religious idealism, the early Caliphate was not devoid of worldly struggles over power and glory.

These antagonisms were exacerbated when the third Caliph Uthman favored his noble Qurayshian relatives with top administrative and military posts, inflaming the anger and jealousy of Muslims from rival lineages, who marched on Medina in protest and, after some days of disputatious negotiation, killed Uthman while the Medinese looked on. With Uthman's death, *fitna*, chaos, was loosed in the world of Islam; it would never again be unified. Uthman's successor, the Prophet's son-in-law Ali, struggled to gain control of the empire, but he was opposed by Uthman's allies, and especially by his distant cousin Muawiya, the military governor of Syria, who swore to revenge Uthman's death and to succeed him as Caliph.

Muawiya was eventually victorious. His advent in 661 inaugurated a secular kingdom that has served the pious ever since as a negative counter to the sanctified rule of his predecessors. Although he did claim legitimacy as a member of Muhammad's family, Muawiya's dynasty, the Umayyad, was the first Muslim government to be validated not primarily because of its moral right, but because it commanded the most powerful army. For the pious, under the Umayyad dynasty Medina gave way to Damascus; faith was displaced by pragmatism and power-seeking; and tribalism and factionalism returned on a vast scale – the period of the charismatic community was over.

The Umayyad dynasty provided the type case for secular rulership to be found from this moment on in Islamic society, wherein authorities rule purely because they have managed to take the throne, without any sacred sanction whatsoever. As Ignaz Goldziher puts it, henceforth the

Sunni Caliph became "nothing but the successor of the one who preceded him, having been designated as such by a human act (election, or
nomination by his predecessor), and not entitled by the qualities inherent in his personality. Most importantly, the Caliph of the Sunnis has
no authority to dispense religious instruction."[5]

Movements of Religious Resistance: Kharijites and Shi'ites

Secular opposition to the Umayyads was relatively disorganized, as the
tribesmen, enmeshed in their own internal battles, could not unite
against the regime. But many Muslims who had participated in the
umma did not accept the disintegration of their unified charismatic community so easily, nor could the old ethic of tribal honor and glorious
revenge ever again hold sway without ambiguity. Even the tribal chief
who gave his men the choice between hell and disgrace was overcome in
time with remorse, and spent his old age in repentance and prayer. In this
morally complex situation, the devout remembered the promises of the
Prophet and the experience of the commune – memories that continue
even today to activate religious resistance to secular government – and
sought more sanctified candidates to fill the post of ruler over a community that would replicate the original solidary umma.

There were two approaches to re-establishing the sacred polity. The
first was taken by those referred to as the *kharijites*, "those who go
out". These originally were early tribal followers of Muhammad who
later favored Ali against the alliance of military elite and Qurayshian
aristocrats. But when Ali vainly sought negotiation with his enemies,
the kharijites rejected him as a poseur and proclaimed new radically
egalitarian religious republics for themselves, wherein only the most
pious and able would rule, regardless of family, ancestral spirituality,
priority of conversion, or any other claim – in some groups, even
women were given the same rights as men! Pitiless opponents to all
who denied the truth of their egalitarian moral stance, they saw themselves as "the people of heaven" battling against "the people of hell".

W. M. Watt has portrayed the kharijites as a retrograde movement of
disappointed tribesmen hoping to reconstitute in new circumstances
and on an Islamic basis the small groups they had been familiar with in
the desert.[6] But unlike the pre-Islamic tribesmen, for them the rule of
the strongest and cleverest was not enough; their leader also had to be
the most devout, and he could be deposed and even killed at any time,
for any moral error, so that commanders rose and fell with rapidity.
Arguments over doctrine also continually split the kharijite bands. Although they were good at fighting, the loosely organized and internally
divided kharijites could not gain any wider legitimacy or establish a

stable governmental structure. They wasted themselves in unwinnable wars against the whole world, and against themselves as well.[7]

Only a few more moderate kharijite groups managed to organize rulership in some remote areas, notably Oman, where the Ibadi branch of the khariji was institutionalized into a full-fledged school of law; here the ruler is still elected by merchant notables and the tribal elite – though since 1741 he has always been a member of the royal Saidi family. Some Ibadi also remain as secretive minorities in out-of-the-way areas of North Africa, such as the Island of Djerba off the coast of Tunisia. Elsewhere, in North Africa, Berbers, rebelling against the center, took up the banner of kharijism to symbolize their opposition. One such group, the Rustamids, managed to establish an ascetic, egalitarian regime that lasted until the tenth century, when it was toppled by warrior tribesmen.

Despite an absence of political success, the kharijite impulse to high morality and political anarchism has had an appeal ever since to rebels who refuse to accept secular rule or elite domination. Even today, modern Muslim radicals are execrated by the orthodox as "kharijites" because of their radical egalitarianism, moral self-righteousness, willingness to use violence against those with whom they disagree, and relentless opposition to central authority. In turn, the radicals denounce their moderate opponents as apostates for accepting the command of the secular state and assert that they alone are true Muslims.[8]

Although the anarchistic kharijites long were a thorn in the side of Middle Eastern regimes, and though their message still has a powerful appeal, a more effective source of sustained sacred opposition to the status quo came from quite the opposite ideological direction. Instead of arguing for a radically egalitarian community of believers who freely elect the man best among them as a leader, these rebels subordinated themselves to a sacred authority whose word was absolute law. For them, Muhammad's charisma was reincarnated in his descendants, notably in Ali, the Prophet's son-in-law and cousin who served as the fourth Caliph after the murder of Uthman. The *shi'ites*, or "partisans" of Ali, argued that, since Muhammad had no sons, Ali had inherited Muhammad's spiritual power and must be recognized as *Imam*, the sacred spokesman for Islam.[9]

For those following Ali or other lineal descendants of the Prophet,[10] the problem of authority was solved by recognizing that one particular kin group had spiritual ascendence above all others, and therefore had the intrinsic right to rule. The Shi'ite belief in the omnipotence of their transcendental Imam incited enthusiasm among the faithful, who could righteously unite behind him in a jihad against the corruption of the center. But, as we shall see, this also meant that their faith was often severely challenged when the dream confronted political reality, and the faithful had either to accept disappointment of their hopes or embark on yet more fervent pursuits of the millennium.

Maintaining Secular Domination

Of course, not all Muslims actively resisted the secular rulership of Muawiya and his successors. The *murjia*, "those who defer", argued that ordinary human beings could not presume to judge other Muslims, but ought to let God judge. For them, it was enough that the rulers defended the faith and acted in public as Muslims ought to act. Only Allah knows what intent lies behind these displays, and human beings are enjoined to suspend judgment. This extreme validation of passivity was later condemned by the mainstream of Islam, but, like kharijism, it does reflect the logic of egalitarian individualism, though taken in an opposing direction. While the kharijites affirmed the requirement of each individual to act on his own moral initiative, regardless of consequences the murjia asserted the inability of anyone to penetrate beneath surfaces and accurately evaluate another person's virtue.[11]

In any case, most Muslims were pragmatic enough to submit to the rule of the Umayyads so long as they followed the minimal obligatory public practices required of all believers: prayer, the recitation of the faith, fasting, abstention from any conspicuous indulgence in forbidden pleasures. The new rulers also displayed the requisite sober and manly personal behavior Middle Easterners have always demanded of their leaders. Even though their abstention in particular was often only a show for the benefit of a Muslim audience, piety of the Umayyads was nonetheless validated by court-supported clerics, who were willing to give their stamp of approval for the sake of the favor of the ruler and the peace of the nation. The absence of any concerted religious condemnation of the Umayyad rulers and their Marwanid successors became characteristic of the attitude of the majority of the clerical class toward secular authority throughout all later Muslim history.

However, the Umayyads and Marwanids were far from being the absolute tyrants that later rulers sought to be. Their rule can rather be seen as a continuation and expansion of a tribal mode of command, constrained not so much by religious compunctions as by necessities of consultation with their rival co-equals and lineage mates among the Arab tribes. Muawiya, in particular, was known as "first among equals" and was renowned for his virtue of *hilm*, a capacity for rational calculation, cool-headedness, and the reconciliation of opposed interests – a value favored strongly by both tradesmen and tribesmen, who traditionally relied on mediation to keep the peace in their turbulent worlds.

Muawiya was a man recognized even by his enemies as a person who combined an unusual capacity to arbitrate disputes and give credence to the rights of others, while at the same time promoting his own position at the center. In this sense, he was very much in the mold of the tribal leader, a man among men, a judge who authenticated his noble birthright by his abilities; yet also accustomed to manipulating for power by playing rivals off against one another to solidify his own position – a technique that has been followed ever since by Middle Eastern leaders who lack the strength to coerce, yet do have the mandate to act as arbitrators.

While Muawiya gained respect and authority from his capacity as a judge and manipulator, his royal ambitions became clear when he was unwilling to consult Arab tribal elders about the selection of his successor. Instead, Muawiya imposed his son Yazid on the community. Perhaps he intended thereby to fend off further warfare among rival claimants; perhaps he realized that the Syrian army, who provided his major support, would only accept his immediate descendant as their commander; certainly his act was interpreted as a move away from both the tribal and the Muslim notion of command, which favored leadership of a *primus inter pares*, elected by consensus of the community elders.

Predictably, Muawiya's maneuver aroused opposition from other potential candidates for the post of Caliph, first from Ali's son, Husain, whose followers saw him as the rightful claimant to leadership of the faithful. The catastrophic failure of Husain's rebellion and his terrible death set its stamp on Shi'ism ever since. More serious at the time was the challenge from Ibn-al-Zubayr, the son of one of the Prophet's companions who was supported by Aisha, the Prophet's favorite wife. After Zubayr's failed uprising, violent civil war ensued, as factional tribal alliances lined up behind various secular pretenders while the Shi'ites tried to hurry the advent of the millennium under a holy Imam, and scattered bands of kharijites, pursuing their radical dream of complete egalitarianism in the community of faithful, fought ruthlessly against everyone.

The eventual triumph of the Marwanid branch of the Umayyad family showed that the centralized and well-organized Syrian army could defeat the fragmented and mutually antagonistic tribes, scatter the kharijite bands, and crush the religious aspirations of those supporting Ali. The army now became more than ever the sole source of dynastic power, and the Marwanids were careful to retain its loyalty by offering faithful soldiers special stipends and privileges, while simultaneously degrading potentially disloyal groups.

Although many governors of safe regions were from the immediate royal family, the regime also made a policy of raising men from low stations to become chiefs and governors of unruly provinces, foreshad-

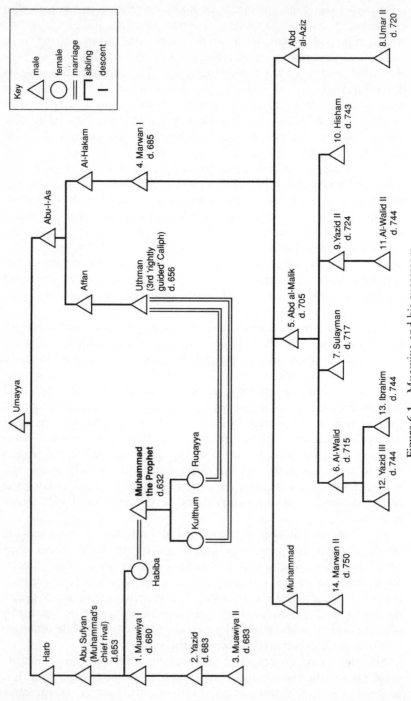

Figure 6.1 Muawiya and his successors.

owing the pattern noted centuries later by Ibn Khaldun of replacing potentially rivalrous members of one's own kin group with more reliable clients and dependents. Under the Marwanids, these newcomers were given very considerable authority in their own domains, which led to a degree of decentralization, but avoided outright rebellion, since their low station meant they could not win the loyalty of Arab troops who retained high opinions of their own nobility and independence.

Meanwhile, in Damascus, the court engaged in a perilous balancing act, playing off different tribal political factions against one another. To buoy up its precarious position, the court expanded the old tribal "blood" ideology to one of Arab nationalism, as all Arabs were reckoned to be intrinsically superior to all non-Arabs. The population of the conquered nations were incorporated into the tribal structure as dependent clients (mawali) protected by the respective Arab clans who had defeated them, much as the Arabs were protected by Allah. Under these conditions, as Goitein notes, "in order to become a Muslim, one had to become an Arab first."[12]

At first, this strategy worked well. Although Arabs contended endlessly among themselves as to which of their lineages was more noble than the others, most of them found it easy to justify the social reality of the distinction between victor and vanquished in terms of "natural" inferiority of the Persians, Berbers, Kurds and Turks, who did not have Arab blood flowing with them, and deserved to be ruled, as was proven by the very fact of their subservience.

To maintain feelings of ethnic superiority, the Marwanids continually sought to keep a distance between the Arab conquerors and their subjects. At the same time, they pursued a policy of continuous expansive war. In this way the rulers made a claim to the only mode of secular authority recognized by the Bedouin – the role of military commander. This two-pronged policy had distinct advantages: Arab soldiers, who were the most dangerous potential opponents to the regime, had their aggressions channeled into interminable struggles on the frontier, where they were kept happy with their share of the booty from their conquests of infidel nations, and were simultaneously reassured of their "natural" superiority over those they conquered.

Yet this latter policy was not without perils: tribal factionalism returned to the fore at a dangerous level, as large lineage segments, newly coalesced together in quarters of the garrison towns, organized as kin-based political units using the ideology of tribal honor to protect their own members and to defeat old enemies. A speech by a new governor of the unruly garrison town of Basra reveals some of the problems the regime had with these powerful factions: "Ye are putting relationship before religion. Ye are excusing and sheltering your criminals, and tearing down the protecting laws sanctified by Islam...

Beware of the arbitrary summons of relationship; I will cut out the tongue of every one who raises the cry...I make every family responsible for those belonging to it."[13]

A ruthless use of force against all opponents, a deep hostility to any factional groups that might unite against the state, a policy of mediation, a reliable payroll, and short stints in battle were the usual means for keeping the army united and the regime in power. However, such a policy ran into trouble when conquest became difficult or impossible, and booty dried up. This is what soon occurred in the inhospitable mountains of what is now Afghanistan, where Arab troops, like so many other armies before and since, came up against intractable resistance. Tired soldiers, weary of incessant fighting for little reward, settled into more sedentary lives as merchants and farmers. In these circumstances, the Marwanid tactics of continual war began to meet opposition, as men found pursuit of their own ventures more appealing than service in the army.

Concurrent with the increased reluctance of soldiers to undertake interminable wars, the maintenance of caste distinctions between Persian and Arab began to break down. By the eighth century, the ranked distinction between Arab superior and non-Arab subaltern was already becoming difficult to maintain, as the regime, following the pattern later outlined by Ibn Khaldun, sought to undermine the power of its tribal armies by increasingly enlisting non-Arab "client" units to fight alongside their Arab co-religionists. In the west, Berbers rapidly converted, and proved themselves equal to any Arab in battle, while in the east, Persian troops also gave a good showing. Meanwhile, the Persian bureaucratic and literary elite quickly adapted themselves to Islam and to Arabic ways and began to assimilate themselves into the Muslim mainstream, where they proved themselves indispensable in maintaining the empire, since the Arab conquerors had no knowledge of or inclination toward participation in government administration, and gladly allowed their new minions to continue in their old posts.

As the defeated people became more integrated into the culture of the Arabs, the reverse process was also occurring. The isolated garrison towns where the Arab soldiers were supposed to retain their purity and tribal asabiyya were rapidly becoming true cities, with expanding bazaars and heterogenous immigrant populations. Especially in the eastern provinces, Arab soldiers learned Persian, began trading and farming, and found the demands of Damascus less and less to their taste. As H. A. R. Gibb writes: "The most striking feature of this period (720–750 AD, the last thirty years of the Umayyad Caliphate) is the division which had begun to develop within the ranks of the Arab conquerors themselves...between those...actively engaged in the military forces of the empire, and those who...had become citizens

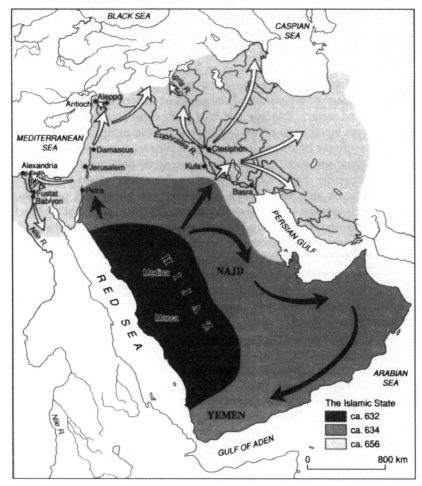

Map 6.1   The early expansion of Islam.

and ceased to be soldiers."[14] This division was loosely attached to the ancient tribal distinction between Qays and Yemen, with allies of Qays becoming associated with the policy of military expansion and Arab superiority, while Yemen was in favor of settlement, trade and assimilation.

Integration was increased as widespread concubinage inevitably resulted in demands for social equality from the sons of Persian, Kurdish and Berber mothers, who cited the strongly egalitarian principles of Arabic kinship and Quranic family law, which make no distinction between half-brothers and full brothers of the same father; each is entitled to the same inheritance and the same respect. Even offspring of slave mothers are legally entitled to be treated in the same manner as their freeborn siblings, while a slave woman who has given birth to the child of her Muslim master can no longer be legally sold.

Along with the equivalence fostered by law and the social structure of descent, conversion of the mawali to Islam allowed these new Muslims and their supporters to use the Quran and Islamic custom to argue for their immediate admission as full members of the community of Muslim brothers and sisters. Reading the holy text, they discovered that if all Muslims are equal before God and in law, then in principle none can be treated as inferior by co-religionists, even if they are not of Arab blood.

All of these pressures led to sporadic attempts, first under Umar II (d. 720), then under Yazid III (d. 744), to reform the system by offering equal rights to all members of the Islamic community and promoting policies that favored trade over war. But these gestures were short-lived, as more conservative and militaristic regimes overturned reforms and heightened resentment among the conquered groups and the assimilationist Yemenite faction. Meanwhile tribal rebels from the periphery and urban proponents of various Alid pretenders to sacred authority tried their strength against the regime, which was itself internally divided and rife with destructive intrigue. The cycle was almost complete, the time was ripe for a new order.

The Abbasid Rebellion

The inevitable successful revolt exploded at last in Khurasan, on the far eastern margins of the realm. In Muawiya's time, this remote Persian province had served as the place to send Muslim warriors who did not quite fit into the existing tribal divisions that segmented the garrison towns. 50,000 troops of various backgrounds had been settled there, not separated from the local populace, as was customary, but intermingled with them. A long period of relative peace attenuated already weakened tribal allegiances and allowed these mixed warriors to settle into farming and trade and to intermarry with the elite of the local society; when a war economy resumed there was widespread dissatisfaction in this region.

The local sense of oppression and alienation was fanned by underground religious revolutionaries, the Hashimiyya, who infiltrated into Khurasan from the city of Kufa, where rebellions in favor of descendents of the house of Ali had flared and been suppressed by the Marwanids. The Hashimiyya, a small but highly organized sect, recognized from experience that an urban revolt in the center of the Empire was impossible, but believed that a revolution from the margins could succeed, and identified Khurasan as the most likely place for such a revolt to begin.

These conspirators had sophisticated techniques of recruitment and organization that closely resemble those used by the al-Qaeda Islamist radicals today. Organized in small segregated cells of zealots under strict central leadership, they maintained absolute secrecy as they spread propaganda throughout Khurasan and inflamed local opinion with millenarian rhetoric. Overt rebellion started in the garrison town of Merv, where 2,200 rebels raised the black banner of revenge and revolt in 747. They soon were joined by thousands more dissatisfied revolutionaries, and the movement began that was to sweep across Islamdom from east to west, ending in 750 in the final downfall of the Marwanids and the ascent of the Abbasids, which meant a shift in power from Syria and Damascus to Iraq and Baghdad and the replacement of rule by noble Arabs to rule by men of mixed ethnic origin. It was the end of leadership by tribal warriors who were simply the best among co-equals, and the beginning of a new imperial absolutism.

Of course, despotism was not what the Hashimiyya partisans promoted in their revolutionary rhetoric. Instead, they rallied followers by crying out against the corruption of the Marwanids and the inequities of their government and by calling for a return to a unified umma where all Muslim brothers would participate equally regardless of race, class or origin. The slogan that the followers shouted as they marched proclaimed support for the Quran, the Prophet, and *al-rida min Muhammad*; that is, for a member of the house of Muhammad who would be elected leader by *al-rida*, consultation and communal choice.[15] The deliberate vagueness of this phrase evoked the idealized image of the original sacred community of believers who elected their ruler cooperatively, and allowed enthusiasts from all parties to assume that their candidate could be the new Caliph.

Cognoscenti, however, knew that in reality the revolt was in support of the descendents of Abbas, the Prophet's uncle, who on the surface had the weakest claims of any of the Prophet's relatives to the mantle of the Imam, but who the Hashimiyya cult believed had been given a secret metaphysical mandate to rule. Though unsure of exactly which member of the Abbasid house would actually wear the robes of the Prophet, the election of the Caliph had, in effect, already been made by an elite consisting only of insiders. Typically, they justified this usurpation by their "special spiritual knowledge" which gave them *carte blanche* to make decisions for all believers.

The leader of the Kufan Hashimiyya conspiracy in Khurasan was a shadowy figure, perhaps an ex-bondservant, who is known only by his pseudonym, Abu Muslim Abdulrahman b. Muslim al-Khurasani ("a Muslim son of a Muslim, father of a Muslim of Khurasan"). This name was meant to indicate that he was neither client nor patron, Arab nor Persian, but was simply a believer from Khurasan. As M. A. Shaban says, "he was a living proof that in the new society every member would be regarded only as a Muslim regardless of racial origins or tribal connections."[16] His integrative policy was also indicated by the fact that recruits were registered not by lineage, as had been Umayyad practice, but by name and place of birth.

With the support of a dedicated and united Khurasani army of fervent devotees, and bouyed by the fervor of Shi'ite revolutionaries who believed they were fighting to bring the reign of a descendant of Ali, Abu Muslim was able to defeat the weakened and internally divided Marwanid forces. But Shi'ite hopes were dashed when the victorious revolutionary forces placed Abu al-Abbas on the throne. Abu al-Abbas soon died, and, after some struggle, his position was taken over by his more effective elder brother, Abu Jafar, who had at first been passed over due to his descent from a Berber slave girl, while al-Abbas had a noble Arab mother.

Because he lacked even the genealogical legitimacy offered by pure Arabic descent, Jafar had to find new ways to maintain and justify his power, and he pursued his goal with ruthless dedication. Having come to power via a conspiratorial movement, he saw sedition everywhere, and no individual was safe from his reach. One of his first acts was to organize the assassination of Abu Muslim, whose influence over the army was dangerous. Although the martyred Abu Muslim has been popularly recalled ever since as a Messianic rebel who remains in hiding, awaiting the proper time to lead his people back to power, there was no organized protest against his murder, and Jafar realized most Muslims were willing to acquiesce to his rule. To further protect himself, he supervised the relentless hunting down of any possible Marwanid pretenders to the throne (one escaped, and set up a rival Caliphate in Spain). And, following the example of Muawiya, he demanded that his son be recognized as his successor.

Centralizing his regime, Jafar planned and oversaw the building of the huge new capital of Baghdad, a circular city constructed at the center of the empire. Unlike earlier garrison cities, which consisted of equal quarters in which rivalrous tribal enclaves of warriors lived, Baghdad was an enormous palace where the ruler was surrounded by his personal dependents and by loyal Khurasani troops, who were isolated from their homeland and reliant on the administration they had brought to power to supply them with stipends.

Jafar kept himself at the core of this complex and ruled for two decades (754–775), holding all the reins of government in his own hands and maintaining a vast system of spies that reported directly to him, even on matters so ordinary as the prices of food in the marketplace. The new circular city symbolized his power and his emphasis on personal control and strong central authority. Jafar also continued, with restraint,

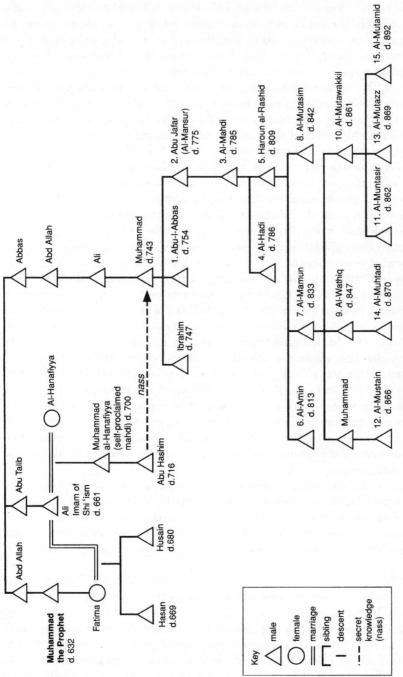

Figure 6.2 Early Abbasid Caliphs.

Key
△ male
○ female
═ marriage
⌐ sibling
— descent
---- secret
knowledge
(nass)

Muhammad
the Prophet
d. 632

Abd Allah

Abu Talib

Al-Hanafiyya

Ali
Imam of
Shi'ism
d. 661

Muhammad
al-Hanafiyya
(self-proclaimed
mahdi) d. 700

Abu Hashim
d. 716

Fatima

Hasan
d. 669

Husain
d. 680

Abbas

Abd Allah

Ali

Muhammad
d. 743

nass

1. Abu-I-Abbas
d. 754

Ibrahim
d. 747

2. Abu Jafar
(Al-Mansur)
d. 775

3. Al-Mahdi
d. 785

5. Haroun al-Rashid
d. 809

4. Al-Hadi
d. 786

8. Al-Mutasim
d. 842

7. Al-Mamun
d. 833

9. Al-Wathiq
d. 847

6. Al-Amin
d. 813

Muhammad

10. Al-Mutawakkil
d. 861

14. Al-Muhtadi
d. 870

12. Al-Mustain
d. 866

13. Al-Mutazz
d. 869

11. Al-Muntasir
d. 862

15. Al-Mutamid
d. 892

to use the same sorts of spiritual propaganda which had successfully mobilized the revolutionary army that had placed him in power. While his predecessors had made minimal claims to religious sanction for their authority, the Abbasid Caliph wore the alleged mantle of the Prophet on his shoulders. Similarly, where the Umayyads and Marwanids, as tribal shaikhs writ large, had simply been known by their personal names, Jafar gave himself the title al-Mansur, the one destined to victory, implying Allah's favor. Playing to the messianic hopes of the masses, his son and successor would be designated by an even more grandiose title: al-Mahdi, the redeemer. With the same ambitions in mind, his famous successor the Caliph al-Mamun took the title Imam for himself, in a vain attempt to present himself as a savior to the Shi'ites and bring about a reconciliation between the Sunni majority and the perpetually rebellious minority of the party of Ali.

But there was a danger involved in exciting enthusiastic expectations among the populace. Millenarian hopes, once aroused, might easily get out of hand. Gnostic communitarian followers of the Hashimiyya believed that the Godly community of true believers should share everything, including, so their opponents exclaimed in horror, property, and even wives – a repetition of the charges made long before against the disciples of Mazdak in the Sasanid era. For example, the Rawandiyya, who held the Caliph Mansur in adulation, came to court to acclaim his divinity, where they caused a scandal by ecstatically leaping from the palace roofs to their deaths, freeing prisoners, and spreading their doctrine of communal sharing of property, transmigration of souls, and the omnipotence of the Caliph. Too much adulation proved to be worse than not enough, and these communitarian dreamers were ruthlessly crushed by the highly practical and puritanical al-Mansur, who favored wealthy capitalists and urban entrepreneurs over millenarian mystics.

So, despite the revolutionary promises of redemption, it turned out that the Abbasid government would not be a return to the sacred rule of the Prophet, but would be a secular administration. In some senses, this meant that the Abbasid dynasty was a continuation of what had preceded it – a dynasty based on the resolute use of power.

The New Hierarchy of the Courtier

But in another sense the Abbasid revolt was a true revolution with profound consequences, since it swept away the claims made by old Arab noble lineages for their right to rule and replaced them with a redefined notion of community and authority. The Caliph al-Mamun explains this new order by saying: "A noble Arab is closer to a noble

Persian than he is to a low-class Arab; a noble Persian is nearer to a noble Arab than he is to a low-class Persian, because noble men form a (separate) class and plebians form a (separate) class."[17]

In this milieu, nobility was expressed and ratified in what Ira Lapidus calls "aristocratic self-cultivation", as expressed in the practice of *adab*, the elaborate Persian protocol mandating a courtier's proper manners and bearing. Those wishing to be recognized as aristocrats could not rely on their bloodline; they had to demonstrate a knowledge of poetry, horsemanship, letter-writing, literature, finance, history and the sciences, along with a background in the subtleties of religious debate. "Gentlemanly in manners, gracious, and sensitive to the nuances of rank and honor," the Abbasid courtier rigorously trained himself to display "a worldly refinement which set him apart from the lowly and justified his claim to power. Indirectly the cultivation of Persian and Greek letters implied a common culture for a heterogenous elite based upon the presumption of inherent aristocratic superiority."[18]

The flowering of refinement at court was an attempt to claim preeminence for deracinated individuals in a world where the old standards for nobility based on lineage or on descent from the Prophet were now challenged by Abbasid cosmopolitanism. Accompanying this change was something more sinister. Assertions of aristocratic rank were now verified only by the approval of the Caliph and his Abbasid relatives – the rest of the Muslims were equal in their shared subjugation. In theory, any of them could be raised or lowered arbitrarily as the Caliph willed, and the disciplined self-cultivation of the courtiers was not only a way to set themselves off from hoi polloi, but also very much an attempt to curry the Caliph's favor. As has so often been the case, a rebellion which was inaugurated in the name of freedom and equality ended by increasing servility.

The heightened authority asserted by the Abbasids was manifested in a greater and greater use of personal clients (the mawali) in the court and administration. After the reign of Mansur, clientage became the essential organizing feature of the Abbasid Caliphate at every level. The mawali included illegitimate and junior kinsmen, manumitted slaves, and freemen in voluntary service. But even though theoretically independent, each was inextricably bound to his elite benefactor. As Jacob Lassner writes: "the mawla no more left the Caliph's service of his own volition than the soldier of the mafia voluntarily abandons his patron's family by invoking his constitutional rights."[19]

The murder of Abu Muslim by Mansur was a lesson taken to heart by all mawali. They realized that their task was not devotion to an abstract ideal of service to the nation at large, but to furthering the personal interests of their particular champion. The mawali themselves had no power base; taken up from the dust, they could be returned to it. To survive, they had to charm and flatter as well as serve. The precarious and personalized form of service offered by these sycophant courtier-administrators allowed the Abbasids to control their subordinates at court and to prevent any attempts by bureaucrats to take power for themselves.

But there was a price for this security: when there was a conflict among the Abbasid elite "clients acting in their own best interests tended to stimulate rather than reduce tensions in an effort to promote the claims of their respective patrons."[20] Under these circumstances, the court became a battleground of rumor, provocation, innuendo and plotting: this was the cost the elite paid for demanding absolute personal authority over their circle of flattering administrators and dependents.

More potentially destabilizing were the ambitions and demands of the military. Despite their claims to religious legitimacy, Mansur and his successors, like the Umayyads and Marwanids who had come before them, were completely reliant on the army to enforce their commands. This relationship was complicated because, as Wellhausen remarks, "the Abbasids were not elevated, like the Umaiyids, over a widespread aristocracy, to which they themselves belonged: the Khurasanites, by whom they were supported, were not their blood, but only their instrument."[21] No longer kinsmen to the ruler, the army were now understood to be servants of their imperial masters, just as the administrators were. However, there was a major difference. These servants controlled the weapons.

The only hope the Abbasids had for keeping power was to maintain the absolute loyalty of this potent military instrument, but they could not rely on the bonds that had been fitfully generated by the shared tribal asabiyya of earlier Umayyad and Marwanid dynasties. The Khurasaniyya army was held together instead by belief in the sacredness of the Caliph and their shared experience of battle, as well as by isolation in the metropolis away from their distant homeland. But the riches and influence they gained as the first supporters of the Abbasid dynasty soon corrupted the integrity and loyalty of the Khurasaniyya; they became wealthy members of the Baghdadi political and mercantile elite and jealously guarded their status even against the Caliph himself, stoutly claiming their entitlements by virtue of past accomplishments, while simultaneously losing their religious awe of the Caliph's person.

To try to balance out the increasingly disruptive Khurasaniyya presence and to acquire a more reliable army the Abbasids began to recruit "slave" troops from more remote districts, most notably from the areas east of the old Sasanid empire. These are the celebrated "Turks" who were generally not Turkish speakers at all, but men from many different ethnic and tribal groups whose chiefs were drawn to service with the Abbasids by promises of wealth and glory. Although they were known as mawali and *abid* (slaves) of the Caliph, these troops were very much like the early Arab adventurers who had fought under Islamic flags not so much for religious reasons, but because of the wealth and power they hoped to gain. Like the original Khurasaniyya army, these new legions too were outsiders to cosmopolitan culture; they too, like their predecessors, were looked down upon as barbarians by the sophisticated inhabitants of the center. But where the Khurasaniyya had mobilized around a messianic promise enunciated by Abu Muslim and embodied in the Abbasid Caliph the "Turks" were gathered around a tribal war leader, a "first among equals" who had to prove himself in battle or else be deserted. They had no higher loyalties beyond their own aggrandizement and their fragile *esprit de corps*.

The reliance of the Abbasids on foreign mercenary troops did eventually break the back of the Khurasaniyya, as Mamun, with support from Turkish mawali, defeated his brother Amin in the great civil war of succession after the death of Harun al-Rashid (809). But the problem of maintaining authority was hardly solved. The Abbasids continued to try to promote their claims to legitimacy but their policies belied their words. As Shaban writes: "The central government acted very much like a colonial power whose only interest was to exploit its domains without regard to the interests of its subjects... The government saw all its duties and responsibilities in terms of enforcing tax-collection, the revenues of which were to support a growing and corrupt bureaucracy and an almost useless army."[22] Local governors were allowed *carte blanche* as long as taxes were paid, while complex networks of patronage links left plenty of leeway for corruption and manipulation, as local notables sought to maximize their own gains, with the peasant often the loser.

The increasing use of flattering honorifics and ever greater pomp and ceremony at the glittering court could not hide the fact that this was a regime where, aside from the king's prime minister, the *wazir*, "the executioner was perhaps the most outstanding figure among the official personnel."[23] This gruesome truth was graphically symbolized by the leather carpet beside the Sultan's throne, which served as the mat upon which the royal executioner summarily practiced his gory craft. Nor could the courtier's cultivation of worldly arts and the discipline of adab offset the discontent rife in outlying regions exploited by the center and among the poor, who were finding it ever more difficult to survive in a polity that appeared to have no sympathy for their plight. It is in this context that the poet al-Sindi exclaimed: "Would that the tyranny of the sons of Marwan would return to us, would that the justice of the sons of Abbas were in hell!"[24]

Under these conditions, popular and regional uprisings were commonplace. The court too began to disintegrate into factionalism, impelled in part by the conniving of client groups supporting their own princely patrons. The motley "Turkish" armies, whose loyalty to the regime was bound only by payment and who had little, if any, sense of connection to the society at large, proved to be even more of a problem than the Khurasaniyya. Various troops solidified around their respective generals and sold themselves to the highest bidder. Provinces became more and more independent, paying only lip service to the ideal of the Caliphate, and were ruled by secular leaders pursuing their own ends. Bankrupt by its profligacy, the Abbasids found power slipping from their grasp, as the Caliphs became puppets in the hands of rival groups of palace guards who allowed them only symbolic authority.

7

Sacred and Secular Rulers

The Quest for the Redeemer: the Qarmati

Two major contenders for power now arose. The first were the Shi'ites. In times of disruption, the party of Ali has always found proponents among the disappointed and disenfranchised who hope for a Messiah. As we have seen, Shi'ites had provided enthusiastic support for the Abbasid revolt, and were sorely disappointed at its result. But the centralized government of al-Mansur broke Shi'ite resistance, aided by their own fragmentation into numerous sects, each supporting different pretenders to the position of Imam. The most numerous Shi'ites were the twelvers, who traced their line to the twelfth descendant of the martyred Husain. They were rigorously suppressed, and withdrew from the political fray. However, other Shi'ites, who branched off at the seventh Imam, assumed a more activist stance, and, despite repression, eventually evolved into a major threat to the weakened Caliphate.

This development took time and was not even; it began with radical oppositional movements that appeared first in the garrison city of Kufa, then spread to Syria, Bahrain, Yemen, and finally to North Africa. They knew themselves generally as *al-dawa al-hadiyya*, the "rightly guided mission", but to Muslims in Syria and Bahrain this sect and its adherents were called the Qarmati, after Hamdan Qarmat, who was their first local *dai* (missionary); elsewhere they were called Ismaili after their founder. In the Syrian desert and in North Africa they were known as Fatimids, stressing the descent of Ismail from the Prophet's daughter Fatima. These latter were eventually to rule Egypt, and to establish the most powerful Shi'ite challenge to Sunni dominance of Islam.[1]

But for the period we are considering (the late ninth and early tenth century), the most dangerous rivals of the Caliphate on the western front were the various groups of the Qarmati, who were mobilized under the leadership of a series of sanctified agents of the true Imam, or under individuals who actually claimed themselves to be the redeemer. The

Qarmati were a chiliastic group of a characteristic Middle Eastern type, appealing to Bedouin rebelliousness, urban dissatisfaction, and angry peasantry for support. They broke from orthodox Shi'ism in their doctrine of the "spiritual initiation" of the Imam, who could be from outside the lineage of the Prophet, and who would be immediately recognized by his personal charismatic radiance. This left the field wide open for any claimant, and broadened the appeal of the movement – though it also involved serious dangers, as we shall see.

Large numbers of enthusiastic youth joined the devotees in their desert settlements. These independent settlements were self-consciously egalitarian, save for absolute deference to the missionaries who claimed to represent the perfect Imam. This paradoxical pattern is typically Shi'ite, since complete submission to the redeemer means that all other forms of distinction amongst the believers, such as blood or occupation, must be obliterated – total sacred authority coincides with radical political egalitarian communitarianism in a kharijism stabilized by acceptance of central command.

Accordingly, in the Qarmatid camps any display of rank or privilege was rejected, and kinship ties to family members who did not support the movement were cut away. These communities also had a just system of taxation, assistance to the underprivileged, high status for women, and government by consultation among a council of respected elders. According to one eyewitness, in anticipation of the foundation of a new sacred society, the Qarmati "assembled their possessions in one place and held them in common, no man enjoying any advantage over his friend because of any property which he owned ... they had no need of possessions because the earth in its entirety would be theirs and no one else's."[2]

The blend of devotion, communitarianism, equity and messianism was a potent mixture, and the Qarmati began to gain numerous adherents among dissatisfied local populations. They terrified the increasingly unpopular regime in Baghdad, who organized pogroms against suspected sympathizers in the city but were unable to control the inroads of the "rightly guided" in the countryside. Allied with nomads from East Arabia and the Syrian and Iraqi desert, the Qarmati were able to raid caravan routes successfully and to threaten the hugely lucrative pilgrimage to Mecca, which they opposed as an impious intrusion of commercialism onto the holy city. They were defeated only with great difficulty, and erupted again a few years later, in 923, when Qarmati from Bahrain under the leadership of Abu Tahir menaced the Abbasid trade life-line in the desert, sacked Basra, massacred pilgrims on the hajj, occupied vital trade ports along the Arabian side of the Persian Gulf, and came very close to conquering Baghdad itself.

With these successes behind him, and anticipating the advent of the mahdi at the astrological conjunction of Jupiter and Saturn in 928, Abu Tahir intensified his relentless campaigns against those whom he regarded as apostate Muslims; in 930, his troops entered Mecca and, in an astonishing act of sacrilege, absconded with the Kaaba. For the Qarmati, however, this act was a symbol of their spiritual ascendence. The corrupt old center of Mecca was to be replaced as the heart of a cleansed and radiant Islamic world by their Qarmati capital of al-Ahsa. From this new sacred city Abu Tahir ruled all of Arabia, inspiring fear or hope in every direction. To him and his enthusiastic followers all the signs indicated that the longed-for moment of world conquest by the rightly guided had come; the Caliphate would soon be held by a true mahdi.

At this fateful moment Abu Tahir's fervent hope for the advent of the millennium betrayed him, leading him to recognize a charismatic young Persian from Isfahan as the long-awaited savior. Believing utterly in the miraculous powers of this youthful self-proclaimed redeemer, Abu Tahir piously turned over his command to him. Unhappily, the supposed mahdi soon proved less than exalted, as he instituted ritual cursing of Muhammad, the worship of fire, and the execution of local notables, including some of Abu Tahir's relatives. In fear for his own life, Abu Tahir declared his protégé a false messiah and had him killed, but this eschatological error demoralized the Bahraini Qarmati community, and cost Abu Tahir his credibility. Many Qarmati now denied their faith, and left Bahrain to serve in the armies of Abu Tahir's opponents. Disappointed in their dreams, the remnants of the Qarmati returned the sacred stone to Mecca, twenty-one years after they had stolen it away. The Qarmatid movement, which had come so near to success, was over, destroyed by its own ambition to proclaim the advent of a redeemer. Its inheritors, the Fatimids, would have more success, but they too would founder on their millenarian expectations.

Pragmatic Tribesmen: Buyids and Seljuks

The Buyids, who were eventually to conquer the Abbasid empire, were very different from the zealous Qarmati. They were pragmatic Daylamite tribesmen from the Elburz mountains to the east of the empire who took advantage of the chaos in Baghdad to expand onto the Iranian plains. As Baghdad collapsed in a welter of internal wars between military factions, the Buyids marched unopposed into the city in 945. The victorious army was led by three brothers who drew glory-seeking tribesmen and adventurers to them by virtue of their successful conquests in Iran. Though they had been recently converted to Islam by zealous Shi'ite missionaries,[3] the Buyids were disinterested in doctrinal disputes.

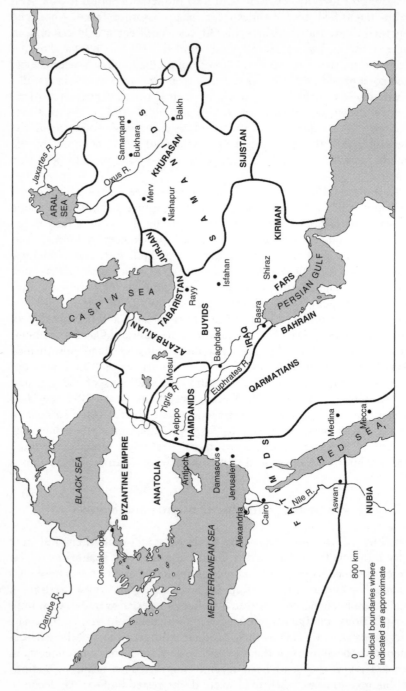

Map 7.1 The central Islamic lands in the tenth century.

For them, Islam was a wide path; they maintained the Caliph as a figurehead, and were tolerant of all forms of religious belief, including Christianity and Judaism, so long as there was no opposition to their rule.

Although they now controlled the shell of what was once the most powerful empire in the world, the Buyids and their Daylamite allies maintained their traditional tribal system of collective leadership and regional automany. M. A. Shaban describes their polity and its principles as follows: "Although other chiefs had placed themselves under Buyid leadership, their individuality and their recent jealously guarded independence in their own mountains would still have to be taken into consideration. Accepting the principle of their own equality under this system of collective leadership, the brothers were in effect setting an example to be followed in the regions, where each one of them would be no more than an equal among equals."[4] Their tribal empire coalesced under central leadership only once in its century of rule; predictably, this was when it was threatened by invasion, and the various segments united under the leadership of the chief whose domain was most endangered. As soon as the threat dissipated, the unity of the Buyids also dissolved.

The Buyids took a laissez-faire attitude towards politics as well as religion; their interest was primarily in keeping order and reaping the benefits of their position of power. Having inherited a bankrupt empire, they were willing to listen to any advice as to how to preserve it, and raised Persian administrators to new positions of authority while also inaugurating the assignment of tax rights to soldiers in lieu of payment – an innovation that would be followed by many rulers henceforth, and would always prove ruinous in the long run.

The Buyid era was marked by the assiduous pursuit of personal advantage within amorphous groups constituted primarily by ties of tribal and soldierly loyalty, cross-cut by patron-client relationships. In such a rapacious and unpredictable environment, the problem of keeping the loyalty of one's supporters was pressing. As Roy Mottahedeh notes, without strong kinship bonds, "the only resource open to these condottieri was an unstinting generosity and a frank avowal that self-interest argued for cooperation in plundering these new conquests."[5] This is the frame of mind exhibited by the deserting troops of an unsuccessful Buyid general. As they rode away, they told their erstwhile leader candidly: "If you become powerful again, we will return to you."[6]

To maintain power and give cohesion to this fragmented world, the Buyids attempted to establish ties of fictive kinship with their allies and subordinates. This system, called *istina*, was meant as a substitute for old tribal bonds of asabiyya, but it proved a failure. Individual self-interest was too strong and group allegiance too weak for fictive kinship to succeed in establishing loyalty to a government with no pretense to legitimacy on any wider ground. Under these circumstances, local communities more or less avoided all participation in the state, relying instead on networks and personal ties with the powerful to influence their foreign overlords. Clerics who served the Buyids, as well as the soldiers who supported them, were popularly regarded as morally compromised. In Motaheddeh's words, Buyid society was "disengaging itself from government and the moral burdens of government, and at the same time giving enormous power to governments."[7] However, the Buyid rulers were unable to take advantage of the power granted them by popular withdrawal from government. Their own internal rivalries, combined with shifts in trade routes, led to a rapid breakdown in the already tottering economy of their realm.

Replacing the faltering Buyids were the Seljuks, another tribal confederation from the east, this time of Ghuzz nomads (renamed Turkmen after their conversion to Islam), who were slowly drifting west in one of history's periodic waves of migration out of the overpopulated steppes of Central Asia into the Iranian plains. As Sunni Muslims, the Ghuzz, under their tribal chief Toghril-beg, were invited by the Caliph to take over from the now enfeebled Shi'ite Buyids, and in 1055 they marched into Baghdad without opposition, to found the greatest empire in Islamdom until the rise of the Ottomans.

The Seljuks were the first Muslim dynasty to forswear completely any pretense of a spiritual sanction for their rule. Leaving the Caliph in charge of prayer and preaching, they frankly declared themselves Sultans, ruling by the sheer fact of "retention of their military supremacy over all rivals."[8] In their regime, as Anne Lambton writes: "Patriotism was an unknown virtue. All the Sultan expected of his subjects was they they should pay their taxes and pray for his welfare, while they expected from him security and justice. The state did not demand, or receive, the loyalty of the common man. Loyalty, so far as it transcended the bounds of the tribe, guild, quarter, or city, was accorded not to the state but to Islam."[9]

In the absence of any constraints placed upon him by judiciary institutions (save the general necessity of keeping the outlines of Islamic practice and local custom intact), the major limitation on the absolute power of the Seljuk ruler was the brake put on by his fellow tribesmen, who demanded the right of consultation with the Sultan and autonomy within their own territories. Following the examples of previous kingdoms, the Seljuk rulers sought to escape these restrictions by increasing usage of slaves and freedmen in the army and administration, while simultaneously sending their volatile Turkmen kin out to do battle as *ghazis* (fighters for the faith) on the remote Byzantine frontier, where they could do little harm and possibly some good. Nonetheless, the Sultans were never able to fully subdue the Turkmen, who continued to make demands for special privileges and personal freedom throughout the Seljuk reign.

Although the Turkmen tribes were an undermining influence, the major threat to the Sultanate was internal. As vertical ties between patron and client, master and slave, became predominant over the horizontal bonds of kinship and alliance between co-equals, the Seljuk regime became ever more despotic and arbitrary, while at the same time circles of clients surrounding various members of the elite struggled with one another for the spoils at hand. As Anne Lambton describes the late Seljuk empire, life at court followed an unhappy pattern which has a familiar ring: "Intrigue and insecurity were the normal concomitants of social life. Men of influence and power accumulated wealth to defend their personal interests against any future intrigues by their rivals, or against a loss of the Sultan's favours, and those who were ambitious for office accumulated wealth in order to buy it."[10]

In such precarious conditions, advisers to the Sultan found they could not follow an honest course (or any course, for that matter) without offending powerful interests, and the death toll among them was high indeed. As David Morgan puts it: "There was no civil service *esprit de corps* in medieval Persia. The way to the top was often that of discrediting – and bringing about the fall of – the current wazir. Only by retaining the support of the ruler and by installing as many reliable people as possible at the lower levels could a wazir hope to remain in office."[11]

Lacking any central, generally agreed upon, conception of the direction that ought to be taken by the state (aside from increasing the wealth and power of its members and maintaining the general outlines of Islamic practice), and lacking any strong ties to the populace, the Seljuk government gradually disintegrated due to a combination of exploitative tax farming (*iqta*),[12] violent factionalism and pervasive mistrust. Within a century, centrifugal forces had torn the empire apart, as various claimants to Seljuk rule disputed with their generals for power in the provinces and in the center itself.

However, at its best, under the rule of the early Sultans who were imbued with a warrior ethic of fairness and considerate of Islamic law, and under the stewardship of an expert Persian administrative corps, the Seljuk regime set a positive example that was not to be met by later dynasties. The disruption their regime caused to Muslim society was relatively small, the Ghuzz nomads who accompanied them probably, on balance, added to the economy by utilizing vacant land for their animals, their court was cultured and hospitable to artists and scholars, and the bureaucracy they inaugurated was usually fair and efficient. The regimes who followed the Seljuks were vastly more destructive and rapacious – none more so than the Mongols and their kin who were to ravage the Middle East throughout the thirteenth and fourteenth centuries.

But even before the Mongol invasions, it seemed that pure rule by force, with even less internal solidarity and empathy towards the subjects than had been shown by the Buyids and Seljuks, was to be one of the most predominant forms of secular governance in the Middle East. As H. A. R. Gibb writes:

> Since the break-up of the Seljuk sultanate at the end of the eleventh century, Western Asia had been parceled out amongst a number of local dynasties, all of them (except a few remote baronies) founded by Turkish generals or Turcoman chiefs, and all of them characterized by...the spirit of personal advantage and aggrandizement which determined their political actions and relationships. It seems well-nigh impossible to discover in the relations of the Turkish princes or the Turcoman chiefs with one another – even when they were members of the same family – any sense of loyalty or restraints in exploiting each other's weakness.[13]

For these military rulers, the answer to the problem of validating domination was simple and might be paraphrased as: "We command because we are strong. Therefore, we deserve our power, and will exercise it as we please." Secular authority was mitigated solely by the requirement of following at least the forms of religion and custom, and by the necessity of keeping the army from rebelling. The Sultan's authority was further magnified by the withdrawal of a citizenry concerned with their own particular freedom from the delegitimized civic world, leaving state government as the domain of human raptors who, in turn, intervened very little in people's ordinary lives except to extract taxes from them and ruthlessly punish any insurrection.

The Religious Option

In the Middle East, millennial rebellions have always rocked secular tyrannies. Sacred resistance to rapacious and delegitimized authority followed in the footsteps of the Abbasids and their Qarmatian opponents, who in turn were emulating the model set by Muhammad himself in his struggle against the oppression of his Meccan cousins. The assertion these leaders make might be stated as: "I rule because God has anointed me – recognize my sacred message and obey." The advantage of this stance is that one can mobilize the people against injustice and take power with a sacred mandate and a claim to legitimacy; furthermore, a capacity to mediate is greatly enhanced if the disputants believe the mediator is speaking with divine sanction.

The disadvantage is that popular expectations of sacred leaders are inordinately high, since Islam is based upon the actual advent of a Prophet who was also a political commander. With this background, followers are easily disappointed by the compromises forced upon any power-seeker who claims a divine right to rule yet who must live in the world of real politics. The reverse danger is that high-minded leaders who refuse to recognize practical limits may break their state apart because of their unrealistic ambitions and the internal schisms they generate. Schism also becomes likely in sacred polities when power changes hands, since authority is based on popular recognition of the leader's charisma; this recognition stands, in principle, against any rationalized succession, so that there is a constant tension between efforts to maintain continuity and expressions of personal holiness.

The dangers of sacred rule can be seen in the trajectory of the great Fatimid Empire, which arose out of an alliance between charismatic leaders and tribesmen in Algeria, extended itself into the east, eventually ruling Egypt from 969 to 1171 and doing battle with the Seljuks for domination over the entire Middle East. Successors to the Qarmati, the Fatimids too practiced an activist brand of Ismaili Shi'ism, but where the Qarmati crumbled when they followed a false mahdi selected because of his personal charisma, the Fatimids kept inheritance of their Imamate within the lineage of Ismail and were able to retain a high degree of cohesion during their conquest of Egypt, where they were strongly supported by their rural tribal allies.

Once victorious, they established vigorous trading partnerships and alliances with Europe and the Byzantines that funneled wealth into their coffers. They were also surprisingly tolerant of religious differences within their realm, which permitted them to utilize experts and administrators who were Sunnis, Jews, and Coptic Christians. This useful tolerance paradoxically correlated with a strong belief that human beings are strictly ranked according to their degree of spiritual enlightenment: those who are higher are the Ismaili brotherhood, who inhabit a plane of true existence; the lower are benighted Sunnis and believers in other religions, who are phantoms unaware of their own unreality. At the highest plane is the Imam himself, the radiant sinless leader of mankind. Believers could easily justify living among and interacting with unenlightened shadow beings, since they felt themselves to be inhabiting an elevated spiritual position which the ignorant masses could not begin to comprehend or approach.

Despite their religiously inspired tolerance, logical brilliance, sophisticated court and entrepreneurial genius, the Fatimids ruined their economy by neglecting the necessary work of repairing canals, and were prey to the same sorts of eschatological difficulties that had beset the Qarmati, though they avoided the Qarmati fiasco over succession by maintaining a strict rule of primogeniture for their Imams. This rule helped prevent destructive battles over who should be recognized as spiritual guide, but did not prevent the Imams themselves from acting disruptively.

The great example is al-Hakim, who ruled the Fatimids from 996 to 1021 and whose regime was beset by a variety of financial difficulties, army revolts, tribal rebellions and the threat of famine. Under these pressures, he announced an often contradictory and shifting series of reforms that sometimes seemed irrational, and also sometimes subverted Ismaili doctrine, seriously testing the faith of his followers. In his later years, the test of faith was intensified, as Hakim became an ascetic, renounced the title of Imam, forbade believers to prostrate themselves before him, and appointed a successor who was not his son, breaking the tradition of primogeniture and threatening the integrity of the royal house; simultaneously, he supported a new revelation, which hailed him as the long-awaited messiah who would shortly initiate the final chapter in human history.

Those who followed this latter revelation are now known as the Druze. They split off from the Fatimid mainstream, and sectarian riots tore Cairo apart. Meanwhile, Hakim, who had begun to take solitary nocturnal walks through the city and countryside, mysteriously disappeared, probably the victim of assassination by one of his family; according to the Druze, however, he had gone into voluntary hiding, and would return in the future to usher in the millennium. Despite Hakim's wishes, his son, a minor, was appointed Imam; the purity of the succession to the Imamate was now deeply in question. The Fatimids never recovered from this period of religious schism. Finally, when the Caliph al-Amir died in 1130 without sons, the regime split into irreconcilable factions, with at least three different pretenders making claims to spiritual authority. Impoverished and wrecked by dynastic struggles, the dynasty fell easy prey to Saladin in 1171.

The Fatimid regime was perhaps the greatest of the religious empires, but it was not the last. Movements to purify the faith and establish a sacred rule led by a messianic figure have recurred periodically in the Middle East. As Ira Lapidus writes, in tribal societies which "did not accept political hierarchy and whose leaders were required to be mediators, the most common form of agglomeration was religious chieftainship under a charismatic religiopolitical leader. The elite religious cadres, ruling subordinate units, were bound together by religious commitment or ideology. In such movements there was an uneasy tension between the religious and prereligious bases of organization"[14] – a tension that has prevailed since the time of Muhammad.

The Almoravids and the Almohads who succeeded them in North Africa and Spain from the eleventh to the thirteenth centuries are the major Medieval dynasties showing this type of political organization.

Each was founded by a puritanical mahdi figure who sought to restore Islam to its original mission by uniting warring tribesmen and urban auxiliaries in a jihad against corruption within Islam and against the Christian infidels. The Almoravids were inspired by a religious scholar and mystic, Abdallah b. Yasin, whom a tribal leader of the Sanhaja tribe had met in Mecca and brought back to his people to serve as judge and teacher. Similarly, the Almohads who succeeded the Almoravids were founded by Muhammad ibn Abdallah ibn Tumart, a scholar who had studied in Mecca and other Islamic centers and then found a following among the tribes of North Africa. Ibn Tumart believed himself to be the promised redeemer, and told his Berber followers that "unity is possible only when the destiny of the people is left to the one who has authority, that is, the infallible Iman exempt from injustice and tyranny...He who does not believe in the Imamate can only be an infidel (*kafir*), a hypocrite, a deviant, a heretic, an atheist."[15]

Although both of these charismatic movements were successful in their time, and provided the energy for Muslim domination over Spain, nothing remains of them today. As in other millenarian rebellions, the original salvational impulse was dissipated and finally evaporated by time and adaption to political reality, as these sacred kingdoms degenerated into secular states, lost cohesion and credibility, and soon dissolved.

Wahhabism, erupting in central Arabia in the mid-eighteenth century, is a more recent version of an Islamic crusade. It was initially less triumphant than the earlier Berber regimes to the west, but it has had far greater longevity. Wahhabism was founded by Muhammad b. Abd al-Wahhab, who, like his Almohad and Almoravid predecessors, had studied in the Islamic centers of Mecca and elsewhere, and preached a strict reform of Islamic practices. As had occurred in many earlier cases, including the case of Muhammad himself, the reformer found his audience not in Mecca but in the hinterlands, this time among the tribe ruled by Ibn Saud in north central Arabia. Under Saud's leadership and inspired by Wahhab's austere teaching, the reformers began a jihad against what they saw a degenerate practices in the Muslim heartland. After the death of Ibn Wahhab, Saud himself became head of the new movement, potently combining tribal and religious leadership. Converting and unifying fellow tribesmen in the tradition of Muhammad's original mission, the Wahhabi managed to take Mecca in 1812, where they destroyed all tombs and sacred sites as conducive to idolatry.

The Wahhabi movement was only put down in 1818, but re-emerged in 1902, when the Saudi chief proclaimed himself the Imam of the Wahhabis and managed to gain control of the entire Arabian peninsula. This was the origin of the modern Saudi state, which is validated by a sacred ideology, maintained by pragmatic tribal alliances, and propped

up by enormous oil revenues that allow the ruling family to offer generous subsidies to placate potential rivals and pacify the tribes. Legitimacy of this state is increased by its control over the most sacred places
of Islam. A policy of settling nomadic groups in religious-military-
farming communities (the *ikhwan*) was an attempt by the regime to
undermine tribal autonomy, inculcate religious enthusiasm, develop a
standing loyal army, and gain acceptance for the state.

Nonetheless, despite its huge wealth, great power, and assertion of
sacred status, the Saudi regime has also had to rationalize its authority
and has been haunted by challenges to its legitimacy. For instance, since
the state had to adapt to secular rule, it stimulated opposition from the
very ikhwan movement that had been its mainstay. As Joseph Kostiner
writes, the ikhwan, who "combined tribal asabiyya and unruliness with
revivalist zeal,"[16] soon began to press the Saudi family to be more
rigorous in promoting Wahhabi doctrine. In response, the ikhwan were
curtailed by the ruler, who in 1919 had his court clerics issue an opinion that the ikhwan version of Wahhabism was not superior to ordinary practice. The 1979 attack on the great shrine at Mecca was another
tribal-religious revolt against what the rebels saw as the corruption of
Saudi rule. Osama bin Laden and al-Qaeda are more recent urban
examples of the same phenomenon.

If religious revivalism in tandem with popular unrest has been fairly
common in the west, it has been more unusual in the east, where,
quoting Lapidus once more, "the most common form of leadership was
the warrior chieftaincy supported by a lineage, clan, or *commitatis* – a
band of warriors who in turn won the allegiance of other such warrior
units and thereby dominated a subject population."[17] The Buyids and
Seljuks were the greatest instances of this type of regime. The major
exception was the rise of the Shi'ite Safavids of Iran and eastern Anatolia, who made the last great attempt, until modern times, to implement
a militant religious regime in the east.

Originating with the charismatic leadership of a lineage of Sufi masters
who bolstered their allure with dubious claims to descent from Muhammad, the Safavids appealed to Persian peasants and townsmen tired of
continuous warfare and the cruelties perpetrated by a series of short-
lived and oppressive warlord dynasties. However, the military force of
the Safavids were recruited from the hinterlands, among Turkmen
tribesmen. As the Abbasids before them, the Safavids enlisted an army
of fervent disciples – the *Qizilbash* (redheads, so named because of
their distinctive headdress) – who, like the Abbasid Khurisaniyya, were
identified not by kinship or lineage, but by the names of their home
districts, emphasizing the syncretic nature of their movement. Qizilbash
loyalty was directed to the sacred person of Shah Ismail Safavi, who said
he was the hidden Imam, the seventh in his line, descended, like the

A Persian Coozelbash.

Plate 7.1 Eighteenth-century portrait of a Qizilbash.

Fatimids and Qarmati, from the seventh of Ali's successors. Utilizing imagery meant to appeal to the widest possible audience (again taking a cue from Abbasid propaganda), he announced himself as both messiah and *Shah* (the pre-Islamic Persian term for king), and demanded absolute and total obedience from his followers. In return, his men would be safe from bullets – or would enter paradise directly if, by chance, the charm against enemy firepower proved ineffective.

The movement spread quickly; in 1501 Ismail occupied Tabriz and declared himself Shah of Iran, simultaneously enforcing the imposition of twelver Shi'ism on the formerly Sunni Persians.[18] Since his power was based on an unstable coalition of tribal warlords and Qizilbash zealots, his regime used techniques we have already seen to gain more authority for itself, such as raising men of lesser standing to offset the powers of the great, and recruiting slaves into the army – although the old reservoir of slaves in Central Asia had now dried up, and fresh sources had to be found in Armenia and the Caucasus. Imported twelver ulema, totally reliant on the dynasty for support, were also brought into the government as judges, administrators and even as military commanders, while

at the same time persecution of Sunni believers was instituted to establish Shiʿism and reinforce faith in the mission of the dynasty.

Even during the reign of the messianic Shah Ismail, the Safavids, like
the Abbasids who are their closest parallels, were constrained by the
unstable conditions in which they found themselves and by the ambiguities of their claim to messianic status. The fervor of the Qizilbash had
to be deferred when a crushing defeat by the Ottoman army in 1514
proved conclusively that the millennium was not going to arrive in the
near future.[19] In response to this disconcerting dose of reality, and in an
effort to escape from too great a reliance on the volatile Qizilbash
while simultaneously broadening the appeal of the regime to the Persian people, the Safavids gradually set aside their claims to be the final
Imams in favor of a more secular role as "protectors" of the faith. By
the reign of Tahmasp I (1533–76) the emphasis had shifted from portrayal of the Shah as the final Imam and toward a more secular ideology of Shahsavani, the love of the Shah.

Meanwhile, Caucasian slaves converted and trained at court assumed
more and more prominent places as the Shah's personal bodyguard and
as an independent army, balancing out the influence of tribal leaders
and Qizilbash. This trend came to a head under the glittering rule of
Shah Abbas (1587–1629), who decisively shifted the center of power to
the court by transferring many of the land revenues collected by Qizilbash chiefs to his own direct control, providing himself with a pool
from which he could directly pay the salaries of his army and thereby
retain their loyalty. Under his leadership, a new circular capital, Isfahan, was built, designed (like Baghdad) to be the symbolic and real
focus of his highly centralized administration. A scintillating and artis-
tic court evolved there, following the tradition of Persian aristocratic
cultivation of adab. This court was increasingly secularized, luxurious
and aesthetically oriented, which meant a greater tax burden on the
peasantry and greater discontent.

The Safavids, now with very little spiritual credit left to them, found
it more and more difficult to cope with the problems of keeping control
over the provinces, maintaining tribal loyalty, and paying off their own
troops. Nonetheless, the centralization and administrative reforms initiated by Shah Abbas kept the empire relatively stable for over a century,
despite these challenges and despite the addiction of later Safavid rulers
to "drink, drugs, and excessive sexual indulgence."[20]

Ironically, the besotted behaviour of the last Safavid Shahs was in
large measure the result of Shah Abbas's own policies. Afraid of
insurrection, he murdered his most promising son and blinded two
others, fragmenting the succession. Even worse, he inaugurated a practice of keeping Safavid princes in the harem, rather than allowing them
to rule a province and learn authority by experience. In consequence, as

David Morgan writes, future Shahs "grew up ill-educated, with no experience of government, administration, or the world in general, and excessively under the influence of women and eunuchs."[21] Proclivities for self-indulgence were enhanced by the belief in court that the Shah, as a holy being, was not constrained by the laws of Islam. Under the increasingly incompetent rule of these divine dissipates (with Shah Abbas II a partial exception), the empire gradually declined, eventually disintegrating into a welter of competing tribal confederacies and war-lords. The Shi'ite ulema also withdrew their support for the Shah. As one told the French merchant Chardin, "our kings are impious and unjust, their rule is a tyranny to which God has subjected us as a punishment after having withdrawn from the world the lawful succes-sor of the Prophet. The supreme throne of the world belongs only to a *mujtahid*, a man possessed of sanctity and knowledge above the common rule of men."[22]

In 1736, the Safavids were finally deposed by Nadir Shah, a Turkish warlord of the old school, who was ousted in turn by Zand tribesmen, who fell themselves to the Qajars, ex-military commanders under the Safavids, who were then deposed by the military rule of Pahlavis in 1924. None of these regimes made any claim whatsoever to religious legitimacy; it was left to Ayatollah Khomeini to rekindle the old Shi'ite spirit of messianic fervor, this time with the ulema themselves as the party of God.[23]

Until Khomeini's revolution, it is clear that Middle Eastern religious dynasties (whether arising in the west or the east), broke apart on the same reefs that had wrecked their predecessors. The necessity of com-promise, the demands of reality, the processes of rationalization, combined with the difficulty of maintaining power in the midst of many strong and rivalrous tribes and other interest groups, inevitably undermined the spiritual legitimacy of each regime. Unable to deliver the promised millennium, they had to settle for mere power holding. If they tried to maintain enthusiasm, like Hakim, they were likely to become the focus of personal charismatic cults that undermined stable government and fractured the community. In consequence, later rulers, though sometimes great men like Shah Abbas, were hard to distinguish from secular Sultans, who governed by virtue of their manipulative ability and their control over troops who were increasingly won over by stipends and grants, not by religious faith in the sovereign. In the end, religious regimes proved to be no more stable or just than rule by kings.

8

Novelties and Continuities

The Ottoman Exception

The huge exception to the rapid turnover of states in the Middle East was the Ottoman Empire, which was the last and in some ways the most successful of cosmopolitan Sultanates. From their power base in Anatolia the Osmanli ruling family governed most of the western region of the Middle East, including all of Arabia and most of the Maghreb, plus much of southeastern Europe. The empire expanded steadily from 1300 up until 1699, and held sway over its enormous territory until modern times; a reign of unprecedented length, coherence and strength. In contrast, the Abbasid Caliphate, recognized as the most powerful of the past, ruled from 750 until 945, but was hardly more than a shadow government with little or no control over its provinces for at least the last eighty years of its life.

Ottoman power and longevity offers a serious challenge to the Khaldunian portrait of the Middle East I have drawn to this point. If the pervasive ethos of egalitarianism and competitive individualism tends to fragment secular and sacred empires alike, why did the Ottomans not succumb to the cycle of decadence and collapse? To answer this question, we need to consider the history of the Empire in the light of its material conditions and social organization.

The Ottomans were descendants of the troublesome Central Asian Ghuzz tribesmen whom the Seljuks had sent west to struggle against the Byzantine Empire. These tribesmen and adventurers developed military emirates along the Byzantine border. The most successful of these was the emirate ruled by Osman, the Ottoman founder. This small military state stood at the very forefront of the battle lines. There, under the pressure of constant military action against the highly centralized Byzantine empire, the Osmanlis themselves developed a centralized "secondary state", to use Morton Fried's terminology,[1] which emulated the Byzantine structure and also built upon the Ottoman's own particular geographical situation and their tribal system. The state that emerged was different in significant ways from earlier Sultanates.

This was partly because Anatolia is unlike the rest of the Middle East in its ecology and mode of production. The great well-watered agricultural plains of Turkey are more suited to sedentary farming than nomadizing; as a result, rather than being surrounded by dangerous and mobile armed tribesmen, as was the case in the rest of the Middle East, most of Anatolia was populated by relatively easily dominated and agriculturally productive peasants. The tribes that did exist had been largely subdued by the Byzantine Empire before the Ottomans arrived.

Another difference from the rest of the Middle East was the Ottoman economic base. Elsewhere, Middle Eastern dynasties were largely dependent upon trade for their surplus, and traders, as we have seen, have no great liking for the ideologies of sacred rank that are favored by the aristocracy of centralized states. Entrepreneurs tend to be pragmatic and flexible individualists, resistant to central regulation as they pursue their own personal projects. The mercantile mentality also has a strong propensity for belief in equal justice under universal law and a faith in individual initiative, adaptability and mobility. All these attitudes and ways of living undercut assertions of ascribed hierarchy. Hierarchy was also undermined in the Middle Eastern trade empires by the fact that trade was easily disrupted, either by external or internal forces. This left the state liable to collapse and falsified elite claims to intrinsic nobility.

In contrast, the Ottoman regime and economy was far more dependent upon warfare and military expansion than upon trade. Throughout its history, all Ottoman administrators were part of the army, and a military tone pervaded the polity. Despite the difficulties of maintaining a war-based economy, the Ottomans found it possible to press into Europe for hundreds of years, building an internal sense of unity upon their own martial history and the ghazi spirit of a jihad against the infidel – a spirit more difficult to stimulate elsewhere in the Middle East, where one's neighbors also have usually been Muslims, and where war generally led armies into impoverished and dangerous tribal hinterlands, not towards greater wealth.

The military tenor of the Empire aided centralization in another way. Warriors, unlike entrepreneurs, are more successful if centrally organized and hierarchically structured; they attach themselves to flags and leaders who can inspire them to self-sacrifice on the battlefield. Where the merchant's virtue is adaptability, the virtue of the soldier is obedience. These military values helped reinforce a strong identification that was enhanced as the Sultanate developed an exceptionally effective slave army, the *Janissaries*, to offset its tribal allies.

More than other Middle Eastern regimes, the Ottomans managed to control and maintain the order and loyalty of their armies. The Janissar-

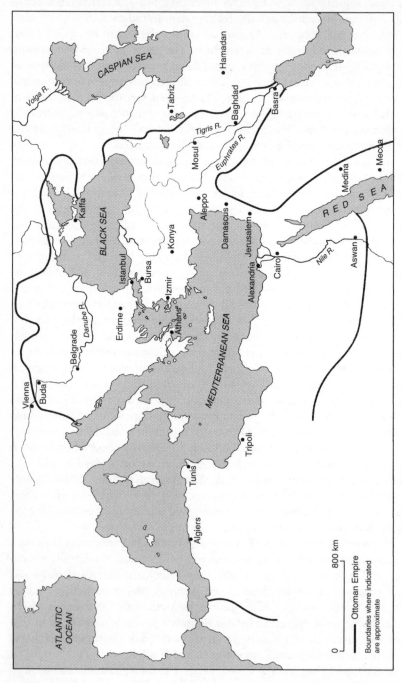

Map 8.1 The Ottoman Empire toward the end of the seventeenth century.

ies lived in isolation and were celibate until retirement; they were also indoctrinated in Sufi discipline, perhaps connected to the early ahi sect, and later were certainly attached to the antinomian Bekhtashi Sufis, whose unorthodoxy set the Janissaries even more apart from the community at large. The elite of the troops and bureaucrats were drafted by the institution of *devshirme*, as Christian children were taken in a levy from their parents, converted to Islam, then rigorously trained from earliest infancy to be members of the court, warriors, and high-level administrators. Only the ulema, of all state employees, were recruited from the free population, the rest were *kul*, slaves of the Sultan, whose whole regime was conceptualized as an extension of his own household, with himself and his immediate entourage cared for by a slave army set off from the rest of the people by background and practice.

All earlier regimes had used slaves to a greater or lesser extent, but the Ottomans had an advantage in that the proximity of Christian Europe (not to mention the large number of Christians within the Empire itself) allowed them a ready supply of loyal slave soldiers and administrators. In comparison, other Middle Eastern states had to import their needed non-Muslim slaves from remote regions of Central Asia, Europe or Africa, risking having their supply cut or interrupted, which would weaken the base of the state.

The Ottomans thus had the following factors that favored the evolution of a strongly hierarchical society: the relative absence of armed and mobile challengers from the surrounding hinterlands; a comparatively easily controlled peasant population and a sufficient food supply; the example and legacy of a highly centralized Byzantine state; an expanding and successful war economy and a correspondingly weak entrepreneurial community; a ghazi mentality that enthusiastically supported struggles against the abutting Christian societies; an easily available supply of slaves who could be trained to be loyal soldiers and administrators.

All this is obvious enough, but a less noted factor of crucial importance is the fact that Turkish descent and marriage systems do not follow the pattern that is typical elsewhere in the Middle East. Distinctions in descent organization and marriage preference may seem esoteric matters to bring within a discussion of political power, but they are not. As we saw in chapter 4, the Middle Eastern sense of asabiyya is expressed in the idiom of kinship, which gives men and women a way of conceptualizing their relationships with one another, and favors a flexible structure of alliance and segmentation that is highly egalitarian. This is not so in the Turkish system.

Both Middle Eastern and Turkish kinship are based on patrilineal descent, and both reckon the intensity of kin ties according to genealogical distance from a common paternal ancestor. As we have seen in looking at Middle Eastern cases, genealogical distance, or segmentation, is simply a way of orienting individuals in patterned relationships of alliance and antagonism in the absence of accepted hierarchies. It serves to organize patrilineal clansmen within a pyramidal structure of allied lineages traced back to a common ancestor, and is the major idiom for validating relationships between individuals in Middle Eastern social organization. In this system, no lineage, clan, or person has any intrinsic right to claim superiority over any other, and such claims are always resisted.

But, as Jean Cuisenier has argued, Turkish kinship adds two more modes onto this simple structure: "Generational distance, or the rank of generation in relation to a common ancestor; and birth order, the rank of brothers in relation to one another."[2] These both express and determine rank and internal differentiation, as elder brothers and the lineages descended from elder brothers are terminologically marked as superior. Turkish kinship is therefore in striking contrast to that generally found in the Middle East. The Turkish form is compatible with cohesive and clearly demarcated clans ranked in terms of power, position, and nobility, while the Middle Eastern is correlated with choice and manipulation in fluid relations of complementary opposition between equal agnatic rivals.[3]

The distinction between the pliable, egalitarian and individualistic structure of Middle Eastern kinship structuring and the more rigid, hierarchical and group-oriented Turkish system is mirrored in the marriage patterns sanctioned in these two societies. In the Middle East, the preferred marriage is to the father's brother's daughter, (technically patrilateral parallel cousin marriage). This is a marriage type that is rarely practiced in Turkey. Father's brother's daughter marriage emphasizes the patriline by idealizing marriage within it ("close to the bone" as Arabs say). But it also has a paradoxical effect of increasing tensions within the lineage, as disputes over the relationship between the married patrilateral cousins may lead to a split between the brothers, who are both the closest of allies and the closest of enemies. Father's brother's daughter marriage is both a symptom and a cause of an ambiguous social order that Robert Murphy and Leonard Kasdan have described as "characterized by the potentiality for massive aggregation of its agnatic units, on the one hand, and atomistic individualism, on the other."[4]

Marriage relationships and descent in Turkey, following an Inner Asian model, indicate quite a different historical pattern: an articulation of society into distinctive and well demarcated clans of superiors and inferiors intermarrying in a pattern known technically as generalized exchange, that is, marriage of men to their mother's brother's daughters. I will not tire the reader with the technical description of this system,[5] since marriage relations structured by generalized exchange have long since lost significance among Turks, as clients, allies, and slaves have replaced subordinate kinsmen in the administration of empire. But the terminology still lingers to indicate the past structure of ranked clans, and Turks still disfavor the close, lineage-disrupting, marriages within the patriline that are preferred by other Middle Easterners.

What this all signifies is that the Ottomans had within their culture a means ready-at-hand for making acceptable claims to genealogical elevation that did not rely on a sacred basis and could be continued from generation to generation. The first son of the first son of the senior lineage had recognized priority, so that all the Ottomans acknowledged without question the intrinsic right of the direct lineal descendants of Osman to rule, just as they accepted the rights of higher ranking local lineages to their authority. In consequence of Turkish recognition of the intrinsic right of the Osmanli family to the Sultanate, there was little factional feuding among competing power groups, and considerable social solidarity. This is in marked contrast to the regions the Ottomans ruled outside Anatolia, where, as H. A. R. Gibb and Harold Bowen note, "it is in fact difficult to overestimate the part which was played in all aspects of the administrative and social life of the Arab provinces by family, group, or tribal rivalries. It was these that stirred the deepest passions of the soul."[6]

Of course, this is not to claim that political rank in the Ottoman central administration was predetermined by lineage seniority alone – military ability and the capacity to lead was crucial in this warrior society. The sons of the Sultan contested violently among themselves for the throne, with the victor putting his rival brothers to death. Only after 1617 was it made law that the eldest surviving male automatically inherit the throne – a law many see as marking the end of the vitality of the ruling house.

However, despite internal struggles over succession, no one questioned the natural right of the Osmanli house to command the realm, and throughout the history of the Ottoman Empire ranking by lineage remained the essential precondition for occupation of the highest levels of administrative and military authority. As Norman Itzkowitz puts it, the steppe ideal that "sovereignty was the prerogative of a single family chosen by God to bear the burden of rule...supplanted the Islamic principle of elective leadership."[7] Other "Turkic" peoples had made this claim previously; only the Ottoman made it so successfully – largely due to the confluence of the circumstances we have already noted that favored centralization and hierarchization.

The ascendance of the Sultan's family and his military retine coincided with a permanent and caste-like social distinction between the *askeri* and the *reaya*; that is, between the military who practiced the "Ottoman way" and the subjects; the latter were marked off from the askeri by sumptuary laws, and were not permitted to bear arms or ride horses. This caste distinction was so absolute that even the Sultan could only elevate a reaya under extraordinary circumstances.

The ideological prop of this system was the ulema, who were integrated into the state in a manner that went far beyond that achieved elsewhere in the Middle East. They were trained in government schools, appointed to government posts, and given immunity from taxation. Most importantly, in concordance with the ascriptive tendencies of Ottoman society, their positions soon became hereditary. In return, the Ottoman clerics recognized the legitimacy of the royal authority exercised by the Osmanli family, and accepted the ranking of persons that the state demanded.

But outside the Anatolian peninsula the typical egalitarian ideals of competitive individualism remained operant, and the Ottoman system had to adapt itself to conditions that were far more turbulent and internally contentious than those prevailing in the heartland of the Empire. However, as outsiders "ingrained (with) the conviction of their superiority" who kept haughtily aloof from the natives, the Ottoman administrators were in a good position to mediate the factional disputes that continually tore more egalitarian societies apart. "By his neutral attitude to the violent local feuds and personal antagonisms of his district he rendered a service to public security and private property, while none knew better how to play off the rival parties for his own ends."[8]

As the above quote indicates, the Ottomans generally governed their segmented, internally rivalrous and egalitarian Arab and Berber subjects through mediation rather than coercion. The competitive egalitarianism of the Middle East made it an easy region to rule in this manner, so long as the autonomy of local groups was respected, and people were allowed to continue their daily affairs with little direct governmental intervention. Far more difficult was any attempt to command by force, which conjured up exactly the unity between local factions that the Ottomans wished to avoid. So, instead of being a despotism, outside Anatolia the Empire actually consisted of "a vast number of small social groups, which may almost be described as self-governing."[9] These autonomous units accepted Ottoman rule because of a fear of chaos should the Porte fall, a shared reverence for the Sultan as the source of justice, a respect for the military force he could muster, and because local notables could use the central administration as the mechanism for balancing out provincial antagonisms.

Under these circumstances the Sultanate achieved an authority never gained by any previous Muslim ruler, an authority buttressed internally by the Turkish faith in the innate privilege of their own nobility. Throughout the region, the populace became accustomed to Ottoman rule, which was not too invasive, and could be useful. The old Middle

Eastern fear of political chaos (articulated in the Quranic proclamation that "fitna (anarchy) is worse than slaughter")[10] led jurists to argue that "whose power prevails must be obeyed"[11] and encouraged the people to remain submissive, if not loyal, to the Ottoman regime. But over time the slave army-administration became complacent, decadent and corrupt; the Sultan, raised within the luxuries and intrigues of court, lost his capacity to rule decisively; the unruly provinces asserted their independence; overtaxation incited unrest; population dropped and dissatisfaction reigned.

Yet the real destruction of the Ottomans was caused not by internal collapse so much as by the inability of the Empire to continue on its old *laissez-faire* pathway in the face of European influence. As a military state, it was set back economically and socially by the cessation of its conquests in Europe and by later European military dominance and the subsequent drying up of surplus. By the end of World War I the Sultanate had lost its effectiveness, and a new Westernized secular society was on the way, led by the rebellious army officers known as the "Young Turks" who rejected the old Ottoman claims to be the cosmopolitan inheritor of the Caliphate, and instead supported Mustafa Kemal's sweeping nationalistic reform movement. But Ottoman glory had proven that a ranked society could rule for a very long time indeed over a culture where rank is denied.

Other Experiments: Cavaliers and Assassins

Aside from the anomalous but enormous success of Ottoman empire, there have been few other attempts to break out of the Middle Eastern cycle of the rise and collapse of dynasties. One remarkable effort was undertaken by the last great Caliph, al-Nasir, who reigned for forty-five years, until he died in 1225 A D. Al-Nasir saw that Seljuk power was crumbling under the burden of factionalism and lack of revenue, and he hoped to re-establish the Caliphate as the moral center of Islamdom.

Influenced by his Sufi adviser Umar Suhravardi, al-Nasir realized that neither his resurgent military might nor the much depleted spiritual legitimacy of the Caliph were sufficient for his task. Instead, he tried a novel approach – a reconfiguration of the men's organizations which provided much of the civic life in urban areas. These clubs, called futuwwa in Arabic, *javanmardi* in Persian, included members from all strata of society, though they served especially as channels for working-class interests and ambitions. Futuwwa and javanmardi both literally mean young manhood, but with the implication of "gallants" or "cavaliers", and the clubs seem to have had a variety of functions, including sports, mutual aid, trade association, and the like. They also functioned as voluntary self-help groups of local militia, patrolling the urban quarters, keeping the peace and protecting the community.

By the time of al-Nasir, the clubs had developed into quasi-religious organizations, with initiation procedures echoing initiation into a Sufi order (though where the Sufi was given a patched robe as a symbol of his vocation, the futuwwa was given warrior's trousers). The members vowed to live up to a code of knightly honor, to avoid impurity, to be chaste, to protect the poor, and to sacrifice themselves for their brothers and for the community. Sometimes participants were asked to give up ties to family in favor of ties to the club. Each town had several rival futuwwa groups associated with specific quarters, and these clubs sometimes battled with one another for the honor of their neighborhoods in the factional feuds that were rife in the cities.

The futuwwa could easily degenerate into mafia-like organizations of thugs maintaining themselves through extortion of protection money (in present-day Arabia and Persia, futuwwa and javanmardi and their descendants the *qabaday* are synonymous with bully and gangster); but they also acted as Robin Hoods, robbing the rich to feed the poor, protecting the quarter from government interference, maintaining local honor, and engaging in egalitarian struggles against all forms of institutionalized authority. In a real sense, the futuwwa were the urban equivalent of the Bedouin. They recaptured the group feeling of the kin-based asabiyya of the tribe by binding themselves together through rituals and oaths; they valued independence, hospitality, loyalty, manly strength, and equality; they opposed the government, preyed upon the wealthy, but were fragmented by continual feuding among themselves. Leadership among them was strictly a matter of personal ability, and they were politically anarchic.

Al-Nasir's predecessors had tried to stop the activities of these gangs, but with no success. As Herbert Mason writes, al-Nasir's inspiration was to conceive of these urban brotherhoods not as enemies of the state, but as "a microcosmic Muslim community within the macrocosmic umma"; he wished to eliminate their lawlessness while expanding their knightly ethic of service and self-sacrificial community action outward toward the Caliphate as a whole, with himself as the moral center of the enterprize.[12] Accordingly, he became a member of a futuwwa club in Baghdad. In 1207, after a quarter of a century as an initiate, he proclaimed himself the *qibla*, pole or central support, of a reinterpreted futuwwa movement, and declared all the brotherhoods everywhere were subordinate parts of his own "authentic" organization. Those who did not agree were banned. He then promulgated decrees outlining the code of chivalric behavior the brothers ought to follow, including Islamic piety, aid and shelter for the weak, obedience to the sacred law, and fraternity and justice. The clubs were united, and were not allowed to quarrel among themselves. In short, the futuwwa were to become a new, urban example of a single Islamic umma, bound together by the personal example and authority of the Caliph himself.

Nor did al-Nasir stop with bringing the urban clubs under his direction; he also initiated other rulers into his brotherhood, including the Prince of Syria and the King of Ghazna; they could then admit their courtiers into the club in a hierarchical system of chivalric legitimation with the Caliph, who combined the roles of founder, spiritual initiator and moral ideal, as its apex. From his position as chief of this spiritual and fraternal order of knights, al-Nasir could also exert influence on other noble members, especially as a mediator in disputes, which ought not disrupt the harmony of the brotherhood.

The incorporative and ascetic movement sponsored by al-Nasir was an extraordinary effort to unite the umma around a new ideal of leadership. Al-Nasir recognized the facts of political decentralization, local autonomy, and social distinction, and sought to bring unity neither through pure power, nor through claims to be the mahdi, but through shared participation in a voluntarily contracted community of mutual respect and aid, based on the self-sacrificing ideology of the futuwwa cavalier, structured by intimate ties of initiation, with the Caliph as the symbolic center. It was a creative effort that took account of Middle Eastern individualism and egalitarianism, as well as the historical desire for a shared ethical community, while relying upon moral suasion, knightly honor, and personal mediation as means for maintaining social solidarity. Al-Nasir's experiment with plural kingdoms united under the ethical authority of the Caliph lasted into the next generation, but was challenged first by rebellions to the east by the Khwarazmshahs, and then was definitively cut short by the devastating invasion of the Mongols, who sacked Baghdad in 1258 and buried all hopes for a renewed Caliphate under pyramids of severed heads.[13]

Al-Nasir's attempt to reintegrate the Caliphate on the basis of knightly honor was paralleled by an equally remarkable (and more successful) effort to solidify and maintain sacred rule. This effort was undertaken by the Nizari branch of the Ismaili Shi'ites (the "Assassins" of fable), who held sway in several small mountain enclaves at the very margins of the Seljuk empire.[14] Because of their fervor and isolation, the Nizari gave rise to legends of hashish-intoxicated madmen and mystical voluptuaries, dying at the whim of their mysterious master. These legends disguised something even more remarkable: a tightly disciplined charismatic community, imbued with a religious spirit that placed their ultimate mission above any personal desire – even above the desire for life.

The movement began under the charismatic leadership of the theologian and mystic Hasan al-Sabbah, the "old man of the mountain". With

pitiless dialectical circularity, Hasan argued for the priority of the Fatimid Imam who, as Hodgson summarizes, "was the only one claiming to
be *his own proof* – and therefore must be accepted, for lack of any other
claimant to fulfill the logical necessity."[15]

Hasan took this argument to its ultimate conclusion, locating the
Imam's authority in the community whose acceptance defines and validates his charismatic mission. In order to manifest the reality of the
distant Imam, the community must devote itself completely and selflessly to bringing about his domination in the world. For this purpose,
any means whatsoever could be employed, including clandestine oper-
ations where fanatical undercover agents remained in place for years,
awaiting the chance to kill their appointed targets. Their most famous
victim was Nizam al-Mulk, the great Seljuk wazir,[16] who was killed in
retaliation, so it was said, for the death of a Nizari carpenter – indicating the millennial egalitarianism of the movement.

But the Nizari had to cope with the collapse of the Fatimids, the
disappearance of the living Imam, and the death of Hasan. Faced with
the ideological and political challenges of defeat and demoralization,
Hasan's successor, Hasan II, responded by declaring that in spite of
appearances the holy war had actually been won and that he himself
was the awaited mahdi come to rescue the faithful. This meant, he said,
that the cycle of time had come to an end, the dead were resurrected,
and his Nizari followers were saved for eternity; it also meant that the
laws of Islam no longer held, since the true believers were now living at
a higher spiritual level and had no need for the outer forms of religious
practice required of mortals. The achievement of eternity was symbolized by the shocking act of abrogating the fast at Ramadan, substituting a feast instead.

In effect, this proclamation offered the Nizari a transcendental escape
from the problem all millenarian sects face: their failure to conquer the
world. Usually this means a gradual secularization, but for the Nizari
weakness and isolation were offset by a withdrawal into a hermetic
world where spiritual status and communion with the living God replaced all other forms of distinction – it was perhaps the most extreme
example in history of a whole community living out the Shi'ite mystical
vision.

Unhappily, heaven on earth proved too difficult to maintain, and after
the death of Hasan's son Muhammad, his successor, Hasan III, declared
that the end of time had itself come to an end; history had begun once
more. In 1210, he repudiated his own divinity, and declared that his
people were now to become orthodox Sunnis. The faithful at once
obeyed their leader's command to deny his right to command and immediately began following Sunni practice while awaiting the next shift in
doctrine. Meanwhile, Hasan III made an alliance with the Caliph al-

Nasir, and the Nizari began slowly rebuilding their political power base. Like al-Nasir's experiment, this effort too was cut short when the Mongols invaded, and conquered the Nizari stronghold of Alamut in 1256, massacring the inhabitants.

Although the Mongol onslaught ended al-Nasir's experiment at revitalizing the Caliphate, it was not the end of the Nizari. Many of the remnants of the sect emigrated to India, where (now known as Khojas) they became associated with trade. The devotees still considered their Imams to be superhuman beings to be obeyed without question. The present Imam, the Aga Khan, is reckoned to be the forty-ninth in the line. He has organized his congregation into a tremendously active and highly innovative cadre, able to adapt rapidly to change and to compete very successfully in the international marketplace, where the sect has become enormously wealthy.

The erratic history of the Nizari sect illustrates the potentials available to a millenarian vision of the world, which so much desires the advent of the mahdi, but which must somehow accommodate itself to the disillusionment and opposition that occur after the redeemer has arrived. Such movements usually end either in collapse or retreat to a more disenchanted worldview. However, as the Nizari sect demonstrates, it is possible for true believers to maintain a sense of spiritual exaltation regardless of (or perhaps because of) experiences of marginality, defeat and fragmentation. By focusing completely on worship of a single sacred leader with the capacity to manufacture a complete and new reality every generation, the inwardly-turned Nizari were able to sustain their community and their faith until today.

In their present incarnation, the Nizari also reveal that the Calvinistic/Muslim orthodox gap between man and God is not necessary for the rational pursuit of economic success. Clearly, contra Weber, there are distinct capitalistic advantages in having one's divinely appointed spiritual guide right here on earth. Of course, it helps if that guide is a Harvard graduate with a shrewd business sense, like the Aga Khan.

Reprise: the Uses and Abuses of Government

What place, then, does the state hold in Middle Eastern culture? The Ottoman Empire was an imposition of a caste-like centralized hierarchy upon egalitarian individualists; al-Nasir's appropriation of the futuwwa ideology was an attempt to use notions of chivalry to legitimize the Caliphate; the Nizari transformations were the responses of a charismatic spiritual minority to extreme pressure. But, as we have seen, the vast majority of Middle Eastern rulers generally failed to hold the loyalty of their people. Muslims, sick of the corruption and venality of the state, have tolerated government solely because it maintained a modicum of order in a world prone to the eruption of anarchy. Having seen the ridda wars, then the catastrophic fighting that arose after the assassination of Uthman, and later the bloodshed that characterized the collapse of dynasties, most Middle Easterners have been willing to recognize any regime that could conserve the peace.

Aside from protection, another important function of the court has been mediation, which derives from the general principles of competitive egalitarian individualism, where local opponents often require some external arbitration to settle disputes among themselves. Men of religious character, learned men, or elders were always the major candidates for such positions. These men could, under proper circumstances, become political leaders, especially in resistance to external threats to local mores and Islamic practice (which were usually seen as one and the same). Muhammad is the paradigm case, and many religious pretenders to power have since used his example as their own validation.

However, the converse trajectory can also occur, as the state apparatus can put itself forward to local people as a disinterested external arbitrator and can be accepted by them, even though they may still refuse to pay their taxes. Yet, in spite of statements to the contrary, the state *does* have an interest in local matters, and that is to use its position as a mediator to gain leverage by favoring the weaker parties in any dispute and undercutting the strength of the main opposition groups. From this perspective, the Middle Eastern Sultan, far from being the absolute tyrant he has often been portrayed as, was in fact a manipulator who ruled by maintaining a delicate balance of power between hostile local rivals.

The unconditional power of the ruler was exercised mainly over those closest to him, most reliant upon him, and least able to escape from him – his clients, advisors, lieutenants, minions, and bureaucrats. Their affluence and power were purely a consequence of his personal whim, and could be withdrawn at any moment; in consequence, they would lose their holdings, their rights to extort taxes, their capacity to dominate others, and perhaps their lives. Ordinary people were usually not directly effected by the intrigues and violence of the courtly world, and may have rather enjoyed the common spectacle of the public fall, humiliation and destruction of the great.

Despite any use or advantage offered by government, it nonetheless remains the case that power in the Middle East has been mostly held by rulers whose authority had very little popular support. As we have seen, even religious dynasties, like purely secular regimes, soon came to rely on their ability to control military force; they too rapidly lost their moral identity, succumbed to luxury, turned to slaves and mercenaries for support, broke apart into rival factions, overtaxed the populace, and fell to new conquerors who would then follow the same cycle.

Naturally, ambitious rulers have always sought to escape this fate by attempting to establish some form of legitimization for their regimes. Early dynasties based themselves on the supposed moral superiority of certain Arabic lineages, due both to intrinsic nobility passed down in the blood and to historic "closeness" to the Prophet. This route became more difficult to follow after the fall of the Caliphate, when rule was often held by foreigners only recently converted to Islam who could make no such claims to condone their authority. Only a few modern regimes in the Arab-speaking countries still attempt to sanction their power on genealogical and historical grounds (Jordan and Morocco are the major examples).

The Abbasids, aiming to solidify their highly centralized authority while undermining the power of all rival lineages, favored a new mode of legitimating hierarchy; they trained courtiers into mastering a distinctive style of speech and behavior that clearly distinguished the elite from plebeians. This form of upward mobility has been favored ever since by cosmopolitan empires, and in its modern guise has been pursued by self-made intellectuals and bureaucrats who wish to be elevated because of their esoteric skills and technical expertise, not for their bloodlines or for their credentials as Muslims. Algeria and Egypt are good contemporary instances where claims to this type of secular authority are made. However, it is noteworthy that rule by a self-cultivated elite can and often does coincide with a disenfranchised general public and a despotic central regime.

Another way to authorize civil authority rests its case on its claims to be, like the Buyids, the fostering protector of the community. This is an assertion especially popular with military rulers, who certainly are not noble, and who have no pretense to being cultivated. Instead, they like to present themselves as parental figures who have the best interest of the country at heart, as they sacrifice themselves to protect the nation. The nationalistic military regimes ruling Iraq and Syria today often use this type of propaganda to quell internal opposition, but like their medieval predecessors, they have had little, if any, real success in winning the hearts and minds of the masses.

The final alternative is to assert a sacred right to rule – the option that Shi'ites have argued for from the earliest days of Islam. Great dynasties of the past have gained their initial successes by claiming sacred foundations, just as modern Iran proclaims its holy destiny under the rule of its ayatollahs, and as Libya organizes inself according to the Green Book of the charismatic Colonel Qaddafi. Meanwhile, in Saudi Arabia, the Wahhabis still assert the spiritual superiority of their Islamic state. But every government which affirms its divine right to authority

Plate 8.1   Nineteenth-century lithograph of a traditional punishment in Iran.

must suffer from comparison to the original umma. Sacred rule is inevitably susceptible to rationalization, fragmentation, and a popular disappointment made more bitter by the great hopes that the movement had aroused.

In sum, all these modes for laying claim to legitimacy, both ancient and modern, secular and sacred, are destined to founder on the rock of the deep-rooted Middle Eastern faith in the fundamental equality of all persons. Within this ethic, noble lineages, civilian "experts", military "protectors" and sanctified preachers must prove their right to rule by deeds that win the approval of the community, not by asserting an intrinsic capacity that automatically validates their authority. Otherwise, their power will rest primarily on pure patronage and coercion, as, in fact, it very often does, today as well as in the past, in Morocco, Algeria, Egypt and Iran as well as in Iraq.

It seems then that Middle Easterners remain caught on the horns of an ancient dilemma, one that dates back to the contest between the warrior kings and communal temples of Sumer. The choice seems to be one of pragmatism or Messianism, with little in between, and those who participate in politics appear to be either Hobbesian manipulators seeking personal advantage or else saintly figures whose heroic attempts to resurrect the prophetic moment are doomed to failure. In this context, the state, at its worst, is a catastrophe to be avoided if possible, suffered if necessary; at its best, it is a protector of the peace and a useful mediator balancing out local disputes, although everyone knows these decisions are manipulated by those in power for their own ends. Small wonder then that the realm of politics has lost its appeal for many Muslims, who have found their refuge instead in religion; a refuge, however, that also reflects the tensions and contradictions of an egalitarian social order – as we shall discover in the next chapters.

Part IV

Sacred Power:
Reciters, Lawyers,
Incarnations, and Saints

9

The Essentials of Islam

The Authority of the Quran and the Necessity of Practice

In the next chapters I want to address the manner in which the community of Islam has dealt with the question of authority after the death of the Prophet and the dispersal of the original community. As we have seen, Sunni Islam is "characterized by the basic equality of all Muslims in the eyes of the law as God's submissive servants, and by the freedom of the individual Muslim in the search for salvation by the doing of God's will."[1] This means that Sunni Muslims have no authoritative body to interpret doctrine, no ecclesiastical council, no synods or Pope, as in Christianity, no Gaon as in Judaism, no sanctified Imam, as in Shi'ism. Nor are there formal priests, an official church or a church hierarchy. In principle, anyone who is able to recite and who knows the ritual can lead the Friday prayer in the mosque, just as anyone capable of reading (or of hearing someone else read) can interpret the Quran. There are not even fixed congregations in the western sense. Any believer can choose to worship at any mosque, to follow any teacher, to accept any of the schools of interpretation of the divine law, including one different from that of his parents or friends. A non-believer can even choose not to accept Islam at all, since it is written that "the truth is from your Lord. Let him who will, believe, and let him who will, reject."[2]

The liberty accorded to personal conviction among Muslims obviously offers great potential for disunity. This danger is countered in part by the believer's trusting reliance on the absolute authority of the Quran. As Louis Massignon writes, "one cannot overemphasize . . . the central position that the Quran holds in the elaboration of any Muslim doctrine, even of the most seemingly heterodox one. Memorized by heart in childhood, the Quran is a real and revealed 'world plan' regulating the experimentation, interpretation and evaluation of every event."[3]

Ideally there should be no need for human initiative when the highest

Plate 9.1   Umayyad mosque in Damascus, Syria.

authority of all has sent down rules to regulate and evaluate every human
action. The only requirement for discovering these sacred dictates is
knowledge of the Book. But there proved to be both theological and
practical difficulties in the utopian vision of a complete and perfectly
legible divine pathway (*Sharia*) that could be easily found in the holy text
and followed on earth. The Quran, being finite, does not and cannot
explicitly cover all circumstances. There are many areas of behavior left
out, some questions are not answered, other precepts are ambiguous, and
sometimes there are contradictions or apparent impossibilities in the text.
Muslim theologians influenced by Greek thought quickly pointed out

these "failings" in the Quran. They argued that educated readers (such as themselves) ought to be able to reinterpret the holy book in order to align it with the dictates of reason. This is the Mutazilite doctrine that was embraced by the Abbasid Caliph Mamun, who hoped to control the experts and thereby gain power over the right of interpretation.

This position was strongly resisted by the "traditionalists", led by Ibn Hanbal. Their argument was simple: "We act according to the unambiguous verses of Thy Book; and we believe in Its ambiguous verses; and we describe Thee according to Thine own descriptions of Thyself."[4] For these men, the omnipotence of God meant that any constraints on Him and on His word – even the constraints of reason – were a form of idolatry. This exclusively textualist vision of Islam was finally completely victorious – in part because of a popular revulsion against the attempt by the Abbasid government to appropriate for itself the right of scriptural interpretation, in part because the traditionalist response was in tune with a general recognition of the feebleness of human reason, which Muslims knew from experience to be incapable of transcending personal interests.

After the victory of Ibn Hanbal and his followers Muslim theologians no longer arrogantly dared to subject God's word to the test of analytical logic, nor could analogy or metaphor be used to interpret scripture; what is said is what is meant – no more, no less. If Allah is portrayed in the Quran with his hand reached toward the sinner, the helping hand is not to be taken as a symbol of God's forgiveness; it must be accepted *bila kayf*, that is, without our being able to specify what it signifies. Reason was not banished – in fact, the use of analytic argument flourished in Muslim scholarship – but it was now firmly limited to explication of the legal implications of the sacred text; it could not be extended to put limits on God. Rather, the believer must accept the sacred word as it is, in its matter-of-fact austerity. Any absurdities this doctrine may seem to entail were taken as indications of human incapacity to grasp the infinite potentiality of Allah's omnipotence.

Instead of a theology of the nature of God, Sunni Islam now offered the faithful a theology of the obligations and prohibitions commanded by Allah, who had given humanity the proper pathway that must be followed over the course of a lifetime in order to reach salvation. Individual devotional practice and acceptance of the Word are what is crucial, not reflection or rationalization. In its emphasis on application, Islam has been appropriately described as a religion not so much of orthodoxy as of orthopraxy, reliant on ritual actions to reveal and inculcate faith.[5] The very word "Islam" signifies an *act* – the initiatory act of surrender and submission to God.

The essential practices required of Muslims are five: the public witnessing of the faith (God is one, and Muhammad is his Prophet),

Plate 9.2   Invocation of the Prophet Muhammad, written by the
Ottoman Sultan Mahmud II about 1838.

prayer, the pilgrimage to Mecca, donation of zakat, and the fast of *Ram-adan*.[6] These shared practices are simple, direct and spiritually compel-ling. Each has a specific and characteristic form and content. The aim of each is to infuse the followers with the necessity of a willed subordin-ation of the self to the dictates of the Muslim community. In return, the believer is offered redemption in the afterlife, and rewarded in the pre-sent. It is a rhythm of active self-abnegation, followed by both an imme-diate and a promised compensation – a kind of sacred behaviorism. It is also a rhythm that continually seeks to reconcile the demands of the egalitarian community with the desires of the individual actor.

For example, consider the practice of prayer (*salat*). Muslims ought to pray five times a day, starting early in the morning and ending in the evening; prayer is a time-consuming and fairly arduous ritual, involving repeated prostrations and lengthy standardized recitations of faith. It is an act of disciplined self-control and an expression of submission to God. But as each person actively submits, he or she is united within the community of equal believers, since all Muslims everywhere pray at the same times of the day, in approximately the same manner, with almost the same words, facing toward the same central point of Mecca. For Muslims, the experience of time itself is structured and sanctified by the cycle of prayer.

Yet while participating in the community, the worshipper can and often does pray alone. Even at the obligatory communal Friday prayer in the mosque, the imam is merely the person standing in front of the congregation. He also prays, and later offers the homily, but he is defin-itely not in control of the ritual, nor is the mosque a shrine from which religious authority emanates. Rather, it is a place of public assemblage – an agora, not a temple. The Arabic term for mosque, *masjid*, simply means the place of prostration, in contrast to the English term "church," which means "the Lord's house."

Along with engendering a potent feeling of solidarity among the individual worshippers, the act of prayer offers each person a sense of exhilaration and profound peace. This is a spiritual state, but it is also at least partially a purely physical consequence of the prescribed regulated breathing, chanting, and rhythmic prostrations of the supplicants, which have a potent physiological effect, as anyone who has studied dissociative states knows. Prayer gives the individual immersion in the disciplined unity of the community, a chance to gain personal spiritual merit by demonstrating submission to God, and a strong sense of physical and mental well-being.

Another pillar of Islam is the *hajj*, the pilgrimage to Mecca – a ritual act that has assumed greater and greater significance in recent years as it becomes more available to the average Muslim. The pilgrimage, like prayer, is both egalitarian and communal – the male and female pilgrims each wear simple clothing and all participate together in the complex and obscure set of rituals and sacrifices that, among other things, are thought to re-enact episodes from the life of Abraham; but the pilgrimage is also individualistic: there is no leader in the ceremony, and each Muslim conducts the ritual alone, even though simultaneously immersed in the surrounding community of equally involved participants, who are each enacting a performance that is thought to benefit both themselves and the entire community.

Like prayer, the hajj too demands great sacrifice, especially when undertaking the trip meant a long and dangerous overland journey through the desert. But the reward is also very great, as the believers all take part in the vast and moving ritual of leveling and identification with Abraham and the monotheistic past that is the climax of the journey – and return to their homelands with greatly enhanced status, to be addressed henceforth by the honorific *hajji*.

A similar pattern is found as well in the injunction to give alms, another required exercise in selflessness for Muslim people. Like the hajj, almsgiving also results in an immediate heightening of secular status, and an even greater hundred-fold return is promised in heaven. Almsgiving too is a purely personal act, done at will, according to one's own lights, but for the benefit of the community at large, and is rewarded by community approval.

The pattern of Muslim practice is clearest in the fast of Ramadan, which is the ninth month of the Islamic lunar calendar.[7] The fast covers the entire month to the sighting of the new moon. During this period from sunrise to sunset it is forbidden to eat, drink, smoke, chew tobacco, or to put anything into the body. According to some of the more zealous, even spittle should not be swallowed, nor should fragrance be inhaled. Sexual contact is strictly forbidden, there can be no forced vomiting, nor retention in the body of anything that would normally be rejected. The fast is not simply a restriction on eating, but a radical limitation on the

Plate 9.3   Elderly man with prayer beads. Southern Syria.

borders of the body, and is associated with maintaining an inviolate purity.

These exacting interdicts are softened by the fact that fasts in Islam, unlike those of other religions, last only from sunrise to sunset. While fasting during the day is total, all restrictions are lifted as soon as the sun sets and "until the white thread of dawn appears to you distinct from its black thread." During this period, the Quran enjoins the believers to "approach your wives...and eat and drink."[8] In point of fact, most Muslims gain weight during the fast. It is estimated that in Cairo, for example, grocery bills are from three to five times higher during Ramadan than at any other time during the year. Not only is more quantity of food usually eaten during the evenings of Ramadan, but the meals are also of higher quality, consisting of feast foods and sweets consumed only on special occasions.[9] The plenty of the evening is accompanied as well with a gathering of friends and family in a joyous celebration of the solidarity of the community. In a similar vein, alms and food are publicly redistributed to the poor by businesses and by those who have any surplus, so that everyone can observe not only the fast, but also the feast that follows it.

Fasting is not regarded by Muslims as a way of atoning for sins through suffering, as it is in the Judeo-Christian tradition. Instead, the sura on fasting says "Allah intends every facility for you; He does not want to put you to difficulties. (He wants you) to complete the prescribed period, and to glorify Him in that he has guided you; perchance ye shall be grateful."[10] By fasting, Muslims hope to gain the mercy of a compassionate deity for the whole community through their own disciplined actions. As an orthodox commentator writes: "The accord and convergence of Muslims on a particular thing, at a particular time, with all the people seeing one thing, lends encouragement to them and makes fasting easy...This concord and unity of purpose is the cause of the descent of spiritual blessings on both the high and the low."[11]

Beneath the hope for blessing is a faith in God's generosity, as evidenced concretely every day in the communal enjoyment of the nightly feast. The faithful, having experienced an immediate return for their efforts, believe that any suffering undergone in fasting will be recompensed a thousandfold in heaven, where a special gateway is opened for those who fast – a gateway equally available to all Muslim men and women, since all alike can undertake and complete the Ramadan fast without imposing too great a burden upon themselves.

The deep egalitarianism of Islam is evident in the restrictions that forbid enthusiasts from continuing the fast beyond the month of Ramadan, though other days in which fast may be undertaken are noted in the Quran.[12] Fasting in Ramadan also *must* be broken every evening by eating and drinking enough to sustain life and health. The temptation to asceticism that is so compelling for certain zealous temperaments is opposed in favor of a balanced normality. Fasting is not a way to show one's special ascetic capacities, but rather a way to help the average person learn self-restraint and live in a more moderate and virtuous manner.

The rhythm of constraint and release, solitude and community, culminates in the great festival of *Eid al-fatr* (literally the lesser festival, but in actuality the major celebration of the year).[13] This celebration is very much an affirmation of participation and renewal, as Muslims everywhere put on new clothes, visit, embrace, share festal food and drink, and congratulate one another for having successfully completed the fast. It is a day for the giving of alms to the poor and for a gathering of all people for prayer in a public space, preferably not in the neighborhood mosque, but outside the town in an open field so that local divisions are ignored for the moment. Men go to the ceremony individually, breaking with the ordinary world, and gather together as a sacred community to hear a sermon extolling the virtues of submission. Forgiveness of all insults and enmity is mandated; debts are cancelled and old enemies hug one another to show their renewed brotherhood.

The music and celebrations that marked the whole month are intensified, and the tombs of the ancestors are visited, reaffirming again the
continuity of the community with its sacred heritage.[14]

Eid al-Fatr is a celebration of the community at large, extending
beyond the family and the mosque to all Muslims, past and present.
Wealth is redistributed, the ancestors are venerated, brotherhood is
enjoined, and community participation is accentuated. Individual sacrifice during the fast is compensated for by shared communal rewards
that reinforce the value of personal self-restraint. The Eid festival repli-
cates the pattern of the entire cycle of the fast, offering immediate
benefit for the individual act of asceticism and a symbolic renewal of
ties with the umma of co-equal believers.

We can see then that fasting in Islam during Ramadan and at other
times is pragmatic, egalitarian, and oriented toward the unity of the
community as well as the salvation of the individual. The personal
restraint and virtue of the faithful during the day are rewarded both by
communal celebration in this world and by redemption in the afterlife.
High and low are leveled through the giving of alms; sharing in hunger
gives the wealthy a sense of the contingency of their plenty and brotherhood with the impoverished, who, like all other Muslims, take part in
both the fast and the feast. Salvation is through the deeds of individuals
in this world, united with their fellows in the performance of socially
and spiritually rewarding acts of self-sacrifice.

The Problem of Salvation

Within this theology of practice there is no original sin. Humans have
been placed on the pathway and given directions, they only need to
heed and obey. The Quran is a light to guide travelers as they work
their way through the darkness of earthly life toward the climactic
moment of the final judgement. Redemption, atonement, an irredeem-
able inner sense of evil – these aspects of Christian dogma are left aside
in Islam where the punishment for turning away from the path is
simple and terrible – God withdraws Himself, and leaves the individual
alone to wander without a beacon in the moral wilderness.

Yet despite the absence of original sin and the emphasis on practice,
Islam is not a religion of positive thinking – a religion of the "once
born", in William James's terms. Instead, according to the Quran,
"the steps of those who fear their Lord should tremble."[15] When the
Quran is cited to them, "they fall down on their faces in tears."[16] All gifts
and all suffering, the believer realizes, are from Allah, who cannot be
fathomed, coerced, begged or persuaded, but will act as He desires. Evil
and suffering are created by God to test the mettle of humanity, but

election to the ranks of the saved cannot be *assumed* to follow from proper practice or good works; salvation is solely a consequence of God's ineffable and unpredictable grace. Al-Ghazali writes that even Muhammad was afraid for his soul, and prayed for refuge "against the evil of things I did and things I left undone."[17]

Fear of the utter power and unknowability of God is mitigated only by reliance on His positive qualities. In the Quran Allah has continually described Himself as merciful and compassionate, and Muslims hope for His forgiveness, since they cannot save themselves or even live in this world without breaking the holy law.[18] Believers are also given hope by sura 7:172, where God tells of the compact He made with humanity before creation, calling all the souls of the future out of the loins of Adam and asking them "Am I not your Lord?" to which they answered "Yea! We do testify!" This was the moment when time was created, and the immeasurable gap between mankind and God instated. Prayer and adoration are the appropriate human response to this gap, as all humanity are witnesses to the omnipotence of the Creator, who, in return, will restore those who honor their covenant back to the state of primordial unity with Him at the end of time.

Notwithstanding God's compassion and His covenant, the Quran also describes Allah as inconsistent and sometimes devious, making misleading statements to prove the faith of men and test the consciences of believers;[19] also, acts which seem evil to men may, in God's eyes, be good, and vice versa.[20] Approaching such a protean God and pleasing Him is no easy task. As one Sufi text puts it:

> To pretend to know Him is ignorance; to persist in serving Him is disrespect; to refrain from fighting Him is madness; to allow oneself to be deceived by His peace is stupidity; to discourse on His attributes is digression; to abstain from affirming Him is foolhardiness; and to consent to being estranged from Him is baseness...Do not let yourself be deceived by God, nor despair because of Him. Do not seek His love, nor resign yourself to not loving Him. Do not try any longer to affirm Him, nor feel inclined to deny Him. And, especially, beware of proclaiming his unity.[21]

This is a paradoxical statement from an antinomian sect, but the impossibility of pleasing an utterly transcendent, unpredictable and indeterminable God left all orthodox Muslims in a state of trepidation and perplexity as to the state of their souls, as attested by al-Ghazali, who writes: "Whoever says 'I am a believer' is an infidel; and whoever says, 'I am learned', is ignorant" and "The farthest removed from (hypocrisy) are those who are constantly afraid of it, while those who deem themselves free of it are they who are nearest to it."[22] In Islam, only God knows the state of a man's soul; the blasphemous drunkard may be saved, the hajji who meticulously prays, fasts, and gives alms to the poor may be damned.

The Charisma of the Prophet

Suffering from a pervasive awareness of their own fallibility and hypocrisy and fearing God's unpredictable wrath, Muslims naturally sought other means to find salvation beyond the study of the Quran and the necessary practices. In particular, they turned their eyes towards the Prophet himself, proclaiming him to be a holy being, a perfect man, sinless, pure and faultless – a symbol of what human beings could be if they realized their Godly nature.[23] Over time, Muhammad was increasingly believed to be capable of miraculous action, foreseeing the future, cursing his enemies, splitting the moon in the sky.[24] His physical abilities became extraordinary as well. A text of the thirteenth century states that Muhammad "could see not only forward but also backward; he possessed the gift of vision in the dark; when he walked by the side of the man who was by nature taller than he, his stature equaled the other man's; when he sat, his shoulder was above the shoulders of all who sat with him; his body never cast a shadow for he was all light."[25] He also was believed to have ascended to heaven while alive, and to have seen the face of Allah; this miraculous event (*laylat al-miraj*) is celebrated today throughout the Muslim world as one of the major holidays of the religion. Believers especially had faith that Muhammad would certainly intercede for them on the Last Day.[26]

Undoubtedly a faith in Muhammad's spiritual capacity to save the faithful helped alleviate the natural anxiety created by the Muslim premise of an absolutely transcendent God. But there is another factor at play which can be explicated by returning to Weber's paradigm of the nature of religion. For Weber the experiential truth of all prophecy – emissary and exemplary alike – begins in the public recognition of the inexplicable appearance of charismatic individuals who are "set apart from ordinary men and treated as endowed with supernatural, superhuman, or at least specifically exceptional powers or qualities."[27]

Charisma differs from other, more instrumental or traditional forms of leadership in that the source of the leader's authority over the follower is not mutual interest, nor shared values, nor the leader's right to rule. From the point of view of followers, the charismatic commands because he has an innate "gift of grace", a mysterious but emotionally compelling power that is "opposed to all institutional routines, those of tradition and those subject to rational management." Rather, as Weber says, "the governed submit because of their belief in the extraordinary quality of

Plate 9.4 The longer Profession of Faith, with decorative *waw* (and)
from an early twentieth-century Turkish calligrapher: "I believe in God
AND in His angels AND in His books AND in His messengers, AND in
the Day of Judgment, AND in the predestination that good AND evil
come both from God, and in the resurrection. I witness that there is no
deity save God and that Muhammad is His servant and His messenger."

the specific *person*."[28] Whatever a prophet says must be believed, because *he* has said it, since it is the emotional compulsion exercised by
him *as a person* that *defines* the religious experience for the faithful.
This was the case with Muhammad, who was loved first, then obeyed;
for his early followers, the content of his annunciation was secondary
to the inspiring emotional impact of his personal presence.

As we have seen, the message offered by Muhammad was an emissary prophecy of unparalleled purity, one which modestly downplayed
his own charismatic role. Obviously, there is a tension between the
message of the ethical emissary who humbly proclaimed himself to be
simply God's "warner" and the follower's own actual experience of
rapture and transcendence in the Prophet's presence. It is this latter
subjective reality that led Muslims to attribute exemplary and irrational
supernatural and salvational powers to the messenger – in other words,
the faithful converted a proclaimed emissary prophet into an exemplary
charismatic. Later, when the Muslim political world was increasingly
disenchanted, the popular focus on Muhammad's miraculous accomplishments and extraordinary personality became even more central, as
the believers sought a savior upon whom they could rely in an uncertain and hostile universe.

Muhammad's charisma can then be seen as a response to the social
reality of egalitarian individualism in the context of the Middle East.
The pressures of this competitive ethic inculcated a wish amongst the
anxious public for an ordering voice that would harmonize the warring
self-interested co-equal rivals into a higher unity. For Muslims, the
Prophet provided that voice, giving shape and moral cohesion to an

inchoate and threatening environment by drawing all his followers into a single moral community, united through shared devotion to the beloved exemplary figure. This shift was symbolized in the change in military tactics that permitted Muhammad's community to be victorious over its enemies. The pre-Islamic ideal warrior was the challenger, who stepped out to defy the assembled foe singlehandedly, and battle itself was a matter of individual combat between heroes. Muhammad stopped this; his men had to obey him, stay in line and fight together, as one.

Because he managed to surmount antagonistic individual differences through his personal charisma, Muhammad's life as an historical individual became a matter of urgent spiritual concern for all Muslims. Love and admiration for Muhammad could be expressed through imitating him down to the last detail – so much so that some of the devout still dye their beards red, since the Prophet is said to have had red hair. This is *sunna*, the Prophet's practice, and many of the characteristics taken as particularly Middle Eastern (clothing, beards, demeanor, etc.) are conscious imitations of sunna. Popular identification with Muhammad is also strikingly indicated in the transformation of names which began in the first centuries of Islam. As Goitein has demonstrated, there was a sudden diminution in the huge variety of personal names that were once characteristic of the Middle East. Within a few hundred years, these old names were displaced by the names of Muhammad and his companions, which were usually coupled with metaphorical names referring to the attributes of God.[29]

Through identification with Muhammad (and, to a lesser degree, in the adoration of his companions and family) Muslims wished to emulate his obedience to the precepts and practices enjoined by the Quran and the community. In this way, they hoped to please God and participate in the spiritually merged umma of co-equal believers, who were also imitating the Prophet. But emotionally speaking, what was really crucial was experiencing the charismatic personal emotional bond with Muhammad; a bond that drew Muslims into the community of believers and simultaneously gave them a sense of personal spiritual expansion that is the hallmark of charismatic discipleship – by becoming like Muhammad they too became closer to his perfection.

Although participation in the personal charisma of the Prophet did overcome many of the tensions between community and individual, the project of imitation and recapitulation also entailed its own contradictions, especially after the death of the Prophet, as scriptural experts (the ulema) made claims to have greater knowledge of Muhammad and his ways, and therefore to have achieved a closer identification with him, introducing a new form of distinction into the umma and also arousing new sorts of resistance to their claims.

10

Recapturing the Sacred Past: the Power of Knowledge

The Authority of History

Because of the nature of its annunciation, Islam is a religion obsessed with history and with the recovery of history. Ordinary Muslims have always sought to know as much as possible about the Prophet's life, his custom, and his words, as well as the lives, customs and words of those who were close to him, and have occupied themselves with seeking to discover and preserve all they could of the millenarian past. These memories serve, with the Quran, as the major source for Muslim moral consciousness.[1]

And so it is that where other religions interpret their holy texts through the decisions of authoritative legislative bodies, or through deduction from general principles, Muslims instead discovered ethical norms and authority through "empirical observation of individual actions which God had approved."[2] These actions could be known only through the collection of historical records of the words and deeds of the founder and his companions. This was the task of the preservers and reciters of sacred history or, as they are conventionally known, the *ahl al-hadith*, people of "tradition."[3]

At first, accounts of holy tradition were casually recounted from memory by anyone who had been with Muhammad at Mecca and Medina, and who had journeyed out with the invading Arab armies to conquer the world. The recollections of these companions of the Prophet naturally reflected their own experiences and personal character, so that different geographical areas developed varying bodies of hadith according to the knowledge of the Muslims who originally settled in them. Also crucial were the requirements of the local Muslim converts, who consulted the early bearers of tradition with their questions about the proper way for a Muslim to behave. For example, as Richard Bulliet has shown, early Iranian hadith are inordinately concerned with matters of pollution, reflecting pre-Islamic Persian apprehensions.[4]

Muslims would come from many miles away to hear the voice of one who had actually heard the voice of the Prophet himself. This immediacy was lost after the deaths of those who were describing what they had really seen and heard of the Prophet and his ways. Believers now could only listen to someone repeating what others had told him, without firsthand experience. Under these circumstances, recitation and remembrance became less informal, and reciters concentrated on developing their memories and eliminating personal biases so they could repeat, verbatim, what they had heard from those before them, without interpretation, comment, elaboration, or condensation.

Oral transmission of the Islamic traditions was greatly privileged over writing. This was partly due to the character of Arabic written language, which leaves the vowel sounds out and so is open to considerable interpretation.[5] An early scholar admonishes students to "strive eagerly to obtain hadiths and get them from the men themselves, not from written records, lest they be affected by the disease of corruption of the text."[6] Orality was also embedded in the traditional poetic culture of the Middle East, and continued to be revered in the equally personalized culture of Islam, where the Quran itself begins with the angel's command to Muhammad to "Recite!" and where reading aloud from the Holy Book has always been considered spiritually efficacious in and of itself, since recitation is regarded as awakening a psychic connection to the original speaker.[7] In the same manner, to recite the traditions aloud is a holy act which puts one momentarily in communion with the Prophet and his companions. In recounting the hadith they had learned, transmitters saw themselves and were seen by others as conduits to exemplary history who gained a penumbra of charisma through their constant recollection and repetition of Muhammad's utterances and acts.

Although becoming a reciter was open to any Muslim, it was not an easy task; proper recitation required a good knowledge of classical Arabic so the texts could be pronounced correctly – anything less would be blasphemous.[8] Reciters also had to have a great capacity for the accumulation and memorization of reports, since the more that was known, the greater one's connection with the past. As Islamdom expanded the most ambitious of these collectors travelled vast distances to discover "rare" hadith or to track down aged reciters whose hadith would be "high", that is, with the fewest number of steps to the original source. Men (and women)[9] who had accumulated a variety of rare and high traditions won special prestige amongst the faithful. Their names too would enter into the *isnad*, or "chain" of transmitters that was recited whenever the tradition was spoken (I heard from so and so who heard from so and so who heard from so and so that the Prophet said ...) assuring them a kind of immortality. As they gained stature as capable and knowledgeable reporters of tradition, these expert individual collectors also began to act as counsels and teachers to their neighbors. In a minor key, they replicated the biography of Muhammad himself, who also was a transmitter of God's word, and a moral exemplar as well.

The reciter's morality was central in deciding the reliability of the traditions he recounted. Naturally, hadith were judged according to historical criterion, such as agreement in time, absence of anachronisms, confirming reports from other sources, and so on. But most of all, they were accepted and arranged according to the *personal* reputation of the carrier. For Middle Easterners the ability to read, learn, and memorize is not sufficient qualification for scholarship. Character and learning go together, memorization and recitation are deeply embedded in the heart, and the proper bearers of knowledge are individuals with impeccable biographies. The learning gained from an untrustworthy or irreligious source, no matter how dazzling, is *a priori* unreliable, much as tribesmen hold the character of anyone not of their own lineage to be fundamentally suspect.

This means that each hadith must be tested by the reliability of the members of its "chain" of transmitters, that is, by its moral genealogy. A plausible hadith with an isnad of dubious repute is rendered suspicious, while an isnad of pious and upright transmitters is considered to be reliable, regardless of the content of the hadith itself. To make these moral judgments, a "science of men" (*ilm al-rijal*), as it was called, grew up at the center of hadith inquiry, using a vast biographical historical literature to establish the moral pedigrees of hadith reciters. These pedigrees, like the lineages of noble tribesmen, validated assertions of moral authority by referring back to one's predecessors. But where the tribesman said: "I am great because I am the son of a great man, who was the son of a great man" the ahl al-hadith said "I am a reliable transmitter, who heard reports recited by a reliable man, who heard the reports of another reputable man, and so on back to the companion who heard the words of the Prophet himself."

The pervasive concern with personal reputation, biography and genealogical history coincides with what Goitein has called the Middle Eastern "passion for identification", that is, "the tendency to ascribe any piece of wisdom, any practice, any incident to a definite person called by name and characterized by some biographical details."[10] In an egalitarian culture, such a concern is understandable, since only character and personal reputation can mark individuals out from the masses; in return, anything distinctive is associated with the accomplishments (or deficits) of a particular person whose standing is passed on by blood or by spiritual osmosis to those who follow him.

Of course, repute had a different content for the hadith reporter than it had for the tribesman, whose heroic standing was gained through resolute self-assertion in battles with his fellows. In contrast, the repute of the hadith transmitter was associated with a lack of arrogance and a sober respectability in the community, as testified to in his biography and the upright character of his teachers and family. Above all, the trusted transmitter must be a moral conformist who "models his conduct upon the respectable among his contemporaries and fellow countrymen ... according to individuals, circumstances and places."[11] To the men of hadith, heroic self-asserting warriors are *ipso facto* incapable of emptying themselves to become the vehicle for truth.

For some time, local reciters continued to serve as unique nodes of knowledge and exemplars of religious morality, each separate from all others, each making a claim to be a receptacle of the sacred words and deeds of the Prophet whilst simultaneously denying any hierarchical organization amongst themselves. The highly informal, opportunistic, dispersed, individualistic form of knowledge of the ahl al-hadith coincided with the gradual erosion of Islamic consensus as the empire expanded over a wider and wider territory. In the absence of any ecclesiastical authority or state control over the dissemination and distribution of knowledge, hadith transmission was becoming more and more localized, and regional schisms were beginning to appear. Questions arose as to how the faithful could discriminate between a true and a false tradition and how the disparate traditions could be culled and codified.

To solve these problems travelling scholars began to collect, validate and publish compendiums of acceptable hadith, setting the stage for more uniform and less personalized instruction in traditions and undermining the autonomy and influence of local reciters. As the derivative charisma of the local reciter became more and more attenuated due to spatial and temporal distance from the original prophetic moment, formal schools were developed in which generally accepted traditions were taught by professional instructors who continued the old oral methods of teaching, but who now used books rather than men as their sources, taking their spoken recitations from the written compilations. By 1300, the unique individual transmitter had been more or less replaced by a professionally-trained college instructor.

The diminution of the individual hadith transmitter's influence was symbolized by the publication of six so-called "canonical" collections of Sunni tradition. Instead of being arranged according to the person who was source of the isnad as was the old format, these hadith were organized according to topic; a less biographical approach that was specifically established to be useful for jurists looking for precedents. These collections were not accepted as final, and Muslim scholars can and do argue heatedly to this day over the validity of a particular tradition. But they were adopted as the standard sources because they integrated hadith into the practice of law. The issuance and acceptance of these compilations was a plain indication that the legal scholar was now predominant over the hadith reciter.

Legalism in Islam

The authority of legalists arises from the same circumstances that led to reliance on hadith scholarship, that is, the attenuation of the charisma of the original umma. This process coincided with the gradual delegitimization of the political world, which meant that justice was not to be found in the official courts. Meanwhile, conquests manufactured many new Muslims who were unfamiliar with the practices that had been followed by the Prophet and his companions. New questions were being asked and new situations were being faced at the same time as the congregation lost its moral cohesion and the political world lost its sacred character. Simply recounting traditions was not enough to retain unity. A class of persons who could respond to these questions and act as decision-makers was required for the evermore diffuse Muslim community. Throughout the region, pious individuals spontaneously began to devote themselves to study of the lore of Islam with a view to using their learning for active guidance of their fellows: these were the legalists (*faqih*) or men of law (*fiqh*).

At first, the faqih overlapped almost completely with the ahl al-hadith. Like the hadith scholars, early legalists had no formal organization, but were available for consultation in their homes or in the mosque, either gratis or for a fee. They soon developed informal study circles to debate questions of doctrine and law with others of similar interests, and, like the hadith scholars, instructed novices who sought them out and paid for the privilege of studying in their circle. There were no schools, no "degrees", no authentication of anyone's credentials. The learned were those accepted as such by their local communities and by the wider community of scholars; acceptance measured by the number of students any faqih had, by the amount they were called upon for consultation, and by the respect they were proffered by the public and by their peers.

The overlap in the social positions of faqih and hadith scholar was matched by the content of their learning, since both were devoted to the study of traditions, along with the necessary reading of the Quran and the sunna. The faqih needed this knowledge to reach decisions in accord with sharia, holy law, which is, in principle, supposed to encompass all human activity. But unlike the hadith scholars, the lawyers soon found they had to develop regulations for matters left unclear by scripture, such as the exact nature of a property transfer. They also had to clarify the weight of any particular rule: was a practice obligatory, merely recommended, or neutral; if obligatory, should failure be punished by men, or left to the discretion of Allah?

Because he wished to apply the knowledge gained from his studies of tradition, the faqih could not just memorize and repeat as did the hadith reciter; rather, he had to understand and implement, always returning to a study of the scripture for inspiration, rather than relying on the opinions of others. "In fact," as George Makdisi writes, the lawyer "must not follow even his own opinion on the same or a similar question; rather he must arrive at a fresh opinion resulting from a fresh effort of research, a fresh effort of *ijtihad*."[12] Ijtihad literally means exertion to the uttermost limit – here it signified a principled effort of personal interpretation to grasp the implications and potentials of the holy texts.

In this early period of individual exertion and interpretation, freedom of religious scholarship – which was the same as legal scholarship – was extraordinarily well developed; as Goldziher remarks, "in the history of Islamic theology a consciousness of being obliged to no one and answerable to no one is often glaringly apparent."[13] This freedom was possible because the absolute authority of the Quran was accepted by all the debaters, as was the fallibility of human reason. Scholars could disagree vehemently with one another while never losing their sense of fundamental concord on first principles. Strict rules of honor governed this scholarly discourse, and writers of opinion were scrupulous in distinguishing their own judgments from those of others; they carefully reported rival arguments, and indicated the degree to which their views and those of their opponents were accepted or rejected by the scholarly community at large. Argumentation was stimulated by the belief that silence indicated assent. These debates did not necessarily end in victory or defeat. As Brinkley Messick writes, "when, as was often the case, positions were taken but the truth of a matter remained uncertain, this could be represented in manuals and other works by the appended formula 'and God knows best'."[14] Conflicting opinions promulgated by reputable authorities were accepted as equally valid for the faithful.

A comparison with the strictly conformist ahl al-hadith is instructive. The hadith reporters gained prestige insofar as they could serve as embodied vehicles for tradition, and lost their authority to a more rational compilation of texts and to the attenuation of their charisma by time and distance. The legalists, in contrast, gained authority by their personal abilities as intellectual interpreters of the Word. The highly competitive environment of professional scholarship pressed them toward demonstrating their grasp of speculative minutiae and their skill in arcane argumentation; this sometimes alienated them from the real moral concerns of the community at large.

From the point of view of the beleaguered hadith scholars, the jurists'

Plate 10.1   A man reciting the entire Quran from memory.
Such experts are paid to recite during ceremonial occasions.

use of reason and analogy to fill in lacunae or resolve apparent contradictions in the holy texts was dangerous anathema. Traditionalists were out-
raged by what they saw as the arbitrary and sometimes trivial manner in
which their sacred reports were used by lawyers whose methods smacked
of sacrilege. In the view of the hadith reciters life ought to be wholly
regulated by simple knowledge of the Book and the sanctified deeds and
words of the Prophet and his companions. There was no room for interpretation and individual decision-making; there was the Word, sunna,
and tradition, and anything else was frivolity at best, idolatry at worst.

   This rancorous dispute threatened the cohesion of Islam but was resolved by the compromise proposed by al-Shafi (d. 820). He argued that
ijma, the agreement of knowledgeable scholars, is needed to decide the
manner in which ambiguities should be understood. In practice, what
this meant was that in the absence of any formal organization to decide
on consensus through deliberation and vote, and lacking an ecclesiastical

hierarchy, the Muslim community itself determined the proper way to interpret scripture and tradition over a period of generations through its approval or disapproval of the findings of scholar/jurists. Ideally speaking this consensus is never final, since an authoritative dissent can, in principle, cause a reopening of any debate if that dissent manages to gain public endorsement and scholarly sanction.

Shafi's intervention allowed Islam to retain its egalitarian and populist character while simultaneously expert legal knowledge was accepted as the arbiter of tradition. Continuity through collective consensus still permitted the theoretical possibility for new ijtihad – a possibility that continues to be the source of intense discussion among contemporary Muslims. In effect, his compromise established the legal scholar as the person responsible for ascertaining the significance and use of religious knowledge. At the same time, the freedom of the scholar to interpret was limited by the necessity of gaining popular approval for any doctrine and by the self-imposed limitation of knowledge to the field of the Quran and the traditions. As a result of Shafi's reforms, the tumult of legalist ideas and arguments did not lead to chaos, as the hadith reciters feared, but was soon rationalized into legal schools and educational institutions which displaced the diffuse and disorganized hadith scholars as independent nodes of legitimate religious authority.

Shafi's reforms and Ibn Hanbal's rigorous affirmation of Muslim traditions served as the inspirational foundations for the formation of two of the named schools of Islamic jurisprudence, or *madhhab* (literally a "chosen way"). In the early days of Islam, there had been hundreds of such schools, each gathered around jurisconsults who held their own personal interpretations of the texts and traditions. But just as hadith scholarship was rationalized in response to the dangerous diffusion of Islam, the legal schools were also consolidated. By 1075 the Sunni madhhabs had diminished to four, which, in imitation of the genealogical chain mode of establishing pedigree, were now named after their supposed founders: al-Shafi, Ibn-Hanbal, Malik b. Anas, and Abu-Hanifah.

At first, these schools were popularly taken up as new identifying emblems for warring factions, and there were violent struggles between the local representatives of madhhabs and their adherents for political as well as ideological domination.[15] However, by the twelfth century, it was clear that none of the schools would ever be able to dominate the others, and a wary truce was called. Henceforth, each school was to be considered equally accurate, since "only God knows" the truth. Though ideally one could choose any school to follow, most Muslims followed the madhhab prevalent in their area. The central Middle East was Hanafi or Shafi, the Malikites prevailed in North Africa, while the Hanbali school remained fairly small, but was intellectually influential.

At this point in time, many Muslims (though not the Hanbali school) agreed that a general consensus of the community had been reached as to the basis of the law, and jurists ought to respect the rules of the madhhab they had chosen to follow. No new madhhabs were to be formed, since the law had solidified – it was "clothed with authority" (*taqlid*). This meant that independent interpretation by juriconsults was supposed to cease; law had become codified and rational, technical expertise and standardized training had replaced ethical imagination and personalized interpretation by ijtihad. Closure was made even more rigorous in the wake of the Mongol invasions, when the shattered community sought to reintegrate itself by extending taqlid through the compilation of standardized texts within each school.

Yet, the continued absence of any central organization enforcing rules, any civil law code, or any standard procedure for appeal to a higher court (indeed, without any hierarchy of courts whatsoever) meant that the jurisconsult still had considerable freedom of interpretation, though he always had to justify his findings by reference to existing law. Still, like judges administering English common law, the Muslim *mufti* (one who issues *fatwa*, legal opinions) had a vast repertoire of case manuals available to him for consultation, as well as a huge range of often ambivalent or even contradictory traditions to confer, giving him a significant range of choice in his decisions. He also could make independent findings in cases not covered by Islamic law. These factors left very large areas open for a jurist's free decisions.

The mufti's interpretive independence was further increased by the fact that he was not employed by the state, answered to no one save himself, and did not have the power to enforce his findings, which the disputants could accept or reject as they pleased. If they did not like one judge's decision, they could always try another, The mufti's job was only to look at the facts and to make a moral finding according to his best extrapolation of the way scripture, hadith, sunna, case law, and common sense could be applied to this particular case, regardless of who was involved. In principle, he ought not even know who was on which side, so that he could treat all claimants equally.

This egalitarian ideal was taken to extraordinary lengths. According to one commentator, disputants, regardless of wealth or rank, should be seated together in a row before the judge, addressed by him in the same manner and given equal opportunity to speak and be heard. The judge should even look at both plaintiff and defendant for the same amount of time and in the same way while they speak. Another commentator remarks that the mufti should treat the opposing parties as equivalent even in matters such as standing up (or not) when each disputant enters, and in the manner of returning their greetings.[16]

In return for his impartial dispensation of equity and justice, the judge was treated with respect by those who appeared before him. Kissing of the judge's hand and honorifics of address were indications of his high position. But it was the mufti's personal reputation for fairness, learning and integrity, not his place in a government bureaucracy, that made him sought out by his fellows. His distance from the state was indicated by the fact that he often held court in his own home, outside his door, adjudicating for whomever came to see him, regardless of their status. Strong and weak alike had access to the court, and there were no guards or officers to keep them distant, except for a scribe whom the mufti paid out of his own pocket.

The Education of the Scholarly Elite

If the multi did not hold authority among the people by virtue of his association with the state, neither could he hope to impress others by his sheer force of personality or claim to be a judge because his father had been one; his position had to be earned, and this could be done in only one way: studying the law. Originally, this had been an informal manner. Jurisconsults, like the ahl al-hadith, had learned law at the homes of their teachers. But by the eleventh century the college of law (*madrasa*) had become commonplace.[17] These institutions were endowed through the private donation (waqf) of a pious wealthy merchant or a state official seeking to propagate his own particular legal faction and expiate the crimes he had committed in pursuit of power. Each college was run by one permanently tenured professor of law who taught students the rules of his madhhab, administered the school funds, and appointed subordinate teachers.   قاضي

Befitting the Middle Eastern ethos, the madrasa education was, as Makdisi comments, "private, individualistic, and personalist."[18] The madrasas were originally independent organizations funded by private donations made by wealthy individuals of their own free will, and were quite beyond the power of government. They had no standardized examinations or bureaucratic hierarchies for certification. Rather, a "personal license was given by the individual professor of law to the candidate after the satisfactory defense of a thesis, or theses, in a formal disputation. In issuing this license the professor acted completely on his own personal authority. He could not be forced to grant it by any other authority, be it the central power, or even a religious body."[19]

The professor could also teach by any method he might choose, select any student (*talib*) who applied to him according to any criteria, and decide when, where, and if the student was ready to gain his license. He could designate his own successor, and could even decide to become a scholar of a different madhhab. The student also had considerable personal leeway. He could decide to study with any professor, follow any madhhab; he could change his course of study, pursue subjects in any order, study any number of subjects, and so on. His only obligation was to master the central legal doctrine of his chosen school.[20]

In other words, as in the legal "system", within the education "system" there was no formal organization, no bureaucratic hierarchy, no standard certification or state intervention. Seniority of professors was determined by peer recognition and by the admiration of the general public (one student remarks that the teachers most sought after were those who "had God's blessings in the religious sciences and feared God the most, those who were older and more powerful and who always had their hands kissed in the street").[21]

As was the case for the transmitters of tradition, the prestige of the jurist did not derive from his academic prowess alone. Alongside a deep knowledge of the holy texts, scholars were also expected to demonstrate purity of character. For the hadith reciter this did not involve much: he merely had to be a person of good repute, conforming to the standards of his community. Any status he had came from the simple act of continuous recitation, which automatically put him close to Muhammad and the original community.

Where the early traditionalists were content with emptying themselves to serve as the passive vehicle of the Word, the jurists had a different vocation. They saw themselves as actively interpreting and implementing holy law in the immoral world. This required a rigorous ethical training which would give the faqih insight into the inner meaning of the text and permit him to stake a claim to personal moral superiority over ordinary men. To accomplish this end required an education that would not only give the student an intellectual grasp of a particular madhhab but also completely transform his character, so that he could interpret the law in a way that was in tune with the higher goals of the religion, and not to further his personal interest.

Selflessness was to be achieved by complete submission to a master who was expected to wield strict discipline over his charges. As Dale Eickelman observes, "when a father handed his son over to a faqih, he did so with the formulaic phrase that the child could be beaten."[22] Violence was just one aspect of a juridical training aimed at breaking the arrogant spirit of the talib. All expression of personality was also prohibited, so that the typically self-assertive boy soon learned proper modesty and silence. As one ex-student recounts: "Going to Quranic school for me, and for all children, was like being taken to the slaughterhouse."[23]

After primary education, the star pupils were sent away to madrasas to become professional faqih. There they lived among an all-male group of peers who all circulated in the narrow orbit of dormitory, mosque, and school. The students were liminal figures, associated with transition and death. It is significant that one of their primary outings was to serve as reciters at funerals and that, in Yemen at least, they were known as *muhajirin*, those who have separated off and dissociated themselves – the same term used for those who accompanied Muhammad in his journey to Medina.[24]

Teaching in the advanced schools generally followed a highly formalized format of question and answer, including commentary and discussion, though the degree to which such discussion was permitted varied from place to place. Most time was spent in memorizing dictated texts and copying the legal manuals which the student was later to use as his standard references – discussion of problems of interpretation was mainly confined to study circles of peers. The educational sequence was from rote repetition to memorization, to writing and finally, for the very best students, to textual analysis and dialectical understanding of specific legal texts, as transmitted through a professor who served as a human link to the original author.

Legal scholars, like hadith reciters, were careful to record exactly from whom they had learned and exactly what texts they had absorbed, since both the personal bond with their instructor and the memorization of textual material were required to verify their moral genealogy and scope of their credentials as jurists and teachers. Because of his disciplined subordination to his masters and to the holy text, the scholar was believed by the populace, and by himself, to have become a conduit for sacred power. He deserved the respect of the layman not simply for his learning, but for his transformed soul, which became, through training, purified, detached from ordinary life and dedicated to the service of the sacred community.

In its ideal form, the traditional Muslim legal/religious educational system was an avenue for upward mobility that ran parallel to and served as a critical commentary upon the political route to authority. In both instances, any Muslim man of sound mind and capacity could, theoretically speaking, succeed, but the modes of achieving authority implied polar differences in personality. A warrior gained his power through the virile *active expression* of his own inner and personal capacities revealed in competition with his co-equals; he submitted to no one, but flaunted his independence and struggled to achieve his personal desires in the world of men. In contrast, the religious acolyte – both hadith reciter and jurist – gained the status of scholar through *passive submission* to a divine force that used him as a vessel and located him within a sacred hierarchy. For the ahl al-hadith, this was achieved by emptying oneself to serve as the transmitter of accurate traditions, while the jurist learned the necessary rigorous suppression of the ego by subordinating himself to his master and to the text in the monklike environment of the madrasa.

Resistance to the Authority of the Learned

Although the learned were held in esteem, their claim to moral authority has never been completely accepted by the egalitarian Muslim masses. Suspicion of the faqih has been metaphorically expressed in popular discourse through a comparison with secular leadership. Sultans and princes are viewed as frankly self-interested individuals reliant on their personal abilities in their eternal struggle to gain and hold power. Their values are the values of manly warriors: bravery, generosity, honor, autonomy, power. Religious figures present themselves as the opposite, that is, as servants of God emptied of personal ambition. But they can then be accused of being the converse of the warrior in other respects as well: effeminate, cowardly, miserly and dishonorable – all of which remain popular stereotypes of the learned among the lay population. The ulema have also often been denounced as hypocrites, disguising their worldly greed and ambition behind their whiskers, turbans, and self-righteous rhetoric. This accusation gains credibility through comparison with the secular leader, whose ability to command is transparently real and immediate, derived from his strength and personal qualities, which cannot be faked, while a pretender to piety is not easily found out. As the Pukhtun say: "Any fool can grow a beard." داير

Popular suspicion of the ulema was increased as many jurists became experts in "permissions" (hiyal) in classical case law that allowed their clients to evade the literal conditions of scripture. As one famous lawyer wrote: "Knowledge means that you are able to grant a permission and base it on the authority of a reliable traditionalist. Anyone can find a restriction easily enough."[25] Powerful and prestigious legal experts also began to socialize and intermarry with the local mercantile and ruling warrior elite. As scholars became influential in the secular world, their community slowly lost its openness, so that eventually only elite families of the learned had the connections and wherewithal to pursue the education required for appointment to lucrative judicial posts. In the power vacuum left after the fall of the Abbasids, some of these elite scholarly families even assumed ephemeral positions of local political authority in the now de-centralized and crumbling eastern empire.[26] The professionalization, wealth, and power of this increasingly closed elite made it progressively more difficult for jurists to present themselves to the layman as disinterested and trustworthy mediators and judges.

The changes in the social position of the jurists coincided with their gradual absorption into the state. As Makdisi writes: "The central power's insidious encroachments on the prerogatives of the Muslim religious intellectual were relentless. From the qadiship, to the professorship of legal studies, and the professorship of legal opinions, it proceeded to the college; so that, under the Ottoman Empire, the Muslim intellectual's institutional projections fell within the central power's all-encompassing orbit."[27]

Absorption of the ulema began with the innovations made in the madrasa system by the powerful Seljuk wazir, Nizam al-Mulk, who in 1067 endowed his own school, the famous Nizamiyya, in the capital of Baghdad. Instead of turning the school over to the control of one permanently appointed independent professor, as had been the custom, Nizam kept administrative control of the school for himself, hiring and firing professors at will. Nizam also established scholarships for students and payment for subordinate teaching faculty. At one stroke, these changes undermined the autonomy of the faculty and enticed pupils and scholars into the new centrally controlled system. By the thirteenth century, the faculty and students of madrasas everywhere in the Middle East were largely dependent on the state.

Coincidental with greater government intervention in education was the creation of official posts for the state-trained ulema. Already by the eleventh century, the mufti, who gave an independent opinion that had no official force, and who was paid by the persons who consulted him or by pious endowment, was beginning to be superseded by the qadi, a government-employed judge whose services were both free and enforceable. A comparison between the two is indicative: where the mufti attracted his clients by his demonstrated moral qualities and intellectual ability, a qadi could be both immoral and ignorant, since his position was granted by the state, not the public; both practitioners used sacred law, but the mufti took the case as a departure for his interpretation of doctrine, while the qadi's judgment was based on testimony, evidence, oaths and other practical information, with doctrine used as a point of reference; the mufti presided informally at home, in the madrasa, or in the mosque, while the qadi was to be found in the official government court, surrounded by guards and other trappings of state power and pomp.

The co-option of the scholar into the state was not easy; there was considerable opposition from both the learned and from the masses, who cited proverbs such as "Of three judges, two are in Hell" and "He who undertakes the judgeship slits his own throat without a knife."[28] Resistance took many forms – an eighth-century manuscript describes the response of one of the local learned whom the military governor wished to appoint as judge. "He went into the bathhouse and used a depilatory and shaved his head ... he dressed himself in his shroud and put on embalming ointments ... Then fell to his knees in front of Husain (the governor) and said: 'By God of which there is no other God than He, I shall never govern for you or for anybody else. You may do whatever you want.'" The governor, impressed, freed him from his appointment.[29] Those of the learned who did accept state positions were often ashamed to admit it: an eleventh-century Shafi jurist only took the post of official qadi with the proviso that he would not be obliged to march in public government processions or given a government salary.[30]

Nor has resistance ceased today. For example, the paramount institution of higher learning in the Middle East, the University of al-Azhar in Cairo (founded by the Fatimids in 970, it is the oldest University in the world), was traditionally the accepted training ground for Egyptian mullahs and teachers. It was integrated into the state by Muhammad Ali in the nineteenth century, when he confiscated all university waqf and turned the professors into government employees, giving the rector the rank of prime minister and an enormous salary. The process was completed in 1961, when the Azhar became a state University offering a secular education alongside the religious studies that had made it famous.

As the University came under state authority, it lost much of its prestige among the populace. In response to suspicions about the moral quality of the modern graduates, local people opened their own informal schools in their mosques to educate themselves in the religious fundamentals. To combat the burgeoning growth of these local non-governmental religious centers, the Egyptian state tried to place them under its direct authority. The largest mosques were annexed by the state and their imams were converted into government appointees. However, shortages in the number of approved preachers and lack of funds to support such intensive local level intervention meant that only about 16 percent of the mosques could actually be controlled by the state, leaving the vast majority at least partially free of state control. Meanwhile, a multitude of popular, egalitarian and informal "voluntary benevolent associations" spontaneously sprang up completely outside both mosque and government control, as self-taught religious leaders gathered congregations around them to discuss and act upon ethical and social issues.[31]

Similar popular movements of resistance to the power of the state over education and law occur to a greater or lesser degree everywhere in the Middle East, since the very illegitimacy of the state pollutes the credentials of the religious teachers and lawyers who consent to work for it. In response, laymen and reformers have always attempted to find a connection to Islam through other, untainted channels, and so develop their own leaders and teachers, who inevitably call for more egalitarian and equitable implementation of the law.[32] Except in Iran, popular distrust of the official ulema is so great today that those offering an "Islamist" critique of the state are autodidacts consciously distancing themselves from the class of the traditionally religiously educated, who are tainted by their graduation from state schools.[33] This reaction is not new – though it has recently taken a radical form in response to the vastly enhanced power of the modern state over education; rather, it is a reflection of ancient cultural suspicions of all forms of authority.[34]

Even the ulema who are uncorrupted by participation in the government are not immune from the cynicism of the people. Distaste for the influence of both the learned and the state has always been expressed through popular avoidance of the government courts as well as the informal courts of the muftis. Local people often preferred instead to maintain traditional mediation processes overseen by tribal and village elders, notables, and friends – though the neighborhood ulema may indeed have some part to play as wise and respected men, giving their opinions alongside others.

This type of egalitarian and informal mediation does not rely on the absolutes of holy texts or bureaucratic regulations to decide right and wrong, but hinges on the go-between's personal knowledge of the disputants, long discussions with neighbors and friends, and the slow negotiation of compromise between co-equal opponents. Instead of taking place at the home of the faqih, or in a court or mosque, proceedings often transpire in the contending parties' residences. Rather than confrontation, there is avoidance, as the mediators try to persuade the antagonists to accept a face-saving settlement that will preserve everyone's honor and avoid interference from outside authorities while maintaining the peace and unity of the community. In place of textual references and legal codes, tribal custom is invoked to convince adversaries to reach an understanding.

However, this traditional form of pragmatic negotiation among co-equals does not offer the transcendental appeal that the faithful hope will permanently cement their community together. Rather the intransigence and jealousy of local rivals can lead to destructive feud and bloodshed despite the best efforts of mediators. As we have seen, the ulema have attempted to overcome such tensions and rekindle spiritual unity among Muslims by recalling and interpreting the words of the holy texts. But the people suspect the learned of hypocritically hiding their own worldly ambitions behind a facade of sactimoniousness and scholarship. Their sacred status has suffered also from the attenuation of hadith reciters' connection with the Prophet, the bureaucratic depersonalization of legal knowledge, and the gradual co-option of jurists into the delegitimized state. Cynicism about the moral integrity of the learned and a desire for a greater sense of spiritual communion has left the door open for the evolution of other more emotional and individualized forms of religious authority. These are the topics of the next chapters.

11

The Partisans of Ali

The Charisma of Ali

The most stable and influential alternative to the increasingly bureau-cratinized Sunni mainstream was that offered by the Shi'ites, the "parti-sans" of Ali,[1] who began as a protest by early Arab Muslims against what they saw as immoral political authority exercised contrary to the true interests of the umma. Today, one can find at least some Shi'ite practitioners almost everywhere in the Middle East: Shi'ites constitute almost the total population of Iran, 55 percent of the population of Iraq, 70 percent of Bahrain, and one-third of Lebanon. It is estimated that Shi'ites constitute perhaps 11 percent of all Muslims, making them the largest non-Sunni sect by far.

In most senses, Shi'ites are indistinguishable from their Sunni broth-ers; like them, they too have a body of traditions which supplement the Quran; they too follow the same essential practices of the recitation of the faith, prayer, fasting, alms, and pilgrimage. In terms of law, the major differences lie in rules for inheritance. Some Shi'ites, unlike Sunni Muslims, allow a woman to inherit all her father's possessions if she has no brothers. Some also permit *muta*, a temporary marriage for pleasure, wherein a woman freely contracts her sexual services over a certain period of time for a negotiated fee.[2] However, neither of these legal permissions have much to do with the essential distinctions be-tween the Sunni and Shi'a faiths.

Ritual discrepancies are more indicative. The Shi'ite call to prayer adds the phrase "I attest that Ali is the *wali* (friend) of God," while the pilgrimage to Mecca is supplemented among Shi'ites by lesser pilgrim-ages to the tombs of the great religious leaders of their past (the Imams). Among the most important are at Najaf, Karbala, Samarra, Mashad, Kazemeyn, and Qum. At these "sacred thresholds" Shi'ites perform some of the same sorts of rites that are performed at Mecca, circumambulating the holy shrine, reading prayers, gaining grace from the presence of the spirit of the entombed Imam.

Plate 11.1 The Persian mosque in Damascus, Syria.

These practices, which focus on the sanctity of Ali and his descendants, are symbolic expressions of the distinctive Shi'ite premise of a charismatic lineage of redemptive figures, who even in death could provide a personal gateway to the divine for the faithful. The logic of the Shi'ite belief is simple. In the Prophet's lifetime, he was the necessary Guide for men to follow. The question was: what shall men do after the Prophet's death? Like the kharijites, the Shi'ites opposed the pragmatic Sunni acceptance of the gradual delegitimization of authority after Muhammad's demise. Unlike the kharijites, they insisted that the righteous ruler cannot be selected by and from the Muslim community at large, which consists of fallible human beings who will necessarily make mistakes in their choices. Nor can ordinary men be expected to understand and implement all the commands of the Book and the traditions without someone to show them the way.

According to the Shi'ites, mankind required what Louis Massignon called an "apodictic proof" (in Persian *hojjat* – an argument beyond contradiction) to draw humanity toward God. Muhammad's charisma served this purpose while he was enunciating Allah's message to humanity. In the absence of such an incontrovertible beacon, men would soon forget the truth Muhammad had shown them and go astray from the straight path of Islam. Human frailty was graphically proven by the wars that erupted after the Prophet's death and the corruption of the Caliphate. Obviously, even after the advent of Muhammad, humans required a heaven-sent leader to shepherd them along the way to salvation, and a just God would not ignore human requirements. Ergo, a living Guide must exist whose self-evident charisma would draw human beings toward righteousness.

The question then was: "Who could this indispensable leader be?" Most agreed that he must necessarily be a member of the lineage of the Prophet, arguing from the cultural belief in the virtue of noble blood. Since Muhammad had no sons of his own, the best lineal candidate was Ali, the son of Abu Talib, Muhammad's father's elder brother and Muhammad's guardian; Ali had married Muhammad's eldest daughter, Fatima, and was his foster brother as well, since he had been raised alongside Muhammad as a child. Finally, Ali had been one of Muhammad's first and most loyal converts and was a stalwart fighter for the faith. Because of this close connection, all Muslims still award the progeny of Ali's son Hasan the noble title of sharif, while those of his second son Husain are honored as *sayyid*. Sunnis also believe that some (not all) of these descendants may manifest special spiritual qualities, and deserve the alms and respect of the faithful.

But Shi'ites went far beyond this. For them, Ali had superhuman characteristics that made him charismatically compelling. A gnostic Shi'ite text quotes Ali announcing: "I am the Sign of the All-Powerful, I am the First and the Last. I am the Manifest and the Hidden. I am the Face of God. I am the hand of God. I am the Side of God...I am he who keeps the secret of God's messenger."[3] Shi'ites believe Ali's unique charismatic power was passed down to one of his descendants each generation, giving every age a hereditary Imam whose very substance is sublime. As Massignon writes, this celestial individual "is divinized *a priori*. He need not examine his own heart, and his intentions must not be questioned. Everything his tongue utters is sacred...The inspired one, in his very whims, is revered as the personal mask through which the incomprehensible arbitrariness of the Creator is shown."[4]

According to Shi'ites, Ali's sacred status as the direct inheritor of the Prophet's mantle and genitor of the line of Imams was proclaimed by

Muhammad himself when he asked a crowd of Muslims near Medina to recognize his son-in-law as "supreme authority."[5] They also cite as proof the gathering of Ali and Fatima, along with their sons Hasan and Husain, under the Prophet's mantle as hostages of his sincerity in a crucial public ordeal he undertook against the Christian community in 632. By acting as the Prophet's juridical substitutes on this occasion they were affirmed to be his closest blood kin. For most Muslims, this simply meant they were recognized as co-responsible with him, according to the tribal custom of shared culpability for blood debt among patrilineal relatives. But Ali's supporters take the cloaking to signify that "the five" participated in Muhammad's initiation into the mysteries of prophethood. They became the supernatural "holy family" of Islam, imbued with special mystical powers as the receptacles of secret knowledge (nass) that had to be kept from the ears of the ordinary persons, who, because of their benighted characters, would use it for destructive purposes.[6]

The great claims made for the sacredness of Ali and his descendants answered the disturbing question of how charismatic authority could be maintained after the death of the Prophet. As noted in Chapter 7, submission to the absolute command of Ali and his family also had the paradoxical effect of reaffirming the essential equivalence of all believers, regardless of their tribal affiliation, their closeness to the Prophet, their history of participation in battle, or their political power and wealth. Only the spiritual authority of the Imam was to be considered worthy of honor: all other claims to superiority were void. Ali himself established this principle by dividing booty equally among all his supporters after his victory at the Battle of the Camel, giving no preference to old Muslims over new converts, or to Arabs over Persians.[7] Because of their principled opposition to every form of privilege aside from rule by their own sacred Imams, the Alid cause has always appealed to the disenfranchised, who have rallied to the Shi'ite battle cry of equality of all achieved through submission to the embodied One.

The Two Faces of Shi'ism

Unhappily for them, the spirited cry of Ali's partisans rarely led to victory. Ali himself was assassinated at a relatively young age by the poisoned sword of a kharijite rebel. As we saw in chapter 6, Ali's sons, the supposed inheritors of his charisma and of the Caliphate, did not accede to his position, which was taken instead by Ali's old rival Muawiya, who founded the Umayyad dynasty. Instead of contesting the throne, Ali's immediate inheritor, Hasan, chose to retire to Medina where he practiced contemplation and spiritual discipline. At Hasan's death, his younger brother Husain, encouraged by his allies from the garrison town of Kufa, did rise in rebellion against Muawiya's son Yazid. But Husain's Kufan allies cravenly abandoned him when the Umayyad army attacked. Cut off by the enemy in the waterless desert, he and his seventy-two companions were pitilessly slaughtered at the battle of Karbala in 680. The histories of these two brothers – the quietist mystic and the tragic rebel – have entered deeply into Shi'ite theology as alternative exemplary models for the faithful to emulate.

The source of the appeal of Hasan's mysticism to Shi'ites is clear enough. Shi'ite faith in their special tie with Allah through devotion to the persons of the charismatic Imams would seem to place them at the center of the universe; yet simultaneously they have suffered the realities of marginalization and oppression. In self-defense, Shi'ites from the time of Hasan have tried to reconcile their high spiritual status with their secular defeats. They did this by asserting that outward appearances (zahir) were false. True reality could be discovered only through the mystical inner knowledge (batin) that the spiritually initiated could perceive behind the mask of materiality. It was argued that in this true inner world human beings were ranked according to the degree of their capacity to experience the love of Allah and the Imams who represent Him – other forms of distinction were a snare and delusion. Therefore, even if the people of Ali do not rule the material world, they do rule the world that is worth ruling – the world of the unseen.

To sustain this position, Shi'ite mystics developed complex theories about the acquisition of spiritual rank, which descended through three different types of relationship: blood kinship with Ali and his family, spiritual initiation, and transmission of secret knowledge (nass). Esoteric knowledge was defended by taqiyya, dissimulation, which was first employed by kharijites to avoid persecution. Later, this practical self-protective device was taken over by the Shi'ite community where it became a discipline of the arcane with a value in itself. According to this discipline, those who know the hidden truth must not divulge it to the unworthy, just as Muhammad did not give nass to any but Ali. To deserve initiation, the seeker had to look beneath appearances and search out an enlightened master who could give his disciples spiritual illumination, which always flowed from above. Sociologists will recognize this as a pattern to be found regularly in secret organizations, where the actual content of the secret is less important than the way its possession unites those who share it into an oppositional community, internally ranked by virtue of the degree of initiation into the inner mysteries.[8]

To maintain this secretive hierarchical world, the experience of initiation could only be expressed in recondite and metaphorical language that excluded all but the few. For instance, a psychology of the states of mind corresponding to different levels of enlightenment was poetically rendered in terms of an alchemical transubstantiation of the soul on its journey from exile in the dark materiality of the west to reunion with God in the light of the east. To facilitate this journey, archetypical forms (*barzakh*) appear in "epiphanic places" such as mirrors or still waters, or in human dreams and fantasies. In these heightened visionary moments when "spirits are corporealized and bodies spiritualized," seekers felt the certitude of mystical communion, which experientially verified their elevated plane of being.[9]

Shi'ite mysticism was marked as well by the scandalous killing of Husain, which was the great turning point in Shi'ite history – the equivalent to Christ's crucifixion for Christians – but in this instance, the believers themselves connived in the death of their savior by their cowardly refusal to rally to him. Shi'ites have ever since sought to redeem their complicity in the political-religious murder of Husain by shedding tears for the martyrs and imitating their suffering during the great holiday of the Shi'ites, *Muharram*, which is a public reenactment of Karbala and a festival of open weeping and bloody self-laceration.

Weeping and whipping oneself, however, is not done only in sorrow, but is also an act of mystical identification; by crying in sympathy and torturing themselves the participants become one with the martyrs, who sit close to God. Like Husain, ordinary devotees too must heroically suffer unjust oppression and cruelty in order to redeem the benighted and corrupt community that had rejected them. In this theodicy of sacrifice martyrdom is conceptualized as Allah's test of His people, who have been given a special task of purifying Islam by their patient acquiescence, much as Ali patiently awaited his eventual nomination as Caliph despite the unfair machinations of his rivals. As the party of Ali agonize and lament over the death of Husain and the other martyrs for the holy cause,[10] they believe their humiliation and grief helps bring the eventual reign of justice – God would not abandon his favored ones.

When the apocalypse comes, it will be ushered in by the arrival of the mahdi, the last Imam, who will return to vindicate the authentic believers in the Final Days, when the wicked will be humbled and the faithful will be exalted. The concept of the redeemer is not Quranic, but was generated out of Christian apocalyptic beliefs and Muslim legend after the assassination of Ali; it developed into an elaborate scheme during the Abbasid Caliphate, when Alid hopes were raised, then dashed.[11] According to this legend, the redeemer will appear portended by the fragmentation of the faith, the advent of false Messiahs, civil war, earthquakes, the rising of the sun in the west, and the resurrection of Christ. Those who had been faithful will be awakened from the dead, as will the evil ones, there will be an apocalyptic struggle, and rewards and punishments will be awarded here on earth, before eternal justice is meted out after death.

In this belief system, the corrupt social world of the day is temporary and precarious, to be destroyed by the arrival of the savior who will deliver those who have steadfastly upheld their faith. Shi'ite believers therefore had to be on the alert for mundane events that might herald his arrival, and be ready to act to hasten the coming of the final Imam, the condemnation of the unjust, and the end of time. Periods of chaos, instability, and blatantly anti-Islamic governments were especially likely to be harbingers of the last moments, and could excite fervid Shi'ite hopes for redemption. Behind Shi'ite quietism then lurks the constant potential for a radical millenarian movement, since a new Husain might appear at any moment – and this time the faithful must not fail to support him.

This ambivalence is evident in the symbolism of Muharram, where self-torture, tears, and martyrdom are characteristically mixed with feasting, drinking of sweets, exuberant music, and other expressions of joy.[12] The parade of self-lacerating devotees marching slowly in unison, whipping themselves or gashing their foreheads, is an unforgettable spectacle that not only demonstrates a communal capacity for self-sacrifice in empathy with past martyrdoms, but also shows the astonishing discipline, unity and power of the devotees. Even more impressive are those men who carry huge decorated metal frameworks on their shoulders, displaying superhuman and death-defying control as they spin with their burdens in front of the admiring crowd. These performances are meant to portray the suffering and endurance of the Shi'ites, but they also express the believers' strength and readiness to redeem the cowardice of their forefathers and fight without flinching when the time of reparation has come.

The two faces of Muharram reflect the two aspects of Shi'ism. One face is quietistic and supplicating, turned away from the mundane and toward the spiritual, remembering the anguish of martyrdom while seeking loving communion with the martyrs in the hope of gaining their mystical intercession in the future. Inferiority and suffering today is accepted as payment for salvation tomorrow. The other is activist, ready to rise in order to bring the Final Days into being and to punish those who have caused unjust suffering and denied Shi'ites the equity promised by the Quran. It is the dialectic between the mystical and activist relationships to oppression and injustice that drives the historical passage of Shi'ite culture.[13]

Shi'ite History: Acquiescence and Rebellion

After Husain's disastrous defeat his direct offspring remained prudently silent. The spirit of rebellion was kept alive by proto-Shi'ite malcontents who argued that the Imamate was not automatically granted by primogeniture, but could leave the immediate line through transmission of nass.[14] Some of these rebels believed nass had been given to a son of Ali and al-Hanafiyya (a woman of the Hanaf tribe) whom he had married after the death of Fatima. This man, Muhammad al-Hanafiyya, was proclaimed the redeemer by the adventurer al-Mukhtar, who rallied his supporters with the cry of "helping the family of the Prophet and revenging their blood."[15] Mukhtar's rebellion was put down with difficulty in 687, but later the Abbasids claimed to have received nass from Muhammad al-Hanafiyya's son, and used this as religious legitimation of their rule.

Most of the supporters of Ali did not accept Abbasid legitimacy, and continued to look to the children of Fatima for their redeemer. However, there was a division among Ali's partisans concerning which of his descendants was properly qualified for the Imamate. Most recognized Muhammad al-Baqir as the fifth Imam, but some favored his half-brother Zayd, the son of a slave woman. This group, the Zaydis, broke with the rest of the Shi'ite community in proclaiming that the Imam need not be of Fatimid lineage, but could be any descendant of Ali who displayed extraordinary political, academic, and spiritual abilities. Recognized as the most moderate of the Shi'i by the Sunni mainstream, the Zaydi came close to the kharijites in their emphasis on demonstrated capacity. Although they were the first Shi'ites to gain an independent state for themselves, their experiment did not spread very far; they were only able to achieve lasting authority within Tabiristan and Northern Yemen.

A more fateful split occurred after the death of the sixth Imam of the main line of Shi'ites, Jafar al-Sadiq (d. 765), a great mystic and alchemist who also was the founder of the Shi'ite school of law. When Jafar died some Shi'ites claimed he had passed on nass to his son Ismail, who had died before his father. They transferred their loyalty to Ismail's son, and became engaged in an active struggle to win victory for him and his descendants. As outlined in previous chapters, these restive adherents of the Ismaili line divided into different parties, each devoted to their own candidates for the Imamate, and evolved various strategies for determining succession to the post. The revolutionary Qarmati went so far as to claim that spiritual adoption could remove the Imamate from the Alid lineage entirely. They splintered when their chosen Imam proved himself extremely fallible. The Fatimids dynasty maintained primogeniture for their leaders, but began to fall apart when one Imam denied his own divinity and a later one had no sons. The suppressed and peripheral Nizari, in contrast, were able to maintain their lineage of living Imams through the centuries.[17]

Where the Ismaili and Zaydi sects followed their various living Imams, most Shi'ites favored a different solution to the problem of maintaining

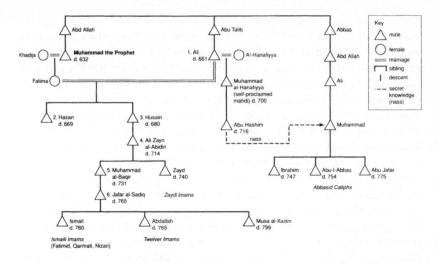

Figure 11.1   Ali and his successors.

the charisma of their leadership. They believed that Jafar had given his spiritual knowledge to his sons Abdallah and Musa al-Kazim. When the eleventh Imam in this line died in 874, apparently without issue, the believers were left in a quandary. They resolved it, and the problems of succession, by asserting that, despite appearances, there must be a living twelfth Imam who could not be seen. He had gone into occlusion, but would return as the mahdi in the Final Days to bring victory to his followers. The occlusion of the Imam eliminated the need to deal with difficulties in deciding who had inherited the nass when there were a number of rival claimants. This Shi'ite sect is known to outsiders as the "twelvers" for the number of accepted Imams in their lineage. They are the people who presently predominate in Iran, and who constitute the vast majority of the partisans of Ali in the world today.

But if the lineage of the Imams had gone into occlusion, the twelvers were then left with the same sort of problem that had faced their Sunni rivals. How could believers have access to legitimate authority when the sacred leader is absent? Like their Sunni co-religionists, the Shi'ites answered this question by relying upon guidance of collections of sayings and deeds of the Prophet, supplemented in their case with similar material from their Imams, and they too developed a learned cadre of

ulema who transmitted these traditions, as well as a circle of highly-
trained jurisconsults/professors who used the scriptures and traditions to
formulate law and as the basis of education. Like their Sunni counterparts, Shi'ite scholars also were wary of association with the state, and
gained stature by their demonstrations of virtue and learning, validated
by the admiration of ordinary people. And, as in Sunni orthodoxy, there
was contestation between those who argued that knowledge of tradition
was sufficient (the *akhbari* school – akhbar are "reports" of historical
traditions)[18] and those legalists who favored a greater range for adaption and interpretation (the *usuli* school).

Here is where the resemblances stop. Among the Sunnis the legalists
and traditionalists were reconciled through Shafi's notion of consensus:
for them, the permissible range of interpretation was limited by ijma,
the agreement of the community, as expressed in authoritative scholarly
opinion written in legal texts. Shi'ite usuli legalists, in contrast, never
accepted community consensus as a way to validate sacred law. Reiterating the Shi'ite argument demonstrating the necessity of the Imam,
they argued that the community was made up of fallible men who
would make mistakes in their decisions. They also maintained that
since the hidden Imam was still alive, though invisible, it was impossible to say that the faith had been completed. Rather, the Imam might
appear at any moment, in a dream or a vision, to bring new illumination to a jurist-sage who could then pass it on to his followers and the
people at large.[19] Finally, they declared that the law must not "imitate
the dead", but should remain open to the reason and intuition of living
jurists.[20] The ideal of a law liable to revision by men who combine
scholarship and insight has dominated in Iran ever since Shi'ism
became its official religion during the reign of the Safavids.

This did not mean that anyone could try to interpret the law for
himself – far from it. As Yann Richard notes, Shi'ism is "both deeply
elitist and pessimistic about the ability of men to steer their own
course."[21] Twelver scholars strongly contended that ordinary persons
were not capable of learning and practicing doctrine properly. Nor was
it enough to leave instruction to learned scholars who could read and
interpret texts to the untutored masses. Instead, human beings need
exemplars who can show the way both by their words and their spiritual aura. It is the ordinary individual's task to search for a learned
master (a "Guide to imitate" – *marja al-taqlid*) who could answer questions and serve as a personal model for the ideal life. Such an inspirational spiritual Guide could grasp the outer shell of the law and its
inner meaning as well; convince by reason, and compel by charismatic
presence.

Twelver Shi'ite emphasis on the follower's personal tie and obedience
to an exemplary leader obviously has an explosive potential for sparking

charismatic movements in which the Guide, or his following, or both, may decide to follow the Nizari example and claim that the hidden Imam has been incarnated and is here to redeem his people. However, this revolutionary potential was limited by the requirement that every candidate for spiritual leadership also had to be a mujtahid, which is the equivalent of a Sunni faqih, a man of special knowledge and sanctity, schooled in law and officially recognized by his teachers and peers as capable of making legal decisions. To become such a man required a lengthy submission to rigorous training, much like that demanded of the Sunni jurist, which inculcated in students a strong respect for tradition and a conservative outlook.

Schooled in obedience themselves, twelver clergy generally believed that quietism was the proper response to secular tyranny. In this, they were like their Sunni cousins, though their arguments for acquiescence were somewhat different, and perhaps even more conducive to passivity. In the first place, as we have seen, in Shi'ism suffering itself has a value, since it increases one's identification with the martyred Imams; resignation will be paid for at the end of time, when the coming of the redeemer ultimately sets things right. Also, if all rulers are in principle usurpers of the crown that rightfully belongs to the hidden Imam, then it really makes no difference who is on the throne, since none truly have any mandate to rule. As Henry Munson comments, "the idea that all governments of men rather than imams are illegitimate can induce resignation as well as revolution."[22]

Quietism was offset, however, by the emphasis in twelver theology on the scholar's ability to interpret the texts personally, according to his own insight and knowledge. Peer recognition of an individual's capacity for interpretation was considered the most telling factor in determining a scholar's rank. In this institutionalized yet charismatic scholastic theological "hierocracy" (as Sayyid Arjomand has called it),[23] the mujtahid who were recognized as able interpreters were authorized to teach and judge. They were called *hojjat al-Islam*, the "proof of Islam," and the most able among them, informally selected by general consensus of their colleagues, were the *ayatollahs*, the "miraculous signs of God." Consensus therefore does not disappear from Shi'ism, but rather than legitimizing the canon of a law school, it is to be continually practiced via the elevation of charismatic spiritual leaders elected by their scholarly peers.

Only ayatollahs were the proper candidates as spiritual Guides for the masses. Only they could write their own independent opinions answering the questions of their followers and freely interpret laws according to their theological knowledge and spritual insight. They also formulated codes of conduct that were binding on their following. Several ayatollahs might disagree in their opinions – the gate of interpretation remained open, and it was up to the follower to decide in his or her own mind and heart which Guide was to be imitated, just as the Sunni can decide which legal school to follow.

The theological independence of the elite Shi'ite clergy coincided with their physical independence. Where Sunni clerics were increasingly drawn into and tainted by service with the state, Iranian scholars retained their separate status and their own informal internal hierarchy. Several factors allowed this. One was the historical failure of the Safavid dynasty to co-opt the ulema, who were disappointed at the dynasty's failure to live up to its millenarian promise. The relatively weak military regimes that succeeded the Safavids were even less able to subdue the clergy, and had to placate them instead, allowing them to solidify their spiritual networks of disciples and to retain their wealth as managers of huge endowments (waqf). Even today, as a group, the ulema are the largest property owners in Iran. Their wealth was supplemented by contributions from disciples, who paid zakat to their chosen Guides. All this gave the elite ulema very considerable discretionary capital which could be spent to maintain their disciples, build mosques and hospitals, and attract support for their causes.[24]

Khomeini's Revolution

Due to their capacity for independent judgment, their reliance on personal charisma, their powerful and hierarchical ecclesiastical organization, their millenarian eschatology and their high degree of financial and political independence, the twelver ulema had sufficient organization, independence, and popular support to stand up against the state. These circumstances help to explain the fact that only in Iran were clerics instrumental in stimulating popular revolts against government policies during the nineteenth and early twentieth century.[25] In comparison, the Ottoman clergy became paid government functionaries, absorbed completely into the state, and lost their connection with the people. When the Empire fell, so did they.

In the twentieth century, the Shah quite rightly saw the independent and wealthy clergy of Iran as the major threat to his power. He expelled them from their old jobs as teachers and judges, replacing them with government appointees. Many were exiled, tortured, and even killed. But the ulema maintained their religious networks and kept their positions as independent preachers and theologians. Secure in these sanctuaries, their exclusion from the state only added to their prestige among the masses, who looked to them for spiritual guidance in an increasingly secularized and alienating environment.[26] Meanwhile, the Shah sought to sidestep Islam entirely by seeking legitimacy in a manufactured connection with pre-Islamic times, while looking to the Christian West as both his model and protector.

Under these circumstances, the rise of ayatollah Khomeini was not a great surprise, at least in retrospect. He was the right man at the right time, who fit the radical role ready made for him to play: a brilliant scholar, a mystical exemplar, a charismatic leader, he drew the materially disaffected and culturally dispossessed to him, and as he did, his own unstated claim to be the manifestation of the redeemer was validated. He repudiated the passive and supplicant attitude of Shi'ism and appealed to its latent dreams of activism and transformation – the believers could now express their spirituality in a cosmic revolution that would overturn all the stultifying dissimulation and corruption of the past and reawaken the sacred community under Khomeini's divine leadership – an eschatological event for which no amount of self-sacrifice was too great. This change was symbolized when the coffins of young people killed fighting the Shah were paraded in the streets during Muharram, and they were compared to the martyrs of Karbala. Meanwhile the Shah was easily portrayed as the modern Yazid, the killer of Husain, and now a puppet of the capitalistic devils in the West.[27]

Khomeini's central claim was that he was refinding a divine order that had been lost – Arjomand calls his message "revolutionary traditionalism".[28] Ironically, the "tradition" that he discovered had actually never existed – though Khomeini and his followers argued that this was only because of a derailing of history from its appointed course by Sunni treachery. From their perspective, the wrong turn of Islam occurred when secular leaders managed to wrest power away from the family of Ali, who, while in occlusion, were represented *in absentia* by religious scholars and jurisconsults. To set right the historical wrong, the learned ulema, as heirs to the Prophet, interpreters of the law, and proxies of the Imam, finally ought to take the authority that had been denied them by secular usurpers and reunite the state and the faith. In keeping with the apotheosis of the ulema, Khomeini himself was referred to as *wali-e-faqih* (the supreme jurist), and *walayat-e-faqih* (rule by the learned) is now taught in Iranian schools as official doctrine.

This in itself was a great innovation, though undertaken in the name of recapturing tradition. As Etan Kohlberg writes, by promulgating the principle of the political and religious supremacy of their own class, Khomeini's ulema have "revolutionized the Shi'ite political ethos whose distinctive mark had been the secularity of temporal rule and the desacralization of political order. To establish and propagate their new conception of authority, the clerical rulers of Iran have incessantly insisted on the sacred character of all authority and thus the thoroughgoing sacralization of the political order."[29]

Under the new sacred polity, the findings of a jurisconsult are no longer conditional or contingent, and ordinary persons can no longer shop around to discover the spiritual leader most in tune with their own predilections. Instead, the old informal contestation between religious leaders for followers in an open spiritual marketplace was to be superseded by a new centralized organization of seventy faqih elected by the people; this assembly would in turn elect an absolute Guide from amongst the ulema most qualified. According to Khomeini, the legislation of this infallible Guide "takes precedence over all other institutions, which may be regarded as secondary, even prayer, fasting and pilgrimage."[30]

In the ideal case the moral authority of Shi'ite absolutism relies upon popular acceptance of the charismatic legitimacy of its spiritual leaders' right to rule, based on a consensus that the very best and most enlightened among the learned has been appointed as Guide to a community of equals united in shared obedience to their sacralized leader. However, the ideal and the real rarely meet in the corridors of power, and it is not surprising to discover that the Guide selected for the Iranian state in 1989 was not one of the ayatollahs democratically recognized by his peers and surrounded by his followers, but was instead a low-ranking cleric who was also a strong supporter of Khomeini. The constitution had to be amended to account for this anomaly. Meanwhile, the famous ayatollah, Kazem Shariatmadari, was summarily ousted from his position as "Guide to imitate" because of anti-Khomeini leanings, as was Khomeini's own designated successor, Husain Ali Montazeri. Under these circumstances, many believers and high-ranking clergy wondered whether, instead of sanctifying government, Khomeini's supporters had been perverted by it.

Such cynicism among the clergy is an indication of the inevitable process of popular disenchantment with a religious revolutionary movement that has necessarily adapted itself to institutionalization and the exigencies of power. When the mosque becomes a center for official propaganda, distribution of spoils and the exercise of coercion, its place as the locus of spiritual opposition to secular inequity is fundamentally eroded; when the faqih who has gained popular support by his resistance to power must wield it himself, he discovers the limits of his mandate; when the eschatological hope for redemption in eternity is manifested in real time, disillusion is sure to result. These are iron laws that Khomeini's charismatic revolutionary movement has struggled hard to overcome – but they are binding nonetheless.

However, there is cause for hope. In Iran, disillusionment with the Islamic revolution has not led to the return of military dictatorship, nor to a search for a new redeemer, but instead to the election of the pragmatic and liberal Muhammad Khatami as President. Perhaps this means it is not Khomeini's charisma, but its rationalization, that will provide the template for future democratic Islamic governments in the Middle East.

12

Sufism in Practice

In Search of the Beloved

Sufism and Shi'ism were, in a real sense, parallel spiritual responses to the breakdown of the original Muslim community. As we have seen, the Shi'ites sought to regain their lost paradise by an unquestioning obedience to the infallible and eternal charisma of Ali and his line. Sunni Muslims rejected the argument for Alid domination out of hand as both unrealistic and tyrannical, but were left then under the sway of an increasingly illegitimate secular state. In this deteriorating ethical environment some devout Muslims tried to find a firm spiritual base for themselves through an intensive study of the life and sayings of the Prophet (hadith). According to Louis Massignon, by the late eighth century a few early hadith transmitters had evolved into the pioneers of Sufism.[1]

What these particular scholars aimed at was personal spiritual transformation. The more ardent and ascetic of them withdrew into remote regions where they emulated the abstemious purity of the first umma and the selfless habits of Muhammad. They also preached to the rural people, who were drawn to the missionaries' austerity, dedication, and learning. Some believe the uniform of the early saintly preacher/ascetics was a rough robe of wool (suf), hence the term *Sufi*.

Though studiedly rejecting cosmopolitan culture, these ascetic moralists were far from humble. As Massignon tells it, they presented themselves as the "apotropaic saints" whom tradition foretold would appear after Muhammad. Like the Imam of the Shi'ites, these walis or "friends of God" believed they were destined to renew the faith and stifle the evil practices of the day. One of the most influential and representative of the early Sufis was Hasan of Basra (d. 728), who was deeply moved by the tragedy of God's distance from man and by the darkness of his era; in response he devoted himself to ascetic practices and adherence to the law. He also was the first to argue for the personal and private "divine intimation" that transcended the sharia and allowed him to speak "in the name of God in the first person."[2]

Hasan and his associates were known as "those who constantly weep". Their sadness accurately reflected the disenchanted tenor of the times, but offered no escape from intolerable conditions and so had little appeal to the masses. A more positive message was required to make Sufism a popular movement. This approach was articulated by Rabiya Adawiyya (d. 801), a former bondswoman, famed for wandering the streets of Basra with a burning torch in one hand and a ewer of water in the other. Her purpose, she said, was to burn paradise and douse hell, so that humanity would no longer worship God out of self-interested hope for paradise or fear of damnation, but only for the proper reason: adoration.[3] She taught that self-immolation in divine love was the only worthwhile end for Muslims. When enfolded in God's embrace she felt herself to have ceased to exist and to have become one with Him.[4]

Rabiya's metaphor of God as the Beloved became the dominant trope for all later Sufi theory and practice, as the value of self-renunciation through love replaced the earlier emphasis on grief. Instead of weeping at the sorrows of the present and praying for the apocalypse, Sufis henceforth would try to gain an intuitive awareness (*marifa*) of the face of the Beloved veiled behind earthly appearances. This could not be accomplished by book learning, but required strict discipline in channeling and controling the passions (*nafs*) that otherwise, like a restive horse, would drag the seeker away from his quest. The pursuit of enlightenment also required a dedicated detachment from the usual preoccupations of humanity. As the Persian mystic Jalaluddin Rumi (d. 1273) advises: "Whatever seems profitable, flee from it, drink poison and spill the water of life, condemn whatever praises you, lend to paupers your wealth and profits! Quit your sect and be a subject of aversion, cast away name and fame and seek disgrace."[5]

The ascetic and world-rejecting spirit of the early Sufis could lead wayfarers to extraordinary lengths. For instance, during his long quest for illumination Abu Said ibn Abi Khayr (d. 1049) is said to have worn only one shirt; he never reclined, leant on a door or wall, or rested on a cushion; he slept (rarely) while standing up in an excavation in the wall. He ate only at night and then only dry bread, and never spoke except when absolutely necessary. Having heard that angels worship God on their heads he had himself regularly tied upside down in a well at night, where he recited the Quran, and begged "O Lord! I do not want myself: let me escape from myself."[6] He humbled himself by acting as servant to wandering dervishes, waiting on them, cleaning their privies, and begging for them. Eventually, he was able, at the age of forty, to experience *fana*, the passing away of the self. Henceforth, he referred to himself in the third person, or as "nobody the son of nobody". He then put asceticism behind him, arguing that it too was a manifestation of egoism, and became famed for his pleasure-loving practices.

By the twelfth century, the individual pursuit of enlightenment had become well institutionalized. Sufi saints like Abu Said founded *tariqas* (lodges – literally pathways) where they were surrounded by pupils (*murids* – one who has made up his will to enter the path, also known as *saliks*, wayfarers).[7] In these lodges the masters taught their pupils the infinite plenitude of God, who has no definite boundaries, but manifests ever unfolding potential. As Massignon explains, the mystical journey therefore cannot seek any conclusive goal, but ends in "a general disposition of the heart to remain always malleable throughout the succession of these states, ... one must not spend time comparing their respective merits, nor become attached to one or another of these instruments of grace as an end in itself."[8]

This meant that unlike the legalist who had a corpus of laws to provide him with a certain baseline for behavior, the mystic had no sure signposts for his quest. Even the holy texts were not a veridical guide, since according to esoteric Sufi teachings what may seem wrong according to the letter of the law may actually be right for the Sufi saint in intuitive communion with a deity who is beyond rules. Similarly, rituals have significance only insofar as they reflect the "heart" of the practitioner, and even acts of piety may be interpreted as obstacles in the path to enlightenment. In these circumstances, how could the murid be sure he was not deluding himself, mistaking his own desires for those of God, and allowing enthusiasm to lead him into heresy or insanity?

The uncertainty and potential for solipsism was countered (at least in part) by the student's immersion into the protective community of brothers where he now lived permanently, sharing out all his worldly goods with his fellows, eating and sleeping with them in a communist community where all distinctions of wealth, knowledge and strength were to cease and the word "my" was anathema. The spiritual "band of brothers" were united under the absolute authority of their *pir* (spiritual guide – also known as *murshid* or *shaikh*) who was conceptualized as the living representative of God on earth who must be obeyed unconditionally – a relationship that transcendentalized the Sunni teacher – student tie and recapitulated in a small and personalized environment the obligation of the Shi'ite to his Imam.

The pir alone could give the blue patched "frock of blessing" and dervish cap to pupils whom he deemed worthy. These symbolic credentials, decorated to designate the novice's spiritual order, marked him as possessing divine grace (*baraka*). The ritual of investiture also required the student to publicly pronounce the oath of allegiance to his teacher, in a way quite parallel to the oath demanded by Sultans of the ulema in ratification of their rule. Then, by putting his hand into his pir's, the

Plate 12.1   *Huwa Allah* – "He is God" – in kufi quadrangular script.

student formally acquired some of his teacher's baraka. Henceforth, he was licensed to act as a spiritual guide, representing his master's school as he instructed his own new pupils on the techniques of enlightenment.

In order to attain his goal, the murid, even more than the student of law, had to enslave himself to his teacher in a relationship of absolute trusting submission (*tawakkul*) that al-Ghazali portrayed as existing on three levels: the first is likened to the trust of man for his attorney; the second is likened to a child's trust in its mother; the third, which is the highest and most difficult, is "cadaver obedience", where the student becomes a limp corpse in the hands of the body-washer.[9] The extent and depth of this relationship is indicated in Sufi manuals: "The student must not argue with the shaikh nor ask from him any proof for what he orders or makes him do, for the shaikhs are the trustees of God ... He should always obey the shaikh and he should serve him with his life and property ... He should not object to anything that the murshid says or does ... He should believe that the shaikh's mistake is better than his own virtue."

Above all, the murid was taught that "nothing is achieved without love for the shaikh, and obedience is the mark of love."[10] By loving compliance to his master, the student could learn to give himself completely to adoration of God, "because love, as all agree, is the negation of the lover's choice by affirmation of the Beloved's choice."[11] The emphasis on unconditional love distinguishes the murid from the scholarly talib, who was obliged to obey, but not to adore, his teacher.

The murid's pursuit of divine love required a rigorous suppression of personal impulse and individual character; he had to be "cut off from humanity for God's sake" and his behavior was "channeled into revealed and correct forms that eliminate idiosyncratic irrational expressions of feeling."[12] To complete his training, he was drawn out of ordinary life and subjected to a complete and arduous regime that filled his entire day and night. Laziness and leisure were to be guarded against as promoting both self-indulgence and introspection. Useless activities, such as digging out and then filling in pits, kept the disciples busy and fatigued, while also demonstrating to them the futility of human endeavor. Service and begging helped humble the wayfarer and the basic ascetic disciplines of "little food, little sleep, little talk" broke down the novice's sense of identity and "polished" away the impurities of personality, leaving him nearer to the ideal state of mirror-like emptiness. Of major importance was a forty-day meditation, where the disciple was secluded in a dark room likened to a tomb, dressed in a shroud, and invited to die to himself.

Violence and arbitrariness were also expected in the pir-murid relationship, and were justified by the argument that ardor for union with the Beloved will be hurtful to the lover, and that the physician must sometimes wound the patient in order to cure him. As Rumi says, "pain is a treasure, for it contains mercies; the kernel is soft when the rind is scraped off."[13] The student was also expected to report all his innermost thoughts and dreams to his teacher, who could then use this information to expose the student's weakness, egoism, ignorance, and impotence, which would help to disintegrate the pupil's worldly identity and facilitate his capacity for absolute self-loss in adoration of the Beloved.

Ecstasy and Remembrance

Having lovingly submitted to his master's discipline, the student then was ready to be emptied of his ego through *wajd*, or "finding"; this was conceptualized as a journey inward, to the depths of the soul, where the manifestation of God was waiting to be experienced.[14] This could be a tumultuous event. One mystic describes his own illumination as follows: "I heard the ringing of bells. My frame dissolved and my trace vanished and my name was rased out. By reason of the violence of what I experienced I became like a worn-out garment which hangs on a high tree, and the fierce blast carries it away piece by piece."[15] According to some accounts, the shock of wajd could render the seeker unconscious for as much as a year.

Once again, the potentially destructive experience of selflessness was kept in check by the pir's continuous monitoring of his pupil, by the support of the other brothers, and by the murid's own expectations. The wayfarer and his teacher anticipated a sequence of psychic stages (*maqam*) that were thought to be markers on the seeker's spiritual journey. These ranked stages (poverty, repentance, trust in God, patience, gratitude, etc.) developed in concordance with the increasing rationalization and centralization of the Sufi orders, and provided a framework the murid could cling to in order to avoid overbalancing into insanity or apostasy. At the same time, a degree of openness was retained and the pathway was lightened by occasional transitory moments of supreme ecstatic grace, *hal*, which gave the traveller the strength to carry on his arduous voyage.

In Hegelian fashion, the stages of enlightenment were understood as reflecting the expansion and contraction of the soul as it moved spirally toward a final reconciliation with God: hope alternated with fear, intoxication with sobriety, presence with absence, unity with separation. The final and highest stages were annihilation (fana), a becoming one with God, which was balanced by *baqa*, a conscious remaining with God while yet retaining one's transformed self. Sufi pupils could be spiritually rated according to the number of these stages they had gone through, though there was great controversy over the weight to be given to the different alternatives, or even their order.

For example, some masters, most famously al-Junayd (d. 910), emphasized sobriety (*sahw*) over intoxication (*sukhr*) and baqa over fana. Hujwiri says "intoxication is the playground of children, but sobriety is the death-field of men."[16] Others, beginning perhaps with Bayazid Bistami (d. 874), made the opposite appraisal. Ever since, Sufism has been split between those seeking ecstatic states (the "drunken" school) and an intellectual minority who say such states must be followed by a return to the normal world, albeit in an inwardly transformed state (the "sober" school).

The ecstatic school relied a great deal on the practice of *dhikr* (remembrance), which soon became the central and defining liturgical ritual[17] of the Sufi orders. This practice may have originated when early anchorites, fearful of forgetting God's bounty, supplemented their isolation and asceticism by fervent repetition of devotional phrases, recited either silently or aloud.[18] As an example, Abu Said's dhikr was "Without Thee, O Beloved, I cannot rest; Thy goodness towards me I cannot reckon. Tho' every hair on my body becomes a tongue, a thousandth part of the thanks due to Thee I cannot tell."[19] He continued to recite this phrase regularly throughout his life, saying it allowed him to "talk to God."

Dhikr were justified via the Quranic admonition to "remember Allah much."[20] Different enlightened seekers, and the devotees who surrounded them, developed their own dhikr with distinctive breathing patterns and often accompanied them with rhythmic bodily movements. For instance, the tariqa Hallajiyya uses a dhikr based on the word "Allah" omitting the initial syllable "al"; it consists of reciting "laha" while bending the head to right, "lahi" while bending to the left, and "lahu" while bending the head down to the heart.[21] Performances also were sometimes heightened by music (*sama*) and dance, though the more austere frowned on these as secular pleasures. These expressions of remembrance were performed both in solitude and within the group in public. During their public performances, the brothers often lost consciousness as they were immersed in God's love, gaining a subjective sense of emotional grounding in the sacred that was not to be found in the fragmented secular world or in academic scholarship or even in the ordinary act of prayer. The dramatic public performances of dhikr drew crowds of onlookers who were inspired and thrilled by the spectacle, and who often became lay devotees of the brotherhoods, donating money and support.

The contrast between Sunni orthodoxy and Sufism is clearly revealed by comparing Friday prayers with a performance of dhikr.[22] During prayers the congregation casually line up in rows facing the back of the prayer leader who is nothing more than an ordinary man representing the community at large; all recite the text individually while prostrating themselves toward Mecca in orderly and sober fashion to demonstrate their free and conscious submission to the moral demands of the religion. The fundamental tension between communal group and free individual is temporarily resolved as each devotee solemnly and voluntarily acquiesces to the community's ethical code, symbolized by prostration.

In dhikr too group and individual are united, but rather than remaining separate and conscious, during dhikr the ecstatic individual is emotionally drawn out of himself and merged within the active charismatic group. In some instances, the participants hold hands and face one another in equal parallel rows, with the leader between them, or the members may circle around their leader, or stand in front of him. Performances of more impoverished and alienated groups tend to be less orderly, more ecstatic, and the performers may use drugs as well as music and dance to help them enter trance. They also may perform acts of extraordinary self-mutilation (eating glass or fire, walking on coals, being galloped over by horses, impaling themselves, etc.), and they may culminate their performance with the curing of diseases under the direction of their master. These are what Victor Turner called the ecstatic "religions of the weak" that offer the faithful a momentary sense of power and control over their lives. On the other hand, performances by Sufi sects with middle-class or elite clientele may be far more refined – more like a concert or music party than an ecstatic occasion. The difference is vaguely comparable to the difference between religious services of Pentecostalists and Unitarians.[23]

But regardless of variations in form, in all Sufi performances of dhikr differences within the group are minimized while the leader stands conspicuously apart and confronts the congregation. He is not one among equals, but acts as spiritual guide, standing above and directing the participants as their absolute superior. His task is to inspire and control the group's emotional climax through overseeing their music, rhythmic movements and synchronized descant. Rather than singly and voluntarily communicating submission to God and His community through prostration, the Sufi brothers collectively are drawn to merger with Him through shared trance. Rather than separately standing behind a symbolic everyman who acts as they do, they face a superior figure who stands apart and draws them toward an ecstatic transcendent state.

Both types of religious experience are characteristic and alternative solutions to the problem of establishing sacred authority in a culture of separate and equivalent individuals. Where orthodoxy accepts human separation from God and from one another and stresses the willed individual submission of the believer to the community of equals united by shared faith in a holy text, Sufism seeks to overcome human differences through the brothers' shared devotion to the charismatic exemplars who offer them a convulsive experience of the ecstatic transcendence of self. By identification with their supernatural mentors, the disciples gain power, at least subjectively, and may eventually become exemplary spiritual figures themselves as well, able to stand outside the ordinary world and inspire a coterie of enthusiastic followers.

The Cosmic Order

The personal relationship between the charismatic exemplary Sufi master and disciple was soon elaborated into a complex hierarchical spiritual edifice. This began as disciples gathered together in a *khaniqa* (a Sufi lodge, *zawiya* in North Africa) to learn from their master, practice the discipline of the group, undertake collective rituals, and participate in the local community. After the founder's death, the tomb of the saint became the center for the proliferation of new devotional cults. Each new cult validated its authenticity by tracing a *silsila* or spiritual genealogy (comparable to the isnad of a tradition or the nass given to Shi'ite Imams) to the sacred founder who himself was spiritually linked back through Jafar to Ali or Abu Bakr, often through the mediation of the great ninth-century Baghdadi Sufi, al-Junayd.[24] By placing themselves in a spiritual line to the founders of Islam itself, and thence to the great saints of yesteryear, the tariqas validated their own present-day authenticity and perpetuated in attenuated and rationalized form the original charismatic relationship between the founding pir and his devotees. They also offered a potentially infinitely ramifying rank order derived from the members' association with their pir's personal charisma.

In radical contrast to Shi'ite claims for the hereditary Imam, among Sufis anyone could become a pir, regardless of history or family – the only criterion was initiation into a brotherhood, the granting of spiritual baraka by one's own teacher, and the unswerving faith of a circle of murids. Pirs also stood in contrast to the orthodox ulema, who had gradually developed caste-like status groups monopolizing formal religious education for themselves. Though Sufis also showed a tendency to hand down positions of authority within kin groups, masters were usually not the children of the scholarly elite, but instead were often of lower and working-class background. Most arose from the people, gained their power by an inner search, not by external learning, and could be recognized by their personal charismatic spirituality rather than by their degrees, official honors, and publications.

The distinction between Sufis and the ulema was physically symbolized by the fact that Sufi tariqas were housed in khaniqas, which were privately endowed institutions (originally they were places where food and housing had been offered to wayfarers), while official worship at the mosque was nominally a state function where one of the duties of the preacher was to invoke the name of the present ruler.[25] As we have already noted, the assimilation of the ulema into the state accelerated after the Seljuk period and culminated in the complete integration of the ulema into the state bureaucracy during the Ottoman Empire.[26]

The Sufis, in contrast, often presented themselves as offering an alternative to the state. The murshid's personal charisma, which drew his disciples to him, was less like the administrative and judicial power of the state-supported legal scholar, and more like the emotional appeal of the tribal warrior, whose manly character won the loyalty of his entourage in the secular world of competing co-equals; this may partly account for Sufism's strong appeal to the military classes. But where the warrior's power was from his personal might and his connection to his noble lineage, the power of the pir was thought to emanate from a much higher source, via his spiritual connection to his teachers, and from them to the deity.

The image of power spreading from a sacred center was elaborated by the Sufis into a totalizing hierarchy of visible and invisible saints based on populist and egalitarian principles of "friendship" and "character." The theory behind faith in the hidden administration of saints went as follows: Muhammad was not only the final Prophet, he was also a Perfect Man, sent by God to maintain the order of the universe. In esoteric language, he was the *Qutb*, the cosmic pivot, who brings the world to perfection. And, as the twelver Shi'ites claimed that each generation must have an Imam, even if hidden, so the Sufis claimed that a Qutb must exist, even though, as "God's bride" he was veiled from ordinary men, and discerned only by the purified elite.[27]

According to many Sufi authorities, the world pivot of the day had legal authority equal to that of Muhammad in his era, since the power of both came from the same source: God Himself. In more esoteric doctrine, a prophet dispenses graces without being transformed, while the saint is transformed without dispensing graces. The saint is therefore superior since he is close to union with God, while a prophet is only

God's emissary. Of course, Muhammad was unique in taking both roles at once. In any case, the Qutb took the place of the Imam in Shi'ite Islam, but without the necessity of being of the Alid line and without the conflicts of loyalty that might ensue were he actually known.

Revolving around the pivot of the universe was an elaborate status order of his khalifa (Caliphs), characterized by Macdonald as "a saintly board of administration by which the invisible government of the world is carried on."[28] These lesser saints had superhuman powers, such as the ability to be in two or more places at once, see into the heart of the disciple and ferret out any hypocrisy, manifest objects at will, curse and bless, and especially the capacity to intercede for their followers on Judgment Day. The hidden order of the "friends of God" became tangible in the local tariqas where the resident pir was the khalifa of a greater pir, who was supposedly under the authority of a still greater master, and so on, extending both to the living seal of the saints himself and back in time to Muhammad, as well as down to the humblest murid just beginning on the Path.

As an ideology of sacred power finding earthly expression in the institutionalized communities of the brotherhoods, the hierarchy of saints provided the popular imagination with a picture of an eternal holy order operating in secret that superseded (at least in imagination) the corrupted and by now crumbled hierarchy of secular power. As Hodgson puts it: "There might no longer be a Caliph with power in the ordinary political sense. But there remained a true spiritual Caliph, the immediate representative of God, who bore a far more basic sway than any outward Caliph."[29]

The Spiritual Division of Labor

In the world of the pre-modern Middle East the charismatic pirs oversaw the mystical aspect of Islam which was personal, mythopoeic, experientially validated, hierarchical, expressive, and heterodox, while the learned ulema more or less dominated the public, the practical-legal, the historically oriented, egalitarian, abstract and scholarly side of Islam. For most Sunni Muslims these two worlds were simply different sides of the same coin, each offering different and complementary forms of insight to the seeker in pursuit of enlightenment. Borrowing from Ismaili terminology, Sufis and scholars alike often argued that the strictures of the law and the texts were God's external message (zahir), aimed at disciplining the intellect, while Sufism offered His hidden message (batin), which touched the true heart. Public rituals and regulations of Islam were the husk beneath which was an inner awareness of a personal relationship with God.[30]

It was therefore perfectly possible during much of Muslim history for an orthodox scholar to be also a Sufi mystic. On the one hand, Sufi scholars included many who were vehemently hostile to all popular forms of saint worship, such as the famous fourteenth-century puritan reformer, Ibn Taimiya.[31] On the other hand, Sufi shaikhs were themselves very often respected members of legal madhhabs. For example, Abdul-Qadir al-Gilani (d. 1160), recognized by his later followers as the Qutb of his time, was a Hanbalite scholar, despite the supposed hostility of Hanbalis to Sufism. In fact, as Makdisi has shown, Hanbalism and early Sufism shared an abiding concern for concerted meditation on the texts as the avenue to spiritual illumination.

The division of labor between esoteric and exoteric worked remarkably well. The ulema maintained tradition and provided the official legal and administrative skills for the people and the court. Sufis had a more pervasive subterranean influence. As they spread throughout the Middle East, the networks of brothers filled important ideological and organizational roles that the universalistic and largely urban ulema could not. For instance, because they stressed the importance of the inner over the outer, or "heart" over "text," Sufis were more willing than the official ulema to tolerate local variation; this made them natural missionaries, and they were usually the ones who brought Islam into the peripheral areas. The drama of the Sufi dhikr also gave the unsophisticated masses in town and country an immediate religious experience and stimulated their faith in a way that the learned study of the texts failed to accomplish.

In towns Sufis also found a receptive audience within the guilds and futuwwa clubs. These closed groups were entered by initiation, practiced secrecy, favored personalized ties of obligation and were based on the hierarchial movement of members up a ladder of expertise; because of their many parallels to the brotherhoods, they easily adopted Sufism as their religion of choice, transcendentalizing their already existent pattern of ranked personal relationships. Until and even into the modern era, Sufi brotherhoods remained tightly integrated into the closed guild and club organization where they formed separate cultic enclaves that helped sustain the integrity of local life. Under Sufi influence, the guilds and clubs also provided urban people with a sacralized social world that countered, and sometimes rose in protest against, the delegitimized central administration.

Sufism had great influence in the tribal regions as well, where the brothers were utilized as sacred mediators and guardians of the peace among rivalrous kin groups who lacked sanctified means for dispute resolution. The khaniqas of the brotherhood generally were strategically located at interstices between tribal groups, where they could function as centers for trade and mediation. There tribal rivals could safely meet,

Plate 12.2 A North African khaniqa in the nineteenth century.

exchange goods, and have their disagreements settled all at once. Because of these services, tribesmen who rejected the secular rule of the Sultan often accepted the religious authority of their local shaikhs, giving them regular donations and providing manpower to protect them – much as the tribes of Aws and Khazraj supported Muhammad at Medina.

These rural brotherhoods furnished a modicum of stability in a hostile environment and established ties between the tribes and the rest of the world through their networks, trade concessions, and urban connections. Successful brotherhoods could even develop their own small sacred empires within the larger secular state, complete with a centralized administrative organization, a leader blessed with baraka, tax collection through voluntary donations and access to the military force of tribal clients. These religious enclaves offered an alternative to secular central authority, and could sometimes rise in protest against state injustice and corruption.

This was especially the case in North Africa, where, for example, the Darqawiyya brotherhood led Kabylia tribes in a revolt against the bey in 1804, while the religious leader of Shararda near Marrakesh rebelled for decades against the Moroccan state at the turn of the nineteenth century, arguing that the government was taxing in a way not permitted by sharia.

But despite their potential for disruption, in general the Sufis were a calming force. Because they could introduce themselves into the moral margins between the tribes and could enter into the guilds and clubs of the urban quarters, Sufis provided local coherence and a sense of spiritual communion in an expanding and complex world that the legalistic and abstract textual scholarship of the ulema could not supply. With their personal charismatic leaders who offered believers an actual experience of religious ecstasy in the performance of dhikr, they gave the ordinary people an escape from the desanctified and fragmented world of the everyday. They were, as Hodgson remarks, "the spiritual cement for the social order."[32] This, however, was not to last, for reasons to be outlined in the next chapter.

13

The Contradictions of
Saintly Authority

The Cult of Saints

The erosion of Sufic influence correlated with a shift of emphasis in the mystic tradition as Junayd's version of private communion and public sobriety lost ground to more magical and delirious forms of Sufism based on the revelatory experiences of a divinized individual. Perhaps the first of these miraculous saints was Bayazid Bistami who in the ninth century cried "Glory be to me" as he was transported in ecstasy; when his scandalized students attacked him, they found their blows miraculously turned back upon them, demonstrating that Bistami had indeed become the pure mirror of God.

For the awed disciples, the transformed saint was a manifestation of the deity on earth, who deserved to be loved unconditionally. Rumi found the image of the divine in a disheveled wandering dervish from Tabriz, Shams al-Din. For Rumi "the sun (shams) of Tabriz is a perfect light, a sun, yea, one of the beams of God!"[1] In his rapture, Rumi went even further: "My master and my shaikh, my pain and my remedy; I declare these words openly, my Shams and my God!"[2] Shams did not deny Rumi's declaration, and affirmed that he was indeed a Perfect Man beyond all convention and law. Under the influence of his beloved, Rumi also felt that he too had escaped the limits of time and space and exclaimed: "Wine is intoxicated with me, not I with it! The world takes its being from me, not I from it!"[3]

Despite such miraculous displays and extraordinary claims to apotheosis by transported saints, for many years ecstatic Sufis were able to continue on their esoteric pathways with very little intervention from the ulema or the secular authorities. This was partly because they followed Junayd's advice to discuss their communion with God cryptically via veiled allusions, much as the Shi'ites hid their beliefs behind dissimulation. Rumi writes: "When the brides of heavenly truth show their faces within you and the secrets are revealed, beware and beware

that you tell not that to strangers, and describe it not to other men."
Further, Rumi pragmatically counsels that it is best to be silent because
if the truth is told by a Sufi "not one person will stay before them or
give them the Muslim salute."[4]

On their side, the ulema, pleased with the division of labor between Sufi
and scholar, felt that so long as the law was obeyed in public, the personal
meanings Sufis gave their teachings and practices were of no concern to
anyone but themselves, since Sunni doctrine held that only God knew
what was in another person's heart. If a man was willing to publicly aver
Allah as the one true God, and Muhammad as his Prophet, he was
accepted by the orthodox as a Sunni Muslim unless he proved himself
otherwise. Only when the mystic was unable to contain his "secret" of
unity was the wrath of the orthodox and of the secular authorities
aroused, since this revelation constituted a direct challenge to their power.

Mansur al-Hallaj was the most famous and radical such challenger.
Born of humble background (his name means "cotton-carder"), Hallaj
was a student of Junayd and others of the "sober" school. But he was too
God-intoxicated to follow his teachers' warnings to be discreet about his
experience. Instead, he declared *Ana l-Haqq*: "I am the Truth" or "my I is
God" and was inspired to rhapsodic poetry by his mystical communion:
"Your Spirit is mingling with my spirit just as wine is mixing with pure
water. And when something touches You, it touches me. Now 'You' are
'me' in everything."[5] In his ecstatic state, he opposed the circumspect
silence of the Sufi spiritual elect and called instead for an egalitarian
sharing of the secret of communion. Rejecting detachment and prudence,
he took off his Sufi insignia and traveled throughout Islamdom, preaching divine love to the masses as well as the nobility, performing miracles
and stirring the people to a sense of Messianic expectation and opposition against the oppression of the regime and the elitism of the clerics.

It is for his challenge to the order of the day, both spiritual and civic,
that he was persecuted, tried, imprisoned, and finally gruesomely tortured and executed in 922 – one of the very few martyrs within Islam.
Those in favor of his death included the Abbasid ruler, who was worried about popular rebellion, the orthodox ulema, who found Hallaj's
pretensions intolerable, and the Shi'ites, who saw him as a threat to
their own hopes for an Alid savior. Most Sufis too abandoned him,
saying he threatened their existence by revealing their doctrines to the
unworthy masses.

What is especially noteworthy is that Hallaj accepted and even welcomed the verdict against him. This was for several reasons. The first
was an overwhelming desire to have a complete and final union with
God. As Hallaj cries: "Between me and You (there lingers) an 'it is I!'

(which) torments...Ah! lift through mercy this 'it is I!' from between us both!"[6]

According to legend, Hallaj laughed and danced on his way to the gibbet, and recited "Kill me, O my faithful friends, for to kill me is to make me live; my life is in my death, and my death is in my life."[7] When his hands and feet were cut off, he did not cry out, and the faithful saw his blood writing "Allah" on the ground.

Aside from his own quest for death, Hallaj also recognized that his ecstatic gnosis pressed against the basic values of Sunni orthodoxy, and elected to sacrifice himself to preserve the sobriety and dogmas of the mainstream. As he told a disciple, "there is no more pressing business for the Muslims than my execution. Try to realize that my execution will be the preservation of sanctions enacted in accordance with the law, for he who has transgressed (the law) must suffer (the consequences)."[8] Since his crucifixion Hallaj has been the hero and patron saint of Sunni artisans, foreigners, outcasts and outlaws who might otherwise have found refuge in the Shi'ite tragedy of Husain. They worship him as a martyr who, by virtue of his sacrifice, can intercede for them with God.

But Hallaj's principled acceptance of the power of the law and his embrace of martyrdom for the sake of the ordinary faithful had little effect on the trajectory of Sufism. Instead, sects such as the Qalandariyya, which had no particular doctrine beyond the achievement of ecstatic states of consciousness, became ever more popular among spiritual aspirants; anti-social wandering dervishes also proliferated, and Sufi masters tended to become magicians rather than moralists, as they tried to command the loyalty of a sensation seeking public. By the thirteenth century, successful tariqas relied primarily upon emotional public preaching, redistribution of wealth in charity, spectacular presentations of dhikr, and the performance of miracles to gain the approval of the populace and donations from lay brothers. The major Sufi rituals became the *mulid*, an annual birthday celebration at the tomb of the founder, where members from the various khaniqas gathered to vie with one another to show their devotion to their venerated patron saints through displays of generosity, feasting, and dramatic demonstrations of athletic asceticism and entranced chanting.

There was a parallel withdrawal from moral activism among mystically inclined Sufi intellectuals as they were increasingly drawn to the esoteric teachings of Ibn al-Arabi (d. 1240). In place of Hallaj's message of ethical self-sacrifice and egalitarian participation in the immediacy of gnosis, Ibn Arabi constructed a complex, hierarchical, pantheistic and contemplative neo-Platonic mystical vision. Adepts of his school spent their time meditating on the forty stages of ascent toward and descent from the loving Perfect Man and pondering the twenty-eight degrees of emanation from the ultimate divine name, each emanation flowering in

Plate 13.1   A religious mendicant.

its own multifarious archetypical forms, all reflecting the perfect love of God. In the Sufi equivalent of the hair-splitting of academic jurists, Ibn Arabi's devotees lost themselves in the abstruse detail of this eternally ramifying mystical universe. For them only those capable of grasping the metaphysical abstractions of the archetypes and emanations could truly experience God; ordinary people were merely "link animals."[9]

Both intellectual Sufism and popular Sufism thus moved away from the ascetic moralism of early practice and toward a more indulgent immersion in contemplation of God's various forms and ecstatic devotion to a charismatic leader, a Perfect Man, to whom the follower is drawn by an intuitive inner compulsion that the devotees likened to romantic love. From this point of view, the living elect are identifiable automatically to their disciples by their spiritual auras – their baraka. As Abu Said put it: "These souls know each other by the smell, like horses."[10]

However, in the absence of any standardized system for ranking and testing, there was rarely any consensus on the quality of spiritual scent an individual exuded. Like the old hadith collectors, serious seekers hunted in remote areas for the hidden and unique spiritual figure, often a beggar or humble artisan, who could be recognized as a great saint only in an intuitive flash of insight, or perhaps in a dream or vision.

The Delegitimization of Sufism

Despite changes in emphasis, Sufis continued to fulfill their function of mediation and leadership among the tribes, while in the cities they offered ecstatic experiences that could lift the poor out of their suffering, if only momentarily. Mysticism also retained its appeal to urban upper classes, who could cultivate their spirituality and elevated tastes simultaneously. Although still popular by the twentieth century Sufism had ceased to be a major moving force in the Middle East, and was increasingly under attack.[11] Why did this occur?

Many commentators have seen the modernizing and debunking influence of western rationalism as the main culprit behind the decline of Sufism. Swayed by the prestige and success of western technology and science, Muslim reformers at the turn of the century saw the practices and beliefs of Sufism as primitive and pagan. They argued that in order to reach parity with the West, Islam should cut away these "residues" and focus on modern aspects of Islam, such as consultation, personal liberty, rationality, and freedom of thought.[12]

These modernist rationalistic puritans gave birth to later oppositional intellectual movements, such as *salafism*, which arose in the 1930s in North Africa as a response to French anti-Islamic propaganda. The salafa reformers called for a return to what they believed to be an original Islam, and in the process vehemently repudiated Sufism as anti-Muslim, primitive, and collaborationist. As Ernest Gellner points out, the rise of anti-Sufism coincided with the heightened authority of the urban administrative and technical class throughout the Middle East. This growing and increasingly culturally dominant segment of society naturally found the universalistic and abstract Islam of the urban ulema more attractive than personalized, charismatic Sufism.[13]

However, as Gellner himself has documented,[14] it is not evident that Sufism in principle is unable to adapt itself to modernity. Because a charismatic leader can make unilateral decisions according to circumstances, with little attention to the restrictions of the law, Sufi groups should, in theory, be able to adapt relatively quickly to modern conditions. The modern-day followers of the Aga Khan, discussed in Chapter 8, are a case in point. It would seem then that Sufis would be favored (or at least not penalized) by a rapidly changing and complex modern environment. But this has not been the case.

Other commentators see the erosion of Sufism beginning in the eighteenth century Wahhabi revival, which promulgated anti-Sufi doctrines such as the prohibition of all worship at tombs and the cessation of Sufi practices such as dhikr. However, al-Wahhab, the spiritual head of the movement, studied in Mecca with al-Sindhi, who was a quietest Sufi, and the form of Islamic puritanism Wahhab preached was very consciously a reiteration of the Hanbalite doctrine, especially as it had been stated by Ibn Taimiya (d. 1328), who was himself a member of a Sufi order. In a real sense, al-Wahhab simply took over the standard Sufi tariqa organization without the overt mysticism.[15]

Nor was the activist moral tone of the Wahhabi movement alien to Sufism. Some Sufi orders, such as the Nasiriyya and the Sanusi, had also responded to the pressures of the time by making purification of Islam and imitation of Muhammad their watchword. These neo-Sufi movements (as Fazlur Rahman has called them)[16] required disciples to become involved in the world in order to transform it. They, more than the zealous and puritanical Wahhabis, gave modern Muslim activism its coloration, and it is no surprise to find that Hasan al-Banna, the founder of the Muslim Brotherhood, began his career as a Sufi, or that Allal al-Fassi, who began the salafa movement, was a member of a famous family of Sufi shaiks in Fez.

If the generally assumed negative relationship between modern puritan reform and Sufism is far from clear, equally unclear is any systematic delegitimizing capitulation by the tariqas to colonialism or to indigenous secular authority. While some Sufi tariqa accommodated themselves to colonialism and secular rule, others did not. The Sanusi of Libya, for example, headed the struggle against Italy, and were strong proponents of a return to original practice. Elsewhere, other Sufi orders, some reformist, others ecstatic, also led their clients against the state, following in the footsteps of the rebellions of the Safavids and the Almohads.[17] Unlike the urban ulema, who were usually easily co-opted into any administration, Sufis often retained their independence and their capacity to act as spokesmen for the people right into modern times.

It is true that western influence, greater state power, and social change have combined to put the legitimacy of popular Sufism in question, but the primary cause for its loss of centrality is deeper. It lies in the internal contradictions involved in maintaining an organization of charismatic personal domination within the egalitarian and pluralistic social world of the Middle East. As an eighteenth-century poet angrily writes: "Would that we had not lived to see every demented madman held up by his fellows as a *pole*! Their ulema take refuge in him, indeed, they have even adopted him as a Lord, instead of the Lord of the throne. For they have forgotten God, saying 'so-and-so provides deliverance from suffering for all mankind'."[18] The exaggeration of powers that the author decries had several sources.

The Exaggeration of Charisma

Partly, Sufi hyperbole about the sacred power of pirs is a consequence of internal struggles over authority within the khaniqas. Since the position of pir was charismatic, it was not automatically handed on within the saint's family, but was transferred to the most spiritually qualified initiate, who might or might not be a family member. In fact, actual ties of blood or spiritual initiation became less and less important over time, as competitors for holy status tried to legitimate their authority through referring to visions only they could see. For example, Ahmed al-Tijani, who founded his influential brotherhood in the mid-eighteenth century, validated his superior spiritual status by declaring that his silsila was only one link long, and came directly from the Prophet Muhammad, who had appeared to instruct him in a dream.

These sorts of unprovable claims left plenty of room for dispute as to the suitability of the inheritor within the tariqa, as disciples and laymen alike aligned themselves in factional alliances around rival contenders for the baraka of the dead saint. Disputes over succession were not only about matters of the spirit; they also were about control over the economic and political resources commanded by the khaniqas. Given the high stakes, it is not surprising that disputes about the sanctity of a claimant often became so intense that they led to splits in the brotherhood, with two or more factions claiming to have the proper silsila, maintaining separate lodges, each vituperatively deriding the virtue of their antagonists' leader, while making extraordinary claims about the spiritual powers of their own pir.

Exaggeration of saintly powers also occurred during disputes that prevailed within the larger mystical community, as several pirs professed to be the present Qutb, or to have elevated positions in the hidden holy administration. Competing claims led to continual debates over metaphysical superiority, as saints engaged in competitive spiritual one-upmanship that is a metaphysical version of the braggadocio and feuds of tribal chevaliers. Spiritual predominance was asserted even by Abdul-Qadir al-Gilani, the modest and tolerant founder of the Qadiriyya, the largest Sufi order, who is reported to have boasted that "my foot is on the neck of every saint."[19] Al-Tijani went even further when he proudly declared himself to be the *Qutb al-Aqtab* (the Pole of Poles) and the seal of the saints, with command not only over all living pirs but over all those who had gone before him as well.[20] Similarly, the Arab poet Ibn al-Farid (d. 1235) ends his great ode on mystical love with these words to his readers: "I found the full-grown men of the tribe (of Sufis no wiser than) little babes. For my contemporaries drink only the dregs of what I left; and for those before me, their (vaunted) merits are my superfluity."[21]

R. A. Nicholson explains the escalating arrogance of saints in this way. "As the Bedouin poet brags about himself in order to assert the dignity of his tribe, so when the Mohammedan saints boast of the unique endowments which God has bestowed upon them, it is not self-glorification, but thanksgiving to Him 'from whom all blessings flow'."[22] This may be so, but a rhetoric of proud self-assertion also coincides with a culture of equality where rank is uncertain. In the competitive world of the Middle East individuals mainly gain respect by personally impressing others. This can be done in part by the simple expedient of stating and restating one's own greatness. Inflationary rhetoric is all the more tempting when the basis of power has relatively little material foundation and rests primarily on others' faith in one's sanctity. The would-be saint seeking disciples and respect is more obliged to brag about his baraka and the spiritual powers of his predecessors and allies than is a warrior whose strong right arm has earned him the support of his men or a scholar who has passed his examinations with flying colours.

The saint's self-glorification is therefore both more ambitious and more dubious than that of the tribesman, who is merely first among equals, a man among men, while the saint is precisely not that, but prides himself on being unified with God. The certitude of a transpersonal union with a higher being is, of course, characteristic of all mystical experience, and everywhere carries with it an element of grandiosity. This characteristic inflation is amplified in Islam, where the theology of an absolute, omnipresent, omnipotent God points in the direction of seeker's complete merger with the deity. Rumi puts the argument this way: "He who says 'I am the servant of God' asserts that two exist, one himself and the other God. But he who says 'I am God' has naughted himself and cast himself to the winds."[23] For the Sufi saint, "naughted" in God, his thoughts now must be God's thoughts, his feelings are God's feelings, and whatever he does must be willed by God.

As we have seen, just such self-loss in God was experienced by the

Sufis as they were taught to "die to themselves" and as they climbed the ladder of inner states toward the ultimate goal of fana. Repeated devotional practices of dhikr also stimulated adepts to moments of ecstatic selflessness. Both reason and action pushed the Sufi pir to have a firm faith in his own transcendent state of unity with an absolute deity. As Rumi exults: "Since my mouth has eaten of His sweetmeats, I am become clear-sighted, and see Him face to face"[24] – an assertion in direct contradiction to the orthodox proclamation of the irreducible gap between an unknowable God and his fallible human creatures who can only rely on Allah's mercy as their sole salvation.

Even if deeply felt, mystic communion is difficult to demonstrate, since, unlike the diploma of the faqih, it is completely internal and invisible. So, in order to symbolize his spiritual authority, the saint studiedly stood apart, and acted in a manner that symbolically marked him off from ordinary men: most dressed in special clothing, had long beards, moved with dignity, showed no overt interest in power, appeared chaste and demure, carried no weapon, avoided politics, and spoke with deliberation. Others, taking the role of dervish, carried a begging bowl and wore a patched robe; they wandered without a home, transformed in ecstatic trance. In all instances, the mystic sought to present himself as beyond the pale of the average man, physically and spiritually.

But because the status of a pir rested primarily on his inner transformation, which was merely symbolized by his outer appearance and actions, and because of the great potential for charlatanism, there was a strong pressure among devotees for some more tangible proof of his Godly qualities. This proof generally took on two forms: the first was the development of a circle of disciples who, as Abu Said put it, could smell the claimant's sanctity; the second rested on the claimant's ability to perform miracles (*karamat*). For example, Rumi's pupils were drawn to him by his astonishing ability to spontaneously recite magnificent poetry, but he was disdainful of his poetic gifts. "I care nothing for poetry" he writes. "It has become incumbent upon me, as when a man plunges his hands into tripe and washes it out for the sake of a guest's appetite, because the guest's appetite is for tripe."[25]

Rumi was right. Disciples were drawn to him by the taste of his poetry, as they were drawn to other saints who displayed less lasting marvels. On their side, the brothers gathered around the pir were impelled to convince potential followers and themselves that their leader deserved their loyalty because he, like Abu Said, had become "nobody the son of nobody" who wanted nothing because he had everything as a result of being "naughted" in God. According to the devotees, the pir therefore cannot sin; a saint who drinks wine turns it automatically into honey.[26] His miraculous powers derive from his selfless merger with the Beloved, and are revealed in his capacity to deliver salvation to the ordinary believer through fusing him into a worshipful community united by the direct experience of grace in the performance of the dhikr.

The faithful murids convinced of the sanctity of their pir were naturally keen to elevate him to ever more Empyrean heights, where he could intercede for them on their uncertain way to heaven and help them on the equally precarious earth. As a result, they tended to assume that every unusual event that happened to them was due to a miraculous intervention by their pir.[27] Murids also gained greater spiritual status among their colleagues through their personal association with a charismatic figure, and were inclined to exaggerate his powers for that reason as well.

With these concerns motivating the followers, it did not really matter much what the saint's doctrine or attitude actually was, so long as he provided a physical presence redolent of sanctity. Puritanical Sufi pirs who made absolutely no grandiose claims for themselves in life very often had them made for them after their deaths by latter-day devotees. For example, worshippers began praying at the tomb of the idol-smashing Ibn Hanbal only forty years after his death in 855, venerating as a saint and spiritual intercessor the man who is today taken as the patron of iconoclastic anti-Sufism. Similarly, the Nasiriyya Brotherhood in Tamgrout, southern Morocco, was founded in the early seventeenth century by Ben Nasir, a Sufi who disallowed ecstatic dancing and trance, condemned magic, favored strict observance of prayer, study, and imitation of the Prophet. Yet after his death, he was attributed with mystical powers, and the brotherhood developed into a standard Sufic cult centered on his tomb.[28]

It seems then that in medieval Middle Eastern culture where legitimate authority and personal security were so hard to come by, any man of religious repute was likely to attract a clientele to his grave.[29] The tendency toward saint worship was furthered by pirs who were persuaded that the ordinary man had to be drawn into religiosity by carnivalesque entertainments and promises of marvels. A puritan Sufi may not have believed in his own magical qualities, but nonetheless might tolerate and even encourage the miracle-seekers flocking to him, and might offer his hand to be kissed by ardent pilgrims seeking some of his baraka.

Ambiguities of Selflessness

In making these extravagant claims for spiritual authority of their leaders, the brotherhoods overturned cultural values of autonomy and equality, and raised questions among the orthodox. Cynics wondered whether the wali given such credit by his devotees might in fact be a hypocrite hiding behind a mask of saintliness while secretly doing what everyone else does. Though his disciples say he is no longer an ordinary human being, he was surely still born from man and woman; whatever his special saintly aroma may seem to be, he still sweats, and perhaps the wine he drinks is not honey after all.

Ambivalence remained even for those who did accept the presentation of the saint as a man lost in God, since the subordination of the self for the sake of a higher power has troubling ramifications in Middle Eastern culture. As we have seen in the case of the ulema, such self-denial stands in complete contrast to the active self-expression required of ordinary men in daily life. Because his training is so rigorous, because his proof of his virtuoso status is solely in his own personal charisma, and because his existential communion with God is expressed in powerful rituals that move the public, the Sufi represents this contradiction in its strongest form. This is especially so when the pir asserts his spiritual authority, yet avoids personal responsibility for his acts by claiming to be an extension of the Almighty. As a result, the very characteristics of the pir that drew his disciples' love have also aroused qualms in the general public, who regarded the friends of God with a mixture of awe and fear that sometimes verged on repulsion.

This attitude is clear in the folk beliefs collected by Westermark in Morocco:

> The same sorts of places – rocks, caves, springs, the sea – as are haunted by *jnun* (malevolent spirits) are also associated with saints – occasionally there is some doubt whether a certain place is connected with a saint or merely haunted by jnun...The relations between saints and jnun are often of a very intimate character. Many saints...rule over jnun, who act as their *huddam*, or servants, and in the so-called *jenn* saints the borderline between saint and jenn is almost obliterated...There are no doubt saints and shereefs who have been habitually and notoriously guilty of great crimes without losing their reputation for sanctity.[30]

These dangerous saints were generally believed by the populace to have magical powers of flight, telepathy, mind-reading, and shape-changing that show their freedom from human constraints and their capacity to invade the personal space of the ordinary man. Along with their awesome and frightening abilities, they were thought as well to be hungry for power, extremely jealous, and suffused with a potent but polymorphous sexuality that can seduce those who go to them for spiritual help. In Swat, men with birthmarks on their faces are still pointed out as the products of their mothers' illicit unions with erotic Sufis.

Pirs could also be violent, as we discover in saintly hagiographies, where an important place is given to miracle competitions between rival friends of God who demonstrated their prowess through displays of spiritual strength, such as reading men's minds, walking on water, and curing the ill. This could escalate into outright combat, as the saints carried on supernatural battles that were analogous to the power struggles waged between tribesmen. Although the weapons of combatants were intangible, they were believed to be just as deadly as spears and swords, and casualties among the murids could be high.

Magical weapons were also used to punish anyone who failed to pay proper respect to the saint. Even animals were not immune. It is said that a bird that flew over Gilani's head without making obeisance was immediately blasted out of the air, while goats eating pasture belonging to a saint would die automatically.[31] Other recorded miracles are rarely the kindly acts westerners might expect. For example, in many popular tales, the saint is a trickster: train conductors who demand a fare from him find their trains suddenly immobilized, their watches stopped – but all comes right again when abject apologies are made. In other cases, the power of the saint is much more frightening: Rumi's mentor Shams magically deafened a pious murid, and forced him to recite in public that "there is no God but God, and Shams-i Tabrizi is his Prophet." When the student was attacked for this blasphemy, Shams roared with such might that he killed one of the attackers, proving his miraculous powers.[32]

Even rulers were not exempt from supernatural punishment if they happened to offend a friend of God. Nicholson tells us that when an emir failed to give a donation to the kindly saint Abu Said (who was known to his disciples as "love's bondsman") he was punished by being devoured alive by his own dogs. Merchants who were stingy in their gifts were threatened with similar fates.[33] These acts of supernatural vengeance and extortion can be read as popular myths of spiritual resistance to repressive authorities,[34] but they are also clearly expressions of the saint's fearsome power to act with a peremptory cruelty that was equal to, if not greater than, the cruelty of the state; a cruelty even more frightening because it could not be escaped or manipulated. In folklore the pir maintains respect much as a Sultan might: through the arbitrary use of brute force.

The truth or falsehood of the beliefs held by the common people about the friends of God is irrelevant for the argument made here; certainly many saints were of a peaceful and kindly character. What is notable is that the Sufi pir, because of his assertion of a special sacredness that emanates from his transfigured person, is a man who has been popularly venerated insofar as he reveals extraordinary powers, but along with respect has always been a marked degree of ambiguity, fear and distaste, as testified in the Moroccan proverb that "God's mercy comes from visiting a saint and going away soon."[35] The pir is always a dangerous figure, followed when he can offer spiritual influence, ecstatic experience, and a variety of worldly connections and services, but abandoned when other sources of leverage and power are available that are less perilous, ambivalent, and demanding.

It is no accident then that the heyday of Sufism was during the Seljuk reign and under the disruptive regime of the Mongols, when the Caliphate had fallen and a purely secular authority had begun to suborn and encapsulate the ulema, leaving the populace with very little in the way of either spiritual resources or legitimate authority. The Sufi lodges with their cosmic hierarchy of charismatics offered Muslim masses the experience of unity under sanctified leadership, as well as an imaginary universal order overseeing the disrupted universe.

But as the Islamicate slowly knit itself together again, Sufi brotherhoods were increasingly obliged to emphasize the miraculous powers of their pirs and to offer the merger of ecstatic trance. These ever more prevalent aspects of Sufism were disturbing to the ordinary man, who was both drawn to and repulsed by Sufic demands for deification of a leader and repudiation of the agentic self; demands that contradicted the sober attitude of orthodox Islam and the dominant individualistic and egalitarian ethic of the culture that Sufism sought to transform through personal charisma. As a result, many Sufi brotherhoods were slowly reduced to meeting places for mystically inclined intellectuals, or to isolated communities for the marginalized, or to popular entertainments. Despite some exceptions, that is largely where they remain today.

Islamists and Sufis

But the lure of the pir's charisma and of the discipline of the tariqa has not lost its salience completely. Even though Sufism has become less central in Middle Eastern Islam, many of its beliefs and practices have been reborn in a new politicized guise within present-day radical Islamist movements, which have arisen as a response to the political and moral crisis in the Islamicate caused by modernization, social transformation, and the challenge of western culture. Under these extraordinary pressures some pious and alienated Middle Easterners, disappointed at the failed promises of Marxism and nationalism, have repudiated their rulers as unIslamic, decried the complicity of the ulema with the state, and called for a new society that, like the original umma, would be ruled by the consensus of virtuous Muslims under the overarching ordinances of the sharia.

These self-designated Islamists have not only contested the moral authority of the orthodox ulema, but have also been overtly hostile to

popular Sufism.[36] They maintain that Sufi practices are immoral innovations, and assert that the praise of Sufi saints and worship at saint's
tombs are practices dangerously close to heresy. But despite their harsh
ideological condemnation of Sufism, Islamist radicals have nonetheless
gathered around charismatic figures and organized themselves in ways
that closely resemble activist Sufi brotherhoods of the past.

For example, the radical Takfir wa al-hijra (infidel and exile) group –
many of whom were imprisoned and executed after their assassination
of the Egyptian minister of religious endowments – advocated a complete separation from society in preparation for their millenarian revolt
against what they imagined to be the diabolical Egyptian state.
Members of the sect were sworn to secrecy, bound together in tightly
controlled and isolated units, rigorously instructed in techniques for
self-purification, and enjoined to complete obedience. All of them were
under the command of an absolute leader, Shukri Mustafa, who
claimed to know the secret meaning of every letter in the Quran, and
whose word was regarded as sacred law.[37] Similar patterns are found in
other radical Islamist sects, and even the relatively moderate Muslim
Brotherhood developed secretive and inclusive cells (called families)
that were held together by rigid discipline and a powerful faith in the
spiritual supremacy of their leader, Hassan al-Banna, who was given
the Sufi title of murshid.[38]

The tendency among Islamic reformers to participate in secretive
charismatic cults is in part a predictable result of the repressive political
regimes of the Middle East which violently persecute all opponents. In
response, activists naturally seek security by gathering in secretive solidary groups knit together through shared beliefs and rituals; such groups
often are also inclined to submit to a leader idealized as divinely inspired. We find cult-like millennial-messianic organizations arising
under similarly hostile conditions in many societies, both Muslim and
non-Muslim. Politicized Sufi sects of the past can be seen as subtypes of
this universal form of protest.

But contemporary Islamists have also been driven to idealization of
charismatic leaders and Sufic organization for reasons more specifically
related to the egalitarian principles of the Middle East and of Islam.
These ideals, taken to their logical extreme, have always led Muslim
zealots to condemn all formal authority structures as immoral impos-
itions, and to argue that "institutional functions are only as good as the
virtue of those who exercise them". The moral leader therefore needs
no official bureaucratic or genealogical qualifications; he can be anyone
at all, so long as he is a male adult Muslim of good health and impeccable character.[39]

It follows then that because personal virtue is the sole criterion for
legitimate authority, the leader of a just government or righteous

organization must "be *index sui*, his own indicator,"[40] followed for his personal qualities alone. In Islamic and especially in Sufi thought, the model for this exemplary and inspiring figure is the Qutb, the pole of the universe, the Perfect Man, the recapitulation of the Prophet, who must be obeyed by those spiritual elect who intuitively recognize his personal right to command. The Islamists are accordingly obliged to search for leaders who, like Sufi pirs, are not known by their credentials, but by their intangible auras – which only the chosen can discern.

Once the true leader has been discovered and recognized, it is the duty of the disciples to emulate him and to offer him their absolute devotion, rejecting the corrupt society around them in order to replicate, within their own band of the spiritually elite, the original umma gathered around the Prophet. A political party organized in this fashion then becomes the equivalent of the Sufi tariqa; a closed society serving as a training ground in purification of the soul, where a hierarchy of dedicated disciples gain sacred knowledge through arduous study of texts written by the leader, public confession of sins, absolute obedience, and practice in self-sacrifice. As Olivier Roy writes, under these conditions, "the degrees of affiliation to the party correspond to stages of personal conversion, of psychological internalization, and not to the simple acquisition of knowledge and techniques. The career of the militant is thus a kind of ladder of virtues, the quintessence of which is embodied in the one who stands at the summit...The stages of 'initiation' are explicitly likened to a mystical initiation."[41]

In these new activist mystical-political cults, the old Muslim dream of the personal redeemer has once again been reawakened among the devotees, only to be dashed anew by the compromises of politics and the repressive power of the state. For some the response has been suicidal acts of terrorism, as fervent disciples hope to frighten the authorities and awaken popular resistance by demonstrating their own selfless faith. This is clearly an act of desperation – a reenactment of the assassination policies of the Nizari, whose marginalization in the Muslim world of the Seljuks led them to follow this same tactic in their own futile pursuit of the millennium.[42] Al-Qaeda is the most recent example of this path.

But most former radicals have renounced violence and have transformed themselves into ulema with madrasas and mosques of their own – often funded by Saudi Arabia. These so-called neofundamentalists are mostly dedicated to creating "Islamic spaces", enforcing purdah, fasting, and general abstinence, and otherwise policing the morality of ordinary persons. Their efforts at purification of the faith have often been encouraged by governments anxious to promote safe expressions of Islamic fervor by drawing religious enthusiasts into the ambit of the state. Although the austerity drives of puritanical neofundamentalists have already made a considerable difference in the tenor of public life in many Middle Eastern societies, the movement itself has not challenged secular authority, nor is it likely to do so. Instead, as Roy writes, "the transformation of Islamist parties into mass movements and the test of power will produce the same results that it has with all other ideologies: the 'pure' will be corrupted or will abandon politics to climbers, careerists, and unscrupulous businessmen."[43] It seems then that either martyrdom or accommodation is the likely end point of Muslim political charismatic movements, even in their new Islamist guise. Under these alienating conditions, it is very possible that Sufism will reemerge as a central part of Middle Eastern culture, offering the disillusioned a more experiential route to enlightenment.

Part V

Dilemmas of Subordination

14

Slaves, Eunuchs, and Blacks

Gelded Warriors: Slaves and Clients

It has often been observed that the Muslim Middle East was unique in world history in the pervasiveness and importance of slavery within its boundaries. As in the West, the slave in the Middle East was bought and sold, could not testify in court, was sexually available to the master, and so on. But unlike the western slave who was valued primarily for hard labor, many slaves in the Middle East were employed as servants in the house, as concubines, and, most importantly, as soldiers and administrators at the center of power.[1]

The evolution of secular government in the Middle East from the ninth century shows the ever-increasing importance of slave warriors and bureaucrats purchased or captured from the manpower reservoirs of Central Asia, Africa, and Europe. These *mamluks*, as they were called, who had been taken from their kin groups and homelands to be sold into service, became the arms and legs of the state and were reckoned as the most powerful persons in the land after the Sultan. The mamluks of Egypt even became kings themselves.

The power of the mamluks grew during the Abbasid era, when the Caliphs employed "Turks" to offset the influence of the Khurasaniyya troops to whom they owed their power. Slaves and clients also entered the administration as the entourages of royalty, undertaking the tasks that free men found beneath their dignity or beyond their capacity. This trend was prefigured by the Umayyad use of men from "inferior" tribes and kin groups as administrators and governors. These were the mawali, the "clients", whose loyalty was to their patrons and who, according to Bernard Lewis, made up the bulk of imperial and metropolitan forces as early as 766.

Ernest Gellner remarks that in the pre-capitalist Middle East, these dependent administrators and soldiers were the equivalents of modern wage workers who, without the refuge of protective lineages or other primary groups, are at the mercy of their employers, and he wryly concludes that "we are all mamluks now."[2] But the parallel is not quite exact, since, unlike today's employees, the mamluks and mawali could not look for a better job, nor could they be fired, though they could be sold or transferred. They were bound unconditionally to their superiors, who had complete power over them, and who also gave them their only opportunity for upward mobility.

As outlined in chapter 4, the preponderance of clients and slaves in the Middle East was classically explained by Ibn Khaldun as a natural result of a ruler's desire to dispense with his co-equal kin, who make claims on his loyalty and who feel themselves to be equally capable of exercising power. It is in this vein that the Seljuk wazir Nizam al-Mulk wrote that "wise men have said that a worthy servant or slave is better than a son... One obedient slave is better than three hundred sons; for the latter desire their father's death, the former long life for his master."[3] Most rulers followed this advice, and relied on servants and slaves to staff their armies and retinue. Mastery demonstrated an individual's masculine capacity to dominate, and provided him with reliable allies who (in theory at least) were selflessly dedicated to helping in his competition against his kinsmen and rivals.

However, the policy of substituting slaves and servants for free men inevitably led, Ibn Khaldun argued, to the loss of the group feeling (asabiyya) that had bound the original conquering tribesmen together. Slaves and dependent clients had no sense of the importance of the shared community, but merely supported their own particular master against all others. They even fomented disunity among their masters in order to further their own interests. According to Ibn Khaldun, without the cohesion and loyalty engendered by group feeling, the dynasty was debilitated, and would finally fall prey to invasion by a more potent band of tribal kinsmen, as yet uncontaminated by the institutions of slavery and clientship. But until that moment came, mamluks and mawali would assume greater and greater power within the regime, where their number and importance would be a clear indicator of the inner infirmity of the regime.

Patricia Crone added another dimension to Ibn Khaldun's theory. For her, the dominance of mamluks in political life after the Abbasid era is actually an indicator of their contaminated status, since the local elite of landed aristocrats, merchants and scholars all had walked out on a state which had "ceased to embody public norms," leaving it to be ruled by a despised cadre consisting primarily of the slaves, mercenaries and dependents of foreign military general/kings.[4]

In the delegitimized state, slaves and servants of the state by and large were better off and more powerful than free men. Yet even the most powerful of them could be deposed and killed at whim, as Harun al-

Rashid pointedly demonstrated when he slaughtered his mighty Barmakid wazir and displayed the man's mutilated body in the public market. In principle, the servants of the crown and the nobility had no lineages, no kin groups, no community outside their barracks and offices. Even their marriages were arranged by their employers, and their children had no rights to inherit their father's power or position.[5] They were, in effect, prohibited from the possibility of constructing futures for their offspring.

Such absolute dependency (even when it coincided with very great authority) was deeply repellent to Middle Eastern culture, where the notions of personal honor, patrilineal continuity, equality, and independence have always been inextricably linked – so much so that the word for freedom (*hurriyya*) also means noble, dignified, generous and good. As Franz Rosenthal notes, this conjunction of meanings "shows the tremendous emotional impact exercised by the concept of freedom, by the feeling of independence, upon the average Muslim."[6] The same ideology retains its attraction today, as tribesmen and proletariat alike agree that freedom and honor are an individual's most precious possessions, not to be sold for any amount.

Within this ethos, being under the yoke of another is regarded as intrinsically debasing and dishonorable; as Ernest Gellner writes, for Middle Easterners "only those who refuse to be governed are themselves fit to rule: political education is to be had in the wilderness alone."[7] The Pukhtun of Pakistan and Afghanistan have a word, *begherata*, which is used for such a person – it not only means a man without independence, but also a coward, a cuckold, a passive homosexual. For them, as for other Middle Easterners, a lack of freedom and the acceptance of servility is metaphorically linked with a lack of manhood.

The link between virility and freedom was not only metaphorical, since in the Middle East, to a degree unknown anywhere else in the world, actual castration was regularly practiced on slaves. There were practical reasons for this. After the operation the slave could be trusted as guardian of the harem. Also, the eunuch was physically sundered from any hope of posterity, which in principle ought to make him even more completely reliant on his master than other slaves, whose break with the future was enforced only by rules prohibiting passing on their power and wealth to their progeny.

But castration also had an important symbolic function. In gelding his slave the master demonstrated his superiority within the framework of an ideology of natural distinctions that dehumanizes and degrades certain categories of person as intrinsically inferior. As we shall see, in the Middle East women have been the major targets of this belief system. By the physical act of castration, which forcibly assimilates the slave into this "naturally" debased non-male category, a symbolic statement is made about the innate inferiority of all slaves and clients who, by extension, belong to the same debased class of humans; the eunuch became physically what it was believed all slaves must be psychologically: effeminate and impotent.

In societies where ascriptive hierarchy is taken for granted, distinctions need not be imposed by such radical measures, since differences of rank are already understood as essential, immutable and God-given. For instance, in the caste society of India, the lower orders were known to be naturally polluted and inferior because of their customs and hereditary tasks, which were believed to be the result of the working of a karmic order that rewarded and punished one's deeds in prior incarnations. The moral distinctions between caste groups were accepted by all, so that the use of mutilation or physical castration of subalterns to symbolize and imprint their inferiority was unnecessary and all but unknown.

In contrast, it is precisely in a society with an all-embracing egalitarian ethic that the pressure is greatest for a superior individual to differentiate himself by rendering his inferiors not only completely dependent, but also symbolically subhuman – an effort which finds its most extreme expression in the actual emasculation of slaves. The prevalence of slavery and eunuchry in the Middle East then can be seen as consequences, both symbolically and practically, of the region's pervasive tenet of egalitarianism as it is enacted within an ideological framework of "natural" masculine superiority.

Race and Inferiority

Another way to dehumanize inferiors among egalitarian individualists is through the ideology of race. As a symbolic marker, race, like sex, has the advantage of seeming natural; it is physically evident, hard to disguise, and can serve as a convenient peg upon which to hang a whole collection of stereotypes that can serve to rationalize inferior status. For example, Louis Dumont has argued that racism does the symbolic work of legitimizing inferior status within the prevailing American egalitarian ethos. A dark skin is understood by many white Americans as a biological and accordingly true sign of subhuman character; people of color can then be regarded as naturally bestial and not qualified for inclusion as human beings and co-equals. The poverty and segregation of blacks is understood as organic and therefore justified.[8]

A similar ideology of race exists in the Middle East as well, where racial prejudice has a long history. According to Bernard Lewis,[9] early Arabs had no real notion of a connection between skin color and character, though they did consider darker skins to be ugly, much like

Plate 14.1   Eighteenth-century portrait of a black slave in Persia.
His dress and the fact that he has been immortalized in a portrait
suggest that he has achieved high social status.

any other physical feature that did not meet their norm of beauty. But
the Arabs had great respect for the dark-skinned Ethiopians who almost
conquered them. And although the children of black slave women
suffered some social opprobrium due to a combination of their ignominious background and culturally unattractive appearance, they could succeed by their skills, so that some became famous warriors and bards.

As one, the black poet Nusayb (d. 726), says: "Blackness does not
diminish me, as long as I have this tongue and this stout heart. Some are
raised up by means of their lineage; the verses of my poems are my
lineage." Antara, the great pre-Islamic poet and warrior, affirmed that
"enemies revile me for the blackness of my skin, but the whiteness of my
character effaces the blackness," while another poet writes that "if I am
black in color, my character is white."[10] Here "blackness" is held, by
both black and white, to be an ugly physical attribute, correlated with a
base lineage, but it could be overcome by a person's intrinsic abilities.

This was changed when the gradual Muslim conquest of Africa
brought Arabs and other Middle Easterners in contact with black cultures which did not have the sophistication or the military capacity of

the early Ethiopians. After these conquests, and the resulting influx of black slaves (generically called *Zanj*), the attitude toward people from Africa changed for the worse. Ibn Khaldun writes: "the Negro nations are, as a rule, submissive to slavery because (Negroes) have little that is (essentially) human and possess attributes that are quite similar to those of dumb animals."[11]

For Ibn Khaldun it is precisely the submissiveness of the Negroes that is taken as proof of their animality. True human beings would not be so tractable, but would fight for their equality. In reality, it was almost impossible for the African countrymen to make any such determined resistance, given the vast technical superiority of the Arab military; their weakness and servility was then interpreted as evidence of their inborn subordinate nature. The great cultural gap between the black pagans and their Muslim conquerors also made it easy for the Arabs to see their African slaves as less than human, since they seemed to share so little with them in terms of belief and culture.

Among the brown-skinned Arabs, whites too were prejudiced against, and conquered light-skinned nations, such as people from the Caucasus, also suffered, like black slaves, from the stigma of subordination. But white slaves, who generally came from more complex, literate and militaristic societies, and who also usually had faith in a monotheistic religion, were more easily assimilated into the Middle Eastern culture. These whites were the trusted military and administrative mamluks, which literally meant "owned", while blacks, who mainly filled menial roles as guards, laborers, and household servants, were known simply as abid, "slaves" – a term which Lewis informs us has become the general word for "black" in some Arab dialects.

Few blacks ever reached the social heights that the white mamluk attained, and when they did it was cause for vicious satirical comment, as blackness and servility became strongly linked in the public mind – a connection made even more compelling by the common practice of castrating black household workers. Hence when a Nubian eunuch became regent of Egypt in the tenth century, he was reviled by the poet al-Mutanabbi, who asks: "Who ever taught the eunuch negro nobility? His 'white' people, or his royal ancestors, or his ear bleeding in the hand of the slave broker?"[12] White mamluk authorities were never the subject of such abuse.

As in the West, black inferiority was understood by Middle Easterners as a natural biological phenomenon, though it was also sometimes justified theologically by reference to the biblical curse on Ham, who was regarded by Muslims as the forefather of the blacks. Black subordinate status was inevitably paralleled to the equally "natural" inferiority of women to men, and the abid were seen as "like women" in their emotionality and lack of discrimination. Other attributed traits served to mark them off from true masculine human beings: they were not only servile, they were dirty, stupid, lazy, cowardly, unreliable and bad-smelling. They were also dangerously and animalistically sexual, and served as the typical seducers in fantasies of wifely infidelity.[13] When viewed positively, they were praised for their simple piety and loyalty, and were often pictured in the role of faithful servant.

These stereotypes, which are troublingly familiar, reflect a tendency to validate inferiority in an egalitarian culture by turning the "naturally" inferior subordinate into a reversed image of the idealized everyman. If brown-skinned true men are brave, emotionally controlled, consistent and honorable, then black-skinned "nonmen" will be the reverse. If true men are constrained in their relations with women, "nonmen" are bestial sexual dynamos. Even the positive imagery of the black has a similar significance: innately servile blacks will readily adapt themselves to loyal service and selfless worship while proud brown-skinned warriors are driven to assert their individuality and personal honor.

Yet, although color prejudice is a deeply-embedded part of Middle Eastern popular culture, it has always been opposed by the egalitarian ethos of Islam. As Lewis tells us, "at no time did Muslim theologians or jurists accept the idea that there may be races of mankind predisposed by nature or foredoomed by Providence to the condition of slavery." As evidence, he notes that the Prophet appointed his black slave Bilal as Islam's first muezzin and reputedly demanded that Bilal be allowed to marry into a noble Arab family, pointing out the direction he wished Islam to take; Lewis also translates al-Sahib ibn Abbad (d. 995) who wrote that "since God created tallness and shortness and the blackness of the Zanj and the whiteness of the Greeks, it is not right that men should be blamed or punished for these qualities, since God neither enjoined nor forbade them."[14] In the Middle East, there have been no lynchings, no miscegenation laws,[15] no legal efforts to differentiate people according to their degree of black blood; with the support of Islam, blacks have generally been able to assert their absolute rights as equals to their white siblings and achieve positions of power and re-spect that until recently were quite beyond what they have gained in America and Europe where color prejudice remains the major mode for justifying the degradation of human beings.

The Categorization of Human Types

Islamic doctrine was not the only source of opposition to racism in the Middle East; the salience of skin color as a marker of inferiority was undermined as well by the proliferation of human differences resulting from the expansion of Islam and the huge variation of persons within the empire. As the Quran says: "Among His signs is the creation of the heavens and the earth, and the variation in your languages and of your colors. Verily in that are Signs for those who know."[16] 'Black', 'white', and 'brown' were difficult classifications to keep distinct in this poly-chromatic world.

The overwhelming diversity of racial types in the Middle East coin-cided with a social universe that was actually highly mobile and rela-tively unpredictable. To keep a sense of control in this fluid environment, Middle Easterners have been preoccupied with typologizing human beings according to a set of expectations and categories based not only on race, but on nation, lineage, occupation, residence, and faith; all separate markers of identity that may or may not overlap in any particu-lar case, and that could be used as indicators of rank.

For example, in any Middle Eastern camp, town or city one can quickly discover current stereotypes about the essential personalities of local lineages and neighborhoods. Some are praised as intrinsically stal-wart, others are condemned as innately cowardly or stingy, and so on. These characterizations vary according to the source, as each tribe or quarter puts itself on the moral high ground, and denigrates the rest. Everywhere similar notions about the typical traits and tendencies of the members of different professions prevail, with some regarded as natur-ally defiled by their occupations. In tenth-century Baghdad, as Mas-signon tells us, these degraded groups included the "blacksmith, butcher, conjuror, policeman, highwayman, police informer, night watchman... tanner, maker of wooden and leather pails, maker of women's shoes, burier of excrement, well-digger, stoker of baths, felt-maker, masseur, horse trader... weavers, ironsmiths, pigeon racers, and chess players."[17]

Each occupation, degraded or not, had its own stereotypical charac-ters and behaviors that were attributed to it by others. For instance, amongst the Pukhtun of Swat, the despised leather-workers (*shah khel*) were regarded as being extremely prone to anger, energetic, reticent, and exceptionally hard-working. They served as the confidants and their wives as the milk-mothers of the warrior nobility. The barber (*nai*) who is paired with the leatherworker as the lowest occupational group of the village, has an "effeminate" personality attributed to him: talkative, un-trustworthy, cowardly, greedy for favors, wheedling, and sexually im-moral. He was the gossip of the village, and his wife the village slut.[18]

Such stereotyping did not only apply to the lower social orders. In sophisticated urban circles the ulema of the various schools were regarded as having specific moral characters: according to Muqaddasi the Hanafite was officious, deft, well-informed, devout and prudent; the Malikite was dull, obtuse, and observant of the Sunna; the Shafi'ite was shrewd, impatient, understanding, and quick-tempered; the Mutazilite was elegant, erudite, and ironic; the Shi'ite was rancorous and loved wealth.[19]

Plate 14.2   Nine of the forty-eight headdress variations recorded in mid-eighteenth-century Yemen. Each headdress indicates significant distinctions of ethnicity, occupation, status, and so on.

Religious categorizations could be considerably more demeaning, as Sunnis degraded Shi'ites, while the Shi'ites returned the favor with added malice. Some Shi'ites even refused commensality with non-Shi'ites, and considered contact with them to be polluting; an attitude that can be understood both as a reaction to their own inferior position and as a consequence of the ancient Persian concern with matters of purity, expressed in an unwillingness to share bread with outsiders. Violent pogroms also sometimes occurred on both sides, reflecting fears of subversion by minority groups with political-religious agendas. But in general, Shi'ite and Sunni have been able to live together in relative peace.

There was also prejudice against non-Muslims (the *dhimmi*), with Jews often singled out as especially unworthy of respect. Yet here too, until recently (with the advent of Israel), discrimination has been relatively minimal compared to the West; except for extraordinary occasions, murder, violence, or humiliation of non-Muslims has never been practiced on any systematic basis or on any wide-scale in the Middle East, nor has bigotry or violence against Jews or Christians been regularly preached from the mosque, except in modern times. Rather, resident dhimmi were regarded as "protected" by the umma. In return, they were required to pay extra taxes and suffered a degree of social exclusion and degradation. At the same time, they were exempt from certain demands. As men without honor, they were not expected to serve as warriors, and ought not be attacked during battles. Jews were also allowed to undertake tasks forbidden to Muslims, such as tin and silver-smithing, and were permitted to give loans with interest. If Jews or Christians converted to Islam they were accorded the same respect and the same legal rights as any born Muslim.

We can see then that religion, occupation, and nationality, in addition to color, were used by urbanites, villagers and tribesmen alike as categories that could legitimize inferiority. But by far the most ubiquitous validation for high and low rank has always been reference to one's forefathers; those who are inferior are conceived of as "naturally" effeminate, impotent or child-like due to their ignoble bloodline, while those who are superior claim descent from a lineage of powerful masculine heroes: this distinction is certified by political reality – we rule, you serve; therefore we are true human beings, while you are damaged or faulty and naturally weak (daif). It is significant in this regard that daif means weak and impotent, but also signifies those without pedigree and unarmed; the daif are powerless because they are ignoble and incapable of fighting.

Images of masculine warrior adults "naturally" dominating womanly, infantile and weak underlings are especially characteristic among Muslim tribal groups. For instance, the Berbers of Morocco believe the lower orders of serfs, smiths, and musicians have wayward or effeminate characters that contrast to the steady, sober, and manly personalities of the tribesmen. Similar beliefs in the blood inferiority of subordinate groups are to be found in the El Shabana Arabs of Iraq, the town of Huraydah in Yemen, the Pukhtun and Marri Baluch of Pakistan, and the Bedouin of Egypt and Saudi Arabia – among others.[20] The imputation of blood inferiority can take on caste-like proportions in practice, as intermarriage and even commensality may be prohibited between the warrior elite and their inferiors. This is precisely the argument made against intermarriage with mawali by Arab purists after the conquests – such a marriage would degrade Arab blood. So too the Pukhtun warrior would never marry a leatherworker or barber; the Bedouin refuse to marry peasants, the Baluch proscribe marriage with their serfs, smiths or musicians, and the people of Huraydah will not eat with a group of "untouchables" who are polluting by their very presence.

The idiom of natural stigma, tainted lineages, pollution, and impotence can be used metaphorically to express the inferiority of those who are obliged to pay taxes and homage to the state. For the Pukhtun tribesmen of the hill country, the lowlander Pukhtun are considered to be permanently degraded because they have given up their masculine prerogatives of autonomy and equality. This is interpreted as feminization or castration; those who submit are no longer deserving of respect and honor. Rather, they are created to be servants, and to be preyed upon by predatory warriors. In Morocco too the tribal Berbers of the hinterlands see themselves as wolves permitted to feed upon "the sheep who have submitted to authority, thereby betraying a loss of moral fibre that might make them royal, and losing it ever more completely through the habits of submission."[21] The Bedouin also believe the peasants whom they dominate are not worthy to rule themselves, but deserve to be controlled by their tribal overlords, who provide them with the authoritative command and protection they need.

This attitude also applied, as we have seen, to those who were the direct servants of the state, who by the Umayyad period were men whom the free Arab warriors held in contempt for their tarnished identities and commoner lineages, since no man of honor would consent to such demeaning service. This attitude is put in verse by a noble Arab poet who calls for a rebellion against the plebeian viceroy Hajjaj because "God and the pride of Ibn Muhammad (b. Ashath) and his descent from a race of kings older than Thamud, forbid us to use ourselves to the rule of wretches sprung from slaves."[22]

All these tribesmen "recognize that people...are divided into a number of different categories, each one of which tends to be occupationally specialized, highly endogamous, and ranked."[23] Each of them, of course, envisions his own people to be of the highest nobility. Yet coincident with the plethora of invidious distinctions, the tribesmen remain egalitarian in their conceptualization of human nature – it is just that very few people qualify as fully human, due to their ignominious ancestry, present weakness, and resultant character flaws.

It is clear then that color and religion have been but two elements among many that have been selected by Middle Easterners to make general characterizations, evolve moral hierarchies and establish expectations in an egalitarian cultural milieu that is highly flexible, opportunistic, and competitive. Of greatest import has been the notion of naturally noble blood validating itself in warrior deeds of conquest; but other stereotypes of national character, religious affiliation, occupation, class, neighborhood, and region also have been used to place others and oneself into "natural" categories that can be used to justify superiority and inferiority. In the United States the absence of such salient social groupings means that color emerges as the overwhelming indicator of "natural" subservience. In the Middle East, on the contrary, there are multiple modes of imputing natural inferiority to others, so that race has been of lesser, though still considerable, importance.

Noble Slaves, Base Freemen

The attribution of "natural" baseness to some populations within an egalitarian culture can never be made without arousing resistance or at least ambiguity, since people will not only search for ways to validate distinctions of rank, but also for ways to obviate, overturn or disguise those very distinctions, and to draw all humanity together into a community of equals. We have seen this to be the case already in the opposition of Islam to all forms of racial prejudice.

On the secular side as well, the very vitriol spewed by "noble" claimants to authority against their "ignoble" rivals illustrates the tensions involved in maintaining an ideology of innate superiority in a society where obstacles of nationality, color, slavery, previous religion, and even emasculation could be and were overcome by ambitious and able men who struggled to climb to positions of power and influence. The Nubian eunuch slave who governed Egypt was remarkable, as was the plebeian viceroy Hajjaj; the ascendance of these men was, as we have seen, greeted with scorn by their noble and freeborn opponents. But what is even more important is that these protests were of no avail. Both men governed nonetheless. The impotent anger of the old elite indicates the relative openness of the system.

In acknowledgment of the realistic possibility for upward mobility and in keeping with the general religious and cultural ethic of equality and achievement, the dehumanization of inferiors has never been complete in the Middle East. As in the case of race, negative stereotypes of all sorts have always generated counterimages in which subalterns are portrayed as human beings whose subordination is merely circumstantial and who have private inner lives, personal honor, and a unique fate. Most importantly, the enslaved and demeaned were understood to have both the desire and the capacity for freedom. This meant that the slave's subservience might only be outward, while inwardly he could retain his independence due to his strength of character. As the black slave poet, Suhaym (d. 660), sang: "If I am a slave, my soul is free because it is noble."[24]

It followed logically that the reverse could also be true; a legally free man could be enslaved by desire, or, even worse, have a naturally sycophantic character. From the perspective of an egalitarian and individualistic ethic, both of these are inherently more despicable than the inferior status of the legal slave, who is forced into thralldom. So it happens that in the Middle East the notion of slaves as "naturally" inferior and deserving of their debased positions is answered by the suspicion that some of them might in fact be innately noble and proud. And, while it is usually taken for granted that freemen are "naturally" superior to their slaves, Middle Easterners also recognize that some of the free may be inherently more base than the slaves they own.

Because of these ambivalences, slavery could be imaginatively transposed from a legal relationship and status position into a matter of personal character; slavery may be debasing, but slaves could inwardly resist their subordination and assert their basic autonomy. Al-Ghazali even warned that citizenry in a state was a greater threat to the human spirit of freedom than actual bondage, since subordination to government requires voluntary acceptance, while slavery is involuntary and forced. The slave, realizing his bondage, can retain his inner autonomy, while the citizen has been tamed into welcoming his own inferiority and accepting his chains[25] – an analysis given force by the fact that the Arabic word for grooming animals is identical with the word for training constituencies in political obedience; siyasah, the art of politics.[25] To a degree, then, slaves are to be envied for the clarity of their forced subordination, while citizens are to be pitied because they have been complicit in their own castration.

Similar ambivalence toward ranking and subordination is expressed in the ethic of the pious Muslim, for whom the "the natural condition, and therefore the presumed status, of mankind was freedom...whoever is not known to be a slave is free."[27] From the orthodox legal point of view, people become slaves of others only due to the vicissitudes of fate; a slave or subordinate is essentially no different from anyone else; all are alike in their fundamental relationship to a God before whom all human beings are equally powerless. The derogatory term for black slaves (abid) therefore also signifies "mankind" as well as "servant of God"; it may be used as a kind of honorific and is the root of one of the most common Muslim names: Abdullah, or "slave of Allah".

Some Sufis, such as Junayd, carried the orthodox validation of subordination even further. He writes: "As long as you have not achieved completely true slavery, you will not be able to reach pure freedom."[28] As we have seen, unconditional obedience and renunciation of the self was required if a Sufi was to claim unity with God and spiritual superiority over other Muslims. This process began with self-abnegation in the master-teacher relationship and could be extended to include submission to political rule; the obsequiousness of the governed, so decried by al-Ghazali, was thereby refigured by some Sufis into an exemplary spiritual discipline. By implication, the servile are actually superior to their political masters, since they are practicing the spiritual discipline of naughting themselves.

However, most orthodox Muslims do not go so far; they do not aim at a reversal of hierarchy so that the politically low become the spiritually high, but rather at a leveling of the ground. This is most explicitly expressed in the hajj which makes absolutely no discrimination between believers on any grounds; all pilgrims of whatever race, occupation, or nation participate equally, dressed in the same simple ritual clothing, all simultaneously follow the prescribed circuit of the kaaba. Even the distinction of gender, which is so deeply embedded in Middle Eastern society, is muted, as women take an equal part in the performance of the hajj. The experience of the multihued and multicultural sacred community during the pilgrimage converted the American black Muslim Malcolm X to orthodoxy, and it has helped make Islam one of the fastest growing religious among American blacks and other disenfranchised groups everywhere.

While Muslim theology preferred to emphasize the leveling of all humans under the authority of an omniscient God, a similar movement occurs from the secular side, but in the opposite direction. Rather than envisioning all men as slaves, ordinary Middle Easterners have usually tried to ignore or obscure relationships of servility. It was taken to be very bad manners to refer to anyone's lack of freedom. Etiquette demanded that slaves not be addressed as abid, but called instead "my boy", "my maid". The much-used term ghulam meant young man, servant, soldier, and male slave – categories which blended one into the other and blurred distinctions of servitude.

Basic courtesy also required all men to treat one another as equals regardless of status – in fact, the presentation of self in the Middle East has very much in common with American where, from colonial times on, "extreme inequalities of material condition were joined to an intense concern for equality of esteem" and where rich and poor "wore similar clothing and addressed each other by first names. They worked, ate, laughed, played and fought together on a footing of equality."[29] Similar institutionalized egalitarian etiquette is very typical of most Middle

Eastern peoples, though often expressed differently from the studied breezy demeanor of Americans. For instance, Gilsenan notes that among the Shadhiliyya Sufis punctilious politeness helps to maintain the appearance of equality despite considerable differences in actual wealth and status.[30] Other Middle Easterners may use elaborate verbal formulas that flatter others and demean themselves as a way of maintaining smooth social intercourse among unequals.

Legally too the line between slavery and freedom was often erased or clouded. For instance, slaves who converted to Islam (Muslims could not lawfully be made into slaves) had the religious privileges that were conferred on any other believer, despite their debased position. As noted in chapter 6, the children of slave women were legally equivalent to the children of a free wife, and had absolute claims to their free father's estate. Even after being manumitted, the slave would keep the tribal name (nisba) of his master, and it was a matter of honor for ex-slaves to rally to the causes of their former masters, and vice-versa.[31] Very often, the relationship was even closer, since slaves or clients regularly served as surrogate parents and wet nurses for sons of chiefs, and later acted as the confidants and advisors for their foster sons. Boys who had suckled at the same breast – one the actual son of the slave wet nurse, the other her princely charge – had a milk relationship almost as strong as blood, and often much warmer than the rivalrous relationships that prevailed among brothers.[32] Such intimate relationships became the model for the role of the wazir, a slave who educated the king and later became his chief advisor.

The relationship between master and slave, superior and inferior, is therefore a complex one in Middle Eastern culture. While distinctions of rank manifestly exist, ideologically and behaviorally these distinctions are often blurred, leveled and even reversed – slaves might be more noble than their masters; abasement could be a virtue; the subordinate might be a closer friend and confidant than one's own peers. Real differences of rank were continuously flattened out by etiquette, ritual, law, religious ideology, and by the potential for both downward and upward mobility.

But paradoxically the leveling impulse to acknowledge the humanity and essential sameness of all persons, regardless of race, nationality, faith, or occupation, also generated a counter impulse to stereotype, categorize, enslave and even dehumanize and mutilate underlings in order to make the ideologically problematic reality of subordination seem "natural" both to the superior and to the inferior. The most powerful symbolic imposition of subordinate status was achieved through rendering a man woman-like by the act of castration, and the metaphor of effeminacy was extended to all inferiors to naturalize their subordination. The question then is: why should women serve as the exemplars of "natural" inferiority in the Middle East?

15

The Ambiguities of Women

Women in Middle Eastern Consciousness

To this point, my narrative has been almost exclusively male in outlook, reflecting Middle Easterners' own conventional vision of the public world, where men reign and all deeds of real importance are thought to take place. Conversely, a woman's world is secret and private, bounded by the walls of her father's house, and then by the compound of her husband and his family. This is the famous *harem*, the protected female part of the household.[1] Women who leave the harem must carry their seclusion with them by veiling themselves, keeping *purdah* from the eyes of strangers.[2] Their obscurity and anonymity in the traditional Middle East (and still today) was such that husbands did not refer to their wives by name – to do so would be scandalous; rather, a man obliquely mentioned "my house" or perhaps, at most, alluded to "the mother of my sons". Similarly, when a man draws up the family genealogy only male ancestors are mentioned, as if the lineage were reproduced by masculine parthenogenesis.

Women are not only hidden; they are also degraded. For example, the Pukhtun of Swat say that their women lack sense and discrimination: "Women have no noses. They will eat shit." For them, women are a separate human species that is naturally stupid, lazy, untrustworthy, polluting, obstinate, emotional, wilful, talkative, greedy, and innately immoral. For men to maintain control of these dangerous and wayward creatures is no easy task; they have to be kept strictly isolated and regularly beaten. As elsewhere in the Middle East, among the Pukhtun, women have served as the pre-eminent and fundamental "natural" category of debased humanity, so that all inferior persons are characterized by extension as exhibiting "feminine" traits.[3]

The popular masculine disparagement of women has been confirmed by the consensus of the ulema, who proclaimed the God-given subordinate status of females in a properly Muslim world. Islam, they said,

Plate 15.1 A bridal procession among the Pukhtun of Swat.
The bride is hidden in the palenquin.

entrusts men with stewardship over women, who would unleash anarchy
unless kept locked behind the walls of the compound under close
watch.[4] The ulema validate their notions by reference to traditions such
as: "Those who entrust power to a woman will never know prosperity"
and "the dog, the ass, the woman interrupt prayer if they pass in front of
the believer."[5] They point to the Quranic injunction that "Men are the
protectors and maintainers of women, because Allah has given the one
more (strength) then the other, and because they support them from their
means...As to those women on whose part ye fear disloyalty and

ill-conduct, admonish them (first), (next), refuse to share their beds, (and last) beat them."[6]

Female inferiority also appears to be encoded in Islamic law which allows men to divorce their wives with ease, while women are prohibited from initiating divorce. This was a shift from pre-Islamic practice, which permitted women freedom to change mates at will. Islam also redefined fornication (*zina*) to include old patterns of temporary, female-initiated sexual relationships or wife "leasing" which now became capital crimes. Muslim men were permitted four wives; women could have only one husband; in legal cases a women's testimony was worth half that of men's; blood money paid for a woman was half that paid for a man; by law, women inherit half what their male siblings do – and are lucky to receive anything in rural societies and among the ordinary urban poor, where all the patrimony usually passes to the sons. Given these negative factors, it is no surprise that everywhere in the Middle East, when a boy baby is born, it is the occasion for noisy congratulations, while silence or condolences greet the birth of a girl.

These negative images have been countered by the same sorts of reversals we have already discovered in reaction to other relationships of subordination. For example, among many Sufis the feminine has been very positively evaluated – God is a bride and enlightenment is a process of unveiling. It was, after all, a female saint, Rabiya, who first enunciated the Sufi faith in divine love. Sufism also favors "feminine" aspects of religion: emotional intuition, ecstatic experience, hidden knowledge, magical practices, and immersion in the encompassing womb of God's love (as exemplified especially in the work of Ibn Arabi).[7] Sufis and other unorthodox groups have also been especially welcoming of women's participation and egalitarian in their treatment of women – factors which have contributed to mistrust of these groups by the larger community.[8]

Yet among the orthodox too the image of women has had positive as well as negative connotations. For instance, like slaves, women have been portrayed as representatives of suffering humanity or been held up as paradigms of strong faith, piety and loyalty. *Rahm* (the womb) has served Muslim polemicists as a model of spiritual communitas, as maternal kinship (*rahma*) encompasses the differentiating patrilineal pedigree (nasab) that is the preoccupation of men and draws the whole community together into the united umma of shared nurturance.[9] As we have seen men who have drunk the mother's milk of the same nurse are tied together in a way that transcends blood.

The imagery of a unified community based upon women reflects a social as well as a metaphorical truth. For example, Carla Makhlouf tells us that urban women in Yemen congregate daily in one another's houses where they dance, sing, gossip, smoke, and amuse themselves in a crowded, egalitarian and uninhibited atmosphere that is quite unlike the mistrustful austerity characteristic of men's gatherings. Similarly, in a Qashqai encampment wary and status-conscious men will not even approach each other's tents, but when the men leave for work the women freely visit, talk, and exchange gifts among themselves, disregarding the rivalries of their husbands and providing their young sons with an experience of community that they will always recall with nostalgia.[10]

A number of Muslim legal rulings also reflect positive attitudes towards women. Of particular significance was the legal prohibition of the pre-Islamic practice of female infanticide. Even more importantly, women in pre-Islamic times were regarded as chattel of their husbands or fathers and could be inherited and disposed of at will. With the advent of Islam, they became shareholders in the family estate, retaining their own individual rights of inheritance which could not be alienated from them by their menfolk. The fact that a woman was entitled to only half of the amount inherited by her male relatives was offset by the dowry of goods, money and sometimes land that a girl was legally entitled to receive from her family when she married. This dowry, usually augmented by a substantial brideprice (*mahar*) from her husband's household, became her own private property, to spend and use as she pleased – though both were usually integrated into the common household resource base. At divorce, a woman could reclaim brideprice and dowry from her husband, and Islamic courts would find in her favor.

The Islamic recognition of the independence of women is especially clear in the negotiation of marriage. As Noel Coulson writes, in Islamic nuptial arrangements the status of the woman changed "from the position of a sale-object to that of contracting party... endowed with a legal competence she did not possess before."[11] As distinct from the sacramentalized marriage of Christianity, matrimony in Islam is understood pragmatically as an exchange of goods and services, reversible in principle, to be bargained over assiduously by the families of the parties involved. In the marriage agreement the woman (through her guardian) trades her sexual and reproductive functions in exchange for a negotiated bride price and for permanent protection and maintenance.[12] If terms were not met, the contract could be annulled and the mahar returned to its rightful owner, i.e. the woman – an arrangement which allowed a wife great leverage in divorce cases and compensated for the husband's preemptory right to revoke the marriage.[13]

As Marshall Hodgson argues, within this legal framework Muslim women actually had greater personal freedom than women in European Christian society, where until recently the wife's property was permanently joined to her husband's and where the conjugal unit took precedence over the individuals who made it up. In contrast, Muslim

232 DILEMMAS OF SUBORDINATION

family law sacrificed the primacy of the family group "in favour of equality of rights on the part of all concerned"[14] – an expression of the deep Middle Eastern values of individualism and equality. The Muslim wife's autonomy is symbolized in her retention of her own family name and in her capacity to earn her own money and run her own financial affairs. Of course, this is not to say that women always take advantage of their legal options – most follow custom, efface themselves, and leave their affairs to men.

Even in matters that seem on the surface to be repressive to women, Islam is ambiguous. For instance, sacred text permits Muslim men up to four wives (concubines are not mentioned), and Muhammad set an exceptional example with his own twelve official marriages. However, Muhammad was unwaveringly faithful to his much older first wife, Khadija, for twenty-five years, and the great majority of his later marriages were simply means to cement relationships with his allies (the first five Caliphs were his in-laws). Perhaps Muhammad's attitude toward polygamy can be best seen in his stipulation that the marriage between his favorite daughter Fatima and his cousin Ali be strictly monogamous (though Ali was also famous for his many temporary marriages).[15]

Further ambivalence can be discovered in the Quranic statement that polygamy is only permitted if a man is able to treat all his wives absolutely equally – a stipulation that many reformers have said is practically impossible to meet except by a saint; therefore monogamy is the only morally secure form of Muslim marriage.[16] In a similar vein, adultery, though punishable by death, can only be proven by the eye-witness accounts of four reliable persons – a condition that renders any confirmation highly unlikely. And divorce, while allowed, was execrated by the Prophet as the most reprehensible of permissible things.

In the modern period, principled religious opposition to the denigration of women has been forcefully proclaimed both from the left (by feminists) and from the right (by Islamists). The first re-examine the basis of women's cultural inferiority by employing alternative evidence from the early period of Islam to question the accuracy of many anti-female sayings that are presently accepted as authentic by the orthodox ulema and by ordinary believers. For instance, Fatima Mernissi argues that Quranic verses which subjugate women to men are negated or at least challenged by a Quranic blessing of both women and men according to their virtues, without reference to their gender: "For Muslim men and women – for believing men and women, for devout men and women... for them Allah has prepared forgiveness and great reward."[17] And she notes as well that the Quran plainly asserts that "women shall have rights similar to the rights against them, according to what is equitable."[18] Mernissi also writes that Muhammad's favorite wife Aisha, herself a famous reciter of hadith, rebuked Abu-Hurayra, the source of the tradition that women defile prayers, as follows: "You compare us now to asses and dogs. In the name of God, I have seen the Prophet saying his prayers while I was there, lying on the bed between him and the *qibla*."[19]

Those claiming a high status for women in Islam cite Muhammad's deep affection for women in general, and for Aisha in particular, and remind us that he chose to die in her room, where he and the first two Caliphs were buried. The honor done to Aisha hardly seems congruent with a belief in female inferiority. As for the right to "scourge" exasperating women, the Prophet himself never beat his wives, but preferred instead to withdraw into solitude when angry with any of them, and told his followers "only the worst among you" would ever resort to violence against their spouses.[20]

The Quranic injunction that called for the wives and daughters of the believers "to cast their outer garments over their persons when out of doors"[21] has also been reinterpreted. Defenders of women's freedom from purdah argue that primitive Islam did not enjoin complete veiling or seclusion for all women; simple modesty seems to have been enough. Actual seclusion was an extraordinary measure applicable solely to the wives of the Prophet in order to allow them some private life, and was unjustifiably expanded in later generations.[22] They note too that demure withdrawal of women from public life and activity was not the practice of the initial Muslim community. Aisha again is cited as an example of a female who participated in public debates, accompanied Muslim troops to war, was a respected reciter of tradition, and even a political leader in her own right.[23] Khadija too is mentioned as an independent woman, a successful entrepreneur who operated her own trading enterprise with the help of her junior partner, her loyal husband Muhammad. If these early women could be such powerful public figures, why should modern women be precluded from the same status?

Like the feminists, Islamists respond to charges that Islam dehumanizes and denigrates women by citing sacred text, but they reach quite different conclusions. They argue in favor of the "immutable and complete difference in the nature of the sexes, which is part of the God's plan for the world."[24] For them, in correct Islamic practice women and men are "equal in humanity and complementary in function",[25] with women acting as reproducers, child-raisers, and preservers of the family while men serve as protectors and wage earners. This view is buttressed by reference to findings from evolutionary biology that purportedly demonstrate women's chemical make-ups and nervous systems naturally suit them to be homemakers.[26]

The modern Islamist view grants women equal status with men so long as the balanced and supposedly innate relationship between the two sexes is maintained. Any shift in the balance is reckoned to be a deviation from God's blueprint and from the natural order; it can only lead to animalistic lust, misery and social collapse – which, they claim, has already occurred in the West. Logically and scientifically speaking, their argument is badly flawed, but it does accommodate the cultural pressure toward equality by presenting women as equal to men while simultaneously "naturalizing" differences in occupation. The seemingly incongruous appeal to evolutionary biology makes perfect sense in this context.

Whether this new rhetoric from both left and right has led men to respect women more remains questionable. Instead, what actually appears to be the case is that modern Middle Eastern women are increasingly isolated in nuclear families, cut away from the support of their patrilineal kin, and obliged to work outside the home to supplement family income, while also being compelled to continue their traditional household tasks, without any help from their male partners (helping would contradict the natural order of things) or any credit (women's work is unimportant and foolish). This is the case in both urban and rural environments, as many studies attest. The rise of neo-fundamentalism, with its emphasis on female purity and cultural integrity, has also eroded earlier Islamist calls for sexual equality.[27]

History, Culture, and Misogyny

We can see then that the record of Islam in relation to women is mixed, but that the balance is tilted toward faith in the autonomy and equality of women.[28] Basic Muslim principles of equity and justice for women can be and have been variously expressed by activists of both conservative and liberal temper, but these principles have definitely not succeeded in dislodging popularly held beliefs in female inferiority. To see why this is the case we need to look not at Islam, but at history and culture.

The first thing we note is the correlation between increasing governmental authoritarianism and the solidification of sexual hierarchy during the Abbasid era and later. Especially crucial was the widespread institutionalization of concubinage, which undercut the claims of a man's legitimate wives just as rulers undercut the claims of their kinsmen by the recruitment of slave armies and bureaucracies. As Abbott writes, for the new elite "acquiring a wife was a much more serious undertaking than stocking up on concubines who could be discarded, given away, or even killed without any questions asked. A wife had her legal rights to property settlement. She had 'family connections'."[29] Under these circumstances, slave women often became the primary consorts of conquering warriors and the mothers of their sons, while free-born women were relegated to seclusion and marginality – positions from which they never escaped.

Control over women through concubinage was nothing new in the Middle East. The Sasanid Empire was famous for the huge slave harems owned by the king and the nobility. In the history of the Middle East we discover many patriarchal practices that long preceded Islam, and that were often transformed and ameliorated by Muslim law.[30] Veiling, for example, has an ancient past. Assyrian tablets dating from the thirteenth century BC prescribe veiling for respectable women, while conversely prostitutes and slaves were forbidden to hide themselves. In these instances the veil was used not only as an indicator of modesty, but also differentiated between rich and poor, free and slave, private and public, moral and immoral.[31] In this light, one could say Islam's egalitarianism is indicated by the fact that, unlike the Assyrians, the Muslims allow *every* woman to veil herself, regardless of her social status.

Besides imposing the veil, most of the pre-Islamic Middle Eastern empires gave women few powers. Females were excluded from the prestigious professions and from public office; divorce was usually difficult for wives, much easier for men, and women were expected to be complaisant and obedient to their husbands, who had the right of corporal punishment over their wives, children, and slaves – a right which continued into Roman law. For instance, a Mesopotamian law code from 3,000 BC says that a woman who contradicts her husband should have her teeth knocked out, while an adulteress could be put to death.

In her account of the history of women's rights in the Middle East, Leila Ahmed writes that although women had handicaps in the most ancient Middle Eastern states, their position gradually eroded from bad to worse, culminating in the Empire of the Sasanids, where huge harems and anti-female laws set a new standard for denying the autonomy of women. Susanid women were not allowed to serve as witnesses, could be loaned out as concubines at the will of their husbands, and were generally uneducated, housebound, strictly segregated from men, and lacked financial resources. The Byzantines were not far behind their Persian opponents in this regard, though there is evidence that some of their women, like later entrepreneurial Muslim women, did have access to independent capital and could participate in trade and finance.[32] Islamic law was, in many senses, a radical overturning of this misogynist history, but, as we have seen, among most people the underlying patriarchal assumptions of female inferiority continued unabated.

Historians and cultural anthropologists usually argue that the steady expansion of male power in the Middle East derived from a complex nexus of influences, including the increased division of labor and concomitant status hierarchies that fueled the growth of the local polities from parochial city-states to cosmopolitan empires. It is often argued that this process necessarily entails greater male dominance, as patrilineal inheritance is initiated to control rights to ever-more valuable permanent property, while patriarchal power is used to retain legal authority over women who could potentially disrupt the solidarity of the group by their marriages and independence.

This transformation is often seen as the culmination of earlier civilizational changes, dating from the substitution of plow agriculture for hunting and gathering, which led in turn to more surplus accumulation, greater distinction between male and female labor, the rise of male elites, and the development of female seclusion as a way of asserting masculine status distinctions. In all cases, subordination of women is tied to the rise of patrilineal and patrilocal social organization, which binds women to their fathers and husbands.

However, things may not be quite so clear-cut. Certainly, the mode of production does make a difference when women's outdoor work is absolutely necessary for survival, as is the case among Middle Eastern nomads, where the necessities of production require women to work unveiled and to take quite substantial part in decision-making, since they have responsibility for the household during the frequent absences of their husbands. But the relative freedom of the Bedouin woman does *not* alter the strongly patriarchal morality of the tribesmen. In fact, nomadic women are actually much less likely than urban women to be granted any inheritance whatsoever, and they are more likely to suffer corporal punishment for adultery or other delicts, despite the protection offered by Islamic law. A simple and cooperative mode of production alters the parameters of patriarchy, but does not necessarily preclude it.

It is also not evident that complexity, patrilineality, and status differentiation implies an ideology of female inferiority. In the Middle East itself we find a powerful counter-example: pre-Islamic Egypt during the New Kingdom was a supremely hierarchical complex society, yet women could own property, inherit, act as legal individuals, make provisions in marriage contracts, initiate divorce, and so on. Marriage, save for that of the Pharaoh, was monogamous. There was no veiling or female seclusion, and women were treated with respect and dignity, despite male dominance in the political, professional and religious spheres.[33] Except for royalty,[34] there was no great concern in Egypt for ensuring the actual paternity of a child, and those without sons commonly adopted an heir – something unheard of in later Muslim Middle Eastern culture or among Egypt's pre-Islamic neighbours.

The reasons for this anomaly perhaps derive from the other unique characteristics of ancient Egypt that were outlined in chapter 3. To

reiterate, where the rest of the Middle East has been typically characterized by strong notions of personal freedom and self-aggrandizement
within an unstable and sparse environment that favored continual internal struggles for ephemeral positions of power among co-equal
rivals, in the fertile, isolated and relatively secure environment of ancient Egypt ordinary men and women were encapsulated in a stable and
hierarchical social order ruled by a sacred Pharaoh and his priesthood.
In this universe they required no notions of "natural" differences of
blood or sex to ratify the taken-for-granted hierarchies of the kingdom;
nor did ordinary Egyptians have any interest in the preservation of their
blood-lines or in controlling reproduction by enforcing female isolation.

Quandaries of Patrilineality

The Egyptian case shows that there is no absolute and necessary connection between social complexity, patrilineality, anxiety over female
purity, and an ideology of female inferiority. That connection requires
faith in an idiom of blood inheritance as the crucial factor in determining identity within an otherwise fluid social world. This factor is
regarded as "natural" by Middle Easterners, but in fact it is perfectly
possible for a patrilineal society to designate children as legitimate by
virtue of adoption – as occurred in Egypt – or simply because they were
born to one's wife, regardless of actual paternity. In other words, the
notion of shared paternal blood was weakly held in the hierarchical
society of ancient Egypt, while it prevailed among their combative (and
ultimately triumphant) neighbors.[35]
    As we have already seen, imagining a "natural" solidary kin-based
community of shared paternal blood lent a putative physical substance
to the group feeling that Ibn Khaldun called asabiyya; this "cultural
imaginary" provided a stabilizing and constructive model for aligning
and motivating social actors in a shifting and perilous environment
where any order at all was hard to achieve. The codification of patrilineal blood rights in Muslim law (which stamped out all traces of earlier
confusing cognatic or matrilineal cross-cutting rights, eliminated inheritance for adopted children, and demanded equal shares for the sons of
slave women) was simply the final step in a long-term process of historical evolution toward a blood-based ideology of patrilineality.
    The hypothesis of a causal correlation between status instability, an
ethic of competitive egalitarianism, a cultural idiom of natural difference located in blood inheritance, and the evolution of patrilineality
and patriarchy is, of course, a tentative one, but whatever the causal
nexus, it is clear that once paternal blood is accepted as the source for
generational linkages between human beings and as the primal founda-

tion for an individual's identity a number of consequences follow – none of them conducive to a congenial and egalitarian relationship between men and women.

This is because the ideology of the centrality of inherited male virtue rests upon an obvious and disturbing contradiction: i.e. even though genealogies and the official organizational model of the society take account only of men, the incontrovertible fact is that the patriline springs from the womb, and that women – outsiders to the patrilineage and men's supposed natural inferiors – are the real centers of the segmentary, masculine social structure in their role as child-bearers and mothers. As Abdella Hammoudi writes, this paradoxical fact of life is "scandalous according to patriarchal norms and yet impossible to avoid"; as a result, men must struggle continually "to transcend the structural contradiction between a patriarchal system and the physical reproduction of lineages."[36]

One way that men try to overcome the "scandalous" physical centrality of wives and mothers is by portraying women as goods purchasable by a bride-price exchanged between fathers and brothers, but this façade of control is undermined by a woman's legal agency in the marriage relationship and the fact that a wife is only conditionally placed under the power of her husband – her paternal kinsmen, not her spouse, remain primarily responsible for avenging her honor and are most sullied by her misconduct. No matter how much bride-price has been paid, it is never enough to break the tie of shared blood and honor. The male attempt to turn women into mere counters in exchanges between men simply does not work – women remain the active human carriers of the reputation and the blood of their lineages.

Father's brother's daughter's marriage, culturally central in the Middle East, can be understood in part as an attempt to overcome this tension by subsuming the mother's lineage into the father's, marrying "close to the bone" so that there is the absolute minimum difference between the marrying groups. But this mechanism does not eliminate the differentiation between the two sides; it simply focuses at the lowest level. Far from stopping hostility, father's brother's daughter marriage can be disruptive of good relations between the very closest of patrilateral cousins.

The exchange of women is disruptive in another sense as well, since in a lineage-based society giving and taking women is always a ploy in the struggle for status between co-equal men. Successful marriage ties to elite lineages can validate one's own nobility, and introduce hierarchy into the egalitarian band of brothers. Conversely, marriage of one's women to an inferior group indicates fallen fortunes.[37] Women then are major elements in men's efforts to overturn the egalitarian ideal; as such they take the brunt of the ambivalence that these efforts arouse – especially when, by the simple act of refusing a marriage arrangement or walking out on an already negotiated union, women can disrupt the ties so laboriously negotiated by their status-seeking male relatives.

Deep cultural anxiety about marriage is revealed at the marriage ceremony in the ritualized enactments of grieving by the bride's family and the exultation and celebration of the groom's people, who have "taken a woman" and gained points in the competitive game of honor. In this context, the importance placed on the symbolic act of proving one's manhood and the power of one's clan by deflowering the virgin bride is very great, and "young men are haunted by the fear of a moment of weakness at that fateful meeting on their first wedding night"[38] – another tension infecting male–female sexual relationships. When (if) the groom does succeed, his deed is trumpeted in the traditional triumphal public display of a bloody sheet hung out after the nuptial night.

However, the exhibition of virginal blood is not for the sake of the groom and his lineage alone, but for the girl and her people as well. The young Middle Eastern bride is far from being the meek or giggly figure often pictured in western fantasy. Like her brothers, she is a proud individual trained to have a high regard for her own status and the status of her family. She too has much at stake in the public exhibition of her lost virginity; her blood is the blood of her illustrious ancestors, and by its display she honors the pride and purity of her line and of herself. To the groom the bloody sheet shows his virility and, by extension, the virility of his lineage; to the bride it is a demonstration of the virtue and value of herself and her people, as well as a validation of her right to her status as wife.

The new bride realistically recognizes marriage as her sole possible avenue to respect, but does not consider herself to be the property of her husband, and only acknowledges that he has certain sexual and legal rights over her. As Paul Vieille writes, for her "the man is the stranger and his family the enemy."[39] She rightly fears the violence of her spouse, the authority of her new mother-in-law, the shameful possibility of childlessness, and above all the prospect that she might be humiliated by divorce or, even worse, the arrival of a co-wife. Her task, as she sees it, is to maximize her position and honor as best she can within the situation that is given her, just as her male counterparts do – though for her the arena of competition is the household and her prime weapon is the production of sons.

She must fight on foreign ground, but in her fraught relationship with her adversaries a woman has many avenues for self-assertion, as numerous anthropological and sociological studies have shown. For instance, in urban environments middle-class women can often personally control the resources they are given at marriage or inherit and can engage in business or invest as they please. However, lower class and rural women may have substantially more mobility and autonomy than their wealthier urban sisters, since less is at stake in inheritance, and because their work outside the home is a necessity for maintaining the household. They can therefore accumulate their own resources and establish their own networks of influence, gaining a degree of personal freedom that is usually not associated with women in Middle Eastern society. Some older women may even achieve positions of significant respect and esteem, acting as consultants to their menfolk and as go-betweens in sensitive marriage negotiations.

Whatever their class situation, age or occupation, women everywhere in the Middle East can all assert themselves by provoking and teasing their husbands, and can humiliate their men by publicly accusing them of impotence or weakness. It is women who are often the most avid defenders of lineage honor, goading their men to act in ways more radical than the men might prefer. Women's control of local information is another resource for them, which they can manipulate to their own advantage. Resistance to male domination can also be displayed covertly in the rhetoric of women's songs and poems.[40]

But a focus on resistance misses the point. For the most part, a woman is not concerned with overturning or opposing the system from which she gains her honorable position. She recognizes that her place is in the home, where she struggles to maintain her own honor, sustain a wary stand-off with her husband, and win the respect of her peers. In this struggle, her sons are her allies. As A. Bouhdiba writes, Arab society, "as masculine as possible, quite gladly abandons the child to his mother."[41] Male abdication means that women are the main influence in boys' socialization. Raised in the company of women, Middle Eastern boys have strong emotional ties to their mothers and sisters, who are their protectors, helpers and mediators. When a man is in trouble, goes a Pukhtun proverb, he will be ashamed to ask help from his father, who will lecture him, but will instead go to his mother or sister, who will intercede for him with no questions asked. In return, he is his mother's ally against his father, and his sister's ally against her husband.[42]

But although women are the source of undemanding affection and approval, to become an adult a boy has to leave the protective refuge of the community of women and find his own way in the rivalrous world of men. In so doing, he learns his mother and sisters are inferior creatures – he can walk freely around the village, while they must remain locked in their compounds or, at minimum, hide behind veils of modesty. Their ways are contemptible and laughable; their smells and their tasks are repellent; they deserve to be isolated in the domestic sphere.

Male hostility toward females is actively inculcated by the women of his household. For instance, as Susan Dorsky reports from Yemen: "A three-year-old continues smacking his nine-year-old sister with a sharply edged toy gun. She forces a smile as she tries to block the blows. Their mother, another woman, and several older boys and girls are present, but do not intervene or criticize the boy."[43] The mother's seemingly paradoxical attitude toward her son's brutality to his sister is a realistic response to the power relationships in the patriarchal family. As Cherry Lindholm explains: "It gives her son practice in the handling of his future wife who is, after all, the mother's future daughter-in-law; it is in the mother's personal interest that her sons should be able to control their wives properly."[44] Raised in this ambivalent setting, men's attitudes toward women are complex and conflicted, composed of the deep ties of dependency and affection fostered in childhood, overlain with later feelings of disgust, antagonism and fear. The ambiguity of the relationship comes especially to the fore when a man must deal with the sexual allure of his wife.

The Dangers of Female Sexuality

Muslim attitudes toward sexuality have always been far more liberal than those of the West. In contrast to Christianity, in Islam there is no feminine responsibility for the fall of man, and eroticism is presented as a good in itself, both a foretaste of heaven and a necessity on earth for the human work of reproduction, as ordained by God. Celibacy is actively opposed in Muslim texts; both women and men are equally responsible for the formation of a child in the womb, women as well as men are thought to experience orgasms, and, like men, women have an equal right to sexual satisfaction – a cultural norm of mutual sexual fulfillment which shows that the fundamental egalitarian precepts of the society are applicable even in the bedroom.

This is all very positive, but the contradictions of the culture also imply far less affirmative responses. For instance, women's sexual power is denied outright by the cultural portrait of women as weak prey who must be protected from lecherous men in the seclusion of the harem. Yet women's real strength is revealed in an alternative image of females as frightening sexual predators. In both instances, women must be caged, but the reasons for their imprisonment differ radically: in the first case she is an innocent lamb, in the second she is a bitch in heat. These two understandings are barely reconciled by the belief that the man is the "revealer of the latent erotic powers of the women",[45] who awakens the virgin to her innate desires, which will henceforth become voracious, requiring all the concentrated attention of a man for satisfaction.

It is from male anxiety about overwhelming female sexuality that the classical pornography of the region took its inspiration, inevitably

Plate 15.2   Women of several generations gathered together for a funeral.
This picture was taken in Swat but in much of the Middle East
women bear the emotional work of mourning.

portraying insatiable wives whose "thirst for copulation is never as-
suaged".[46] Popular wisdom asserts that once aroused the sexual desire
of a woman is nine times greater than that of a man, who will have no
power to withstand her irresistible advances.[47] As a Moroccan man
tells Lawrence Rosen: "Women have very great sexual desires and that's
why a man is always necessary to control them, to keep them from
creating all sorts of disorder, to keep them from leading men astray.
Why else do we call women *hbel shitan* (the Rope of Satan)? That is
why women must be cloaked when in public, live in houses with small
windows placed so that others cannot see in, and married off before
they can give their fathers any trouble."[48]

As Abdellah Hammoudi writes, male anxiety about women is dis-
closed symbolically in "the mass of ambivalent images portraying her, in
which healing and danger are mixed."[49] Woman's touch renders a man
ritually unclean; her menstrual blood is defiling, as is sexual contact with
her.[50] In addition, women are commonly thought to have special relations with dark spirits and the occult. It is they who know how to
prepare magic spells and poultices, they are the fortune-tellers and the
main clients of shrines and saintly mausoleums, where their emotional

supplications and ecstatic behavior stand in sharp contrast to male restraint. These female supernatural activities and supplications often aim
either at producing and guarding her sons or at binding her husband to
her, since it is through parental and sexual control over men that women
gain their authority.[51]

Male fear of the power of women to seduce them is so marked that
in several controversial books Fatima Mernissi has claimed that "the
whole Muslim social structure can be seen as an attack on, and a
defense against the disruptive power of female sexuality."[52] Mernissi
argues that in Islam piety is constrained and rational, while women are
erotic and irrational – they may tempt men from the straight path by
their lust. In order to avoid this peril, learned texts tell devout men how
to control and monitor their sexual lives and thereby maintain the
proper priority of reason over passion. Mernissi concludes that "the
Muslim system is not so much opposed to women as to the heterosexual unit. What is feared is the growth of an involvement between a man
and a woman into an all-encompassing love, satisfying the sexual, emotional and intellectual needs of both partners. Such an involvement
constitutes a direct threat to the man's allegiance to Allah."[53]

In a similar vein, but without reference to Islam, Paul Vieille writes
that there is a basic tension between the amorous passions of lovers and
the restraint required of hierarchical male–female relationships. Woman
as an erotic actor "represents the eruption of spontaneity in the culture
that comes from above"; her conduct is in the "domain of the incomprehensible."[54] Vieille argues that the compelling sensuality of female
eroticism endangers male superiority and causes men to malign and
resent women.

However, neither of these perspectives pays attention to the question
of exactly why women's sexual desire, which is explicitly a God-given
thing to be enjoyed as well as a necessity for reproduction, should be
thought to be such a force for chaos. Mernissi, in the tradition of the
Muslim scholar, cites religious texts as her proofs, but the texts themselves transmute into religious language a social reality which is not
analyzed. Vieille is closer to the mark when he rightly notes that the
status distinction between male and female is threatened by sexuality,
but the distinction itself is taken for granted.

The cultural source of ambiguity about female sexuality is easy
enough to discover; it rests in the paradox of Middle Eastern patrilineality. We have seen that it is through her reproductive capacity that a
woman creates and unites the patriline in her role as mother, preserving
the social structure and projecting it into the future through her sons.
However, she can negate all her creative work by taking a lover. In doing
so, she will ruin the honor of her men and undermine the basis of the
blood-based patriline – destroying herself into the bargain. Women's

sexuality is both the basis and the potential ruination of the whole masculine social order.

Even in her wifely role, women's allure poses an unresolvable dilemma to men; her sexuality is necessary for reproducing the lineage,
yet a wife's sexual seductiveness draws her husband away from where
his first loyalties should be in daily life: to his co-equal lineage brothers
and neighbors. This is why the Pukhtun say that a man who loves his
wife becomes weak, why the Iraqis say "women who hear soft talk
misbehave",[55] and why break-ups of the extended family are always
blamed on the machinations and selfishness of incoming wives. As both
the sources and the ultimate challengers to the patriarchal system,
women must always be guarded against – especially in terms of their
sexuality. It is in this sense that woman's eroticism is indeed an eruption
of the incomprehensible into the masculine world.

We can say then that the Middle Eastern customs of veiling, isolat-
ing, and denigrating women are not an invention of Islam, or a demonstration of women's frailty, but an expression of and defense against
women's erotic capacity for both creation and destruction within a
patriarchal system based on an ideology of blood inheritance. The practices and the symbolism that surround women reveal their hidden potency, their paradoxical capacity to nurture and seduce, and the fear
they arouse in men. As the feminist novelist Nawal El Saadawi writes,
in the Middle East "woman is powerful and not weak, positive and not
passive, capable of destroying and not easily destructible ... if anyone
needs protection it is the man rather than the woman."[56]

16

Escapes from Distinction:
Love and Friendship

Romantic Love

So far, I have argued that Middle Eastern male-female relationships are constructed upon deep contradictions that lie at the root of the whole social order: women's culturally elaborated inferiority in the Middle East is a symbolic expression of their ambiguous structural position in a patrilineal–patrilocal culture that bases itself upon an idiom of shared paternal blood. The threat women offer to this structure is met by a strong naturalizing of their subordination and a concerted effort to control their sexuality and agency.

But the cultural assertion of female inferiority is at odds with the general ethos of human equality, autonomy and competitive individualism, which is expressed in women's rights to sexual satisfaction, in their legal control over their own resources, and in their attempts to maximize respect and honor for themselves and their lineages. Covert recognition of women's threatening powers is also revealed in the unorthodox spiritual forces they are thought to control, in their emotional potency, and in their capacity for sexual seduction.

Within the traditional Middle Eastern context women are known to be dangerous and divisive creatures. At worst, their promiscuity can destroy a man's honor, resulting in a kind of social death; even if faithful, their sexual wiles can entice him away from his most important strategic loyalties to other men and from his spiritual commitment to God. Yet women, as the centers and sources of the family, also provide a model of unity and nurturance, as expressed in their capacity to come together in informal private communities of friends. Women are at the core of the society as mothers and are also its most dangerous enemies as seductresses. The complex symbolism surrounding women both reflects and masks their pervasive ambivalent influence, and colors all relationships with inferiors.

Given this context, it would seem then that any mutuality and respect between a husband and wife would be all but impossible. Of course, this is not the case. Shared trust and deep affection between husband and wife certainly do exist and have existed in the Middle East, as couples grow together and weather the storms of their relationship. Nonetheless, such ties stand in opposition to the whole texture of a patriarchal social construction of reality. As Fatima Mernissi puts it, rather than being trusted helpmates, women in the Middle East continue to be understood as a "source of subversion (that) is endogenous... violently intimate, insidiously, tenderly internal to the Muslim family."[1]

Yet paradoxically it is in the Middle East that we find the most passionate expressions of what we know as romantic love: the heartfelt adoration of another person. In the Middle East, this emotion has often been apostrophized as the most valued of all experiences. As a fourteenth-century poet wrote: "The heart of one who has never loved was a hard, inhuman heart." For some of the enamored, love was superior even to the bliss of heaven. For example, consider the verses of the ninth-century poet Said b. Humayd: "If we achieve Paradise, it will hold both of us, if such is His will. Or, if He wills, He will throw us into the fire. When it burns hot, kisses will cool us both, And the coolness of sucking (saliva) will arouse us in pangs of love, so that at last all those who are there eternally will say: Would that we altogether had been lovers."[2]

Aside from its eternal, ennobling and delirious qualities, love in the classical Middle East also had other characteristics that western readers will recognize. Among the Sufis, love was spiritualized to represent the highest form of bliss in merger with God. God wishes to kindle love in the human heart, and the jihad of lovers is "to be killed by the sword of attraction, fallen on the threshold of coquetry and liberality."[3] Such ecstatic love is selfless: "Perfect Love proceeds from the lover who hopes naught for himself; What is there to desire in that which has a price? Certainly the Giver is better for you than the gift."[4] Love also involves suffering and self-sacrifice: "A soul that thinks to meet with no suffering in love, when it addresses itself to love, is spurned. No spirit that was given repose ever gained love, nor did any soul that desired a tranquil life ever win devotion. Tranquility! how far is it from the life of a lover! The garden of Eden is compassed about with terrors."[5]

The passionate spiritual love between the seeker and the deity that was apotheosized by the great Sufi poets was a transformation of idealized relationships between human beings, and reflected even more ancient stories and legends of the Middle East, which are full of tales of empassioned lovers who waste away and die when deprived of their beloved's company. The Persian epic of Laila and Majnun is perhaps the most famous case, as Majnun (literally, the madman) wanders distractedly through the desert, reciting poetry inspired by his unfulfilled love for Laila, who has been married to someone else by her parents.

Eventually, he dies of his love, as does Laila, and the two lovers are united in death as roses growing from their adjacent tombs intertwine.

These tales of passion and loss are not just fictional creations – they are the stuff of real life. As Massignon writes: "It is not rare for an Arab who has fallen in love to die, for he 'burns' and is consumed, body and soul. The desert has no distractions or 'substitute' capable of diverting him from the image of beauty that flames in his solitary memory."[6] Recorded cases of self-inflicted death are often the result of love, as a man mistakenly kills his beloved and then slits his own throat in remorse, or a lover commits suicide at the death of his beloved, or a man dies when his ardor is unrequited.[7]

According to many commentators, it is from this fervent Middle Eastern tradition that the notion of romantic love came to the West, spread by returning Crusaders.[8] Whether this is historically accurate or not, certainly the experience of passionate attachment to another human being who is regarded as uniquely compelling and almost deified is a deep part of both western and Middle Eastern culture. But the way this experience has typically been played out is very different indeed. In the West the historical course love has taken has combined sexuality, idealization and marriage. We take this configuration as normal, but it is actually quite unusual in world cultures. According to some historians, this singular combination is a consequence of the unraveling of the extended family and the atomization that occurred with the industrial revolution, combined with a demographic shift that permitted longer attachments. Others argue that instead of being a consequence of capitalism, romantic love is its precursor, growing out of conditions favoring social mobility, free choice, late marriage, individualism, and relative wealth that prevailed in northern Europe from very early times.[9]

Whatever the history of love in the West, it did not follow the same trajectory in the Middle East, where relative poverty and the importance of the lineage made for a different social environment. As in the courtly love of medieval knights, in the Middle East romance and marriage are never connected. Love is always between those who are not bound by legal ties and contractually obliged to engage in sexual intercourse – such mundane and negotiated relationships between corporate groups are the very antithesis of passionate romantic idealization. This makes sense in the context of the Middle Eastern marriage relation, which was, as we have seen, a political contract binding families together and not a matter of the heart.

Even more remarkable for modern western sensibilities, but also comparable to the medieval courtly tradition, sexuality itself was often detached from love. Ibn al-Jawzi (d. 1200) who was the most prolific Medieval writer on romantic love, writes that the convention of chastity derived from the early Bedouin, who "loved passionately but spurned physical union, believing that it destroys love. As for the pleasure resulting from union, it is the affair of animals, not of man." This hypothesis was validated by the philologist al-Asmai (d. 828) who did research among the remote tribes. He writes: "I said to a Bedouin woman: 'What do you consider love to be among you?' 'Hugging, embracing, winks, and conversation,' she replied. Then she asked: 'How is it among you, city-dweller?' 'He sits amidst her four limbs and presses her to the limit,' I answered. 'Nephew,' she cried, 'this is no lover, but a man after a child!'"[10]

Traditionally, the high evaluation of chaste love (*hubb udhri*) is traced to the seventh-century Bedouin Yemeni tribe of the Banu Udhra, who supposedly believed that "to die of love is a sweet and noble death." According to Massignon, udhritic love was linked to a deep notion of the "election to a religious and sacrificial life by the unexpected appearance of a 'kindred soul'."[11] The transcendent other who inspired this elevated state was believed to be a pure spirit embodied in a human being, and the relationship was not to be soiled by physical contact. Instead, the beloved was internalized through avid contemplation, so that eventually the two became one. Taha Husain has linked the rise of chaste udhritic Arab poetry in the seventh century to economic crisis, arguing that a hard life of poverty predisposed Arabs to a love that is asocial, and ends in death. His thesis remains controversial, but it is certainly true that udhritic ideals and the detachment of marriage from passion has long permeated Middle Eastern experience. Why this should have occurred can only be understood by reference to cultural context.

An especially useful case for this purpose is the nomadic Marri Baluch of the rugged Southeastern deserts of Iran, who were studied by the anthropologist Robert Pehrson. The Marri, like so many Middle Eastern peoples, live in a harsh, isolated and unforgiving environment. Also typically, they reside in small camp settlements that are patrilineal, patrilocal, and patriarchal. Oganized according to segmentary principles of opposition within an overarching political confederacy headed by a court-appointed leader called the Sardar, they are highly individualistic, self-interested and competitive. According to Pehrson, the Baluch expect opportunism and manipulation from all social transactions; secrecy and social masking are at a premium, and collective action and cooperation minimal.

Among these people, romantic love is greatly appreciated and idealized; it "is a thing of surpassing beauty and value"[12] that is based on absolute trust, mutuality, and loyalty between the lovers, who are lost in adoration for one another; such a relationship is to be pursued at all costs, even at the price of one's life. For the Marri, romance can never lead to marriage, but rather must be a secret liaison with a married woman of a distant camp. This is a dangerous matter, since other camps are hostile, and adultery is punishable by death. Romance for the Marri is thus both the stuff of dreams and of daily drama, as frustrated lovers may commit suicide, or successful lovers may be caught and killed, and thereby become celebrated in the romantic poems and songs that are the mainstay of Marri art. As one Marri woman says, "It is very great, very hard, to be a lover for us Marri."[13]

All this can be related to the social organization of the Marri, who, like many other Middle Eastern people, live in small extended family units. Although they are ruled by a central authority who is nominally absolutely powerful and religiously sanctioned, these local units, permeable and shifting as they are, have considerable local autonomy. Within their groups, members have rights and duties to one another, which are legitimated by close blood ties and co-residence. Participation in blood feuds, payment of fines, rights to pasturage and the punishment of adultery all are incumbent on this minimal group. The campsite is not, however, a place of cooperation and friendship. The herdsmen, despite their ties, work separately, have their own tents and property, cooperate as little as possible, and are mutually suspicious and rivalrous. If they could, they would separate, but the need for defense and a varied labor pool keeps the camps together; it is a need validated by the rights and duties of kinship and the honor of shared paternal blood.

Within this structure, Marri men continually manipulate to get a share of the power and status that derive from the center. By gaining a loyal following among his cohorts, the poor herdsman can hope to become the local factotum of the Sardar, gaining points over his nearest, and most disliked, lineage mates and rivals. As is the case throughout the Middle East, a major way men try to accomplish this is through establishing alliances with other powerful families by marriage; the wedding of a sister or daughter is essentially an effort to bind men together, and has little to do with the preferences of the couple.

Marri men therefore use marriage in an instrumental fashion to establish relationships which will help them to pursue their political interests. This means that women, despite their seeming independence at work and freedom from veiling, are treated as chattel, to be controlled and dominated for the honor and benefit of the household head. As a Marri woman says, "You know what rights a woman has among us Marris. She has the right to eat crap – that's all."[14]

Within (and in reaction to) this conflicted and misogynist environment, romantic love, with all its great risk, is the only relationship in the whole of Marri culture that is not simply a means to the instrumental ends of personal power and prestige. Instead, it is understood by men and women alike to be of ultimate value in and for itself. The Marri themselves specifically contrast romance with marriage. For them, marriage is a public and sanctioned relationship between superior men and inferior women, often within the camp and the lineage, and always among allies; it is pre-eminently politically motivated, and it is expected to be cold and hostile at best. It is, in fact, shameful even to show affection for one's spouse in public.

Romance, on the contrary, is secretive, private, and conducted with strangers who are actually potential enemies. Its only possible political consequences are disastrous enmity and feud. Love has the potential for dividing groups while it unites the lovers; in contrast marriage aims to solidify groups, permitting no attraction within the asymmetrical couple. In marriage, the woman is inferior and despised, while in romance she is honored as an equal and revered by her lover. In romance, the lovers assert their own desires for mutuality and passionate recognition as they meet face to face – unique individuals acting outside the strangling ties of the group.

As in chaste udhritic love, the Marri claim that a true romantic relationship, again in stark distinction to marriage, is not sexual. According to the Marri, when lovers meet, they exchange tokens of mutual affection, talk heart to heart, without dissimulation, and are often moved to spontaneous recitation of poetry. Lovers must be chaste because sexuality, culturally understood as an expression of male power over women and as the origin of the masculine lineage, imposes an element of oppression and subordination that the romantic ideal of equality, passionate mutuality, creativity and personal respect between lovers cannot permit. Perhaps this is an ideal which may be met only in rare cases, but ideals must not be set aside as illusions. The way people believe things ought to be tells us much about the core values that actually motivate their actions.

For the Marri, then, romance is a pure, equalizing, creative and mutual relationship shared with a distant, idealized and beloved other; it is consciously perceived as negating the rivalries of power, the inferiority of women, and the constraints of the marriage tie. It is personal, free, passionate, and of surpassing value as the highest expression of the self. In this relationship sexuality, which is associated with hierarchy and domination, is suppressed in favor of chastity. I believe that this romantic complex is characteristically Middle Eastern, and recurs with variations throughout the region. It is an emotional construct appearing within a deeply competitive and ethically egalitarian social formation where women are nonetheless marked as inferiors and where both sexes are immersed in the never-ending rivalries of a competitive segmentary system. Romance in the Middle East opposes and yet reflects the social order in which it appears – offering an alternative world in which reproduction and lineage are unimportant and men and women can escape from their antagonisms and meet, for a fleeting moment, as equals, as individuals, as creative actors, and as lovers.

Love Between Men

There is another alternative which also overcomes the obstacles of the distinction between the sexes and the ambiguities of reproduction: love between men. This is a delicate subject, since homoeroticism is strongly repudiated in the texts of Islam, where it is viewed as an offense against God's natural order. But in ordinary life, homosexuality has traditionally been quite common in much of the Middle East, and has met with very little opprobrium. Moreover, it has been lauded by poets and mystics as a relationship of surpassing beauty, and in this guise has provided the material for many of the great Middle Eastern romances, which stand very much in contrast to the exclusively heterosexual romances of the West and resemble instead the idealized love between men immortalized in the literature of ancient Greece.

In fact, as we have seen in the case of Rumi's adoring praises of Shams al-din, much of Sufi poetry is openly homoerotic, though this eroticism is usually interpreted metaphorically. Nonetheless, some Sufis have been accused of the "love of beardless youths" and of young princes who "have faces like those of women and are a greater temptation than virgins";[15] in its mildest form, this form of love continued the chaste udhritic tradition of the "amorous regard" of a living person as a way to gaining closeness to God. As we shall see, homosexual love has also had a powerful symbolic role in the larger culture, where it can serve as a fantasy of a world without the tensions and ambivalences that surround male-female relations.

Yet those ambivalences also enter into homosexual love affairs, so that the active "masculine" partner is regarded as simply fulfilling the expected dominant male role; the passive partner, in contrast, is held in contempt as "feminine". Yet even the despicable passive homosexual may be redeemed if he ceases his practices, marries, has children, and gains respect – which happens relatively often, since the demeaning position of sexual passivity is not generally understood as an unalterable essence for a man (as it is for a woman), but only as a condition which can change according to circumstances. This is especially so when the passive partner is obliged to submit because of his subordinate role. For example, apprentices are often supposed to be sexually available to their bosses and young scholars to their teachers – as inferiors they are culturally expected to take effeminate roles. Or a young man may perform as a woman sexually in order to earn money in a society where female seclusion is strongly enforced. In these circumstances, demeaning activities may be excused if they stop when the boy has moved out of the apprentice role, or when he has earned enough money to stop acting as a prostitute, marry and establish a household like a proper man.[16]

The relative tolerance toward and even high evaluation of homosexuality in the region (despite orthodox sanctions against such practices)
helps substantiate my case that it is social organization, not Islam, which
is at the root of sexual attitudes in the Middle East. The socially
engendered contradictions and ambiguities that surround women not
only make extramarital sexual encounters with women difficult to
achieve, but also imbue heterosexual desire with an aura of ambiguity
and fear. In the great Middle Eastern love stories heterosexual lovers
never touch one another, but die apart; though tortured by desire,
Majnun refuses to embrace his beloved Laila, because for him she has
become an abstract essence infused into the universe – in her actual
person, exhibiting all the flaws and dark powers of the feminine, she
could never serve as the expression of God, which he wishes her to be.
Instead, she would be, at best, the mother of his sons and his entrance
into the ordinary world of ambivalent relations between men and
women.

Love between men, on the other hand, is uncontaminated by the
ineradicable stain of female inferiority and the complexities of reproduction. Unlike women, men are independent and, in principle, all equals –
although their intrinsic equality is indeed sullied by the humiliation that
is understood to be a consequence of sexual penetration. This unfortu-
nate reality can be etherialized by spiritual notions that the dominant
other is infused with God; submission and passivity then becomes a
discipline leading to enlightenment – a transformation that is valorized
in poetry where submission in love and images of slavery are mingled:
"Do not censure me, for I am not the first free man to become through
love a slave of those he loves."[17] The type case is the famous love affair
between the great King Mahmud of Ghazna and his slave Ayaz, a
Turkish officer, where the ruler actually became a slave of his slave
through love – an image many Sufis found to be an irresistible metaphor
of the quest for enlightenment. These factors help make homosexuality
into what Hammoudi has called a "utopian fantasy" in the Middle
East.[18]

As a fantasy and as an actual encounter, the main cultural function of
homosexual love is to provide a symbolic as well as experiential counter to the very real tensions between men and women that mar the
mundane world. However, the dream of love between men is just that –
a dream. It seeks to deny the woman's central role as reproducer of the
patrilineage and caretaker of the family, and ignores the disgrace of
male submission to a dominant sexual partner. This means that the
homosexual bond can only be, at most, a temporary and tainted escape
from the ordinary strains and contradictions that characterize the necessary connection between men and women.

"I Am You": Idealized Friendship

Far more influential than homoeroticism has been another relationship
between men which, like idealized heterosexual romance, is chaste.
This is male friendship, which is extremely highly valued by Middle
Eastern society, and which, like love, has been taken as exemplary of
the relationship between man and divinity, especially by Shi'ites, whose
Imams called themselves the "friends of God". This intense form of
friendship must not be confused either with the casual, easily termin-
ated, plural friendships that are characteristic of the West, or with the
warm and intimate community of complaint and hospitality shared by
Middle Eastern women. Instead, as Katherine Bateson and her colleagues report, male friends are required to manifest "total vulnerability
and availability to the demands and needs of the other." A man's friend
"is expected to help him in trouble, to support, sympathize, and be
loyal and sincere in his friendship. He neither blames nor accuses but is
expected to be patient and understanding, someone on whom one can
depend. One not only expects these qualities in his friends, but is obliged to reciprocate." Friendship is also a relationship of supremely
compelling emotional commitment. As a poet writes: "Separation from
the friend for one moment is like Judgment Day. Should their love take
them to Hell, for the friends Hell is paradise."[19]
   These are criteria that would seem to have much in common with
qualities westerners associate with romantic love, and, in truth, the two
are hard to distinguish. Like love, true friendship is dyadic, and a man
can really have only one boon companion, whom the Pukhtun call a
"naked chest" friend, a person whose heart is open, who immediately
intuits and meets one's needs and whose trust is absolute. Friendship is
also equalizing and selfless, and must transcend the rivalries and self-
serving maneuvering of lineage mates. Therefore friends, like lovers, are
not likely to be found among one's close and rivalrous relatives, but are
characteristically outsiders from whom nothing is demanded or granted,
and who are free to respond solely according to sentiment. Still, the
course of friendship is not smooth; the demands on the relationship are
so absolute and so intense that betrayal and jealousy are commonplace,
and friends, like lovers, are more often than not bitterly disappointed in
their hopes for complete understanding and total loyalty.[20]
   The nature of extraordinary friendship is symbolized in the notion
that two persons can share the same essence, and that ideal friends are
"kindred souls" who have sought out and interiorized one another to
the degree that they have actually become one being – it is a transformation of udhritic love in which the "amorous regard" of the lover for
the beloved is reciprocated, and each partner finds his true self in the

gaze and empathetic mirroring response of the other. In Persian this
state of mutual identification is indicated by the term for friend (*dost*),
which is said to come from *du ast* ("is two"), indicating that friends are
"one in essence, two in reality and by designation".[21] It is said that the
unity of ideal friends is so complete that a blow to one will raise a welt
on the body of the other and that at the death of a friend, the other will
automatically waste away; the actions of the friend are also attributed
to the other, and the two bear joint responsibility for their deeds.

These fantasies of the absolute identification of friends run parallel
with the Sufi formula of "I-am-you" used by Hallaj and other ecstatic
mystics bent on describing their ecstatic merger with God. As Hallaj
wrote: "Whenever something touches You, it touches me. Now 'You' are
'me' in everything."[22] Desacralized and applied to individuals as an indication of mutual respect, this formula entered into ordinary discourse
where it could easily descend to absurdity. As one official writes: "I have
sent you so-and-so who is I as I am you. Thus be I-am-you to him"![23]

But there is a deeper meaning behind the formula. Just as Sufism
allows the lonely individual in a harsh world an escape from his isolation in ecstatic union with a God who may be embodied in the form
of the teacher, or as udhritic love permits self loss in amorous regard of
the beautiful kindred soul, or as romantic enchantment lifts the lover
out of his ordinary being in selfless service to his beloved, so does the
dreamt-of friend offer a similar experience, but on the mundane plane,
and without the psychically intolerable burden of submission to a superior entity. Rather, in this secular version the friends are equivalents:
each needs and reflects the other, without subordination or distinction.

Friendship thus conceived is a very old notion that serves as a model
for an idealized masculine relationship where selfishness and selflessness
are harmonized, where equals who are images of one another unite as
one yet retain their separateness; it serves as a relief from the eternal
antagonism between co-equal men and from the hierarchical contempt
that tends to pollute male–female relationships. In idealized friendship
the self-seeking individual can freely and unhesitatingly surrender himself to his alter who is actually himself, his absolute equal and reflection, whose ambitions are the same as his own, and who can therefore
be trusted and loved completely.

The problems of distinction that plague egalitarian culture vanish in
the longed-for experience of perfect identification, as do the inequities
that result from personal greed and the endemic struggle for honor.
Egoism is reconciled with self-effacement in the shared umma of the two
friends; the treasured self is simultaneously sacrificed and deified, over-
coming the tensions that always accompany the participation of the
individual in the rivalrous community of co-equal men. The Middle East
is the home not only to premises of human equality and competitive

individualism but also to fantasies of romantic bliss and perfect camaraderie. My argument is that the latter are a product of, and an escape from, the former: the culture of struggle and warfare among equals is also the culture that dreams of absolute love and perfect friendship.

Part VI

Conclusion

17

Problems and Possibilities

The Command of the Powerful

The cultural heritage of the Middle East, as I have drawn it, is structured by an ancient antagonism between unstable urban civilizations and armed peripheries. This fluid and unreliable setting has favored an entrepreneurial ethic of risk-taking, individual initiative, adaptiveness and mobility among opportunistic co-equals who struggle over ephemeral positions of power and respect, constrained only by participation in a framework of elastic patrilineages. In this competitive environment, secular authority has been thoroughly pragmatic and desacralized. As Hodgson writes, "everyone knew well enough that in fact the king was a mere man among others. In himself he was a mere six feet of flesh, with passions like any other man, by no means unassailable."[1] In reaction to this disenchanted political world, the unifying message of Islam proclaimed a community of saints serving a sacred commander, providing an example that serves still to inspire reformers.

Of course, the Middle East is a vastly different place now than it was in the days of Ibn Khaldun, al-Ghazali and Hallaj. For one thing, the periphery no longer has much power; the advent of the airplane and tank has negated most of the military threat the tribes might offer and impoverishment has made them subservient. As a result, the state, with its learned servants, its bureaucrats and sycophants, now holds more or less complete sway – aided often by fortunes in petrodollars which allow it to assuage tribal pride with bribes.

The expanded power of the state has coincided with the enormous growth of the cities, where diverse populations live in polyglot neighborhoods instead of kin-based quarters and work in huge factories instead of local shops. Under these conditions, old values have been challenged and new ones forged. Ties of blood, once so crucial, have been undermined by the competing claims of class, union, party, and nation. Colonialism and post-colonialism have also greatly disrupted the universe of the past, casting into doubt much of what had been assumed for millennia. New ideologies – communism, capitalism, socialism, and nationalism – have appealed to an expanding and evermore youthful populace torn from its roots in tribe and quarter. Islam itself has changed, as autodidact Islamists and neofundamentalists challenge the state-supported teachings of the modern ulema. Even the old dichotomy between men and women has been tested. Women are entering the workforce in ever-increasing numbers and the extended family has been eroded, leaving husbands and wives alone together within nuclear households.

Yet certain continuities remain: the value placed on personal honor and respect, the contradictory attitudes surrounding the position of women and other "inferiors", the central importance of Islam as the overarching source of identity and hope, and above all a ubiquitous sense of the precariousness of life and the tenuousness of power, coupled with a disrespect for aristocratic privilege, a competitive urge, a faith in the essential equality of persons (except those excluded by their "natur-ally" subordinate characters), and a belief in the potential for individual empowerment and status in the face of arduous odds – these are the pervasive ethical undercurrents of Middle Eastern culture, and would seem to provide the basis for the rise of a modern civil society.

Unhappily, as Walid Khalidi laments, this potential has not been realized: the political order of the region has failed "to approximate in any of its constituent sovereign states to minimal levels of genuine power sharing or accountability in government, much less to self-governing parliamentary institutions operating within democratic forms and constraints."[2] The repressive regimes of the contemporary Middle East have been variously explained as structural remnants of colonial-ism, as western puppets, as consequences of the transition from trad-itional to modern society, and so on. In this final section, I do not wish to dispute any of this conventional wisdom, but merely suggest some historically-grounded hypotheses that flow from the cultural premises I have sought to elucidate in the previous chapters.

To do this, we need first to clear away some possible misapprehen-sions. Under the influence of Rousseau's positive portrait of equality, westerners like to believe that competitive aggression does not coincide with egalitarianism, which is imagined as a relationship of harmony between like-minded individuals sharing their benefits amongst them-selves within a communal atmosphere of familial concord. Anthropolo-gists sometimes perpetuate this halcyon image in their depictions of small-scale communities where personal ambition is denied in favor of participation in the group, where the hunter is anxious to give away his kill, and where leadership is forced on self-effacing and reluctant candidates.

As we have discovered, this has hardly been the case in the Middle East. While generous sharing has always been highly valued, charity has also been viewed as a personal assertion of the magnanimous individual's noble character, displayed to win points in a perpetual game of honor with local opponents. Leadership and dominance, far from being avoided, have been eagerly sought, and avidly contested, while rivalry with one's nearest relations is still considered a fact of life. The prevalent attitude was best expressed by a ninth-century philosopher al-Muhasibi who wrote that human beings are naturally motivated by "a dislike of being unable to attain someone else's station". Even brothers can and should compete for the love of their parents. To make his case, Muhasibi cites a poem: "I am envied. May God increase the envy of me! May nobody live one day without being envied!"[3] How could such a self-aggrandizing value system coincide with the ethic of equality? Isn't the latter simply a mask for the former, adopted by the successful to gull the losers?

I hope I have shown that this is not the case, and that the elite and the deprived share a faith in equity that coincides with strong personal ambition. The seemingly counter-intuitive intertwining of egalitarian belief with individual self-seeking and continual contestation has perhaps best been explained by Alexis de Tocqueville, who, reasoning from the American case, argued that an absence of ascribed social positions in an open-ended egalitarian society logically led to status anxiety, restlessness, and intense competitive struggles between co-equal individuals:

> Some men still enjoy great privileges, but the possibility of acquiring them is open to all. From which it follows that those who possess them are constantly preoccupied with the fear of losing or sharing them...
> The immediate result is an unspoken warfare between all the citizens. One side tries by a thousand dodges to infiltrate, in fact or in appearance, among those above them. The others are constantly trying to push back these usurpers of their rights. Or rather the same man plays both parts, and while he tries to insinuate himself into the sphere above him, he fights relentlessly against those working up from below.[4]

For Tocqueville, then, the ethic of egalitarian individualism in America tends to *increase* competition in the unending struggle for positions of rank precisely because these positions are intrinsically unstable, impermanent, and difficult to measure. The Middle East case is parallel, despite the fact that, unlike the unadulterated individualism of America. the Middle Eastern lineage structure brought people together in patterned alliances. However, these linkages have never precluded internal antagonism. As the Swasa merchants put it: "We are brothers, but when we evaluate the inventory we are enemies."[5]

Whether in America or the Middle East, as a vision of the world, competitive egalitarian individualism has an inherent dilemma – that is, how to conceptualize the actual relations of hierarchy and command which must exist in any complex social formation. In Middle Eastern secular politics the answer to this question has been simple. As Fredrik Barth writes: "It is the fact of effective control and ascendancy – not its formal confirmation or justification – that is consistently pursued." For the leader, and for his subjects, political domination in itself was unambiguously seen as a goal to be achieved simply because power obliged the deference of others and thereby affirmed the ruler's personal strength and glory. Acceptance of command by the ruled similarly "entails accepting the validity – though not necessarily the morality or desirability – of his positions and acts; it implies a confirmation of his value, in terms of ideals of strength and wholeness. It is incompatible with a record of failures or ineffectiveness by the person; whereas it is fully compatible with fear of the person."[6]

Compliance in the Middle East therefore has very often been a direct result of fear, since otherwise a man would not willingly obey another man who is, in principle, no better than he is. The degree of fearful deference reveals concretely the power and renown of the one who commands. As Pukhtun proverbs have it, "where there is the sound of a blow, there is respect," and "he who has power to fight need not negotiate"; sentiments echoed in tenth-century Baghdad: "If you are an anvil, suffer – if you are a stick, make someone suffer."[7] Similarly Henry Munson remarks that in Morocco "all forms of hierarchy are seen as involving hitting and being hit."[8] Force is its own best argument, and the state is popularly understood, in Clifford Geertz's words, as a "machine less for the governing of men...than for the amassment and consumption of the material rewards of power"; a machine characterized by "a constantly rearranging kaleidoscope of political constellations centering around rising and falling strong men."[9]

The pervasive lack of any form of legitimacy for government is not just "superstructure" – it has significance for the actual capacity to hold command. Ruling by pure force, no secular leader can credibly claim any intrinsic right to the wealth or power he manages to accumulate; as a result, his position can be continually and convincingly challenged by new claimants, who are willing to risk being struck down by the king in the hope of taking his throne for themselves. For these reasons, secular power can be fleeting – if the heroic leader shows any signs of weakness today he is abandoned tomorrow... or perhaps sooner. In such an uncertain and treacherous environment, the maintenance of rule did not often coincide with mildness and idealism, though few monarchs would be quite so frank as Muhammad Ali, the powerful nineteenth-century ruler of Egypt, who proclaimed that "a great king knows nothing but his sword and his purse; he draws the one and fills the other; there is no honor among conquerors!"[10]

We have seen that mainstream Muslims (though not the Shi'ites) were obliged to accept the reality of the situation and admit that no one group or person has any intrinsic spiritual claim to authority over any other – rather, political power lay in the hands of the mighty. Typical of this realist trend is Muhammad al-Ghazali who laments in the Seljuk era that "this is a time when the opinion of the people is depraved and the people are all evil doers and evil intentioned."[11] Under such circumstances, he argues that submission to an unjust government is better than the horrors of disorder. Pragmatically, al-Ghazali accepts the fact that, in his degenerate days, government "is a consequence solely of military power, and whosoever he may be to whom the holder of military power professes his allegiance, that person is the Caliph."[12]

In a similar vein, three hundred years later, Ibn Jamaa, chief qadi (judge) of Egypt, baldly asserts that "if the office of Imam is vacant... and there aspires to it one who does not possess the qualifications for it but who imposes himself on the people by his might and his armies... obedience to him is compulsory... this is in no way invalidated by his being barbarous or an evil-doer, according to the most authoritative opinion."[13] Ibn Jamaa goes on to argue that "the sovereign has a right to govern until another and stronger one shall oust him from power and rule in his stead. The latter will rule by the same title and will have to be acknowledged on the same grounds."[14]

The bare expression of arbitrary and coercive secular power remains the case today. In modern Morocco, usually portrayed as the most legitimate and orderly of Middle Eastern governments due to the king's sacred lineage and his long heritage of authority, Muhammad Guessous writes that "political power is seen essentially as a source of evil and harm, and those who hold power tend to be unjust, to break the law, and to play with other people's lives... Injustice is the rule, the abuse of power is the rule; the proper, adequate use of power is the exception."[15]

Among ordinary Muslims, the arbitrariness of the state and its coercive character means that "political roles are selected against, politics is associated with destructiveness, and much activity associated with it is regarded as antireligious, immoral and injurious to the social fabric."[16] This is an attitude that goes back to the fall of the early Caliphate. Ironically, the pious withdrawal of the righteous from the political fray has done much to further an acceptance of tyranny, which will be avenged in the afterlife, but must be suffered in the here and now. This passive attitude is often ratified by citation of the saying: "If they (the rulers) do evil and rule you ill, then punishment will fall upon them and you will be quit of it, for they are responsible for you, but you have no responsibility."[17]

In fact, ruthless exploitation by authorities has often been expected by subjects who did not find it especially troubling that those in power should take advantage of their opportunity to enrich themselves and punish their enemies. This is partly because, as H. A. R. Gibb and Harold Bowen put it: "There was none so low as might not hope, by some turn of fortune's wheel, to be set in a position of authority, however subordinate, and so to share in its perquisites." Under fluid social conditions, "those whose turn had come enjoyed an opportunity which would probably be brief and therefore to be made the most of."[18] From this perspective the depredations of power-holders were regarded not as reprehensible acts but as rational and normal.

Moral opprobrium of tyranny has also been lessened by the masculine ethic of competitive individualism. Those who are successful in political maneuvering are admired as brave, self-controlled, aggressive, intelligent and capable natural leaders, doing what all men would do, if they could. Those without power, whether avoiding or flattering their rulers, nonetheless frankly envy and wish to emulate those who command them. As one of my informants, a poor laborer, told me fervently: "the khans sit upon the necks of the poor. God grant that I may become a khan!" Other tribesmen told me their leaders were "real Pukhtun"; that is, just like them, only more so. In the same vein, the anthropologist Robert Fernea describes the traditional tribal leader in rural Iraq as "a kind of ideal Everyman in the eyes of the tribesmen";[19] when he arrogantly rides by on his white horse, his subordinates feel pride in his power and manly demeanour, which they see as reflecting their own honor and manhood.

An acceptance of tyranny is also a realistic protection against the chronic precariousness of the environment. From ancient times, Middle Easterners have had a strong fear of the chaos that would ensue were human beings, with their aggressive natures and selfish ambitions, allowed free license. Given the history of the region, the typical dread of anarchy is surely not unwarranted. One certain prophylactic against chaos is a strong hand – following the saying that "sixty years of an unjust Imam are better than one night without a Sultan."[20] This attitude is reflected in other popular proverbs recorded by Louis Massignon from tenth-century Baghdad: "When power is fair, subjects abuse it"; "Rather the abuses of power than the fairness of subjects," and "Worship the monkey when he is powerful."[21] Similarly, modern Moroccan proverbs cited by Muhammad Guessous seem to show a longing for domination by force. For example, "The stick is the only thing that will prevent rebellion and dissidence"; or, "An unjust government is better than bad citizens"; or "Starve your dog and it will follow you." The general rule seems to be: "if you are going to be eaten, let yourself be eaten; but if you can eat others, then eat them."[22]

Egalitarian Individualism and Despotism

But there is more to the much discussed "fatalism" of the Middle Eastern populace than a simple hope that they too might someday get their chance to take a share in the spoils of state power or manipulate the state to their advantage, or the acceptance of exploitation as a rational act, or their identification with the ruler as "an ideal Everyman", or even the realistic horror of the chaos that is likely to ensue if no one has a firm grip on the reins. Ironically, Middle Eastern acquiescence to despotism also springs directly from the values of egalitarian individualism – a point first made by Tocqueville in his warning to Americans about the potential for dictatorship in the United States.

Tocqueville feared that American egalitarian individualists, pursuing their own ends, would gladly give up their civic responsibilities to a tyrant if, in return, they were allowed to continue their personal activities.[23] Until recently, this has been the case in the Middle East, where persons seeking respect and honor for themselves and their lineages asserted themselves in contests with their antagonistic co-equals in their local clans, camps and neighborhoods; as long as these rivalries were permitted and intervention from above was minimal, individuals were generally quite willing to allow the central government free rein in its own domain, and used it only for purposes of mediation or, at best, recruited it as an ally in local rivalries.

Tocqueville also thought the danger of dictatorship could be avoided by educating the populace in republican virtue through active participation in local democratic organizations. One might think then that extensive participation in local affairs by Middle Easterners would be a training ground for popular participation in civil society. As we have seen, the Middle East has long been characterized by multiple local-level institutions that strongly affirm each male participant's personal responsibility for himself as well as the absolute right of all members to take part in local political discussion and activity. Among the Pukhtun, for example, *jirgas*, or informal counsels, periodically brought together the interested men of neighborhood, village, or region to discuss and decide local issues.

Similarly, even though the Basseri shepherds of Iran were administered by an appointee from the King, the actual headmen who were his representatives in local camps had no real power to make arbitrary decisions, but had to rely on "compromise, persuasion, and a keen awareness of the drift of group opinion."[24] This pattern was not confined

Plate 17.1 Boys learn the competitive skills of adulthood through play.

to the hinterlands. In urban crafts guilds members gathered regularly in meetings to debate issues, admit members and hold group rituals. Strong solidarity was expected among members, despite actual differences in wealth and power.[25]

These patterns are typical. Everywhere, Middle Eastern men from both the city and the countryside have traditionally met in local assemblies to weigh issues, debate, contend, and make collective decisions about their affairs, which could mean deciding when to move the herd, settling a dispute over land, admitting a member to the guild, debating the rights of a neighbor to blood money, agreeing to take part in a camel raid, and so on. But, despite Tocqueville's predictions, this democratic local-level participatory system has never translated into public participation in the society at large.

In part, this must be because in the Middle East the realm of citizenship and the realm of the state are mutually exclusive – the practice of democratic action is *only* possible as long as the state is excluded, since any secular governmental hierarchy is by definition oppressive and illegitimate. Beyond the particular loyalties of the clan and beneath the universal faith offered by Islam, the intermediate structures of state and civil society have been viewed by the pious as the location for corruption, and by the opportunistic as an arena for personal aggrandizement. In neither case was it a realm for the exercise of corporate morality. The despotism of the center can therefore be understood not as a result of an *absence of* any democratic and egalitarian tradition, but rather as a *response to* just such a tradition taken to its extremes.

Without a legitimate state sphere for public service, the Middle Eastern traditions of democracy, equality, and participation in the rivalries of the local polity trained men to value their freedom from domination, but did not lead to any wider sense of citizenship or community beyond the local necessities of mutual defense and aggression. The public world was conceived solely as an arena for individual pursuit of glory by free agents who hoped to become tyrants themselves, and felt no great moral horror at another man's enactment of the cultural ideal. Fredrik Barth explains the logic of this position:

> Independence and personal sovereignty were highly, perhaps inordinately, valued; but they were conceptualized as goods for each to seek for himself, not as rights for all, to be collectively safeguarded by all. A person who commanded effective and sufficient sanctions to dominate and exploit others was not particularly condemned and his acts were not collectively resisted – indeed he would rather be admired and sought as ally and leader, unless he was so feared for the threat he might pose to one's own autonomy that one sought to build a defensive faction against him.[26]

This pattern serves as a lesson that we should be careful not to romanticize democratic and egalitarian local structures in themselves; when individuals lack a public goal or a legitimized governmental framework, and are motivated solely by a desire for personal aggrandizement, local independence may easily coincide with national repression, and democratic communities may produce aspiring dictators rather than participatory citizens.

Within this ethic, those who have power are limited not by any civil constraints, but only by their own willing conformity to the constraining framework of religion and custom, which can restrict the range of tyrannical behavior very considerably. Such conformity is correlated, as Tocqueville again has remarked,[27] with a competitive egalitarian social order and an absence of clear status markers. This absence stimulates not only competition, as mentioned earlier, but also a deep fear of appearing out of place, and a subsequent compulsive accommodation of the self to the social surround. As the Pukhtun say, the bravest man will not go against custom.

Under these conditions, the leader too is obliged to adhere to local mores and religious beliefs. This is not hypocrisy. In an insecure world, the leader must play an appropriate part in order to retain his own self-esteem as well as the respect grudgingly granted him by his subjects.

Both leader and follower expect that the power-holder will act in the manner that publicly displays the cultural ideal of proper behavior. In the Middle East, this means offering generous gifts to the poor and to favorites, judging cases with an eye to fairness, and displaying the requisite Islamic behavior, sober demeanor and manly bravery expected of a warrior–ruler. In this manner, the expression of power by a leader can be mitigated by the very same egalitarian individualistic value system that has made secular leadership illegitimate and coercive. But as custom is eroded by the conditions of modernity, this mitigating factor may also disappear, leaving government without any responsibility whatsoever beyond maintaining itself through coercion and terror. This, perhaps, is what has occurred in modern Iraq.

Resistance to Authority

Yet, despite the harsh realities of everyday politics, Muslims have never lost their millennial hopes, and their dream of reconciling egalitarian individualism with a sacred community where the faithful willingly submit to a divine law. So, even as imperial power has become "illegitimate in the most literal sense of the word,"[28] the age of Muhammad, and the "rightly guided" Caliphs, is everywhere recalled as the ideal against which contemporary reality is invidiously compared.

For example, although the Moroccan king is perhaps the best ensconced and most "legitimate" of Middle Eastern rulers, his official exaltation has not stopped reformers from castigating him for "eating the flesh, drinking the blood and sucking the marrow of the bones and the brains" of his subjects.[29] And the passive acquiescence to power we find in popular proverbs and traditions can be contrasted to numerous other oppositional proverbs and traditions such as: "the oppressor is cursed by God and despised by the people"; "man owes no obedience to rulers who disobey God" and "a kiss on the hand means hatred of it."[30]

Popular insurgency against tyranny and injustice has a long history in the Middle East. Zayd ibn Ali, leader of a rebellion in 738, called on all Muslims "to wage Holy War against oppressors and defend those who have been abased, to give pay to those who are deprived of it and to share the booty equally among those who are entitled to it, to make good the wrongs done by the oppressors," while a contemporary tribesman complained against Abbasid despotism as follows: "Our booty, which was shared, has become a perquisite of the rich; our leadership, which was consultative, has become arbitrary; our succession, which was by choice of the community, is now by inheritance."[31]

Nor was the voice of resistance heard only from soldiers. In 840 the scholar and writer al-Jahiz forcefully rebutted the doctrine of quietism, arguing that if kingly "misconduct reaches the degree of unbelief, if it passes beyond error to irreligion, then it becomes a greater error even than that of whoever refrains from condemning them and dissociating himself from them."[32] Similarly, al-Ghazali, who grudgingly admitted the necessity of despotic kingship, warns his readers: "Woe to him who is forced to serve the Sultan, for he knows neither friend, kinsman, nor children, neither respect nor reverence for others,"[33] and elsewhere concludes that "it is a religious obligation to avoid the authorities... The scholar should neither see, nor be seen by them."[34] Other theologians said that even walking in the shade of the prince's palace was a sin, since this would mean taking shelter from the sun in the shade of a building erected from the proceeds of injustice. For these righteous Muslims, the self-styled "Shadow of God" could not even rightfully shelter his pious subjects from the heat of the day.

The same voice of discontent and opposition remains compelling today. For example, a poem written by Iran's Ayatollah Khomeini against the evils of Iran's monarchy echoes the complaints of earlier reformers and radicals: "O monarch! The affair of Islam and the Muslims is in disarray, on a festive day when all should be singing joyously. See on every side the heads are bent down with grief!" Elsewhere, Khomeini calls for the election of "a just monarch who will not violate God's laws and will shun oppression and wrongdoing, who will not transgress against men's property, lives and honor."[35]

Although the protests cited above are directed against despotic and corrupt governments, it is noteworthy that the egalitarian and individualistic ethos of the Middle East holds so deep an antipathy to secular hierarchy that the *content* of authority may not necessarily be relevant: a prince might exercise his command in a kindly, gentle and fair manner; nonetheless, as Dale Eickelman points out, the very fact that another person is dominant is by definition unacceptable to the one who has been dominated, since the principle of human equality means that "in so far as a person is obliged to defer to the wishes of others, his autonomy and social honor are diminished."[36] Within this belief system, deference is humiliating, to whomever one defers, and all yokes, however light, are too heavy to bear with honor.

The Middle East then is characterized by a complex and ambiguous political milieu wherein men vie with one another for the pleasures of power, but where the winner of the contest is not left in peace to enjoy his rewards. Rather, the ethic of masculine self-assertion, the lack of legitimacy in the state, and the equivalence of actors impels the dominated to plot continually against the victor in hopes of recapturing their lost honor. The incessant splitting of factions and treachery by those closest to the ruler that is implicit in this world view means the leader's overthrow is always potentially in the offing. It is a Hobbesian universe from which none can withdraw for fear of being destroyed by their surrounding enemies and where continous machination is necessary simply to stay even. Paradoxically, it is also a world where the relative autonomy of the local level allows men to withdraw from the larger life of the state, and can permit a despot to remain in the palace, manipulating competing local rivalries to his own advantage.

This is a harsh picture, but one that is not unrealistic, given the actual ecological, social and historical conditions of the Middle Eastern social world. But, as I have noted, such authority has never been accepted or legitimized by the masses, nor have the pretensions of kings to heavenly sanction ever been acknowledged either by clerics or by popular opinion. The spirit of revolt burns even brighter today as the newly potent state seeks to expand its domain and intrude itself into the previously autonomous realms of local politics.

In response, ordinary Muslims, threatened by the inequities and violence of secular politics and disillusioned with the failures of western ideologies, have again imagined the possibility of a redeemer, the mahdi, who will bring an end to inequality, injustice and cruelty, smiting the wicked and knitting the fragmented world together again in a community of submission to Allah and his messenger. Natural human aggressiveness and selfishness could be curbed, and the ancient Sumerian contest between the cooperative temple, the independent clan and the tyrannical prince could be resolved if all parties were to coalesce around the message of the charismatic "warner" who was anointed by God, yet still a man among men. The depth of this yearning is evidenced in the rallying cry of the Puritan kharijites of Islam's first decades – *la hukm illa li llah* (no judgment but that of God alone) which is echoed in the slogan of the modern Muslim brothers – *la dustur illa l-Quran* (no constitution other than the Quran).

The sacred community grouped around the God-given text voiced by a charismatic emissary who is simultaneously a man like any other stands at the origin of Islamic political memory and as the end point of Muslim political aspiration. It is a religious message extraordinarily egalitarian in its denial of any special qualities to its Prophet, save the fact of his iteration of the Holy Book; it is also a religious message that, more than any other, combined the state and the church in an expansive holy empire. And, above all, it is a message that seeks to replace despotism with a sacred community of the righteous, bound not by self-interest, but by submission to the word of God and His emissary.

But the quandary remains: How could anyone be certain that someone claiming to be a sacred leader actually is speaking for a higher power, and not for personal interests? Those who repudiate any earthly authority may wish for domination by a transcendental heavenly voice – but that voice, which has already been supplied in sacred text, is nonetheless always interpreted by a human agent, who has desires, alliances, and ambitions like every other human being. Any claims to sacred authority are bound to be rendered questionable by the exigencies of secular power, and political failures must lead to an even greater disillusionment with government among the faithful.

Reliance on personal morality to provide order, instead of developing political institutions, also implies a further paradox. As Olivier Roy writes, "on the one hand, as the logic goes, the existence of an Islamic political society is a necessary condition for the believer to achieve total virtue; but on the other hand, such a society functions only by the virtue of its members, beginning with its leaders." In other words, "no Islamic state without virtuous Muslims, no virtuous Muslims without an Islamic state." This circular reasoning leaves reform minded Muslims unable to think practically about civic life, which is left to be exploited by ambitious groups united by self-interest and led by opportunistic power-seekers.

The only course out of this political quagmire is a slow process of gradual democratization and open debate, demonstrating to the people that the state is indeed their servant, not the instrument of the ruler, and that it can function with integrity in its own sphere, despite the imperfections and immoralities of fallible human beings. How – or whether – this can be accomplished is a question that only the future can answer.

"Everything is perishing except the Face of God" (Quran 28:88) in mirror script. Egypt, sixteenth century.

Chronology of Events

Dates	Middle East	Elsewhere
9000	BC	
	8350?: Jericho founded. First walled town	
8000		Rice cultivated in Thailand
7000		First cultivation in Greece
6000	6250?: Catal Huyuk founded in Central Anatolia. Site of early pottery and woolen textiles.	
5000	Colonization of Mesopotamian plain.	
4000	Bronze casting.	
3500	Wheel and plough invented. Pictographic writing in Sumerian seals. Expansion of trade in Sumeria controlled by rival temple complexes.	
3000		Indus Valley civilizations.
	2815–2294: Old Kingdom in Egypt – Age of the pyramids.	
	2750?: Gilgamesh rules in Uruk.	
	2590: Great Pyramid at Giza.	
2500	2500: Fall of Kish.	
	2350–2300: Empire of Akkadian King Sargon I – the first in world history.	
	2254–2218: Reign of Naram Sin – pinnacle of military rule in Sumeria.	
	2112–2006: Dynasty of Ur III – Sumerian temple land expropriated.	
	2100–1700: Middle Kingdom in Egypt.	England: Stonehenge built. Beginnings of Mycenaean civilization.
2000		1760–1122: Shang bronze age culture in China.
	1750–1792: Reign of Hammurabi.	
1500	1575–1200: New Kingdom in Egypt.	
	1200: Gilgamesh epic written.	
	1193: Destruction of Troy.	

Dates	Middle East	Elsewhere
	1116–1077: Tiglath-pileser I founds the Assyrian Empire.	
1000	1000–965: King David temporarily unites Israel and Judah.	
	720: Tiglath-pileser III conquers Samaria.	776: First Olympic Games. 753: Traditional date for foundation of Rome.
600	586: Nebuchadnezzar destroys Jerusalem. 553: Death of Zoroaster. 553–529: Cyrus II founds the Persian Empire.	486: Death of Siddhartha Gautama, founder of Buddhism. 479: Death of Confucius 443–431: Periclean age.
	332–330: Alexander the Great conquers Egypt and Persia	332: Foundation of Mauryan Empire.
250		274–232: Asoka rules India. 264–241: The first Punic war 221: Shih Huang-ti unites China. 112: Opening of the Silk road across Central Asia. 44: Julius Caesar dies. 43AD: Romans invade Britain.
	30AD: Jesus of Nazareth is crucified.	98–116: Rome reaches its apogee under the rule of Trajan.
100	70: Romans destroy the Jewish temple in Jerusalem. 105: Nabatean kingdom in Arabia is annexed to Rome.	105: First use of paper in China.
200		122–127: Hadrian's wall built. 220: Han dynasty ends.
	226: Battle of Ctesiphon establishes Sassanian Rule in Iran and Iraq. 273: Rome conquers Arab kingdom of Palmyra. 276: Mani, founder of Manichean sect, is crucified	
300		304: Huns invade China. 314: Edict of Milan – Pope recognized by Latin Christians. 320–510: Gupta dynasty in India. 360: Huns invade Europe.
400		410: Visigoths sack Rome. 430: Death of St Augustine. 453: Death of Attila the Hun.
	485–531: Mazdak attempts egalitarian reform of Sassanian empire.	486: Merovingian Franks rule in Gaul. 497: Franks convert to Christianity.
500	525: Fall of Himyar. Ethiopians occupy southern Arabia.	520: Invention of the decimal system in India.

Dates	Middle East	Elsewhere
	527–565: Reign of Justinian. Byzantium at its peak. 531–579: Reign of Chosroes I. Sassanian empire is at its height.	
550	550: Marib dam in Yemen breaks – catastrophe for Arabian agriculture 570: Birth of the Prophet Muhammad in Mecca 575: Sassanians occupy southern Arabia.	538–617: Sui dynasty reunite China. 542–594: bubonic plague devastates Europe. 590–604: Gregory the Great reigns as Pope.
600		600: Mayan civilization is at its apogee.
	612–19: Sassanians occupy Syria, Eastern Anatolia and Egypt. 622: Muhammad's Hijra to Medina. Year zero of the Islamic calendar. 624: Battle of Badr. First Muslim victory over Meccans.	618–907: Tang dynasty rules in China.
625	627: Meccans unsuccessfully besiege Medina in the Battle of the ditch. 628: Byzantine army under Heraclius defeats Sassanians. 630: Heraclius restores the true cross to Jerusalem. 630: Muslims occupy Mecca. 632: Muhammad's death. 632–634: Caliphate of Abu Bakr. Arab tribes defeated by Muslims in riddah wars. 634–644: Caliphate of Umar. Sassanian and Byzantine armies defeated as Islam expands across Arabia, Egypt and Persia. 638: Muslims conquer Jerusalem. 644–656: Caliphate of Uthman. Expansion continues. Quran is standardized.	645: Buddhism reaches Tibet
650	656–661: Caliphate of Ali. First civil war. 656: Ali defeats Aisha and Zubayr at the Battle of the Camel. 657–658: Ali battles his cousin Muawiya, the governor of Syria, to a stalemate at Siffin. Kharijites repudiate Ali. 661: Ali is murdered by a kharijite. Muawiya becomes Caliph. *661–750: Umayyad rule. Damascus replaces Medina as Muslim center. Arab Expansion continues.*	
675		676: Korea united.

Dates	Middle East	Elsewhere

680: Death of Ali's son, Husain, at the battle of Karbela.
687: Suppression of Shi'ite rebellion led by al-Mukhtar in favor of Ibn Hanifiyya.
692: Muawiya dies. Second civil war over succession of his son Yazid I.
692: Dome of Rock in Jerusalem completed.

Buddhist temples built in Nara Japan.

700   705: Great Mosque in Damascus completed.

Rise of Kingdom of Ghana.
712: Arabs conquer Seville.
712: Muslim conquest of Sind and Samarkand.
714–741: Reign of Charles Martel in France.

717–720: Reign of Umar II, conciliatory Umayyad caliph.
725   726: Death of the black Arab poet Nusayb.
728: Death of Hasan al-Basra, early Sufi ascetic who emphasized the fear of God.

China: Introduction of printing.

732: Battle of Poitiers ends Muslim expansion in France.

743: Revolt by Zayd, founder of Zaydi branch of of Shi'ites.
744–50: Third civil war.
747: Abu Muslim leads rebellion in the eastern province of Khurasan.
750   750: Khurasaniyya forces defeat Marwan II, end Umayyad rule.

750–945: Abbasid Dynasty rules most of the Middle East. Baghdad replaces Damascus as capital.

751: Arabs in Samarkand learn the use of paper making from the Chinese.

754–775: Rule of al-Mansur, the first great Abbasid Caliph.

Muslim traders reach Chinese ports.

762–763: Foundation of Baghdad, the new capital of the Abbasids.
765: Death of Jafar al-Sadiq, the sixth Shi'ite Imam.
766: Mawali make up the bulk of the Abbasid imperial forces.
767: Death of Abu-Hanifa, founder of the Iraqi school of law.
775   786–809: Caliphate of Harun al-Rashid, zenith of Abbasid culture.
788: Shi'ite Idrisi build capital in Fez.
795: Death of Malik b. Anas, founder of the Maliki school of law.

794: Japanese capital moves from Nara to Kyoto.

Dates	Middle East	Elsewhere
800	801: Death of Rabiya Adawiyya of Basra, female mystic who proclaimed God's love. 813–833: Caliphate of al-Mamun, supporter of Mutazilite theology. 820: Death of al-Shafi, consolidator of Islamic law and founder of the Shafi legal school.	800: Charlemagne crowned Emperor of Rome – foundation of the Holy Roman Empire. 846: Arabs sack Rome.
850	855: Death of Ibn Hanbal, founder of the Hanbalite legal school. 861: Turkish troops murder the Caliph. 869–883: Zanj slave revolt in Iraq. 873: Eleventh Shi'ite Imam dies without issue, leading to the twelver doctrine of the occlusion of the living Imam. 874: Death of Bayazid Bistami, the first of the ecstatic "drunken" Sufis. 890–906: Rise of millenarian Qarmati bands in Arabia.	Mayan culture collapses. 859: Norsemen enter the Mediterranean. 871: Alfred halts the Danish conquest of England. 878: Arabs conquer Sicily.
900	900: Zaydi Shi'ite state established in Yemen. 909–902: Fatimids expand in North Africa. 910: Death of the quietist Sufi master al-Junayd, originator of most Sufi tariqa. 922: Martyrdom of al-Hallaj, Sufi ecstatic. 923: Bahraini Qarmati under Abu Tahir sack Basra. 930: Abu Tahir's men enter Mecca and abscond with the Kaaba. *945–1055: Buyid dynasty of Daylamite nomads rules Persia and most of the central Middle East from Baghdad.*	
950	951: Disappointed in their mahdi the Qarmati return the Kaaba to Mecca. 965: Death of al-Mutanabbi, poet in the classical Arabic style. *969–1171: Fatimid dynasty rules much of the Western region of the Islamicate from Cairo.* 970: Establishment al-Azhar mosque by Fatimids. Al-Azhar is the oldest scholarly institution in the world. *976–1161: Ghaznavid rule in eastern Persia, Afghanistan and Northern India.*	960–967: Sung Dynasty unites China. 967: Fujiwara clan dominate in Japan.

Dates	Middle East	Elsewhere
		987–996: Hugh Capet rules France.
	996–1021: Reign of al-Hakim as Fatimid Imam	989: Prince of Kiev converts to Christianity.
1000	1000: Death of al-Muqaddasi, world traveler and observer	1000: First Iron Age settlement in Zimbabwe.
		1000: Vikings discover America
	1020: Death of Firdawsi, Persian epic poet and author of the Shahnameh.	
	1037: Death of Abu-Sina (Avicenna), Iranian Platonic philosopher.	
	1038–1063: Reign of Toghril-Beg, who expands Seljuk rule west.	
	1040: Seljuk Turks, migrating into eastern Persia, defeat the Ghaznavids.	
	1049: Death of Persian Sufi master and preacher Abu Said.	1045: Chinese invent movable type printing.
1050	1055–1118: Seljuks rule Persia and the central Middle East from Baghdad.	
	1056–1147: Puritanical Berber Almoravid (al-Murabit) dynasty rules Morocco, expands into Africa and Spain.	
	1062: Almoravids found Marakesh.	
	1065–1067: Foundation of the Nizamiyya madrasa in Baghdad; beginning of the absorption of religious institutions by the state.	1066: Normans conquer England
	1070–1080: Seljuks occupy Syria and Palestine.	
	1071: Seljuks defeat Byzantines in the Battle of Manzikert.	
1075	1075: Consolidation of the four Sunni legal schools completed.	
	1090: Nizari Ismaili under Hasan-i-Sabbah conquer Alamut, begin their long battle with the Seljuks.	
	1092: Assassination of the great Seljuk vizier, Nizam-al-Mulk, by the Nizari.	
	1094: Death of Fatimid Caliph Mustansir. Split in Ismaili movement, with Hasan-i-Sabbah leading extremist wing.	
	1096: First Crusade. Franks invade Syria and Anatolia.	
	1099: Crusaders take Jerusalem.	
1100	1111: Death of Muhammad al-Ghazali, Sunni theologian who synthesized orthodoxy and Sufism.	1114: Chichester cathedral founded.
		1119: Bologna University founded.
	1123: Death of Umar Khayyam, Persian poet and mathematician.	
1125	1130: Death of al-Sanai, great Sufi poet.	

Dates	Middle East	Elsewhere
	1130: Fatimid caliph al-Amir dies without sons, fragmentation of the empire.	
	1130–1269 Almohad Sufic reformers rule in North Africa and Spain.	
1150		1154: Chartres cathedral begun.
	1160: Death of Abdul-Qadir Gilani, founder of the largest Sufi tariqa, the Qadiriyya	
	1171: Saladin conquers Fatimid Empire.	
	1180–1225: Reign of al-Nasir, the last great caliph, who attempted to use futuwwa clubs as a basis for reorganizing Islam.	
	1187: Saladin takes Jerusalem from the Crusaders.	1193: Zen Buddhist order founded in Japan.
	1198: Death of Ibn-Rashid (Averroes), philosopher and author of commentaries on Aristotle.	
1200	1200: Death of Attar, Persian allegorist.	
	1210: Hasan III, Imam of the Nizari, repudiates his divinity	1215: Magna Carta.
	1220–1369 Age of Mongol Domination.	
	1225: Almohads abandon Spain.	1227: Death of Gengis Khan.
	1235: Death of Ibn al-Farid, Arab poet and mystic.	
	1240: Death of Ibn al-Arabi, Sufi mystic and esoteric monist.	
1250	1256: Mongols conquer Alamut, Nizari stronghold.	
	1258: Mongols devastate Baghdad, ending the caliphate.	
	1259–1517: Mamluks (Turkish slaves) rule in Egypt and Syria.	
	1273: Death of Persian mystic and poet Jalaluddin Rumi, founder of the Mehlevi Sufi order.	1271–1295: Marco Polo's travels.
	1290–1326: Osman, first Sultan of the Ottomans, leads expansion into Anatolia.	1290: Jews expelled from England.
	1291: Crusaders expelled from Syria	
1300		1321: Death of Dante.
	1328: Death of Ibn Taimiya, Hanbalite jurist and scholar.	1337: Beginning of the hundred years war in Europe.
		1346–1350: Black death ravages Europe.
1350	1369–1405: Timurlane raids the Middle East and India from Samarkand.	1354: Ottomans enter Europe, occupy Gallipoli.

Dates	Middle East	Elsewhere
	1377: Death of Ibn Battuta, Arab geographer and world traveler.	1389: Battle of Kosovo. Ottomans defeat Balkan armies.
	1390: Death of Hafiz, poet of Shiraz	1398: Timurlane sacks Dehli.
1400	1402: Timurlane defeats the Ottomans at Ankara, forcing a retreat.	1400: Death of Chaucer.
	1406: Death of Ibn Khaldun, sociologist.	
		1415: Battle of Agincourt.
		1431: Joan of Arc burned at stake.
		1445: Gutenberg Bible is printed.
1450	1453: Mehmed the conqueror captures Constantinople for the Ottomans and renames it Istanbul, city of Islam.	
	1453–1924: Ottoman Empire rules Anatolia, the central Middle East and North Africa, and expands into east and central Europe.	
	1492: Death of Jami, often called the last great poet of Persia.	1492: Voyage of Columbus.
		1492: Fall of Grenada – Arabs and Jews expelled from Spain.
		1497: Vasco da Gama rounds the Cape of Good Hope, outflanking Muslim traders to India.
1500	1501: Shah Ismail Safavi, Sufi saint, captures Tabriz.	1500: Beginnings of the Renaissance.
	1501–1722: Safavid dynasty rules Persia. Shi'ism becomes the official religion.	1507–22: Muslim dynasties establish rule in Sumatra and eastern Java.
	1508: Safavids take Baghdad.	
	1514: Safavids defeated by Ottomans.	
	1516–1517: Ottomans conquer Egypt, Syria and Arabia.	1519–1522: Magellan circumnavigates the globe.
	1520–1566: Suleiman the Magnificent oversees the flowering of the Ottoman empire.	1521: Martin Luther outlawed – beginning of the Reformation.
	1524–1576: Tahmasp I strengthens Shi'i dominance in Safavid empire.	1521: Ottomans sack Belgrade.
		1526: Babur establishes the Mughal Empire in India.
		1529: Ottomans besiege Vienna.
		1543: Ottomans conquer Hungary.
		1545: Council of Trent; Counter-Reformation begins.
1550		1556–1605: Reign of Akbar the Great, zenith of the Mughals.
		1564: Birth of Shakespeare.
		1571: Ottoman navy defeated by Hapsburgs at Battle of Lepanto.
	1587–1629: Reign of Shah Abbas I, who breaks power of the Qizilbash. Apogee of Safavid rule.	1588: Spanish Armada defeated by the English.

Dates	Middle East	Elsewhere
	1598: Shah Abbas I builds the new Safavid capital of Isfahan	
1600		1603–1867: Tokugawa shogunate. 1606: Ottoman war with Hapsburgs ends in a stalemate. 1610: Beginning of the scientific revolution.
	1623–1640: Murad IV subdues independent Janissaries; revives Ottoman empire. 1639: Ottomans take control of Iraq, defeating Safavids.	1618: Outbreak of the Thirty Years War in Europe.
1650		1644: Manchus overthrow the Ming Dynasty. 1659–1707: Regime of Auragnzeb, the last great Mughal. 1661–1715: Reign of Louis XIV. 1683: Ottomans fail in second siege of Vienna. 1699: Treaty of Karlowitz: Ottomans lose Hungary to Hapsburgs.
1700	1720–1730: Tulip Age: Ottoman effort to Westernize ends in revolt. 1726: First Ottoman printing press. 1735: Wahhabi movement begins in Arabia. 1736–1747: Rule of Nadir Shah in Iran.	1718: Ottomans lose Belgrade.
1750		1740–1780: Frederick the Great of Prussia. 1770: Russians destroy Turkish fleet. 1775: American Revolution.
1800	1789–1807: Selim III fails to reform Ottoman. 1792: Death of Muhammad Wahhab. 1794–1924: Qajar Dynasty in Iran. 1798–1801: Napoleon occupies Egypt. 1801–1804: Wahhabis conquer central Arabia. 1805–1848: Muhammad Ali rules in Egypt. 1808–1839: Sultan Mahmud II centralizes and modernizes the Ottoman Empire. 1811–1818: Wahhabis defeated by Egyptian armies. 1822: First printing press in Egypt. 1830: French invade Algeria.	1789: French Revolution.
		1833: Slavery abolished in British empire.
1850	1839: British occupy Aden. 1839–1876: Tanzimat western reforms lead to bankruptcy in Ottoman empire.	1854–1876: Crimean War.

Dates	Middle East	Elsewhere
		1861: Emancipation of serfs in Russia.
		1863: Emancipation of slaves in United States.
	1869: Suez Canal opened.	
1875	1881: French rule in Tunisia.	
	1882–1907: Lord Cromer is proconsul of Egypt.	
	1892: Shah of Iran cancels tobacco concession to Europeans after popular and religious resistance.	
1900	1902: Ibn Saud leads Wahhabi movement.	
	1905: Muhammad Abduh, modernist Islamic reformer and rector of al-Azhar, dies.	1905: Theory of relativity.
	1906: Hasan al-Banna, founder of the Muslim Brothers, is born (d. 1949).	
	1908–1913: Young Turk movement.	1910: Slavery abolished in China.
	1911: Italy conquers Libya.	
	1914: Egypt named British protectorate.	1914–1918: World War I.
	1917: Balfour Declaration promises Jews a homeland in Palestine.	1917: Russian revolution.
	1919–1922: Turkish war of independence.	
	1924–1938: Rule of Mustafa Kemal (Ataturk) in Turkey. Caliphate abolished. Civil court replaces sharia.	1922: Marcel Proust dies.
1925	1925: Reza Shah founds the Pahlavi dynasty in Iran.	1929–1939: Great Depression.
	1932: Ibn Saud establishes the Kingdom of Saudi Arabia.	
	1935: Rashid Rida, leader of Salafiyya, dies.	
	1936: Arab revolt in Palestine.	1939–1945: World War II.
	1946: Jordan, Lebanon and Syria recognized as independent.	1947: Pakistan and India independent.
	1948: Creation of the state of Israel.	1949: Communist victory in China.
1950	1953: Republic declared in Egypt.	
	1956: Suez crisis. Britain gives up power in Aden and the Suez.	1957: First space satellite launched.
	1961: Al-Azhar becomes a state University offering secular education.	
	1962: France withdraws from Algeria.	1963: President Kennedy assassinated.
	1967: Israel defeats Arab forces in Six-Day war.	1965–1973: Vietnam war.
1975	1973: Arab oil embargo.	
	1975–1987: Civil war in Lebanon.	
	1979: Egypt and Israel sign peace accord.	

Dates	Middle East	Elsewhere

1979 Ayatollah Khomeini overthrows
the Shah.
1979 Messianic Muslims occupy the
Great Mosque in Mecca.
1979–89 Soviet occupation of
Afghanistan.

1980   1980–88 Iran–Iraq war.
1987 Anti-Shi'ite riots in Mecca.   1989 Berlin Wall demolished.

1990   1990–2 Iraq invades Kuwait, defeated
by USA led coalition.
1991 Treaty gives Syria control over
Lebanon's foreign relations.
1992 Civil war in Algeria after election
victory of Islamic party is overturned.
1993 Israel and PLO sign Oslo accord.
1994 Civil war in Yemen.

1995   1995 Israeli Prime Minister Yitzhak
Rabin assasinated by right-wing Jewish
activist.
1996 Islamic coalition victorious in
Turkish election.
1996 Taliban occupy Kabul.
1997 Islamic coalition in Turkey
overthrown.
1997 Moderate Mohammad Khatami
elected President of Iran in surprise
landslide.
1999 Deaths of King Hasan II of
Morocco, King Husein of Jordan.
1999 Abdelaziz Boutefika becomes the
first civilian President of Algeria.

2000   2000 Israel withdraws from Lebanon.
2000 Failure of Camp David summit.
2000 Death of Hafez Asad, ruler of
Syria.
2000 Palestinian popular uprising.
2001 Taliban defeated and deposed by   2001 Terrorist attack on US
USA and Northern Alliance.
2002 Hamid Kharzi appointed interim
Prime Minister of Afghanistan.

Notes

(Among the anthropological sources on the Middle East, those I find most useful for introductory purposes include Eickelman (1987), Gilsenan (1983) and Gellner (1981). See also Coon's classic study (1951), which is unsurpassed for its technical detail.)

Chapter 1: The Middle East: Assumptions and Problems

1 See Southern (1962) for a catalogue of attitudes.
2 Hegel (1953: 24).
3 Daniel (1960).
4 Weber (1978: 625–7, 976–8).
5 Hodgson (1974, vol. 3: 158).
6 Baring (1908, vol. 1: 7).
7 Baring (1908, vol. 2: 164).
8 Said (1979: 12).
9 Said argues that all efforts at cultural comparison are "generalities whose use historically and actually has been to press the importance of the distinction between some men and some other men, usually towards not especially admirable ends." For him the notion of "culture and cultural comparativism" is an oppressive act of force, "which spawned ethnocentricism, racial theory and economic oppression" (Said 1979: 45, 146; see also Abu-Lughod 1993). For a response, see Lindholm (1995a).
10 Needham (1978: 3).
11 See Coon (1951) for the best statement of the physical and geographical limits of the Middle East.
12 Leach (1961).
13 Arkoun (1994).
14 See Dumont (1970) for the standard argument on this.
15 See Gellner (1983) for a clear statement of this position.
16 Rosenfeld (1965: 174).
17 Antoun (1967: 295).
18 Khan (1958: 47).
19 Black (1972: 616).
20 Rabinow (1977: 116). This egalitarian attitude is in marked contrast to the European Mediterranean where the poor are thought to have less honor than their superiors (Stewart 1994: 132).
21 Lewis (1988: 64). This is not only true in the central regions of the Middle East, but also in the supposedly more hierarchical society of Iran. As Sir John Chardin wrote in 1720, Persians often took their names from the calling of their ancestors, "whether

Liberal or Mechanick, by which they rais'd themselves in the World...and what is Remarkable, as very Praise-worthy in my Opinion, that they are not ashamed of bearing these Sir-names after they become Rich, are raised to the highest Dignities, and are put into the greatest Employments. This is because they are rais'd by the Sciences, by their Employments and especially by their Riches. There are but very few who are tied to it by Descent" (Chardin 1927: 197).

22 Lewis (1988: 23).
23 Hodgson (1974 vol. I: 344, 253).
24 See Lindholm (1992).

Chapter 2: Ways of Living

1 As Paul Dresch puts it, in this ancient region, "there is no need to invent the state" (Dresch 1990: 260).
2 The exact date of the introduction of the camel is not known. Camels were certainly plentiful by 1000 BC, since the Bible describes invading Midianites as having thousands of camels.
3 Cole (1975).
4 The Bedouin's virtually obsessive interest in the personality of the individual is revealed in the "almost unlimited amount of synonyms for the ideas of character and character traits" found in ancient tribal texts. See Goitein (1977: 5), and Goitein and Von Grunebaum (1975).
5 Ibn Khaldun (1967: 108, 119).
6 Irons (1979: 362); see also Burnham (1979).
7 See Bulliet (1975) for a history of this extraordinary process.
8 Gellner (1981: 31).
9 See Barth (1961) for an example, though Barfield (1993) notes that sloughing off of excess population only operates in situations where nomads have no other sources of income, such as raiding, and where there is a deficit in the sedentary population.
10 See Mernissi (1991: 135–6).
11 See Tapper (1979). See also Barfield (1993) who distinguishes Central Asian horse nomads from Middle Eastern pastoralists. As we shall see, the social structure of the Central Asian nomads is significantly different from their Middle Eastern counterparts.
12 Barth (1959a: 9).
13 The Khamseh confederacy of Iran, for instance, was organized by the Qajars under the leadership of the Qavam merchant family from Shiraz.
14 See Tapper (1990), Beck (1990) for recent articles on this topic.
15 Black (1972: 617).
16 Beck (1990: 216).
17 Beck (1986: 200).
18 For a discussion, see Salzman (1979).
19 Michael Meeker (1979, 1980) argues for a contradiction between the freedom and violence of a nomadic ethic and the diligent labor involved in farming. See Lindholm (1981a, 1995b) for my response.
20 Davis (1977: 99)
21 See Gilsenan (1993) for a modern case.
22 Davis (1977: 80).
23 This is in sharp contrast to the Greek *polis*, which was differentiated from the country by the presence of government offices as well as by the communal civic spaces of gymnasium, theater, market, and fountain. It is noteworthy as well that there was no civic responsibility for education or amusement in the traditional Muslim city. See von Grunebaum (1961). See also Kennedy (1985) who shows the evolution of this urban form precedes the Muslim conquests.

24 Lapidus (1969: 73). See also von Grunebaum who writes that the Muslim town was "merely a functionally unified, administrative entity with a more or less stable complement of settlers or inhabitants" (1961: 142).
25 See Massignon (1963) for the relationship between these clubs and trade guilds.
26 Chardin (1927: 251).
27 See Udovitch (1977) for more on this topic.
28 For this formulation, see Weber (1958).
29 Traveling and trading in the Persia of the late seventeenth century, Chardin was astonished to discover that "every one is at Liberty to go where he pleases, and there is no need for a Pass, they having free Egress out of the Kingdom without it" (1927: 130).

Chapter 3: Traditions of Authority and Freedom

1 See Firdawsi (1967), Sells (1989)
2 Von Grunebaum (1970), van Ess (1970).
3 Gibb (1955: 126).
4 Rosenthal (1960: 13).
5 Zaehner (1961).
6 See Yar-Shatar (1968).
7 See Lambton (1980).
8 Lapidus (1982: 52).
9 Crone and Cook (1977) entitle their book on early Islam *Hagarism*, commemorating the Islamic claim to be descended from Abraham's wife Hagar and her son Ishmael.
10 See the essays "Religious Rejections of the World and Their Directions" and "The Social Psychology of the World Religions" in Weber (1946) for Weber's most succinct statements.
11 Of course, this is the "ideal typical" form of high Buddhist tradition, found most purely in the Hinayana school. It has little to do with popular Buddhism, which is far more personalized and miraculous in character. Yet the high culture values do permeate to the level of the masses, informing local concepts of the nature of ultimate reality and the possibilities of social and moral action in a way that is quite different from the Muslim tradition.
12 "One responsible lifetime; one transcendent God – and one righteous community. To assert the priority of the moral universe over the natural called for all three" (Hodgson 1974, vol. 1: 132).
13 There are alternative values manifested within orthodox Islam itself and in the Shi'ite and Sufi paths which will be explored later in more detail.
14 See Weber (1946, 1978).
15 Chang (1983).
16 See Geertz (1980), Tambiah (1976) for examples in south-east Asia.
17 Note that Weber is not making Wittfogel's claim for a correlation between the rise of despotic states and the development of irrigation systems. Rather, he is arguing that different types of state and different types of legitimizing ideology correspond to various modes of production.
18 See Kalberg (1994) for an outline of Weber's views on the origins of monotheism.
19 Kohl (1989: 238).
20 Frankfort (1948: 5).
21 Frankfort (1948: 5).
22 Kovacs (1989: 4–5, 19–20). Kovacs' is the most scholarly translation. For more literary versions, see Sandars (1972), Mason (1972a).
23 Kovacs (1989: 4, 20, 21, 10).

24 See Jacobsen's articles "Primitive Democracy in Ancient Mesopotamia" and "Early Political Development in Mesopotamia" reprinted in Jacobsen (1970).
25 Jacobsen (1970). See also Saggs (1962) who bases his work on Jacobsen's argument. This is a controversial assertion, since the temples did develop into highly centralized and tyrannical institutions, as Marxist scholars have pointed out. But, as we shall see, the evolution of tyranny is not incompatible with an ideology of equality.
26 For an alternative perspective see Crone (1986), who argues that "tribal" kinship organization does not precede the state, but is a response to the evolution of central- ized authority. Her hypothesis is a reasonable reaction to Adams's (1966) argument that kinship in pre-dynastic Sumeria must have been of a conical or hierarchical type. However, as we shall see, the conical kinship structure is not presently characteristic of the Middle East, and probably never was. Rather, we find a more egalitarian type of kinship organization that is quite compatible with the data Crone cites.
27 Saggs (1989: 31).
28 Frankfort (1948: 215, 218).
29 Lamberg-Karlovsky (1989). The payment of one-fifth of personal profits into the community coffers can be seen as a precursor to the Muslim institution of zakat.
30 Diakonoff (1969).
31 Frankfort (1948: 221).
32 The pragmatic orientation of nomadic warriors remains striking, though they are also equally prone to conversion to messianic movements.
33 True to the pattern of repeated nomadic sedentarization and integration into urban society that we find throughout Middle Eastern history, many of these "barbarians" had previously been assimilated into Mesopotamian culture and were already farmers, merchants, and administrators within the empire.
34 The debtor orientation of ancient law parallels later Islamic prohibitions on usury.
35 Quoted in Saggs (1989: 162).
36 Diakonoff (1969: 185).
37 Diakonoff (1969).
38 Lamberg-Karlovsky (1989: 266).
39 Frankfort (1948: 311).

Chapter 4: The Social Construction of Egalitarianism

1 Ibn Khaldun (1967: 91).
2 Ibn Khaldun (1967: 122).
3 Ibn Khaldun (1967: 96).
4 Ibn Khaldun (1967: 146).
5 Quoted in Ayalon (1975: 49).
6 Ibn Khaldun (1967: 111).
7 Ibn Khaldun (1967: 97-8, 146).
8 Ibn Khaldun (1967: 99, 148).
9 Ibn Khaldun (1967: 100).
10 For example, Lois Beck has shown that the Qashqai confederation of Iran was in fact a collection of disparate tribal elements brought together in the eighteenth century. However, recent tradition claims a common origin (Beck 1990).
11 Saggs (1989: 182).
12 Quoted in Stewart (1994: 85).
13 Gibb and Bowen (1963: 277).
14 Cuisenier (1975). Kinship terminology in the region nonetheless retains bilateral elem- ents.
15 See Murphy and Kasdan (1959, 1967) for this important argument.

16 Bacon (1958).
17 Wellhausen (1927: 320).
18 Murphy and Kasdan, (1959: 27).
19 See Sahlins, (1961) for the original formulation of this model.
20 Peters, (1960: 31).
21 Fernea (1970).
22 Hart (1970: 70).
23 See Lindholm (1981b, 1982, 1995b) for more.
24 Meeker (1979: 207).
25 Cole (1975: 73).
26 Montagne (1973), Gellner (1969: 67), Hart (1970: 45), Barth (1959b, 1965).
27 Barth (1959b: 15–19).
28 Thus Patricia Crone, writing about Medieval factions, notes that "clearly, had one faction succeeded in eliminating the other, it would have split in two itself" (Crone 1980: 233).
29 Salzman (1978: 62).
30 Peters (1967: 276).
31 Dresch (1986: 321). For a more recent discussion of the pros and cons of segmentary lineage theory, see the exchange between Gellner and Munson (1995).

Chapter 5: The Prophetic Age

1 Wellhausen (1927: 3).
2 The major exception was the Nabatean buffer kingdom on the Roman border. See Bowerstock (1983).
3 This region is, in fact, a very ancient cosmopolitan center; it was in what we now call Bahrain that the great commercial entrepot of Dilmun flourished four millennia ago as a hub of trade with Mesopotamia, Egypt and points east.
4 The metaphor of the hijra has been used ever since by Muslim political activists who consciously seek to replicate Muhammad's sequence of revelation, struggle, exile to the hinterland and triumphant return.
5 Quran 96: 1–2.
6 A "Muslim" is one who is submitting. The root of both Islam and Muslim is *aslama*.
7 Shaban (1971: 9).
8 Quoted in Kister (1979: 4).
9 The actual polytheism of the ancient Bedouin, and especially of the Quraysh, is a matter of much dispute, since they are presented in Islamic tradition simultaneously as pagans and as the devotees of the God of Abraham. As we shall see in later chapters, even after the advent of Muhammad, Muslims have continued to worship local saints while averring their faith in Allah as an absolute deity.
10 This is disputed by Crone (1987) who argues that Mecca was not a pre-Islamic pilgrimage site. Rather, she believes that nearby pagan sanctuaries and marketplaces have been conflated with Mecca because Meccans used these sites for trade.
11 See Watt (1988) and many other of his books. Kister (1965a, 1965b, 1972) and Shaban (1971) also give accounts of the pre-Islamic trade of Mecca and the relationships of Mecca with its allies.
12 Watt (1988: 51).
13 Crone (1987: 151).
14 Crone (1987: 237, 236).
15 For the standard statement on nativist movements, see Wallace (1956).
16 Crone (1987: 245).
17 Quran 41:6.

18 Quran 6:50.
19 Quran 88: 21–22. At the same time, the faithful were also enjoined to obey God and His messenger.
20 Quran 16:93.
21 Quran 4:97.
22 Crone (1987: 240).
23 Dabashi (1993: 49).
24 Watt (1988: 25).
25 Quran 2:256.
26 Quran 4:59.
27 Crone (1987: 237).
28 See Eickelman (1976) for an account of one such site. Of course, not all sacred sites are overseen by holy men, nor do all holy men have an association with a sacred site. But the combination is a common and potent one in terms of the potential for expansive political organization.
29 Serjeant (1981a: 1–2). However, Crone (1987) has noted that sacred enclaves under the authority of a holy guardian are not common in northern Arabia, where Medina is located. Instead, she believes the Medinese adopted Islam as a political act. From my point of view, there is no contradiction here, since war leaders have first to reconcile rivalrous tribesmen before leading them in battle.
30 Torry (1892: 48). See also Gellner (1983), who, like Rodinson (1973) and Hodgson (1974) argues that the Middle Eastern cultural ethos was (and remains) uniquely mercantile and amenable to capitalism.
31 This is not to say that conversion was wholesale or immediate, or even necessarily motivated by the liberating message of Islam. Rather, it seems that conversion was a gradual process of assimilation and adaption. See Bulliet (1994) for more on this.
32 For Shi'ites only Ali is recognized.
33 Cornelius (1979: 51).
34 Crone and Hinds (1986: 27).
35 Quoted in Dabashi (1993: 83).
36 Letter from Ali in 658 AD quoted in Jafri (1979: 12). Later Caliphs, though no longer accepted as "rightly guided" nonetheless continued to use a public rhetoric of service and justice. For instance, the Abbasid Caliph al-Mamun wrote: "It is incumbent upon the Caliphs of God to obey Him regarding such of His religion and of His servants as are placed by Him in their keeping and care; and it is incumbent upon the Muslims to obey their Caliphs and to help them to establish God's justice and his equity, to make the highways safe and prevent bloodshed, and to create a state of concord and unity of fellowship." Quoted in Crone and Hinds (1986: 135).
37 Quoted in Crone and Cook (1977: 225).
38 Quoted in Kister and Plessner (1990: 53).
39 See Watt (1956), Nagel (1982). Crone (1988) argues that it is possible the Quraysh were not so elite as they later claimed, noting that merchants have traditionally not been held in great esteem by the Bedouin.
40 Wellhausen (1927: 71).
41 See Watt (1956) for genealogies.
42 Wellhausen (1927: 80).
43 Quoted in Crone and Cook (1977: 225).
44 Quoted in Kister and Plessner (1990: 53).
45 Quran 49:13.
46 For instance, in the tenth century Abu al-Hasan al-Amiri writes disapprovingly that pre-Islamic Persian rulers "forbade their subjects to advance from one rank to another higher one. Such an attitude results in preventing many good qualities from achieving

equitable distribution. It incapacitates noble souls and discourages them, so that they do not aspire to high rank." Yet only a few sentences later he says that "it is proper for us to realize that the pride a person might take in Islam is greater or less, corresponding to the closeness of that person's relationship or contact with Muhammad" (Quoted in Rosenthal 1956: 52).

Chapter 6: Early Struggles for Authority

1 Wensinck (1932: 13).
2 Wellhausen (1927: 25).
3 As is typical in such blocs, splits and cross alliances were commonplace. Qays was traditionally divided between Mudar and Rabiah, and Rabiah often allied with Qahtan against Mudar, especially among settled populations of Christian converts in Iraq and Syria. Non-Arabs usually affiliated with Qahtan and Rabiah, though some allied with Mudar, especially the Tamim branch (Hodgson 1974, vol. 1: 229).
4 Quoted in Wellhausen (1927: 207–8).
5 Goldziher (1981: 183).
6 Watt (1973).
7 See Dabashi (1993) for more on the difficulties of maintaining authority solely by delegation "from below".
8 See chapter 13 for more on contemporary Islamist movements.
9 In Sunni Islam, the imam is the leader in prayer in the mosque. For Shi'ites, he is the sinless and infallible inheritor of Muhammad. When used in the latter sense, the term will henceforth be capitalized. See chapter 11 for more on Shi'ism.
10 In a controversial article, Watt (1961) argues that Shi'ites of this period are descended from southern tribes of Yemen who aim to recapitulate the charismatic central authority they had known before Islam, while kharijites are northerners pursuing an indigenous ideal of tribal community. However, it is not clear that early leaders of Yemen were actually charismatic in the Weberian sense, nor is it evident that the kharijites rejected charismatic leadership. In fact, it could be said that the Shi'ites were more bureaucratically inclined than the kharijites, since they were willing to accept a leader based on lineage rather than on demonstrated personal ability.
11 As Madelung (1992) has pointed out, this portrait, more or less taken for granted by Muslim theologians, is in fact a distortion of the actual teachings of the early murjia. Although they did emphasize faith over acts, they were not actually politically passive, but were at odds with the Umayyad dynasty because they advocated suspending judgment on Ali's rule and because they favored justice and equity for non-Arabs.
12 Goitein (1966: 5).
13 Ziyad B. Abihi, quoted in Wellhausen (1927: 122–3).
14 Gibb (1962: 62).
15 See Crone (1989).
16 Shaban (1971: 183).
17 Quoted in Kister and Plessner (1990: 50).
18 Lapidus (1988: 97). Adab also can mean courtesy grounded in religious humility.
19 Lassner (1980: 98).
20 Lassner (1980: 16).
21 Wellhausen (1927: 559).
22 Shaban (1976: 89).
23 Wellhausen (1927: 561).
24 Quoted in Lewis (1973: 252).

Chapter 7: Sacred and Secular Rulers

1 For standard accounts, see Daftary (1990), Lewis (1940).
2 Al-Nuwayri, quoted in Lewis (1974: 64).
3 They were members of the Zaydi.
4 Shaban (1976: 161).
5 Mottahedeh (1980: 80).
6 Quoted in Mottahedeh (1980: 144).
7 Mottahedeh (1980: 190).
8 Morgan (1988: 36).
9 Lambton (1968: 205).
10 Lambton (1968: 251).
11 Morgan (1988: 31).
12 Iqta was a Middle Eastern tradition, but became predominant during the Seljuk regime. Initiated as an aid to the financing and administration of a widespread empire, the major forms of iqta involved a land grant with the expectation of military service in return (the "military" iqta), or simply the appointment as a provincial governor (the "administrative" iqta). Under strong rulers, the system was efficient, but as the Seljuk Sultans lost power, the holders of iqta soon began to resemble independent princes.
13 Gibb (1962: 95).
14 Lapidus (1990: 29).
15 Quoted in Munson (1993: 49).
16 Kostiner (1990: 231).
17 Lapidus (1990: 29).
18 The reasons for this are unclear, since the founding ancestor of his order was certainly a Sunni, and his Qizilbash followers were not Shi'ites. Shah Isma'il himself had been raised in a Shi'i environment, and possibly was influenced by this heritage.
19 Though travelers' accounts show that Qizilbash devotion to the Shah remained deep even into the 1540s. See Morgan (1988: 118).
20 Morgan (1988: 147).
21 Morgan (1988: 142). A similar policy has often been pointed out as a major reason for the low quality of later Ottoman sultans.
22 Quoted in Morgan (1988: 147).
23 See chapter 11 for more on Khomeini and Shi'ism in general.

Chapter 8: Novelties and Continuities

1 Fried (1960)
2 Cuisenier (1975: 67 my translation).
3 Cuisenier (1975: 480).
4 Murphy and Kasdan (1959: 23).
5 See Lindholm (1986) for a detailed discussion.
6 Gibb and Bowen (1963: 206).
7 Itzkowitz (1972: 38).
8 Gibb and Bowen (1963: 207).
9 Gibb and Bowen (1963: 211).
10 Quran 2: 191.
11 A phrase of Maliki jurists quoted in Lewis (1988: 102).
12 Mason (1972b: 120). See Massignon (1963) for the relationship between the clubs and artisan guilds.
13 See Bartold (1968) for an account.

14 For accounts of the assassins see Lewis (1980), Hodgson (1955), Daftary (1990).
15 Hodgson (1955: 56).
16 In their use of assassination the Nizari were precursors of modern terrorists. Their killings, however, were never indiscriminate.

Chapter 9: The Essentials of Islam

1 Makdisi (1983: 85).
2 Quran 18: 29.
3 Massignon (1982 vol. III: 4).
4 Dhahabi quoted in Makdisi (1962: 70).
5 See Smith (1957) for this formulation.
6 Some Muslim radicals now say jihad, holy war, should also be seen as compulsory. For some of a "kharijite" persuasion, this can be taken as a physical war against those considered infidels, who can often be fellow Muslims regarded as apostates. For others, jihad can be understood as an inner struggle against oneself.
7 The lunar calendar is eleven days shorter than the solar calendar, meaning that there is a rotation of Muslim holidays every thirty-two years. Part of the genius of Muhammad was to create a new way of measuring time which would effectively remove all Muslim holidays from any previous connection to seasonal celebrations.
8 Quran 2: 187
9 The more austere do not indulge themselves, and it is considered correct to eat no more during Ramadan than one would eat ordinarily. But it is noteworthy that everyone *is obliged* to break the fast and to eat *at least* as much as it eaten when one is not fasting.
10 Quran 2: 185.
11 Shah Waliullah, quoted in Nadwi (1972: 195–6).
12 None of these fasts are obligatory, as the Ramadan fast is, though they are considered spiritually and physically beneficial. But in any case to fast for more than four days in succession (save during Ramadan and the six days immediately after Eid) is deemed wrong by the commentators (see Gibb and Kramers 1965: 504–7).
13 *Eid al-Adha*, the greater festival, is also a commemoration and re-enactment of sacrifice which involves a great communal feast – usually of a sheep which has been cleansed by fasting, slaughtered and shared out with family, dependents and the poor.
14 See Lane (1871 vol. II: 238) for a full description of this holiday as kept in Cairo in the mid-nineteenth century; Jomier and Corbin (1956) for a later view of the same festival, Goitein (1966) for a general statement on fasting.
15 Quran 39:23.
16 Quran 17:109.
17 Quoted in al-Ghazali (1963: 130).
18 In their stress on God's forgiveness, Muslims are more like Lutherans or Pentecostal Christians than they are like Christian fundamentalists.
19 Quran 74: 31.
20 Sura 39:48 in which God says that on Judgment day "there shall appear to them, from God, things they have never reckoned on" has been interpreted in commentaries to mean that what was thought good may be reckoned in the final balance as evil.
21 The Akhbar al-hallaj quoted in Massignon (1982 vol.II: 87).
22 Cited in al-Ghazali (1963: 134, 128).
23 See Andrae (1936) for historical material on this transformation. As we shall see, much of this ideology has a basis in Sufi theory, especially that of Ibn Arabi.
24 This is the miracle that provides the iconography for the Ottoman symbol of the crescent moon with a star between its points.

25 Quoted from al-Sharani in Goldziher (1981: 189).
26 The theory that saintly mediators are a psychological response to an absolutely om-
    nipotent and transcendent God was first posed by David Hume (1976), and was
    applied to Islam by Ernest Gellner (1981).
27 Weber (1946: 47–8).
28 Weber (1946: 52, 295).
29 Goitein (1977). But this should not be taken as a supression of individuality – highly
    personal, descriptive and often insulting nicknames continued to be used in ordinary
    life. See Antoun (1968) for the variety of nicknames and the manner in which abusive
    nicknames are a way of asserting equality within the local context.

Chapter 10: Recapturing the Sacred Past: the Power of Knowledge

1 Hodgson (1974, vol.II) calls this the kerygmatic mode of religious experience, in which
   the ultimate is sought in the moral events recorded in history. Recalling this historical
   revelation permits re-imagining one's own life within the historical religious drama.
2 Hodgson (1974 vol.I: 321).
3 These "traditions" are not to be taken in the usual English sense of unwritten custom.
   Over time, they have been carefully codified and collected in texts, and very often
   explicitly repudiate ordinary usage. Hadith writers saw themselves as maintaining the
   true tradition which had been revealed by Muhammad. See Hodgson (1974, vol. I:
   63–7).
4 See Bulliet (1994)
5 From very early on, in fact, Muslim linguists and ethnographers travelled into remote
   parts of Arabia to recapture pure Arabic grammar and practice in order to elucidate
   the Quran and the traditions. Makdisi (1985) argues that this movement was the
   direct inspiration for renaissance humanism in the West. The humanistic canon of
   grammar, poetry, rhetoric, history, and moral philosophy were also the subjects studied by early Muslim investigators seeking to clarify their cultural history. Influenced by
   the scholastic style, yet reacting against the Muslim concern for Arabic, westerners
   turned their attention to ancient Greek and Latin.
6 Quoted in Messick (1993: 23).
7 Recitation of the Quran was the only miracle that Muhammad ever claimed to have
   accomplished, and Muslims say the uniquely elevating emotional and aesthetic quality
   of the Quran is definitive proof of its divine origin. To this day, one of the major
   religious and aesthetic experiences of ordinary Muslims is listening to experts chant
   Quranic verses in Mujawwad style, which uses melody, repetition, ornamentation, full
   voice, and intensity to "reach the hearts" of the audience (see Nelson 1986).
8 The conservativism of Arabs in regard to language is correlated with their sense of the
   sacredness of the spoken Quran. In the modern Middle East almost all written Arabic
   is in classical style, which is very different indeed from ordinary spoken language. The
   Western equivalent would be if our newspapers were written in Chaucerian English.
9 It is an indication of the nature of the category of hadith transmitter that both male
   and female Muslims could fill the role, since it only required that one be upright,
   reliable and act in a respectable manner according to one's station in life. One of the
   most famous early transmitters was Aisha, Muhammad's favorite wife.
10 Goitein (1977: 15).
11 The jurist al-Nawawi quoted in Messick (1993: 161–62).
12 Makdisi (1985: 82).
13 Goldziher (1981: 164).
14 Messick (1993: 34)
15 These disputes could be lethal. For example, in Nishapur endemic warfare between

Hanafi and Shafi factions helped lead to the abandonment of the city. See Bulliet (1972, 1976).
16 Abu Shuja and al-Nawawi cited in Messick (1993).
17 Possibly these institutions, like so much else in Islam, are a result of innovations in Iran, especially Khurasan.
18 Makdisi (1983: 81).
19 Makdisi (1983: 82).
20 Makdisi (1981) has argued forcibly that the classical Muslim system of higher education, with its stress on academic freedom, original doctoral work, the thesis defense, and the achievement of orthodoxy through scholarly consensus is the direct precursor of the western University. See also Makdisi (1990) for the relationship between Muslim scholarship and western humanism.
21 Quoted in Eickelman (1992: 117).
22 Eickelman (1992: 105). His account is of early twentieth-century Morocco, where memorization was especially stressed. But the absolute authority granted the teacher is typical. See Makdisi (1981), Fischer (1980) for other examples.
23 M. al-Akwa quoted in Messick (1993: 75).
24 See Messick (1993: 81, 83). See also Lane (1871) for a description of the ritual roles fulfilled by Quranic schoolboys in Egypt.
25 Sufyan al-Thawri (d. 778), quoted in Goldziher (1981: 56).
26 In Bukhara one family of ulema actually dominated the city from the eleventh to thirteenth century, while in Samarqand "the demon of sovereign rule laid an egg" in the head of another scholar, who led a momentarily successful rebellion in 1098. See Bulliet (1994: 143).
27 Makdisi (1985: 87).
28 Quoted in Messick (1993: 143).
29 Quoted in Bulliet (1994: 58).
30 Cited in Makdisi (1983).
31 Gaffney (1987) estimates that there are 40,000 such associations. The government controls and regulates 6,000 of the best established.
32 See Gaffney (1987), Antoun (1989), Mullaney (1992).
33 See Roy (1994) for this terminology. As he has documented, self-taught Islamist scholars are presently being replaced by a new ulema trained in neofundamentalist schools that are ostensibly separate from the state, and are funded by groups such as the Muslim Brotherhood or the Wahhabis. Many Middle Eastern governments have welcomed this new form of religious scholarship, which is both politically conservative and socially puritanical. See chapter 13 for more on modern Islamist movements.
34 See Peters (1987) for an example in the eighteenth century of a "fundamentalist" uprising.

Chapter 11: The Partisans of Ali

1 Shi'ah means the partisans or party, with the assumption that they are the party of Ali. In this chapter, I follow general usage to refer to the adherents of this party as Shi'ites rather than Shi'i, which would be more correct. See chapters 6 and 7 for more on Shi'ite political movements.
2 See Haeri (1989) for the definitive work on this topic.
3 Quoted in Corbin (1971–2, vol. I:96).
4 Massignon (1982, vol. III: 35). See Crone and Hinds (1986) for a contrary argument, in which the Caliphate is likened to the Imamate. However, I believe there is a distinction to be made between obeying God's deputy and worshipping God's divine incarnation.

5 Naturally these claims are not accepted by Sunni Muslims, who deny the authenticity of the traditions, or say that Muhammad simply was defending his nephew in a local dispute.

6 See Massignon (1982, vol.I: 299–303); Amir-Moezzi (1994, 1983).

7 Other Shi'ite heroes have set similar examples. For instance, Abu Zarr al-Ghifari, an early companion of the Prophet, eschewed luxury, called for redistribution of all spoils, and was exiled for his beliefs.

8 For a good example of the way this mechanism can work, see Bainbridge and Stark (1980).

9 For much more, see the translations in Corbin (1977) and his four volume work (Corbin 1971–2).

10 In Shi'ite belief, all of their Imams have been treacherously murdered, usually by poison, by their Sunni enemies.

11 Sunni Muslims also have a notion of the mahdi which can be called upon to legitimate religious uprisings, but it is far less developed than among the Shi'ites. See Madelung (1986) for more.

12 See the collection edited by Chelkowski (1979) for more on this unique holiday.

13 See Mary Hegland (1983) for a portrayal of the tensions between these two ways of understanding Muharram in modern Iran. See also Richard (1995), Chelkowski (1979).

14 Watt (1973).

15 Cited in Goitein (1966: 195).

16 For more on the Yemen and the Imamate see Dresch (1989), Caton (1990), Crone and Cook (1977).

17 The Nizari experiment was not unique. Other excluded Shi'ite groups have also maintained oppositional pockets of charismatic esotericism within the Muslim mainstream, centered around an embodied mahdi and hierarchical control over hidden knowledge (batin). Some of these, such as the Druze and Yazidi, have been actively persecuted. Others, such as the Alawi of Syria and Lebanon, have managed to gain considerable political power.

18 The technical distinction between hadith and akhbar is that hadith give Prophetic authority to some doctrine, while akhbar give information about a particular incident of the past, and only incidentally serve as moral guides. See Humphreys (1991: 83).

19 Usuli believe that a person must reach truth either by mystical insight or by proficiency in legal texts. Mullah Muhsin al-Fayd al-Kahani (d. 1680) probably followed the mystical route. See Kohlberg (1987).

20 In permitting interpretation the Shi'ites came close to readopting the Mutazilite position that reason could be used to understand God's demands. But for the Shi'ites, reason had to be combined with spiritual authority.

21 Richard (1995: 91).

22 Munson (1988: 28).

23 Arjomand (1984).

24 See Keddie (1972).

25 The most famous are the tobacco boycott of 1890, in which a British monoply was successfully challenged by a fatwa, and the constitutional revolt of 1906–9, where some ulema played a major role in mobilizing resistance, though most of them were terrified at the thought of a popular uprising.

26 See Kohlberg (1988).

27 See Fischer (1980), Beeman (1983) for more on the symbolism of the revolution.

28 Arjomand (1988).

29 Kohlberg (1987: 123).

30 Ayatollah Khomeini quoted in Richard (1995: 86).

Chapter 12: Sufism in Practice

1 Massignon (1954).
2 Massignon (1982 vol. I: 383).
3 See Smith (1984). Women have been accepted in Sufi circles more readily than else-where in the public world of Islam, but only if they are celibate. In contrast, men are usually expected to combine the mystical quest with a home and family life.
4 Rabiya was not the only mystic to rely on the imagery of love. As Schimmel (1975) points out, the sixth Imam, Jafar, had earlier made use of the same concept.
5 Rumi (1975: 90–1).
6 Quoted in Nicholson (1921: 16).
7 Abu Said perhaps founded the first tariqa, but it is likely that institutionalized brother-hoods really began in the far East, in Khurasan, as a response to the highly unstable social conditions there.
8 Massignon (1982, vol. III: 25).
9 See Watt (1953). The same metaphor of "cadaver obedience" was used by the Jesuits and later by the Nazi SS. For a discussion of the uses and abuses of techniques of identity transformation, see Lindholm (1990).
10 Quoted in Gilsenan (1973: 75), Ajmal (1984: 241).
11 Al-Hujwiri cited in Lapidus (1988: 197).
12 Lapidus (1984: 57).
13 Rumi (1975: 90).
14 For this reason, Schimmel (1975) defines wajd as "instancy" rather than ecstasy.
15 Al-Jili (d. 1406) quoted in Nicholson (1921: 129). Compare the statements made by shamans recorded in Grim (1983) and I. M. Lewis (1971).
16 Quoted in Schimmel (1975: 129).
17 The term is Gilsenan's (1973), and the following discussion owes much to his analysis.
18 Muhammad reportedly taught silent dhikr to Abu Bakr, while Ali was taught to recite dhikr aloud.
19 Quoted in Nicholson (1921: 5).
20 Quran 33: 21.
21 As reported in Massignon (1982 vol. II: 29). This is a particularly powerful dhikr, to be used only in private by those who have been well instructed. Let the novice be warned.
22 Of course, Sufis perform prayers exactly as do all other Muslims.
23 For discussion and comparison of the dhikr of some Sufi sects, see Gilsenan (1973), Massignon (1954), and Lane (1871). For the notion of "religions of the weak" see Turner (1982), Lewis (1971).
24 See Trimingham (1971).
25 Thus the "doctor" and "saint" distinction made so forcefully by Gellner (1981).
26 This contrast, however, must not be taken too far. Some Sufi tariqas have also dis-credited themselves through service to an irreligious state.
27 They argue Muhammad was indeed the seal of the Prophets, but was not the last pole. His job was to prophecy *and* to be the divine grace that holds the world together. The Qutbs to follow only have the latter responsibility.
28 Macdonald (1909: 163).
29 Hodgson (1974, vol. II: 228).
30 This is in radical contrast to the twelver Shi'ite ideal of uniting charisma and learning in the Guide.
31 See Makdisi (1974).
32 Hodgson (1974, vol. II: 230).

Chapter 13: The Contradictions of Saintly Authority

1 Rumi (1975: 6).
2 From the *Diwan-e-Shams* quoted in Arasteh (1965: 64).
3 Rumi (1975: 32–3).
4 Rumi (1972: 81, 141).
5 Hallaj quoted in Massignon (1982 vol. III: 41).
6 Hallaj quoted in Massignon (1982 vol. III: 47).
7 Quoted in Massignon (1982 vol. I: 600).
8 Quoted in Massignon (1982 vol. I: 289).
9 See Massignon (1952).
10 Quoted in Nicholson (1921: 56).
11 Significantly, in the Middle East it is only in Turkey that Sufism remains truly central. This is partially attributable, I would argue, to the deep connection between the ulema and the Ottoman state, which led to a delegitimization of orthodox learning and a correlating popular interest in Sufism – an interest heightened by Ataturk's efforts to crush all forms of religion not controlled by the state apparatus and by Turkish acceptance of hierarchy. It is also significant that Sufism remains powerful in the far more hierarchical societies of South Asia and Southeast Asia. See Werbner (1995) for more on this.
12 The connection with the Mutazalites is clear, and was evoked by reformers.
13 See Gellner (1983) for this argument.
14 Gellner (1981: 99–113).
15 Voll (1987).
16 Rahman (1982).
17 For instance, in Turkey Naqshbandi Sufis led a rebellion to free Kurdistan in 1925, while more recently in Afghanistan the same order allied itself with Islamist resistance parties. Sufi led uprisings continued in Pakistan's NWFP even after the departure of the British. I have already mentioned a few of the many revolts that occurred in North Africa under Sufi leadership.
18 Al-Badr al-Hijazi quoted in Arberry (1950: 128).
19 Quoted in Schimmel (1975: 247). Tijani, in typical fashion, goes him one better by saying "my feet are upon the neck of every one of Almighty God's walis from the time of Adam until the horn (of the Hereafter) is blown" See Abun Nasr (1965: 39).
20 See Gilsenan (1973).
21 Quoted in Nicholson (1921: 264).
22 Nicholson (1921: 173).
23 Rumi (1972: 56).
24 Rumi (1972: 166).
25 Rumi (1972: 85–6).
26 See Munson (1993).
27 Gilsenan (1973) notes that the more educated, respectable and wealthy members of brotherhoods see karamat as connected to learning and character, while lower status members will look for more magical proofs, and cite dreams and voices as evidence of their master's powers.
28 See Hammoudi (1980), Miller and Bowen (1993). For a similar case among the Sanusi of Libya, see Evans-Pritchard (1949).
29 A story heard from Morocco to Northern Pakistan illustrates the point. A holy man venturing into the tribal area meets a group of locals, who ask him his occupation. He responds that he has come to bring them the benefits of his spiritual knowledge. In response, they kill him in order to acquire the baraka of his tomb. See Serjeant (1981b) for a version.

30 Westermark (1926: 389, 228, 238).
31 Hodgson (1974 vol. II: 227); Serjeant (1981b).
32 Cited in Hodgson (1974 vol. II: 245).
33 Nicholson (1921).
34 See Geertz (1968) for such a reading and Munson (1993) for a response.
35 Quoted in Westermark (1926: 228).
36 See Roy (1994) for this terminology.
37 See Youssef (1985) for this example and others.
38 See Mitchell (1969) for the Muslim Brotherhood, Roy (1994), Abun-Nasr (1985), Youssef (1985), Choueiri (1990) for other examples.
39 It is for this reason that the leader is generally designated the emir, or the murshid, not the Caliph, since the Caliphate is associated with the lineage of the Quraysh.
40 Roy (1994: 62, 43).
41 Roy (1994: 69). Islamist technical terms are often taken directly from the vocabulary of Ismaili and Fatimid missionaries. See Roy (1994: 101).
42 See chapter 8. Political assassination is hardly a Muslim phenomenon, and can occur wherever a powerless group resist a coercive authority. But assassination in the Middle East has always reflected the egalitarian and anti-authoritarian ideology of larger society. Assassination of innocents, however, is a wholly modern phenomenon.
43 Roy (1994: 195). For a more positive view of Sufism today, see Paulo Pinto's excellent doctoral thesis *Mystical Bodies: Ritual, Experience and the Embodiment of Sufism in Syria* (Department of Anthropology, Boston University 2002).

Chapter 14: Slaves, Eunuchs and Blacks

1 Only in China was comparable use made of castrated slaves, though not in such numbers.
2 Gellner (1990: 115).
3 Nizam al-Mulk (1966: 121).
4 Crone (1980: 87).
5 This is an ideal. In fact, as ex-slave and client groups became new power blocs they acted to protect their own interests by attempting to bequeath their estates and rank to their sons. This became commonplace among the Ottomans and Mamluks, and has often been cited as a cause for the eventual decay of these regimes.
6 Rosenthal (1960: 120).
7 Gellner (1981: 28).
8 Dumont (1970).
9 Lewis (1990).
10 Nusayb quoted in Lewis (1990: 29); Antara quoted in Lewis (1990: 24); Suhaym quoted in Rosenthal (1960: 91).
11 Ibn Khaldun (1967: 117).
12 Quoted in Lewis (1990: 59–60).
13 For instance, the erotic primer *The Perfumed Garden* (Nafzawi 1964) has as one of its main themes the humiliating passion of upper class women for a phallic black slave.
14 See Lewis (1990: 87: 33).
15 The closest thing to such a law is the legal doctrine of *kafaa*, which required husband and wife to be equals. This could be interpreted as social or moral equality, but could also be invoked to prohibit marriages that were racially mixed.
16 Quran (30: 22).
17 Massignon (1982 vol. I: 267).
18 See Lindholm (1986, 1995b) for more.
19 See Massignon (1982, vol. I: 266–8).

20 See Fernea (1970) on El Shabana, Bujra (1971) on South Yemen, Lindholm (1982, 1995b) on the Pukhtun, Pehrson (1966) on the Marri Baluch, Marx (1967) and Cole (1975) on the Bedouin.

21 Gellner (1981: 30).

22 Quoted in Wellhausen (1927: 247).

23 Cole (1984: 184).

24 Suhaym quoted in Rosenthal (1960: 91).

25 Cited in Rosenthal (1960: 105). Compare Rousseau's vision of human degradation due to envy and vanity.

26 Lassner (1980: 94).

27 Lewis (1990: 6).

28 Quoted in Rosenthal (1960: 111–12).

29 Fischer (1989: 754).

30 Gilsenan (1973).

31 Egyptian mamluks, for example, took on the nisba of their present owner, as well as names of previous owners. The most important nisba for freed slaves was that of their manumittor (see Ayalon 1975).

32 See Musil (1928: 277) for an Arab example; also Goitein (1966: 192). The shah khel among the Pukhtun served the same function, as noted above.

Chapter 15: The Ambiguities of Women

1 Harem derives from the root h-r-m, which also is the root of haram (sacred, forbidden) and of *hurma* (honor).

2 There are any number of variations on the veil, ranging from the all enveloping black *burqah* of Afghanistan, which leaves women only a grid to peer through, to the diaphanous Ottoman *yashmaq*, which elegantly covers the hair and lower part of the face.

3 See Hammoudi (1993) for examples.

4 Fitna, the term for chaos and anarchy, has at its root precisely the fear of female promiscuity.

5 Cited in Mernissi (1991: 56–7).

6 Quran 4.34.

7 Ibn Arabi cites two women as his major spiritual mentors and uses the union of male and female as the metaphor of the completion of the quest for divinity. See Murata (1992).

8 The Bekhtashi dervishes treat women as equal members of the brotherhood and radical kharijite groups of early Islam permitted a great degree of female power, including, in one instance, the leadership of women (Dabashi 1993: 131). The Qarmati also opposed polygamy, concubinage, the marriage of young girls, and the veil (Ahmed 1992).

9 See Antoun (1989) for this analysis.

10 Makhlouf (1979), Beck (1978: 357); see also Wikan (1991) for Oman. Of course, women's solidarity and friendship does not preclude competition. They are as concerned as their men with their own honor and pride, and contend for status among themselves through elaborate displays of hospitality and demonstrations of wealth. However, women's exclusion from the serious public business of political struggle does permit them a cordiality and openness that is absent among men meeting as rivals in continuous struggle. Also, whatever their personal differences, women can always find comfort and solidarity in their shared complaints against men, whereas men prefer to pretend that women do not exist.

11 Coulson (1964: 14).

12 In Iran a woman's virginity is explicitly referred to as "her capital". See Haeri (1989: 67).

13 For some of the ways in which women's absolute rights over their mahar gives them a capacity to negotiate for their own benefit see Mir-Hosseini (1993).

14 Hodgson (1974, vol. I: 341).
15 Similarly, Middle Eastern Muslim men typically do not wish their daughters to be subjected to the humiliation of a co-wife, but may want to take a second wife themselves.
16 Among the Pukhtun the only polygamous man cited as living up to the Quranic requirement was an individual who did indeed treat his wives equally – he avoided them both like the plague.
17 Quran 33:35
18 Quran 2:229, see also 4.1, which remarks that women are persons created with a "single soul" like men.
19 Quoted in Mernissi (1991: 70).
20 Ibn Sad quoted in Mernissi (1991: 157).
21 Quran 33:59.
22 Again, see Mernissi (1991) for a clear statement of this argument.
23 Aisha's participation on the losing side in the Battle of the Camel played a major part in discrediting further female political activism. See Spellberg (1991).
24 Stowasser (1993: 15). For a good account of this new rhetoric, see Metcalf (1987).
25 El-Amin (1981: 92).
26 For example, see Sayyid Qutb quoted in Choueiri (1990: 128).
27 For women's work see Papps (1993), al-Khayyat (1990) and Friedel (1991a, 1991b). For the neofundamentalist perspective see Roy (1994).
28 For alternative views on this see Stowasser (1984), Abbott (1942), Ahmed (1986).
29 Abbott (1946: 67).
30 In this regard, see especially the work of Deniz Kandiyoti (1991, 1992) and Germaine Tillon (1966).
31 See Lerner (1986).
32 Ahmed (1992).
33 Ahmed (1992).
34 Among royalty the concern for blood purity led to incestuous marriages between brothers and sisters. Yet even here adoption sometimes occurred, as is attested in the story of Moses.
35 Cross-culturally, patrilineal-patrilocal organization seems to be favored in antagonistic environments where male solidarity is requisite for survival. In the Middle East, the Tuareg are the sole exception.
36 Hammoudi (1993: 155, 8).
37 See Conte, Hames, and Cheikh (1991) for recent essays on this contradiction.
38 Hammoudi (1993: 47).
39 Vieille (1978: 469).
40 Abu-Lughod (1986).
41 Bouhdiba (1977: 128).
42 According to al-Khayyat the rise of the nuclear household in urban society has meant that "the traditional conflict between a wife and her in-laws is replaced by a conflict between the husband and his in-laws" as men seek to isolate their wives completely in order to better dominate them (1990: 122).
43 Dorsky (1986: 87).
44 Lindholm (1982: 56).
45 Vieille (1978: 463).
46 Quoted in Sabbah (1984: 27).
47 Vieille (1978).
48 Quoted in Rosen (1978: 568).
49 Hammoudi (1993: 155).
50 The orthodox assume that these prohibitions are given in Islam, but modern feminists

claim that Muhammad opposed these ancient pollution beliefs, which they say derive from patriarchal Judaism.
51 See Lindholm (1981c, 1982).
52 Mernissi (1975: 14).
53 Mernissi (1975: viii).
54 Vieille (1978: 471).
55 Quoted in al-Khayyat (1990: 79).
56 El Saadawi (1980: 100).

Chapter 16: Escapes from Distinction: Love and Friendship

1 Sabbah (1984: 35).
2 Quoted in Rosenthal (1987: 12, 14).
3 Hallaj, quoted in Massignon (1982: Vol. II: 87).
4 Abu Said quoted in Nicholson (1921: 5).
5 Ibn al-Farid quoted in Nicholson (1921: 205–6).
6 Massignon (1982: Vol. I: 348).
7 Cases cited in Rosenthal (1946).
8 For an account of the pros and cons of this controversy see Boase (1977), Bell (1979).
9 See Stone (1988), Shorter (1977) for examples of the first position, MacFarlane (1986) for an example of the second.
10 Quoted in Bell (1979: 33–4, 134).
11 Massignon (1982: Vol. I: 348, 349).
12 Pehrson (1966: 65).
13 Pehrson (1966: 62).
14 A Marri woman, quoted in Pehrson (1966: 59).
15 Quoted in Bell (1979: 21).
16 See Wikan (1991) for a case of the latter. There is little literature on female homosexuality in the Middle East, though it is reputed to have been common in the great seraglios of the Turkish pashas, where male company was scarce.
17 Quoted in Rosenthal (1960: 9).
18 Hammoudi (1993: 166).
19 Bateson (1977: 270) on Persia; Melikian (1977: 182) on Saudi Arabia; Rahman Baba, quoted in Lindholm (1982: 240) on the Pukhtun.
20 For more on friendship among the Pukhtun, see Lindholm (1982).
21 Rosenthal (1977: 39).
22 Quoted in Massignon (1982 vol. III: 41).
23 Quoted in Rosenthal (1977: 43).

Chapter 17: Problems and Possibilities

1 Hodgson (1974, vol. I: 283).
2 Walid Khalidi quoted in Makiya (1993: 282). For more on the problems and possibilities of civil society in the Middle East, see Norton (1995); Goldberg, Kasaba and Migdal (1993).
3 Quoted in Rosenthal (1990: 10).
4 Tocqueville (1969: 566).
5 Quoted in Waterbury (1972: 232). However, a Swasa who fails in business is rescued by his lineage, who will not allow the destruction of any of their number, though such a man is permanently disgraced among his peers.
6 Barth (1985: 175, 178). Barth is speaking specifically of Swat, but his statements are accurate in general. Goitein makes the same argument about the Medieval Islamic

society: "actual possession of power is the necessary and sufficient argument for the exercise of authority, irrespective of the ruler's personal qualifications" (Goitein 1966: 204).

7 Quoted in Massignon (1982, vol. I: 268–9).
8 Munson (1993: 144).
9 Geertz (1979: 141, 239).
10 Burkhardt (1829: 149).
11 Quoted in Lambton (1954: 53).
12 Quoted in Gibb (1955: 19).
13 Quoted in Seligman (1964: 19).
14 Quoted in Von Grunebaum (1956: 169).
15 Quoted in Dwyer (1991: 120).
16 Antoun (1989: 202). Antoun is writing about the TransJordan, but the views are characteristic.
17 Quoted in Seligman (1964: 17).
18 Gibb and Bowen (1963, vol. I: 205).
19 Fernea (1970: 142).
20 Cited by Ibn Taimiyya, quoted in Rosenthal (1973: 6).
21 Quoted in Massignon (1982, vol. I: 268–9).
22 Quoted in Dwyer (1991: 121).
23 Tocqueville (1969).
24 Barth (1961: 81).
25 Vatter (1993). See also Singerman (1995) for a contemporary example.
26 Barth (1985: 169).
27 Tocqueville (1969).
28 Crone (1980: 63).
29 The seventeenth-century reformer al-Hasan al-Yusi, quoted in Munson (1993: 29).
30 Quoted in Munson (1993: 143); Goitein (1966: 156); Serjeant (1977: 238).
31 Quoted in Lewis (1988: 144).
32 Quoted in Lewis (1973: 255).
33 Quoted in Lambton (1980: 425).
34 Quoted in Goitein (1966: 206).
35 Imam Khomeini quoted in Algar (1988: 275, 276).
36 Eickelman (1976: 143).

References

Abbott, Nabia 1946. *Two Queens of Baghdad: Mother and Wife of Harun al-Rashid*. Chicago: University of Chicago Press.
—— 1942. Women and the State in Early Islam. *Journal of Near Eastern Studies* 1: 106–26.
Abu-Lughod, Lila 1993. *Writing Women's World: Bedouin Stories*. Berkeley: University of California Press.
—— 1986. *Veiled Sentiments: Honor and Poetry in a Bedouin Society*. Berkeley: University of California Press.
Abun-Nasr, Jamil 1965. *The Tijaniyya: A Sufi Order in the Modern World*. London: Oxford University Press.
Adams, Robert McC. 1966. *The Evolution of Urban Society*. Chicago: University of Chicago Press.
Ahmed, Leila 1992. *Women and Gender in Islam: Historical Roots of a Modern Debate*. New Haven: Yale University Press.
—— 1986. Women and the Advent of Islam. *Signs* 11: 665–91.
Ajmal, Mohammad 1984. A Note on Adab in the Murshid-Murid Relationship. In: Barbara Daly Metcalf (ed.), *Moral Conduct and Authority: The Place of Adab in South Asian Islam*. Berkeley: University of California Press.
Algar, Hamid 1988. Imam Khomeini, 1902–1962: the Pre-Revolutionary Years. In: Edmund Burke III and Ira Lapidus (eds), *Islam, Politics and Social Movements*. Berkeley: University of California Press.
al-Ghazali, Mohammad 1963. *The Foundation of the Articles of Faith*. Translated by Nahih Amin Faris. Lahore: Ashraf Press.
—— n.d. *The Confessions of Al-Ghazzali*. Translated by Claude Field. Lahore: Ashraf Press.
al-Khayyat, Sana 1990. *Honour and Shame: Women in Modern Iraq*. London: Saqi Books.
al-Mulk, Nizam 1966. *The Book of Government or Rules for Kings*. New Haven: Yale University Press.
Amir-Moezzi, M. A. 1994. *The Divine Guide in Original Shiism*. Albany: State University of New York Press.
—— 1983. Le Shi'isme doctrinal et le fait politique. In M. Kotobi (ed.), *Le Grand Satan et La Tulipe*. Paris: Institut supérieur de gestion.
Andrae, Tor 1936. *Mohammed: the Man and his Faith*. London: Allen and Unwin Ltd.
Antoun, Richard T. 1989. *Muslim Preacher in the Modern World: A Jordanian Case Study in Comparative Perspective*. Princeton: Princeton University Press.
—— 1968. On the Significance of Names in an Arab Village. *Ethnology* 7: 158–70.
—— 1967. Social Organization and the Life Cycle in an Arab Village. *Ethnology* 6: 294–308.
Arasteh, A. Reza 1965. *Rumi the Persian*. Lahore: Ashraf Press.
Arberry A. J. 1950. *Sufism: The Religious Attitude and Life in Islam*. Chicago: University of Chicago Press.

REFERENCES

Arjomand, Said Amir 1988. *The Turban and the Crown: The Islamic Revolution in Iran.* New York: Oxford University Press.

—— 1984. *The Shadow of God and the Hidden Imam.* Chicago: University of Chicago Press.

Arkoun, Mohammed 1994. *Rethinking Islam: Common Questions, Uncommon Answers.* Boulder: Westview.

Ayalon, David 1976. Aspects of the Mamluk Phenomenon: the Importance of the Mamluk Institution. *Der Islam* 53: 196–225.

—— 1975. Preliminary Remarks on the Mamluk Military Institution. In: V. Parry and M. Yapp (eds), *War, Technology and Society in the Middle East.* London: Oxford University Press.

Bacon, Elizabeth 1958. *Obok.* New York: Wenner-Gren.

Bainbridge, William and Stark, Rodney 1980. Scientology: To Be Perfectly Clear. *Sociological Analysis* 4: 128–36.

Barfield, T. 1993. *The Nomadic Alternative.* Englewood Cliffs, N. J.: Prentice-Hall.

Baring, Evelyn (Lord Cromer) 1908. *Modern Egypt.* 2 vols. New York: Macmillan.

Barth, Fredrick 1985. *The Last Wali of Swat.* New York: Columbia University Press.

—— 1965. *Political Leadership Among Swat Pathans.* London: Athalone.

—— 1961. *Nomads of South Persia.* Boston: Little, Brown.

—— 1959a. The Land Use Pattern of Migratory Tribes of South Persia. *Norsk Geografisk Tidsskrift* 17: 1–11.

—— 1959b. Segmentary Opposition and the Theory of Games: a Study of Pathan Organization. *Journal of the Royal Anthropological Institute* 89: 5–21.

Bartold, Vasilii 1968. *Turkestan Down to the Mongol Invasions.* London: Luzac.

Bateson, Mary, et al. 1977. Safa-yi Batin: A Study of the Interrelation of a Set of Iranian Ideal Character Types. In: L. Carl Brown and Norman Itzkowitz (eds), *Psychological Dimensions of Near Eastern Studies.* Princeton: Darwin Press.

Beck, Lois 1990. Tribes and the State in Nineteen and Twentieth-Century Iran. In: Philip Khoury and Joseph Kostiner (eds), *Tribes and State Formation in the Middle East.* Berkeley: University of California Press.

—— 1986. *The Qashqa 'i of Iran.* New Haven: Yale University Press.

—— 1978. Women among Qashqa 'i Nomadic Pastoralists in Iran. In: Lois Beck and Nikki Keddie (eds), *Women in the Muslim World.* Cambridge: Harvard University Press.

Beeman, William 1983. Images of the Great Satan: Representations of the United States in the Iranian Revolution. In: Nikki Keddie (ed.), *Religion and Politics in Iran.* New Haven: Yale University Press.

Bell, Joseph Norment 1979. *Love Theory in Later Hanbalite Islam.* Albany: State University of New York Press.

Berque, Jacques. 1978. *Cultural Expression in Arab Society Today.* Austin: University of Texas Press.

—— 1955. *Structures Sociales de Haut Atlas.* Paris: Universitaires de France.

Black, Jacob 1972. Tyranny as a Strategy for Survival in an "Egalitarian" Society: Luri Facts Versus an Anthropological Mystique. *Man* 7: 614–34.

Black-Michaud, Jacob 1975. *Cohesive Force.* New York: St. Martin's Press.

Boase, Roger 1977. *The Origin and Meaning of Courtly Love.* Manchester: Manchester University Press.

Bouhdiba, A. 1977. The Child and the Mother in Arab-Muslim Society. In: L. Carl Brown (ed.), *Psychological Dimensions of Near Eastern Studies.* Princeton: Darwin Press.

Bowersock, G. 1983. *Roman Arabia.* Cambridge: Harvard University Press.

Bujra, A. 1971. *The Politics of Stratification.* Oxford: Oxford University Press.

Bulliet, Richard 1994. *Islam: the View from the Edge.* New York: Columbia University Press.

—— 1976. Medieval Nishapur: a Topographic and Demographic Reconstruction. *Studia Iranica* 5: 67–89.

—— 1975. *The Camel and the Wheel.* Cambridge: Harvard University Press.

—— 1972. *The Patricians of Nishapur: a Study in Medieval Islamic Social History.* Cambridge: Harvard University Press.

Burkhardt, John 1829. *Travels in Arabia.* London: Henry Colburn.

Burnham, Philip 1979. Spatial Mobility and Political Centralization in Pastoral Societies. In: L'équipe écologie et anthropologie des sociétés pastorales (eds), *Pastoral Production and Society.* New York: Cambridge University Press.

Caton, Steven 1990. *Peaks of Yemen I Summon: Poetry as Cultural Practice in a North Yemeni Tribe.* Berkeley: University of California Press.

Chang, K. C. 1983. *Art, Myth, and Ritual: The Path to Political Authority in Ancient China.* Cambridge: Harvard University Press.

Chardin, Sir John 1927. *Travels in Persia.* London: The Argonaut Press.

Chelkowski, Peter (ed.) 1979. *Ta'ziyeh: Ritual and Drama in Iran.* New York: New York University Press.

Choueiri, Youssef M. 1990. *Islamic Fundamentalism.* Boston: Twayne Publishers.

Cole, Donald 1984. Alliance and Descent in the Middle East and the "Problem" of Patrilateral Parallel Cousin Marriage. In: Akbar Ahmed and David Hart (eds), *Islam in Tribal Societies: From the Atlas to the Indus.* London: Routledge and Kegan Paul.

—— 1975. *Nomads of the Nomads.* Arlington Heights: American Museum of Natural History.

Combs-Schilling, M. E. 1989. *Sacred Performances: Islam, Sexuality and Sacrifice.* New York: Columbia University Press.

Conte, Edouard, Constant Hames and Abdel Wedoud Ould Cheikh (eds) 1991. *Al-Ansab: Anthropologie historique de la société tribale arabe.* Paris: Éditions de la Maison des Sciences de l'Homme.

Coon, Carlton 1951. *Caravan: The Story of the Middle East.* New York: Holt.

Corbin, Henry 1977. *Spiritual Body and Celestial Earth: From Mazdean Iran to Shi'ite Iran.* Princeton: Princeton University Press.

—— 1971–2. *En Islam iranien, aspects spirituels et philosophiques,* 4 vols. Paris: Gallimard.

Cornelius, A. R. 1979. The Concept of the State in Islam. *Hamard Islamicus* 1: 39–55.

Coulson, Noel 1964. *A History of Islamic Law.* Edinburgh: Edinburgh University Press.

Crone, Patricia 1989. On the Meaning of the Abbasid Call to al-Rida. In: C. E. Bosworth, et al. (eds), *The Islamic World from Classical to Modern Times: Essays in Honour of Bernard Lewis.* Princeton: Darwin Press.

—— 1987. *Meccan Trade and the Rise of Islam.* Princeton: Princeton University Press.

—— 1986. The Tribe and the State. In: John A. Hall (ed.), *States in History.* Oxford: Basil Blackwell.

—— 1980. *Slaves on Horses.* Cambridge: Cambridge University Press.

Crone, Patricia and Cook, Michael 1977. *Hagarism: The Making of the Islamic World.* Cambridge: Cambridge University Press.

Crone, Patricia and Hinds, Martin 1986. *God's Caliph: Religious Authority in the First Centuries of Islam.* London: Cambridge University Press.

Cuisenier, Jean 1975. *Économie et Parente: leurs affinités de structure dans le domaine turc et dans le domaine arabe.* Paris: Mouton.

Dabashi, Hamid 1993. *Authority in Islam: From the Rise of Muhammad to the Establishment of the Umayyads.* New Brunswick: Transaction Publishers.

Daftary, Farhad 1990. *The Isma'ilis: Their History and Doctrines.* Cambridge: Cambridge University Press.

Daniel, Norman 1960. *Islam and the West: The Making of an Image.* Edinburgh: University of Edinburgh Press.

Davis, John 1977. *People of the Mediterranean.* London: Routledge and Kegan Paul.

Diakonoff, I. M. 1969. *Ancient Mesopotamia: Socio-Economic History*. Moscow: "Nauka" Publishing, Central Dept. of Oriental Literature.

Dorsky, Susan 1986. *Women of "Amran: A Middle Eastern Ethnographic Study*. Salt Lake City: University of Utah Press.

Dresch, Paul 1990. Imams and Tribes: The Writing and Acting of History in Upper Yemen. In: Philip Khoury and Joseph Kostiner (eds), *Tribes and State Formation in the Middle East*. Berkeley: University of California Press.

——1989. *Tribes, Government and History in Yemen*. Oxford: Oxford University Press.

——1986. The Significance of the Course Events Take in Segmentary Systems. *American Ethnologist* 13: 309–24.

Dumont, Louis 1970. *Homo Hierarchicus: an Essay on the Caste System*. Chicago: University of Chicago Press.

Dwyer, Kevin 1991. *Arab Voices: The Human Rights Debate in the Middle East*. Berkeley: University of California Press.

Eickelman, Dale 1992. The Art of Memory: Islamic Knowledge and its Social Reproduction. In: Juan Cole, (ed.), *Comparing Muslim Societies: Knowledge and the State in a World Civilization*. Ann Arbor: University of Michigan Press.

——1985. *Knowledge and Power in Morocco: The Education of a Twentieth Century Notable*. Princeton: Princeton University Press.

——1981. *The Middle East: An Anthropological Approach*. Englewood Cliffs: Prentice-Hall.

——1976. *Moroccan Islam: Tradition and Society in a Pilgrimage Center*. Austin: University of Texas Press.

El Amin, Nafissa Ahmed 1981. Sudan: Education and Family. In: Philip Stoddard, David Cuthell, Margaret Sullivan (eds), *Change and the Muslim World*. Syracuse: Syracuse University Press.

El Saadawi, Nawal 1980. *The Hidden Face of Eve: Women in the Arab World*. London: Zed Press.

Evans-Pritchard, E. E. 1949. *The Sanusi of Cyrenaica*. Oxford: Oxford University Press.

Fernea, Robert 1970. *Shaiykh and Effendi*. Cambridge: Harvard University Press.

Firdawsi 1968. *Shahnameh*. Chicago: University of Chicago Press.

Fischer, David 1989. *Albion's Seed: Four British Folkways in America*. New York: Oxford University Press.

Fischer, Michael 1980. *Iran: From Religious Dispute to Revolution*. Cambridge: Harvard University Press.

Frankfort, Henri 1948. *Kingship and the Gods: A Study of Near Eastern Religion as the Integration of Society and Nature*. Chicago: University of Chicago Press.

Fried, Morton 1960. On the Evolution of Social Stratification and the State. In: S. Diamond (ed.), *Culture in History: Essays in Honor of Paul Radin*. New York: Columbia University Press.

Friedel, Erika 1991a. *Women of Deh Koh: Lives in an Iranian Village*. Harmondsworth: Penguin Books.

——1991b. The Dynamics of Women's Spheres of Action in Rural Iran. In: Nikki Keddie and Beth Baron (eds) *Women in Middle Eastern History: Shifting Boundaries in Sex and Gender*. New Haven: Yale University Press.

Gaffney, Patrick 1987. Authority and the Mosque in Upper Egypt: the Islamic Preacher as Image and Actor. In: William Roff (ed.), *Islam and the Political Economy of Meaning: Comparative Studies of Muslim Discourse*. London: Croom Helm.

Geertz, Clifford 1980. *Negara: The Theatre State in Nineteenth Century Bali*. Princeton: Princeton University Press.

——1979. Suq: The Bazaar Economy in Sefrou. In: Clifford Geertz, Hildred Geertz and Lawrence Rosen (eds), *Meaning and Order in Moroccan Society*. Cambridge, Cambridge University Press.

——1968. *Islam Observed: Religious Development in Morocco and Indonesia*. New Haven: Yale University Press.

Gellner, Ernest 1990. Tribalism and the State in the Middle East. In: Philip S. Khoury and Joseph Kostiner (eds), *Tribes and State Formation in the Middle East*. Berkeley: University of California Press.

——1983. *Nations and Nationalism*. Ithaca: Cornell University Press.

——1981. *Muslim Society*. Cambridge: Cambridge University Press.

——1969. *Saints of the Atlas*. London: Weidenfeld and Nicolson.

Gellner, Ernest and Munson, Henry 1995. Segmentation: Reality or Myth? *Journal of the Royal Anthropological Institute* (N.S.) 1: 820–32.

Gibb, H. A. R. 1962. *Studies on the Civilization of Islam*. Princeton: Princeton University Press.

——1955. Constitutional organization. In: M. Khadduri and H. Liebesny (eds), *Law in the Middle East*. Washington DC.: Georgetown University Press.

Gibb, H. A. R. and Bowen, Harold. 1963. *Islamic Society and the West*, vol. I, part I. London: Oxford University Press.

Gibb, H. A. R. and Kramers, J. (eds) 1965. *Shorter Encyclopedia of Islam*. Leiden: E. J. Brill.

Gilsenan, Michael. 1993. Lying, Honor and Contradiction. In: Donna Lee Bowen & Evelyn Early (eds), *Everyday Life in the Muslim Middle East*. Bloomington: Indiana University Press.

——1983. *Recognizing Islam*. New York: Random House.

——1973. *Saint and Sufi in Modern Egypt: An Essay in Comparative Religion*. Oxford: Clarendon Press.

Goitein, S. D. 1977. Individualism and Conformity in Classical Islam. In: A. Banani and S. Vryonis Jr. (eds), *Individualism and Conformity in Classical Islam*. Wiesbaden: Otto Harrassowitz.

——1966. *Studies in Islamic History and Institutions*. E. J. Brill: Leiden.

Goitein, S. D. and Von Grunebaum, G. 1975. The Hero in Medieval Arabic Prose. In: Norman Burns and Christopher Reagan (eds), *Concepts of the Hero in the Middle Ages and the Renaissance* Albany: State University of New York Press.

Goldberg, Ellis 1992. Smashing Idols and the State: The Protestant Ethic and Egyptian Sunni Radicalism. In: Juan Cole (ed.), *Comparing Muslim Societies: Knowledge and the State in a World Civilization*. Ann Arbor: University of Michigan Press.

Goldberg, E., Kasaba, R., and Migdal, J. (eds) 1993. *Rules and Rights in the Middle East: Democracy, Law and Society*. Seattle: University of Washington Press.

Goldziher, Ignaz 1981. *Introduction to Islamic Theology and Law*. Princeton: Princeton University Press.

Grim, John 1983. *The Shaman: Patterns of Siberian and Ojibway Healing*. Norman: University of Oklahoma Press.

Haeri, Shahla 1989. *Law of Desire: Temporary Marriage in Shi'ite Iran*. Syracuse: Syracuse University Press.

Hammoudi, Abdellah 1993. *The Victim and Its Masks: An Essay on Sacrifice and Masquerade in the Maghreb*. Chicago: University of Chicago Press.

——1980. Sainteté, Pouvoir et Société: Tamgrout aux XVII et XVII Siècles. *Annales: Économies, Sociétés, Civilizations*: 615–41.

Hart, David 1970. Clan, Lineage, Local Community and the Feud in a Riffian Tribe. In L. Sweet (ed.), *Peoples and Cultures of the Middle East*, vol. II. Garden City, NY: Natural History Press.

Hegel, G. W. F. 1953. *Reason in History*. Indianapolis: Bobbs-Merrill.

Hegland, Mary 1983. Two images of Husain: Accommodation and Revolution in an Iranian Village. In: Nikki Keddie (ed.), *Religion and Politics in Iran*. New Haven: Yale University Press.

Hodgson, Marshall G. S. 1974. *The Venture of Islam: Conscience and History in a World Civilization*, 3 vols. Chicago: University of Chicago Press.
—— 1955. *The Order of Assassins: the Struggle of the Early Nizari Isma'ilis Against the Islamic World*. 's-Gravenhage: Mouton.
Hume, David 1976. *Natural History of Religion*. Oxford: Oxford University Press.
Humphreys, R. Stephen 1991. *Islamic History: A Framework for Inquiry*. Princeton: Princeton University Press.
Ibn Khaldun, 1967. *The Muqaddimah*. Princeton: Princeton University Press.
Irons, William 1979. Political Stratification Among Pastoral Nomads. In: L'équipe écologie et anthropologie des sociétés pastorales (eds), *Pastoral Production and Society*. New York: Cambridge University Press.
Itzkowitz, Norman 1972. *Ottoman Empire and Islamic Tradition*. Chicago: University of Chicago Press.
Jacobsen, T. 1970. *Towards the Image of Tammuz and Other Essays on Mesopotamian History and Culture*. Cambridge: Harvard University Press.
Jafri, S. 1979. Conduct of Rule in Islam (In the Light of a Document of 38/658). *Hamard Islamicus* 2: 3–34.
Jomier, J. and Corbin, J. 1956. Le Ramadan, au Caire, en 1956. *Institut Dominicain d'Études Orientales, Mélanges* 3: 1–74.
Kalberg, Stephen 1994. Max Weber's Analysis of the Rise of Monotheism: a Reconstruction. *British Journal of Sociology* 45: 564–83.
Kandiyoti, Deniz 1992. Women, Islam, and the State: A Comparative Approach. In: Juan Cole (ed.), *Comparing Muslim Societies: Knowledge and the State in a World Civilization*. Ann Arbor: University of Michigan Press.
—— 1991. Islam and Patriarchy: A Comparative Perspective. In: Nikki Keddie and Beth Baron (eds) *Women in Middle Eastern History: Shifting Boundaries in Sex and Gender*. New Haven: Yale University Press.
Keddie, Nikki 1972. The Roots of the Ulama's Power in Modern Iran. In: N. Keddie (ed.), *Scholars, Saints and Sufis*. Berkeley: University of California Press.
Kennedy, H. 1985. From Polis to Medina: Urban Change in Late Antique and Early Islamic Syria. *Past and Present* 106: 3–27.
Khan, Ghani 1958. *The Pathans, a Sketch*. Peshawar: University Books.
Kister, M. J. 1979. Some Reports Concerning Al-Taf'if. *Jerusalem Studies in Arab and Islam* 1: 1–18.
—— 1972. Some Reports Concerning Mecca: From Jahiliyya to Islam. *Journal of the Economic and Social History of the Orient*. 15: 61–93.
—— 1965a. Mecca and Tamim (Aspects of their Relations). *Journal of the Economic and Social History of the Orient*. 8: 113–63.
—— 1965b. The Campaign of Huluban: a New Light on the Expedition of Abraha. *Le Museons* 78: 425–36.
Kister, M. J. and Plessner, M. 1990. Notes on Caskel's Gamharat an-nasab. In: M. J. Kister (ed.), *Society and Religion from Jahiliyya to Islam*. Aldershot: Variorum.
Kohl, Philip 1989. The Use and Abuse of World Systems Theory: the Case of the "Pristine" West Asian State. In: C. C. Lamberg-Karlovsky (ed.), *Archeological Thought in America*. Cambridge: Cambridge University Press.
Kohlberg, Etan 1988. Imam and Community in the Pre-Ghayba Period. In: S. A. Arjomand (ed.), *Authority and Political Culture in Shi'ism*. New Haven: Yale University Press.
—— 1987. Aspects of Akhbari Thought in the Seventeenth and Eighteenth Centuries. In: Nehemia Levtzion and John Voll (eds), *Eighteenth-Century Renewal and Reform in Islam*. Syracuse: Syracuse University Press.
Kostiner, Joseph 1990. Transforming Dualities: Tribe and State Formation in Saudi

Arabia. In: Philip Khoury and Joseph Kostiner (eds), *Tribes and State Formation in the Middle East*. Berkeley: University of California Press.

Kovacs, Maureen. 1989. *The Epic of Gilgamesh*. Stanford: Stanford University Press.

Lamberg-Karlovsky, C. C. 1989. Mesopotamia, Central Asia and the Indus Valley: So the Kings were Killed. In: C. C. Lamberg-Karlovsky (ed.), *Archeological Thought in America*. Cambridge: Cambridge University Press.

Lambton, A. K. S. 1980. Islamic Mirrors for Princes. In: A. Lambton (ed.), *Theory and Practice in Medieval Persian Government*. Aldershot: Varorum.

—— 1968. The Internal Structure of the Saljuq Empire. In: J. A. Boyle (ed.), *Cambridge History of Iran*, vol. 5. Cambridge: Cambridge University Press.

—— 1954. The Theory of Kingship in the Nisihat ul-Mulk of Ghazali. *The Islamic Quarterly* I: 47–55.

Lane, Edward William 1871. *An Account of the Manners and Customs of the Modern Egyptians, Written in Egypt During the Years 1833, –34, and 35 Partly From Notes Made During a Former Visit to that Country in the Years 1825, –26, –27, and –28*, 2 vols. London: John Murray.

Lapidus, Ira 1990. Tribes and State Formation in Islamic History. In: Philip Khoury and Joseph Kosiner (eds), *Tribes and State Formation in the Middle East*. Berkeley: University of California Press.

—— 1988. *A History of Islamic Societies*. New York: Cambridge University Press.

—— 1984. Knowledge, Virtue and Action: The Classical Muslim Conception of Adab and the Nature of Religious Fulfillment in Islam. In: Barbara Daly Metcalf (ed.), *Moral Conduct and Authority: The Place of Adab in South Asian Islam*. Berkeley: University of California Press.

—— 1982. The Arab Conquests and the Formation of Islamic Society. In: G. H. A. Juynboll (ed.), *Studies on the First Century of Islamic Society*. Carbondale: Southern Illinois University Press.

—— 1969. Muslim Cities and Islamic Societies. In: I. Lapidus (ed.), *Middle Eastern Cities*. Berkeley: University of California Press.

Lassner, Jacob 1980. *The Shaping of Abbasid Rule*. Princeton: Princeton University Press.

Leach, Edmund 1961. *Rethinking Anthropology*. London: Athalone Press.

Lerner, Gerda 1986. *The Creation of Patriarchy*. Oxford: Oxford University Press.

Lewis, Bernard 1990. *Race and Slavery in the Middle East: An Historical Inquiry*. Oxford: Oxford University Press.

—— 1988. *The Political Language of Islam*. Chicago: University of Chicago Press.

—— 1980. *The Assassins: A Radical Sect in Islam*. New York: Octogon Books

—— (ed.) 1974. *Islam from the Prophet Muhammad to the Capture of Constantinople*. New York: Harper and Row.

—— 1973. *Islam in History: Ideas, Men and Events in the Middle East*. New York: The Library Press.

—— 1940. *The Origin of Ismailism: A Study of the Historical Background of the Fatimid Caliphate*. Cambridge: Heffer and Sons.

Lewis, I. M. 1971. *Ecstatic Religion: An Anthropological Study of Spirit Possession and Shamanism*. Harmondsworth: Penguin.

Lindholm, Charles 1995a. The New Middle Eastern Ethnography. *Journal of the Royal Anthropological Institute*. (N.S.) 1: 805–20.

—— 1995b. *Frontier Perspectives: Essays in Comparative Anthropology*. Karachi: Oxford University Press.

—— 1992. Quandaries of Command in Egalitarian Societies: Examples from Swat and Morocco. In: Juan Cole (ed.), *Comparing Muslim Societies: Knowledge and the State in a World Civilization*. Ann Arbor: University of Michigan Press.

—— 1990. *Charisma*. Oxford: Basil Blackwell.

—— 1986. Kinship Structure and Political Authority: The Middle East and Central Asia. *Comparative Studies in Society and History* 28: 334–55.

—— 1982. *Generosity and Jealousy: The Swat Pukhtun of Northern Pakistan*. New York: Columbia University Press.

—— 1981a. History and the Heroic Pakhtun. *Man* 16: 463–67.

—— 1981b. The Structure of Violence among the Swat Pukhtun. *Ethnology* 20: 147–56.

—— 1981c. Leatherworkers and Love Potions. *American Ethnologist* 9: 512–25.

Lindholm, Cherry 1982. The Swat Pukhtun Family as a Political Training Ground. In: Steven Pastner and Louis Flom (eds), *Anthropology in Pakistan: Recent Sociocultural and Archeological Perspectives*. Ithaca: Cornell University Press.

Macdonald, Duncan 1909. *The Religious Attitude and Life in Islam*. Chicago: University of Chicago Press.

MacFarlane, Alan 1986. *Marriage and Love in England: 1300–1840*. Oxford: Basil Blackwell.

Madelung, W. 1992. Murjia. In: C. Bosworth et al. (eds), *Encyclopedia of Islam* (New Edition), vol. VII: 605–7. Leiden: E. J. Brill.

—— 1986. al-Mahdi. In: C. Bosworth et al. (eds), *Encyclopedia of Islam* (New Edition), vol. V: 1230–8. Leiden: E. J. Brill.

Makdisi, George 1990. *The Rise of Humanism in Classical Islam and the Christian West with Special Reference to Scholasticism*. Edinburgh: Edinburgh University Press.

—— 1985. Ethics in Islamic Traditionalist Doctrine. In: Richard Hovannisian (ed.), *Ethics in Islam*. Malibu: Undena Publications.

—— 1983. Institutionalized Learning as a Self-Image of Islam. In: Speros Vryonis (ed.), *Islam's Understanding of Itself*. Los Angeles: UCLA Press.

—— 1981. *The Rise of Colleges: Institutions of Learning in Islam and the West*. Edinburgh: Edinburgh University Press.

—— 1974. Ibn Taimiya: a Sufi of the Qadiriya Order. *American Journal of Arabic Studies* I: 118–29.

—— 1962. Ash'ari and the Ash'arites in Islamic Religious History: Part I. *Studia Islamica* 17: 37–80.

Makhlouf, Carla 1979. *Changing Veils: Women and Modernization in North Yemen*. Austin: University of Texas Press.

Makiya, Kanan 1993. *Cruelty and Silence: War, Tyranny, Uprising, and the Arab World*. New York: Norton.

Marx, Emmanuel 1967. *Bedouin of the Negev*. New York: Praeger.

Mason, Herbert 1972a. *Gilgamesh: A Verse Narrative*. New York: Mentor.

—— 1972b. *Two Statesmen of Mediaeval Islam: Vizir Ibn Hubayra (499–560 AH/ 1105–1165 AD) and Caliph an-Nasir li Din Allah (553–622 AH/ 1158–1225 AD)*. The Hague: Mouton.

Massignon, Louis 1982. *The Passion of al-Hallaj: Mystic and Martyr of Islam*. Translated by Herbert Mason, 4 vols. Princeton: Princeton University Press.

—— 1963 La "Futuwwa" ou "Pacte d'Honneur Artisanal" entre les Travailleurs Musulmans au Moyen Age. In: Y. Moubarac (ed.), *Opera Minora*, vol I. Beruit: al-Maaret.

—— 1954. *Essai sur les Origines du Lexique Technique and de la Mystique Musulmane*. Paris: J. Vrin.

—— 1952. L'alternative de la pensée mystique en Islam. Monisme existentiel ou monisme testimonial. *Annuaire de College de France*. 52: 189–91.

Meeker, Michael 1980. The Twilight of the South Asian Heroic Age: A Rereading of Barth's Study of Swat. *Man* 15: 682–701.

—— 1979. *Literature and Violence in Early Arabia*. London: Cambridge University Press.

Melikian, Levan 1977. The Modal Personality of Saudi College Students. In: L. Carl Brown (ed.), *Psychological Dimensions of Near Eastern Studies*. Princeton: Darwin Press.

Mernissi, Fatima 1991. *The Veil and the Male Elite: A Feminist Interpretation of Women's Rights in Islam*. Addison-Wesley Publishing: Reading MA.
—— 1975. *Beyond the Veil*. Cambridge: Schenkman.
Messick, Brinkley 1993. *The Calligraphic State: Textual Domination and History in a Muslim Society*. Berkeley: University of California Press.
Metcalf, Barbara 1987. Islamic Arguments in Contemporary Pakistan. In: William Roff (ed.), *Islam and the Political Economy of Meaning: Comparative Studies of Muslim Discourse*. London: Croom Helm.
Miller, James and Bowen, Donna Lee 1993. The Nasiriyya Brotherhood of Southern Morocco. In: Bowen, Donna Lee and Evelyn Early (eds), *Everyday Life in the Muslim Middle East*. Bloomington: Indiana University Press.
Mir-Hosseini, Ziba 1993. Women, Marriage and the Law in Post-Revolutionary Iran. In: Haleh Afshar (ed.), *Women in the Middle East: Perceptions, Realities and Struggles for Liberation*. New York: St. Martin's Press.
Mitchell, R. P. 1969. *The Society of the Muslim Brothers*. Oxford: Oxford University Press.
Montagne, Robert 1973. *The Berbers, Their Social and Political Organization*. London: Frank Cass and Company.
Morgan, David 1988. *Medieval Persia 1040–1797*. London: Longman.
Mottahedeh, Roy 1980. *Loyalty and Leadership in an Early Islamic Society*. Princeton: Princeton University Press.
Mullaney, Frank 1992. *The Role of Islam in the Hegemonic Strategy of Egypt's Military Rulers (1952–1990)*. Cambridge: Doctoral thesis, Dept. of Sociology, Harvard University.
Munson, Henry 1993. *Religion and Power in Morocco*. New Haven: Yale University Press.
—— 1988. *Islam and Revolution in the Middle East*. New Haven: Yale University Press.
Murata, Sachiko 1992. *The Tao of Islam*. Albany: State University at New York Press.
Murphy, Robert and Kasdan, Lawrence 1967. Agnation and Exogamy: Some Further Considerations. *Southwestern Journal of Anthropology* 1: 1–14.
—— 1959. The Structure of Parallel Cousin Marriage. *American Anthropologist* 19: 17–29.
Musil, Alois 1928. *Manners and Customs of the Rwala Bedouins*. New York: American Geographical Society.
Nadwi, S. Abdul Hasan 1972. *The Four Pillars of Islam*. Lucknow: Academy of Islamic Research.
Nafzawi, Umar bin Muhammad 1964. *The Perfumed Garden*. Translated by Richard Burton. New York: Castle Books.
Nagel, H. M. T. 1982. Some Considerations Concerning the Pre-Islamic and the Islamic Foundations of the Authority of the Caliphate. In: G. H. Juynboll (ed.), *Studies on the First Century of Islamic Society*. Carbondale: Southern Illinois University Press.
Needham, Rodney. 1978. *Primordial Characters*. Charlottesville: University Press of Virginia.
Nelson, Kristina 1986. *The Art of Reciting the Quran*. Austin: University of Texas Press.
Nicholson, Reynold Alleyne 1921. *Studies in Islamic Mysticism*. Cambridge: Cambridge University Press.
Norton, A. R. (ed.) 1995. *Civil Society in the Middle East*, 2 vols. Leiden: E. J. Brill
Papps, Ivy 1993. Attitudes to Female Employment in Four Middle Eastern Countries. In: Haleh Afshar (ed.), *Women in the Middle East: Perceptions, Realities and Struggles for Liberation*. New York: St. Martin's Press.
Pehrson, Robert 1966. *The Social Organization of the Marri Baluch*. New York: Wenner-Gren.
Peters, Emrys 1967. Some Structural Aspects of the Feud among the Camel-Herding Bedouin of Cyrenaica. *Africa* 37: 261–82.

—— 1960. The Proliferation of Segments in the Lineage of the Bedouin of Cyrenaica Libya. *Journal of the Royal Anthropological Institute* 90: 29–53.

Peters, Rudolph 1987. The Battered Dervishes of Bab Zuwalya: A Religious Riot in Eighteenth-Century Cairo. In: Nehemia Levtzion and John Voll (eds), *Eighteenth-century Renewal and Reform in Islam*. Syracuse: Syracuse University Press.

Quran, The Holy n.d. Medina: King Fahd Holy Quran Printing Complex.

Rabinow, Paul 1977. *Reflections on Fieldwork in Morocco*. Berkeley: University of California Press.

Rahman, Fazlur 1982. *Islam and Modernity: Transformations of an Intellectual Tradition*. Chicago: University of Chicago Press.

Richard, Yann. 1995. *Shi'ite Islam: Polity, Ideology and Creed*. Oxford: Basil Blackwell.

Rodinson, Maxime 1973. *Islam and Capitalism*. New York: Pantheon.

Rosen, Lawrence 1978. The Negotiation of Reality: Male-Female Relations in Sefrou, Morocco. In: Lois Beck and Nikki Keddie (eds), *Women in the Muslim World*. Cambridge: Harvard University Press.

Rosenfeld, Henry 1965. The Social Composition of the Military in the Process of State Formation in the Arabian Desert. *Journal of the Royal Anthropological Institute* 95: 75–86, 174–94.

Rosenthal, Franz 1990. The Study of Muslim Intellectual and Social History: Methods and Approaches. In: Franz Rosenthal (ed.), *Muslim Intellectual and Social History*. Aldershot: Variorum.

—— 1987. Reflections on Love in Paradise. In: John Marks and Robert Good (eds), *Love and Death in the Ancient Near East*. Guilford: Four Quarters Publishing.

—— 1977. "I Am You" – Individual Piety and Society in Islam. In: Amin Banani and Speros Vryonis (eds), *Individualism and Conformity in Classical Islam*. Wiesbaden: Otto Harrassowitz.

—— 1960. *The Muslim Concept of Freedom Prior to the Nineteenth Century*. Leiden: E. J. Brill.

—— 1956. State and Religion According to Abu 1-Hasan Al-Amiri. *The Islamic Quarterly* 3: 42–52

—— 1946. On Suicide in Islam. *Journal of the American Oriental Society* 66: 239–59.

Rosenthal, Von Erwin I. J. 1973. The Role of the State in Islam: Theory and Medieval Practice. *Der Islam* 1: 1–28.

Roy, Olivier 1994. *The Failure of Political Islam*. Cambridge: Harvard University Press.

Rumi, Jalaludin 1975. *Teachings of Rumi: The Masnavi*. Translated and abridged by E. H. Whinfield. New York: Dutton.

—— 1972. *Discourses of Rumi*. Translated by A. J. Arberry. New York: Samuel Weiser Inc.

Sabbah, Fatna A. 1984. *Women in the Muslim Unconscious*. Oxford: Pergamon Press.

Saggs, H. W. F. 1989. *Civilization Before Greece and Rome*. New Haven: Yale University Press.

—— 1962. *The Greatness That Was Babylon*. London: Sidgwick and Jackson.

Sahlins, Marshall 1961. The Segmentary Lineage: An Organization of Predatory Expansion. *American Anthropologist* 63: 322–43.

Said, Edward 1979. *Orientalism*. New York: Vintage.

Salzman, Philip 1979. Inequality and Oppression in Nomadic Society. In: L'équipe écologie et anthropologie des sociétés pastorales (eds), *Pastoral Production and Society*. New York: Cambridge University Press.

—— 1978. Does Complementary Opposition Exist? *American Anthropologist* 80: 43–70.

Sandars, N. K. 1972. *The Epic of Gilgamesh*. New York: Penguin.

Schimmel, Annemarie 1975. *Mystical Dimensions of Islam*. Chapel Hill: University of North Carolina Press.

Seligman, H. 1964. The State and the Individual in Sunni Islam. *Muslim World* 54: 14–26.

Sells, M. 1989. *Desert Tracings: Six Classical Arabian Odes*. Middletown: Wesleyan University Press.

Serjeant R. B. 1981a. Documents in the Constitution of Medinah. In: R. B. Serjeant (ed.), *Studies in Arabian History and Civilization*. Aldershot: Variorum.

—— 1981b. Haram and Hawtah: The Sacred Enclave in Arabia. In: R. B. Serjeant (ed.), *Studies in Arabian History and Civilization*. Aldershot: Variorum.

—— 1977. South Arabia. In: C. A. O. van Nieuwenhuijze (ed.), *Commoners, Climbers and Notables*. Leiden: E. J. Brill.

Shaban, M. A. 1976. *Islamic History A D 750–1055 AH 132–448. A New Interpretation:* vol. 2. Cambridge: Cambridge University Press.

—— 1971. *Islamic History A. D. 600–750 A. H. 132: A New Interpretation*, vol. 1. Cambridge: Cambridge University Press.

Shorter, Edward 1977. *The Making of the Modern Family*. New York: Basic Books.

Singerman, D. 1995. *Avenues of Participation: Family, Politics, and Networks in Urban Quarters of Cairo*. Princeton: Princeton University Press.

Smith, Margaret 1984. *Rabia the Mystic and Her Fellow Saints in Islam*. Cambridge: Cambridge University Press.

Smith, Wilfred C. 1957. *Islam in Modern History*. Princeton: Princeton University Press.

Southern, R. 1962. *Western Views of Islam in the Middle Ages*. Cambridge: Harvard University Press.

Spellberg, Denise. 1991. Political Action and Public Example: A'isha and the Battle of the Camel. In: Nikki Keddie and Beth Baron (eds) *Women in Middle Eastern History: Shifting Boundaries in Sex and Gender*. New Haven: Yale University Press.

Stewart, Frank 1994. *Honor*. Chicago: University of Chicago Press.

Stone, Laurence 1988. Passionate Attachments in the West in Historical Perspective. In: W. Gaylin and E. Person (eds), *Passionate Attachments*. New York: Free Press.

Stowasser, Barbara 1993. Women's Issues in Modern Islamic Thought. In: Judith Tucker (ed.), *Arab Women: Old Boundaries, New Frontiers*. Bloomington: Indiana University Press.

—— 1984. The Status of Women in Early Islam. In: Freda Hussain (ed.), *Muslim Women*. New York: St Martin's Press.

Tambiah, Stanley 1976. *World Conqueror and World Renouncer: A Study of Buddhism and Polity in Thailand against a Historical Background*. Cambridge: Cambridge University Press.

Tapper, Richard 1990. Anthropologists, Historians, and Tribespeople on Tribe and State Formation in the Middle East. In: Philip Khoury and Joseph Kostiner (eds), *Tribes and State Formation in the Middle East*. Berkeley: University of California Press.

—— 1979. Access to Grazing Rights and Social Organization Among the Shasevan Nomads of Azerbaijan. In: L'équipe écologie et anthropologie des sociétés pastorales (eds), *Pastoral Production and Society*. New York: Cambridge University Press.

Tillon, Germaine 1966. *Le Harem et les Cousins*. Paris: Éditions du Seuil.

Tocqueville, Alexis de 1969. *Democracy in America*. Garden City, NY: Doubleday.

Torry, Charles 1892. *Commercial-Theological Terms in the Koran*. Leiden: E. J. Brill.

Trimingham, J. 1971. *The Sufi Orders of Islam*. Oxford: Oxford University Press.

Turner, Victor 1982. *The Ritual Process*. New York: Aldine.

Udovitch, Avrom 1977. Formalism and Informalism in the Social and Economic Institutions of the Medieval Islamic World. In: A. Banani and S. Vryonis Jr. (eds), *Individualism and Conformity in Classical Islam*. Wiesbaden: Otto Harrassowitz.

van Ess, J. 1970. The Logical Structure of Islamic Theology. In: G. von Grunebaum (ed.), *Logic in Classical Islamic Culture*. Wiesbaden: Otto Harrassowitz.

Vatter, Sherry 1993. Journeymen Textile Weavers in Nineteenth-Century Damascus: A Collective Biography. In: Edmund Burke III (ed.), *Struggle and Survival in the Modern Middle East.* London: I. B. Tauris and Co.

Vieille, Paul 1978. Iranian Women in Family Alliance and Sexual Politics. In: Lois Beck and Nikki Keddie (eds), *Women in the Muslim World.* Cambridge: Harvard University Press.

Voll, John 1987. Linking Groups in the Networks of Eighteenth-Century Revivalist Scholars: the Mizaji Family in Yemen. In: Nehemia Levtzion and John Voll (eds), *Eighteenth-Century Renewal and Reform in Islam.* Syracuse: Syracuse University Press.

von Grunebaum, Gustav 1970. The Sources of Islamic Civilization. *Der Islam* 46: 1–54.

—— 1961. The Structure of the Muslim Town. In Gustave von Grunebaum (ed.), *Islam: Essays in the Nature and Growth of a Cultural Tradition.* London: Routledge and Kegan Paul.

—— 1956. *Medieval Islam.* Chicago: University of Chicago Press.

Wallace, A. F. C. 1956. Revitalization Movements. *American Anthropologist* 58: 264–81.

Waterbury, John 1972. Tribalism. Trade and Politics: The Transformation of the Swasa of Morocco. In: Ernest Gellner and Charles Micaud (eds), *Arabs and Berbers.* Lexington: Lexington Books.

Watt, W. M. 1988. *Muhammad's Mecca: History in the Qur'an* Edinburgh: Edinburgh University Press.

—— 1973. *The Formative Period of Islamic Thought.* Edinburgh: Edinburgh University Press.

—— 1961. Kharijite thought in the Umayyad Period. *Der Islam* 36: 215–31.

—— 1956. *Muhammad at Medina.* Oxford: Clarendon Press.

—— 1953. *The Faith and Practice of al-Ghazali.* London: Allen and Unwin.

Weber, Max 1978. *Economy and Society.* Berkeley: University of California Press.

—— 1958. *The Protestant Ethic and the Spirit of Capitalism.* New York: Scribners.

—— 1946. *From Max Weber: Essays in Sociology.* New York: Oxford University Press.

Wellhausen, Julius 1927. *The Arab Kingdom and its Fall.* London: Curzon Press.

Wensinck, A. J. 1932. *The Muslim Creed: Its Genesis and Historical Development.* Cambridge: Cambridge University Press.

Werbner, 1995. Powerful Knowledge in a Global Sufi Cult: Reflections on the Poetics of Travelling Theories. In: Wendy James (ed.), *The Pursuit of Certainty: Religious and Cultural Formations.* London: Routledge.

Westermark, Edward 1925. *Ritual and Belief in Morocco,* vol. 1. London: Macmillan and Company.

Wikan, Unni 1991. *Behind the Veil in Arabia: Women in Oman.* Chicago: University of Chicago Press.

Yar-Shatar, Ehsan 1968. Mazdakianism. In: Ehsan Yar-Shatar (ed.), *The Cambridge History of Iran,* vol. 2, part 2. Cambridge: Cambridge University Press.

Youssef, Michael 1985. *Revolt Against Modernity: Muslim Zealots and the West.* Leiden: E. J. Brill.

Zaehner, Robert 1961. *The Dawn and Twilight of Zoroastrianism.* London: Weidenfeld and Nicolson.

Index

Abbasid dynasty 96–104; army in 97, 102–3; compared to Umayyad 102, 103; courtiers in 100–1; despotism of 100, 103–4; egalitarian ideals of 97–8, 101; Hashimiyya conspiracy and 96–7; Khurasaniyya warriors and 97–8, 102–3; Mutazalites and 140–1; policy of 98–9, 103–4; Qarmati raids on 106; sacred authority of 97, 100, 102, 174; slaves and clients in 102–4, 213; 'Turkish' resistance to 103–4, 268; women's subordination in 234

Abbot, N., on effects of concubinage 234

Abu Bakr (first Caliph), character of 84–5; conditional authority 80; leadership of 85

Abu Jafar (Abbasid Caliph) 98–100; on clientship 51

Abu Said (Sufi saint), austerities of 182–3; dhikr of 186; on recognition of saints 198; selflessness of 182, 202; violence of 205

Abu Tahir (Qarmatid commander) 106–7

Abu Talib (Muhammad's uncle), on prostration 68

adoption, inheritance and 236, 237; spiritual 174

Ahmed, L., on women's history 235

Aisha (Muhammad's favorite wife), independence of 232–3

Al-Azhar (Egyptian University) 165

Al-Banna (founder of Muslim Brotherhood), as Sufi 199, 207

Al-Basra (Sufi saint) 181–2

Al-Farid (Arab poet), on mystical powers 201

Al-Ghazali (Seljuk theologian and Sufi), on avoidance of the state 269; on hypocrisy in Islam 147; on subordination to the state 225, 263; on trust in Sufism 184

Al-Gilani (founder of Qadiryya order), on his spiritual supremacy 201

Al-Hakim (Fatimid ruler) 114

Al-Hallaj (Sufi martyr) 195–6; death of 196; on friendship 254; on gnosis 195

Al-Jahiz (ninth-century scholar), on right of rebellion 269

Al-Jawazi (essayist), on sex and love 247–8

Al-Junayd (Sufi saint), emphasis on sobriety 186; on slavery as freedom 226; as Sufi founder 188

Al-Mamun (Abbasid Caliph), Mutazalites and 140; on nobility 100–1

Al-Mansur, see Abu Jafar

Al-Muhasibi (philosopher), on rivalry 261

Al-Muqaddasi (traveller and essayist), on the character of the ulema 220

Al-Murrah (Bedouin tribe), migration of 20; state and 19

Al-Mutanabbi (poet), on race and nobility 218

Al-Nasir (Caliph) 127–9; as initiate of men's club 128

Al-Shafi (jurist) 157–8

Al-Sindhi (poet), on Abbasid corruption 103

Al-Tijani (Sufi saint) 200; as 'pole of poles' 201

Algeria, secular authority in 133, 134

Ali b. Talib (fourth Caliph) 87, 89, 169; battle of camel and 170; death of 170; egalitarianism of 170; as friend of God 167; marriage of 231; patience of 172; as Sufi founder 188; as superhuman being 169–70; on the virtue of the ruler 80; see also Shi'ism

Allah, see divinity

alliances, structure of 55, 60–1; marriage 238, 249; see also segmentary lineage system

Almohad dynasty 114–15

Almoravid dynasty 114–15

America, see Christian west

Antara (pre-Islamic poet), on race and honor 217

Antoun, R., on equality 11

Arab 7; blood ideology of 81, 93; as cultural designation 22; early history of 65–73; as language of Quran 20, 152; pre-Islamic religion of 69; race and 216–18; see also Bedouin

Arjomand, S., on Khomeini 179

Arkoun, M., on 'cultural imaginary' 10

asabiyya (group feeling) 52, 53–5, 58, 62, 102, 123; fictive kinship as substitute for 109; among men's clubs 128; naturalization of 237; see also kinship; segmentary lineage system

INDEX

INDEX 319

324   INDEX

Sumeria, *see* Gilgamesh; Mesopotamia
Syria, secular authority in   133

taxation, Islam and   68, 74; iqta (tax farming)
111; Shah Abbas's policy of   118; state
and   103; tribal rejection of   25–6, 85;
twelver ulema and   178
terrorism, Islamist   208; Nizari   130
Tocqueville, A., on competition among
equals   261; on conformity   267; on local
democracy   265; on tyranny   265
Torry, C., on mercantile imagery in Islam   77
trade   30–2, 40, 95; contradictions of   71;
Islamic view of   77–8; Mesopotamian   30,
40, 43, 45; nomadic   24; pre-Islamic   66,
69–71, 72; rise of Islam and   70–1, 79;
shifts in   31, 69, 110; state and   30–1, 45,
106, 110; values and   30–2, 45, 78, 90; *see
also* contractualism; mercantilism
traditionalism   141; and jurists   157; *see also*
hadith reciters; ulema
trait complex, Middle Eastern   8, 10
tribesmen, compared to tradesmen   31–2, 78,
90; Islam and   72–6, 78, 81; mediation
among   23, 58, 90, 265; rank among   223,
264; religious leadership among   72, 88,
114–16; secular leadership among   20,
23–5, 26, 51, 90, 116, 222, 265–6; state
and   20–1, 23–5, 26, 27, 28, 35, 40, 42,
46, 48, 51–2, 62, 65–6, 71, 72, 81–2, 85–7,
88, 90–1, 93, 96, 106, 107–9, 110, 113–16,
120, 121, 123, 193; Sufism and   191–3;
values of   19–21,
24, 25–7, 50, 71, 72, 81–2, 153–4, 201,
222–3, 224, 265–6; *see also* Bedouin; Lur;
mountaineers; nomads; Pukhtun; Qashqai.
twelvers (Shi'ite sect)   175–80; rank
among   177–8; revolution
among   178–80; scholarship
among   176–8; succession among   175–6;
ulema among   178; *see also* Shi'ism

ulema (the learned)   155–66, 175–8; character
of   156, 161–3, 177, 220; charisma
of   177; compared to warriors   162–3;
compared to hadith reciters   155–6, 156–7,
162–3; consensus among   156–8, 159, 176;
delegitimization of   163–6; hypocrisy
and   163; independence of   159, 178;
interpretation and   156, 159; as
mystics   191; Ottoman   123, 126, 178;
opposing state   164–5, 267; passivity
of   162, 177; persecution of   178; as
rulers   163, 178–9; Shi'ite   175–8; Sufism
and   183, 184, 188–9, 190–3, 194–5;
training of   160–3, 177; validating
state   12, 90, 126, 177, 199; *see also* hadith
reciters; Islam; law colleges; madhhab;
spiritual authority
Umar (second Caliph)   85; on equality in
Islam   82; on nobility in Islam   81
Umayyad dynasty   87–96; clients in   213;
compared to Abbasid   102, 103; fall
of   96–8; leadership in   90–1; opposition
to   88–90; policy of   94; reform in   96
Ur-Nammu (Sumerian ruler), on justice   47
Uruk (Sumerian city)   18; expansion of   44–5;
rule of   42–3; trade in   45
Uthman (third Caliph), death of   87

Veille, P., on husband and wife relationship   239
virginity   239; *see also* sexuality

Wahhabi (Saudi sect)   115–16; as anti-
Sufi   199; resistance to   116; rule of   116,
133
waqf (religious endowment), confiscation of by
state   164; Iranian ulema and   178;
Mesopotamian temples and   44;
Universities funded by   160; *see also*
taxation
warriors, authority and   90–1, 109, 112, 121,
153–4, 162, 163, 222–3; compared to
hadith reciter   154, 162–3; compared to
jurist   162, 163; compared to Sufi   189;
and non-Muslims   222; organization of in
Islam   79, 150; values of   19–21, 24,
25–7, 50, 81–2, 112, 121, 153–4, 162, 189,
201, 219, 222–4; *see also* leadership; noble
lineage; state; tribesmen
Watt, J., on kharijites   88; on pre-Islamic
trade   69–71
wazir (prime minister), instability of   111; milk
relation with   227
Weber, M., on prophecy   36–40, 148–9; on
Sultanism   5
Wellhausen, J., on the Abbasid army   102; on
blood bonds in early Arabia   65; on the
early Islamic army   85–6; on genealogies
of poets   81–2; on heroes   82; on
rivalry   58
Wensinck, A., on rebellion   85
Westermark, E., on the ambiguity of saints   204
women   228–44; ambivalence of   238–9, 240,
241–5, 252; autonomy of   231–2, 238,
240; character of   228, 239, 241–4;
children and   240; community of   230–1;
compared to western   231–2; concubinage
and   234–5; divorce and   231, 235; fear
of   243, 252; feminist view of   232–3;
honor of   239, 240; inferiority of   215,
228, 235; inheritance by   167, 230, 231,
236; Islam on   228–30, 231–3; Islamist
view of   233–4; labor of   235; love
and   243, 249–50; magic and   242–3, 245;
among Marri Baluch   249; marriage
contract and   231–2, 238; modern
condition of   234, 260; Muhammad's
attitude toward   233;
neofundamentalist views of   234; among
nomads   236; patriarchy and   235–45; and
pilgrimage   226; positive views of   230,
232–4; powers of   240, 242, 243–4, 245;
pre-Islamic treatment of   234–7;
responsibility for   238; rights of   231–2,
234–6, 239; rivalry among   240–1;
seclusion of   228–9, 233, 235, 242; self-
assertion by   239–40; sexuality
and   241–4, 252; subordinate males
as   215, 218, 220, 222, 223, 228;
Sufi imagery of   189, 194, 230; temporary
marriage of   167; *see also* family;
inferiority; marriage;
patriarchy; rank; sexuality
writing, invention of   44–5;
suspicion of   152

zakat, *see* taxation
Zaydi (Shi'ite sect)   174